THE DEED OF READING

THE DEED OF READING

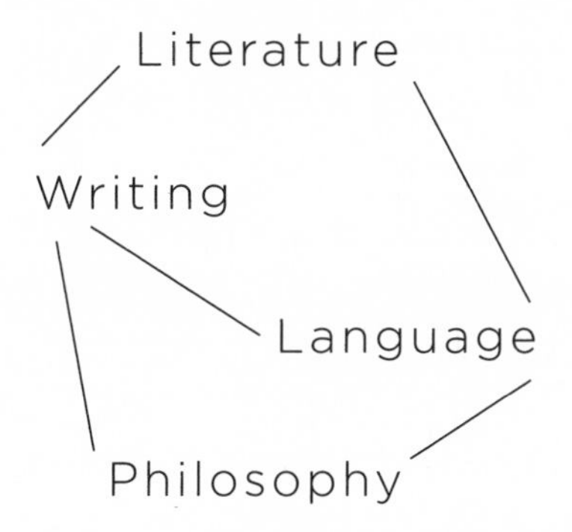

GARRETT STEWART

Cornell University Press
Ithaca & London

Copyright © 2015 by Cornell University

All rights reserved. Except for brief quotations in a review, this book, or parts thereof, must not be reproduced in any form without permission in writing from the publisher. For information, address Cornell University Press, Sage House, 512 East State Street, Ithaca, New York 14850.

First published 2015 by Cornell University Press
First printing, Cornell Paperbacks, 2015

Printed in the United States of America

Library of Congress Cataloging-in-Publication Data

Stewart, Garrett, author.
The deed of reading : literature * writing * language * philosophy / Garrett Stewart.
pages cm
Includes bibliographical references and index.
ISBN 978-0-8014-5421-9 (cloth : alk. paper) —
ISBN 978-1-5017-0048-4 (pbk. : alk. paper)
1. Literature—Philosophy. 2. Books and reading—Philosophy. 3. Language and languages—Philosophy. I. Title.
PN45.S854 2015
801—dc23 2015012130

Cornell University Press strives to use environmentally responsible suppliers and materials to the fullest extent possible in the publishing of its books. Such materials include vegetable-based, low-VOC inks and acid-free papers that are recycled, totally chlorine-free, or partly composed of nonwood fibers. For further information, visit our website at www.cornellpress.cornell.edu.

Cloth printing 10 9 8 7 6 5 4 3 2 1
Paperback printing 10 9 8 7 6 5 4 3 2 1

To Stanley

for introducing so much to literary study,

including Tim Gould to me

To Tim

for teaching us the full reach of Cavell's philosophic thought

CONTENTS

THE DEED OF READING

FORE WORD

The one real criterion for anybody's *reading* is the conscious act of reading, the act of reading the sounds off from the letters.

Ludwig Wittgenstein, *Philosophical Investigations*, 69 no. 159

Literary ethics or verbal ethic? There is of course no reason to choose. But many a distinction to be made. We have come to this: "It is not unusual in literary studies to treat language as transparent, and thus irrelevant."[1] Thus writes a professional linguist, in the year 2012, from her institutional base in an English department at a major Canadian university. It is in fact very common lately not to "treat language" at all in the analysis of literature, as if it were no more than the readily legible conveyance of expressed ideas, whether urgently identitarian, ideologically suspect, or anything in between. And when one hears that things are changing slowly, in some collective rediscovery of verbal structure in literary reading, not only is prose usually forgotten, but the neoformalist contenders adduced seem in the main committed more to a fresh study of the forms (categorical) of verse production, meter most prominently of late, than to the more deep-seated study of literature at large by way of its linguistic formation.

And the more ethicist, in one sense, the critical instinct becomes (the more expressly committed, for instance, to a moral or political barometer in taking the measure of character and event in narrative evidence), the more likely, and for no good reason, is "actual reading," with its ethic of verbal attention, to be sidelined—as implicitly irrelevant if not downright indulgent. Such is the frequently unstated bias, though nowhere openly legislated. By "actual reading" I mean, in the long run, something more (or something more basic) than a semantically valorized "close reading," though certainly including anything regularly intended by that term—but something more ingrained as well, involving a deeper cognitive investment in verbal decipherment. This deed of attention entails an etymology prior to any philosophical elaboration. *Ethos*: spirit of a community. *Ethike*: the set of obligations that structure any such human collective. But if the community is not simply obliged by social contract or conditioning but is bonded by a sense of origins in shared discourse, then poetic utterance concentrates a signature effect of the human: language per se listened to as one of literature's "ends" as well as its premise.

By stressing in what follows an embodied speaker at the reading (more palpably than the writing) end of literary production, I build on two of my leading theoretical influences (early and late) in the matter of poetic formation: the Geoffrey Hartman of "Ghostlier Demarcations" brought together with the Giorgio Agamben of *The End of the Poem*. For each, we may say, the gesture of language has its intrinsic *zoe*, its anatomical form, as well as its subjective *bios* and attendant sociology. Exactly fifty years ago at the so-called English Institute, Hartman addressed something more deeply instituted, and constituted, than any one language, let alone than academic departments devoted to English literature, inflecting the point with one of his familiar allusions to Wallace Stevens: "Myth and metaphor are endued with the acts, the gesta, of speech; and if there is a mediator for our experience of literature, it is something as simply with us as the human body, namely the human voice. . . . To envision 'ghostlier demarcations' a poet must utter 'keener sounds.'"[2] In such gesta begins an ethos. Whereas the work of literary ethics, plural(ist), typically concerns social action under representation, an ethic of reading goes underneath—and back before. The ethos of a social body involves depiction and its ironies; an ethos of embodied reading is singular, intimate. And because this singularity is at the same time held in common, it is the precondition for community as well as for representation, for social space all told.

So it is that the embodied channels of speech—as manifested in a reader's own contact with the page—direct us in this way, along this route of production, to Agamben's understanding of poetic ends, where the event of closure does not dispel, but rather installs by renewed anticipation, the possibility of a text being sounded each time anew on the reader's inner ear: a circulating speech act rather than a delivered message. It is this act of readerly contact and transference that, brokered by style, grows into a renewable and transparent cultural *contract*, a deeding of authority with no deceptive subclauses in finer print than the others, all of it continuously renegotiable by the silent voice of recognition. This mode of engagement is more than some committed responsibility to what is written, ethical in that "disciplined" (or even everyday) sense. Rather, it extends (or descends) to an ethic of obliged response that taps those rituals, and rules, of language that may be said, when the mood is right, to get us where we live—as well as to where a given text is going, powerfully compounded in the process by a formative sense of where (if only to a certain depth) the language itself is coming from.

Without some closeness of approach, there is no sense of depth whatsoever. Yet there seem ways of "being philosophical about" even a widespread professional indifference to literature as language (amounting almost to a disciplinary amnesia) that are more than merely idiomatic—and, hence, more than quietly defeatist. One such way, as already broached, is to enlist the literary commentary of certain actual philosophers, like Stanley Cavell and Agamben—writers interested profoundly in literary linguistics—who do have some English department following, if increasingly for other than their most literary work. But a foot in the door, even if not metrical, may pry open a wider angle of linguistic vigilance in the consideration of both fiction and verse.

From Philology to Philosophy

Philosophy recommends itself in this sense not because it has something new to say (which it may) about literature or writing separately, but because it can help find in literary writing a tacit philosophy of language in its own right that would otherwise fall beneath the bandwidths of prevailing reconnaissance in the contextual and political—and even the formalist—study of texts. Certainly some of the best questions are liable to get lost as a result of the culturalist tendency; recovering incipient linguistic curiosity is one way to start retrieving them. What, in the event of reading, constitutes its immediately verbal deed? And why would this both obvious and elusive thing about literature elicit the fascination of a young reader (read: student) new to the task of literature, as my own teenage experience will soon be recovered to illustrate? And do so in a manner that retains its charge even when a professional vocabulary rises to the once unschooled occasion? That's why I've wanted to look back at the first poem I remember taking seriously, or let's say the first poem I tried seriously taking the measure of—precisely because to do so was for me then such a stretch: a stretch matched in fact by, and fitted to, the elasticity of the poem's own wording.

The philosophy came much later—and in a manner flagged by the quadratic spectrum of this book's subtitle. The topic isn't, and at this brief length couldn't be, literature and philosophy, nor even the philosophy or aesthetics of literature. There is little Aristotle to speak of, a mere mention of Kant, next to no Nietzsche, and even Hegel and Heidegger mostly as encountered by later philosophers and media theorists—Jacques Derrida only in the background among them, Friedrich Kittler more prominent. Nor, more narrowly yoked, is this a book about literature *as* philosophy in some generalized thematic sense, let alone about pockets of philosophizing in literature. It is a book about literature as writing—about lexicon, syntax, and figuration—as these aspects in themselves are angled toward their most immediate interface in philosophy: namely, an account of human language. Literature seen in part as a linguistic event is seen at times as a philosophy of that event's enabling conditions. That's the sliding scale of my subtitle. Literature writes philosophy when it takes writing itself, as language, up and on—though less as topic or theme than as endemic and plumbed condition.

As both Agamben and Cavell, along with other theorists of metaphor and related linguistic functions, will differently help bring to focus, literature, philosophically read, becomes the inquisition of its own medium. It is then that questions attached to a ventured ontology of human speech take shape as a tacit theory of literary communication.

Derek Attridge's latest book, *Moving Words*, is incontestable on one among many points: that "the event of the poem takes place as part of the event of its reading" and is as such a "*formal* event." His italics there intend to keep company with over a decade's worth of resuscitated (even when not dramatically renovated) formal analysis whose contributions he begins by reviewing—even as he resists the frequent (though not inevitable) codification implied by the labels "formalism," "formalist," and especially "new formalism."[3] My particular emphasis on the linguistic deed of the reading "event" takes its own different distance from the routine nomenclature of this welcome trend in recommitted formal attention, this resistance to the strictly contextual in the reading of a text within its historical moment of production.[4] Returning us not to some previous methodological rallying cry (reminiscent of New Criticism) but to the germinal force of language itself, what happens in the passages I consider, from prose and poetry alike, may be approached by something I am calling a *formative* sense of their linguistic energy, rather than a formal*ist* one (let alone formal*istic*).

There is no undue polemic in my emphasis, no sense of a lamentable rigidity or aggressiveness that needs checking. Form-attentive critics don't, at their most illuminating, tend to insist on the kind of cemented methodology the *ist* might suggest. Nor, for that matter, do all who claim some at least loose allegiance to the so-called neoformalist camp (its prefix as much an implicit corrective, if only by label, as *New* historicism was) necessarily hoist their banners as if in an overthrow of the old. But both the *ism* behind the one term and the implied schism of the other may mislead—as Susan Wolfson has shown by way of securing her own alternative and more immediate emphases ("reading *for form*"; "*formal* charges").[5] Formal apprehension in reading is all one needs to insist on in an ethic of literary engagement: namely, so she shows, the *charge* of reading in its double sense, what both galvanizes and obliges us. But with it may, and in a writer like Agamben certainly does, come the formative: the whole human ethos of acquired and achieved rather than inbred speech as an ontological vanishing point no less definitive for being undefinable.

Even as contextually minded and politically driven a critic as art historian T. J. Clark has taken recently to defining his formal terms.[6] He begins a recent piece by reminding us that aesthetic form borrows from and typically arrests the repetitive patterns human perception finds in nature and makes them mean, makes them human. For Clark insists that any "theory of form is weak to the extent that it does not address form's semantic force" (5)—even as he resists the theorization of such force in anything resembling a semiotics of form. As a "controlled repetition" (7; think literary rhyme, say, as well as chromatic echo in painting), form is to be understood less as passive, relaxed, distracting, than as "an operation on the world"—this, rather than "a set of equivalents to a world in place" (7). So Clark can sum up this way in closing his brief position paper: "The point is that form—repetition—is change" (7).[7]

Put otherwise, form is the shape of change—or the shape by which change becomes legible. So "formal reading" would be a reading for difference within repetition: the differences both across a given text and of it (or its details) from its predecessors. This, so far, might certainly seem all the terminology, at least all the methodological terminology, we would need to rely on: the formal charges of formal change. I wish simply to stress within this focus—in the spirit of analogy offered by Clark to nature's own developmental repetitions—that beneath surface variety there is often "a kind of patterning that points to an order of orders, a deep structure, underlying the accidents of growth" (6) or say (in another of his terms), undergirding the "mutation" (5) of surface features. Agamben, as Cavell before him, helps in steering us toward just this dimension, where origins are made immanent in their ends—steering us, that is, toward what we might call (after Clark's "order of orders") the "form of forms" (or in Coleridge's terms, the *forma informans*). By this I mean the lingual conditions of literary formation, or again the formative aspect of the formal, whose consideration is all the less "formalistic" for accessing this level of generativity (and gesture) rather than fixed pattern.

Clark, as noted, sees form-as-change working its changes upon natural pattern in the aesthetic pressure toward meaning. Beyond this, I find the formative cast of literary writing as witnessing to the nature (the given) of language as its own system of meaning, whose productive options remain felt in the local mobilizations—and "mutations"—of the textual speech act. Methodologically conceived, then, the formative, as a fact of language, is simply one facet or aspect of formal apprehension. It is part of what we read for in the cued intuition of how reading itself works—works both technically and emotionally. If form is change, repetition with a difference, it may in the process reveal the transformative operations that feed it. What emerges around the hinge of such perception, in the reversible swivel from words back to wording and out to world, is almost an inferential ratio and proportion—or more like a textual chiasm: the formal (as point of departure) is to the formative it alone can reveal as a verbal ethic is to a literary ethics—the one means as the only way to the other's felt manifestation. From the evident wording is precipitated both the meant sense and the linguistic event of its generation.

Who can doubt that verbal texture derives from a deep fund of linguistic possibility underwriting the patterning of a lexical or syntactic formation? But how is this underwriting to be read? And why? Answers begin at another level of the doubtless. For such surface texture is so far from "transparent," even when called refracted and prismatic, as to resist any wholesale subservience of form to content by which the shaped phrase could be thought to disappear altogether into the phrased shape or event. To read as if the surface were so dissoluble—which operates in certain circles as the ungoverned rule of literary commentary, the tendency rather than the rare pragmatic exception—is, for instance, to encounter ethical events *in books* rather than their construction *in words*. The former is where literary situations are prized only for a human complexity fuller and more nuanced than the categorical instances of moral philosophy. What "actual reading" registers instead is the fostering energy of language in action rather than just in use, its formative pressure. In helping to characterize such a textual response within a general formal persuasion, and in full support of the latter's methodological commitments, the localized epithet *formative* is thus "transferred" here with a quite specific purpose, deliberately twofold in its flip from cause to effect, and *pointedly* so—aimed from the received structures of language plumbed and activated by a given phrasing toward the reading moment fashioned (or say, informed) by their recognition. No hermetic stylistics is on call in these pages. The readings are in their own way resolutely contextual. But the context, before all, is language.

The coming experiment is to test the bearing of philosophy on literature—and on the interpretability of its words—by considering philosophers who themselves treat the literary text as active readers of its linguistic operation and philological sedimentation. That's what draws these pages at length to the ordinary language analyst in Cavell (reading Shakespeare and Poe and Emerson), more briefly to the exegete of virtuality and its immanence in Gilles Deleuze (reading Dickens), in passing (on Mallarmé) to the deconstructor of the lexico/syntactic divide in Derrida, to the sociocultural metalinguist in Kittler (on Goethe and the hermeneutic urge of German Romanticism), and at greater length to the poetician of the vernacular in Agamben (reading not just Dante and Italian Romanticism but Dickens, too, and at greater length Melville). In each of their thinking, literature under the aspect of writing (like cinema under the aspect of film, which, as it happens, Cavell, Deleuze, Kittler, and Agamben all take up elsewhere in their work) comes under description as a philosophy of representation and its medium.

From Tropology to Linguistic Topography

Such issues of literary language, of literature as language, have, of course, waxed and waned in academic currency. But even when something like a philosophy of reference was quite prominently convened for discussion under the banner of literary theory, the conversation was at key points unduly constrained. What my approach, hinted at so far, might sound closest to is that of the philosophically inflected essays collected by J. Hillis Miller in *The Linguistic Moment*, a book "about moments of suspension within the texts of poems . . . when they reflect or comment on their own medium."[8] After calling "this suspension the linguistic moment," Miller's further clarification is more revealingly cued to his method: "It is a form of parabasis, a breaking of the illusion that language is a transparent medium of meaning" (xiv). Literature's linguistic turns serve to uncurtain the theater of its own opaque shadow play and its choric exposition at once. The "linguistic moment" in Miller is thus identified by—and perhaps overly identified with—that rhetorical trope named in turn for the moment in classical drama ("parabasis") when an audience is addressed directly, dispelling, one might say, the diegesis by its exegesis. Typical of deconstruction in its "Yale" phase, the question of linguistics tends to reduce in most every case (certainly in Miller's own case studies, for instance, on poets from Wordsworth to Stevens) to the deviations—and evasions—of tropology: where the trope is stressed as a "turning" from literal to strictly figural referent. What results is less a relation of Signifier to signfied on the linguistic (Saussurean) model of S/s than a deflected S\s—and a reflexive one at that: namely, the turning back on itself of the text as such, in other words as a figure for its own writing.

On this understanding, any question of what the text is about—or turns about, even in the disclosed pivotal "moment" of linguistic witness—is indeed rhetorical: a question of rhetoric per se, as signaled, for instance, by that evoked classical trope in Miller's summary. Case closed—or felt by some readers to be too soon foreclosed in its own tropology. This is because the narrowed question of rhetoric at stake, in what might well be specified as "the rhetorical moment" rather than "the linguistic moment," is, for the most part, allegorical only of itself. The writing's own apparent disclosure of a particular self-figuration becomes the troping of the whole text in extrapolated rhetorical terms: providing, say, not only a wholesale parabasis (auto-staging) but elsewhere a metalepsis (authorial cause intruded as aesthetic effect), a catachresis (figuration eclipsing all claims on the literal), a prosopopoeia (the featuring forth of the intangible).[9] And so on.

The gains in rhetorical attention under this analytic mandate were as hard to deny at the time as to find in active engagement since. Yet even in the first flush of its influence, deconstruction's way of singling out tropology from the whole spectrum of linguistic operation—at the expense, to begin with, of phonology or morphology, of grammar and its syntactic patterning—served to curtail the imagined leverage of such a verbal "moment," its potential analytic torque. By such self-inflicted constriction, the reflexive angles of the linguistic moment suffered from a limited range of motion not just in gaining purchase outside a given writing in the discursive field of context but—more to the point here—in connecting with a broader base of stylistic (and hence linguistic) operations. It is this expanded verbal field—a more widely gauged topography and its undertext—from which analysis might have tapped not so exclusively into the tropology of referential subterfuge but into a fuller philology, and ultimately philosophy, of alphabetic language in action. In short, the linguistic moment wasn't linguistic enough.

To say so is to take up a theme in my own writing that runs from 1990's *Reading Voices* through the "microstylistics" (across a broader range of effects, lexical and syntactic as well as phonemic) of *Novel Violence*.[10] In each case the phenomenological space of literary action is taken to be a space not just brought out but entirely brought off by phrasing. At the minimal level of subsyllabic (phonetic) accretion, words in cross-coupled formation, precipitant and disappearing, keep lugging on, plugging on, ferrying description on the punctually broken backs of lexical script and its at times replete interstices. That, I argued years ago, is writing read: the reading that voices. To vary the epigraph from Wittgenstein, text need not sound itself off (or out) to be called *read*; the "conscious" liftoff from alphabetics into phonetics (and thence semantics) is the only "criterion" of the reading deed—all that philosophy (in our ensuing chapters) wants to make us more than ordinarily conscious of. With my previous emphasis on record, therefore, this book need not concentrate so exclusively (as a definitive limit case) on the zero degree of writing in the phonemic space between isolated word units, words you knit together on the run. Broader spans of collocation, suspension, elision, and ligature can now, as they do the reader at large, concern the chapters ahead. And in prose narrative as often as in poetry.

From Phonautography to Narratography

It takes other than the naked eye to make good on the principle that reading voices. An extravagant exception—and a brief technological digression—can gird the rule. Almost two decades before Edison's first sound recording, speech sounds found their momentary signatures. A French typesetter (of all things)—dramatically overstepping his alphabetic bounds—managed to "imprint" the human voice on soot-treated paper in a way that has recently been scanned by lasers and recovered for playback and reproduction.[11] The traditional page reconfigured as "phonautograph"—with the term's portmanteau suggestion of an automatized visual tracing of the phonetic register—was in the late 1850s not only the technical fulfillment of earlier European Romanticism, with its emphasis on phonemic mimesis in a poetics of unmediated natural transmission. It was also the dawn of a new technical epoch in aural culture. There were now other ways to log speech than by hand. And the voice-graph's continuum with literary Romanticism is apparent not least in its settling for the transcribed and legible *look of sound* rather than its ambient remanufacture: its sheer graphonic status, as it were, with no fantasy—or only a fantasy—of audition. In its short-lived transitional status between technological storage paradigms, the phonautograph suspends the very distinction, in media archaeology, between script and groove, typeset and phonographic trace.[12]

This is where phonetics, lexically enacted, connects with an expanded but comparable range and rotation of syntactic process equally prey to the uncertainties of temporal uptake in the unrolling pace of designation. Grammatical as well as lexical points of contact are often vulnerable to the pressure of unexpected phrasal turns. Those spinning mid-Victorian cylinders would, in this figurative sense, have been a not inappropriate surface on which to register that particular semantic loop taken up in the second half of this book as the phrasal counterpart to cross-lexical drift: namely, syllepsis, which regularly involves one verb either predicating two objects in different sequential senses, sometimes literal versus metaphoric, or otherwise unfurling across divergent idiomatic registers—in any case broaching a structural mismatch in the process of supposed syntactic "coordination." A philosophical case in point to come, for Gilbert Ryle's anti-Cartesian philosophy of mind, is Dickens's implicit mind/body slide in *The Pickwick Papers* when noting of Miss Bolo that she "went straight home, *in a flood of tears and a sedan-chair*" (chap. 35). As much as with the phonetic split ends of the lexicon (if this exit were put otherwise, say, as "She wept as she was swept away"), such higher-order phrasal effects (of ambiguous grammar rather than syllabic juncture) are susceptible as well to those "strange attractors" capable of denucleating grammatical armatures as much as eroding lexical autonomy.

At each level of such tension and dispersal, and with many an effect in between, the time-based medium of writing incurs its own time loops, second thoughts, and purposive recursions, whether in the split second of juncture, the logically dropped beat of conjunction, or in any number of other extended verbal syncopations. Literary writing at moments like these, unraveled to the constituents of speech itself and its paradigms of alternation, invites a philosophy of language as much as a literary criticism—in the form, let us say, of a linguistic rather than strictly semantic decipherment. With such attention applicable as much to the phonetic and syntactic "microplots" of prose narrative as to the recognized compressions of verse patterning, this is how my former call for a "narratography" of fiction—answering to a topography contoured, and a depth stratified, by more than the turning of tropes—finds itself complemented in the second half of this book by a prosaics of linguistic potential that there are good reasons, so we'll see, to think of as proto- rather than neo-formalist.

From Deed to Ethos

At which point no little bafflement arises over why the former "linguistic turn" and the current "ethical turn" have to seem (especially in proximity to the neoformalist "return") not just decades but worlds apart, so wholly incompatible in the scale of their notice. In fact, they don't. With fiction or poetry, something specifically literary—literal, textual—is directly entailed in the responsible temper (and tempo) of reading. Paying heed in this way keeps the mind afloat on what it decodes, inner ears alert to divergences within the written, interpretation nervous and on edge, exercising discriminations subtler than anything (grammatically, let alone culturally) prejudged. But so little unanimous has such an assumption been in literary studies recently (the assumption that literary reading is first of all an event of language and a deed of responsibility to it) that this notion can only reformulate itself in the mode not of a received axiom but of a proposal to be tested, like all hypotheses, on fresh evidence—and this in the spirit not of complacency but of new advocacy.

Put the proposal this way: that the minuscule but scarcely minor discriminations upon which intensive reading must rest, even in its constant renegotiation—and must rest its case in the end—are not just the facilitators of an other-directed vigor of response to various representations but, rather, a kind of ethical calisthenics in their own right. They exercise attention at its point of departure. Following on the academy's counterswing, roughly three decades ago now, from the strenuous medium-specificities of deconstruction to a more politically cued sense of textual transaction with the world, the so-called ethical turn concerns literature's place, literature's interface, in our textual consideration of the Other. Implementing this rather than simply complementing it, a deliberate verbal *ethic* rather than a generalized literary ethics keeps faith instead, or first of all, with the words on a page as the necessary, crucially nuanced, conduit of any such mediated encounter with things other.

The emphasis to come in these chapters (and its sponsoring evidence) is highly selective, even eccentric at times, if only in order to anchor the principle more vividly. But even in the most general terms, I make no apologies for the familiarity of all this about literature being alive only in its words. That's the trouble: we used to know it full well. Why has it come to this pass, then, where literature, rather than requiring a unique and refined pedagogy all its own, is now so often only pedagogic in itself: exemplary, identificatory, imbued with "otherness" only in its representations, not in its words? Literature instructs us in alternatives, in the very fabric of alterity, without being seen any longer to practice what it preaches. It is no longer responded to as the work of internal differentiation, nor as different enough in this respect from other discourses to demand a specialized analytic apparatus. Again and again, that is, a text is asked to testify to the Other without performing the heuristic of overcome alienation on itself. Or say, literature is found witnessing to difference without enlisting it. The same is true for cinema studies with no filmic (or now digital) texture on call. Or of art history when it is all history and no art.

Though schooled in an interpretive culture of acknowledged difference and its politics of identification, academic readers as such are not always comparably adept—even professional ones, or professors in training—at that very different instinct, even before it could become a skill: letting go of the written as regimented signification only then to find, outside the efficiencies of representation, an otherness made intimate in the power of language itself. Call this more closely verbal task a disidentification ethic. It operates within, across, and athwart the events of address or characterization—at the level of the word, the phrase, the clause, sometimes at the hinge points of phonemic aggregation itself. Just such verbal cleaving and dis-identity, this multifaceted and syncopated overlap of wording and even grammar, is what makes poetry poetry, but also, in fiction, prose prose. This is also what alone makes for a fully nerved reading of literary reverberation as such, unsettling the molds of character and event in fiction, persona and expression in verse, so that the subject lent out in reading and the perspective conjured by it come to intersect, mediate, remeasure, and disquiet each other. And even empty each other—as we will see in Agamben's emphasis on "desubjectification." With its instigation or trigger in the force of phrase, it is at this intersection, this interface, where literary meaning plies its trade—and takes its play. And pays its dues. It is also, as we are to find from various angles, where philosophy meets linguistics in delimiting the ethos of the human, its locus of community, in the powers, but first of all the potential, of communicability itself.[13]

The Coming Terrain

Hence the ground plan of this book. With implications for a philosophy of language in action, the deed of reading takes shape here in a kind of circulatory economy, with its own brand of deficit expenditures. I begin in Chapter 1 by calling to mind my own earliest remembered encounters—and collisions—with literary density. Then, with an emphasis on the English Romanticism of Wordsworth and Shelley and their Victorian legacy, the treatment of verse flux and compression (Chapters 2 and 3) listens in part for the toll that a phonic apprehension of speech sounds can take on the punctual and self-regulating thrift of written meaning, less through overt aural wordplay like "toll," however, than in a more oblique and, so to say, glancing fashion. Yet such a verbal surcharge is often heard still, even in being only half glimpsed across the pitch of script. For all this and more takes place in a manner deeply embedded in the variable linguistic "support" (and condition) of human speech, with the givenness of language intuited anew, when not exactly audited, in its various phrasal takings.

In the same spirit, Part 2 moves from this formative poetics to a "prosaics of potential" that is often more broadly gauged across syntactic spans in narrative phrasing. Yet even here we begin with a certain phonemic crisis in Cavell's approach to the writing of Poe, as well as a grammatical one (incurred by the syntactic trope of syllepsis) that I find brought in tow by his narrator's strained, manic phrasing. This discussion lays the (shifting) groundwork, in turn, for a chapter on comparable syntactic effects in Dickens and others, in which that perverse sublexical slippage noted by Cavell in Poe is scaled up to the further tax exacted by the byplay of sylleptic syntax (and its figurative fallout) on the forward momentum of narrative—yet recouped in other ways that certain philosophers of metaphoric language, polled as we go, have been attentive to. From there, we move forward to contemporary writing in the aurally contoured style of Toni Morrison—as foregrounded by the very lessons of literacy and its obliteration in her 2008 novel, *A Mercy*.

At which point analysis has in fact rounded back to the question launched in Chapter 2 concerning the matter (via Agamben) of a medium's own *transmissibility* rather than just its role in transmission. This is an unstable state where phrasing might be said, in its very saying, to retain the human potential for utterance by keeping its possibilities still presently in action, in transformation, as we read. Instances by then will have been variable but steadily accumulating from chapter to chapter. In each verse and prose text differently (that difference being exactly the point)—and with or without the recurrence of an almost linguistic gothic in some of these writings—both literary diction and the syntax of its distribution are ghosted in this way by the unruly returns of their own undertext. And there is reason to think that such matters may still have their due hearing in literary debate. Despite the setbacks of presumed verbal "transparency" in too much culturalist literary discussion, an optimistic note can be sounded in preparation for the coming chapters. One needn't, I suspect, be drawn habitually to the inner contours of literary writing (as I confess, and soon show, myself to have been from early on) in order to regret the deflated status of verbal alertness, the late vacuum of silence around phrasing as such in prose and poetry alike—and to want some of the air let back in, so that imaginative writing might breathe a bit (even if still silently) before being called to one account or another in its historical and social bearings. Or before being imagined (under the often medium-effacing wrench of the "cognitive turn") as putting us directly in mind of the world, or in touch with other minds, rather than of given words for it and them.

So a word more on the word-skirting bias of this latest turn—as it develops, curiously enough, alongside the fitful emergence of certain neoformalist tendencies, if not tenets. When neuroscience allows us, as it now does, to locate exactly where and how sectors of the brain differentiate phonemic features in the listening act, it is closer to an ethic of attention in literary criticism, it seems to me, than when—often absorbed by literary accounts into a broader ethicist trend in the exploration of affect and empathy—similar science is brought forward to explain our evolved cognitive functions in the hardwired recognition of bodily and facial gestures. As intriguing as these latter interdisciplinary applications can seem, one may still wish to remember that some bodies and faces are only written into being, and different as such from ones coming through to us visibly from their own places in the world—and that in this respect the etymology of words, for instance, in contrast to the evolution of brain structure, may therefore have a good deal more to say about their particular constitution. For all the ways in which emotive reactions to events both experienced and merely depicted can be traced to common functions of the brain's electrochemistry, one may still want to bear in mind the very different means (or intervening mediations) by which characters versus people, textual events versus lived actions, *come to mind* in the first place: in the minding of words.

Some fairly widespread desire to keep hold of these methodological differences is therefore the best hope for a book like this in finding more readers out there, readers at least vaguely impatient with the disciplinary dispersals incident to cultural and cognitive studies, than the few who—in respect to (and for) intensive verbal attention—might populate a choir of the already faithful. I mean more readers than just those with a pluralist tolerance for other ways of doing literary business than the ones currently fashionable. I mean, more particularly, those further readers harboring a genuine sense that something fundamental—albeit in deference to issues even arguably more burning—has gone missing. And there's a resulting extra hope on this book's part: that the polemic to come, mostly tacit, though flaring up at times, might seem welcome even to those largely immune to the specific approach, through linguistics and philosophy, that it attempts. A book's motives can be timely even if the proposed corrective may not fully satisfy—or seem overdone in one direction or another; or seem (a more bracing complaint, this would be) not to have gone far enough.

Confess, did I say?—to that early interest in what I would later hear called the "languageness" of literature. Well, it's closer to that, certainly, a confession, than to credentialing, let alone a boast. It's inveterate, my slow reading. Nothing in itself to be proud of. In an often fumbling rather than systematic fashion, the instinct to *read the words*—rather than just through them to their point—has been with me from the start of my self-conscious reading life. Which began rather late, and swamped itself at times in admittedly modest overreaching. Trying to get into the swim, I often drifted out of my depth. My attentiveness to wavering and oscillation in the pace of serious writing, I later realized when coming to examine and rechannel it in college, was only the potential virtue of a true defect. Early on, it was simply that I was often unsure about exactly what I was reading, sentence by sentence, in my teenage forays—and well before I gathered that this referential dislocation can be the very point of some texts. Not as many as threw me, though. Frequently upended and forced to reread, all I could do was let myself be tossed forward again from word to word.

In thinking back to these moments, and knowing better than to plume myself on some bold will to multivalence, I do recognize at least a willingness to rest unsure. In giving some sense of this in retrospect, the coming autobiographical excursus will be brief and merely strategic—zeroing in on a representative poem from the shelves of memory (a rhymed lyric by Richard Wilbur) as a sample proof text. Beyond autobiographical accuracy in regard to my early taste, the text in question serves to look straight into the teeth of both a large portion of contemporary academic discourse and especially its political allergies—in whose name literary criticism, as such, is often defamed or silently avoided—and go directly back to the work of a New Critical standard-bearer in Wilbur, singling out a poem whose reflexive thematic of fluctuant beauty is as apparently shuttered from politics and from cultural contestation (if only apparently, as I'll try showing) as it is possible to be. So in what follows I'm letting a finely wrought minor piece of lyrical description, cashed out at the end with an earned perceptual generalization, carry the initial weight of a claim for the verbal challenge—lexical, syntactic, and figurative all at once—of literature at large. What will seem incomplete about this procedure—so obviously left hanging in the coming memories of poetic "induction" and its frequent hazings by complexity—is exactly what the subsequent philosophical discussion is brought in to develop.

So let me offer a borrowed anecdote by way of parable. As it happens, a far more prominent autobiographical memoir than my brief recollections to come, a 2010 magnum opus by Stanley Cavell, actually limns the border between philosophy and literature that my own much later work here, like Cavell's many books before it, attempts crossing.[14] Writing of his efforts, as a doctoral student in the mid-1950s, to come to grips with J. L. Austin's extended dimension of performativity in the promissory overtones of a phrase like "I know," Cavell remembers sensing, as recounted in *Little Did I Know*, that there are more ways than one to "*give others your word*" (321). He is led by this progress of thought to a conception that "reveals human speech to be radically, in each uttered word, ethical" (321). But such a thought, though shaping his later career, had in those student days to be, as it were, *utterly* repressed within the halls of Harvard's philosophy department. The tacit interdict is in fact recalled, in Cavell's own phrasing, with a wry overtone of literary echoism in the necessary choking back of any such "uttered" thought even in clutched and tentative form: "To have *muttered* such a thing then would have seemed, well, literary" (321; my emphasis on the slant rhyme declining from insight to its untransactable deed in context). To prize the "given" word in this way, yet on good philosophical grounds—and to appraise as steadily as possible its contract with us—is exactly what is meant from here out, and exemplified, as an ethic of attention.

If all this was about the farthest thing from the mind of a high school literary initiate, let that be one yardstick of the more considered method these chapters, whose interdisciplinary reach was achieved only long after, are hoping to demonstrate. And it is none too soon to say that if you are able to contain your curiosity about budding teenage hunches concerning the challenge of literary phrasing, you can certainly skip the freestanding first chapter—or save it for later, when what comes of it can be more fully read back into it—and fast-forward straight past Richard Wilbur to William Wordsworth on the way to that prose poetics of the novel after Romanticism where the lack of a serious linguistic attention in standard commentary is perhaps most apparent. By then, certainly, it should be clear that the true spur to this book is an interest in the "languageness" of language itself, not simply of literature (as in the high-structuralist touchstone—and its mostly poetic rather than prose evidence). Hence the frequent transit, to come, from criticism to language philosophy and back again. The uncertain high school kid just entering the workforce, and later the college applicant pool, who was coming to take compensatory pleasure in certain accidents of phonetics and syntax like the too little difference between "you're A's" and "your raise" or the unflagged prepositional detour in the bumpy roadwork of a phrase—a rough phrase at that—like "scholarships for merit and certain degree programs only" would, nonetheless, never have believed there could be a coherent book in the likes of this: in the conceptual space, that is, between these two differently scaled registers of linguistic instability (cross-word phonetic ambiguity versus syntactic forking, though each a hitching glitch in its way, sublexical on the one hand, metagrammatical on the other). Let's hope he would have been wrong.

Long grown up since, and when writing recently on Victorian fiction for an anthology called *The Feeling of Reading*, on the affect of this literary institution, I deliberately concentrated on the feel of actually doing it, actually reading.[15] Here too: an emphasis not solely on what one is reading *about* in literature, but on what one *is about* while doing so. And this well before, and quite separate from, any more radical recognition that subjectivity itself may be only about language to begin with. In taking stock of reading in this fashion, emphasis falls not only on what moves you, but on what propels you forward through the chord changes of response. At which point one may notice that affect is not simply delivered, but actually taken up, by wording's own flow, where a reader may often be moved by sheer exposure to the inner workings of the only medium (as Agamben will insist in pursuit of its poetics as well as its elusive ontology) shared by consciousness and text: moved, that is, by the never quite overcome mystery of human language itself.

A more recent monograph in part on the feeling of reading bears directly on the link between ethics and affect in the latest paradigms of nineteenth-century scholarship. Examining the tension between lyric arrest and biographical drive in Victorian fiction—the former surrendering persona and subjective agency as well as suspending the emplotment of developmental characterization—Elisha Cohn proposes an affect theory not exclusively beholden to a progressive fictional aesthetic of self and other in social sympathy, but rather stylistically registered by moments of narrative suspension in a poetics either of reverie or of lassitude.[16] It is at this prompting sensory level, for instance—well short of any communal orientation in the work of fiction, yet bound up no less in the deep impersonal basis of all shared knowing in words—that formative linguistic energies, as my own study seeks to illustrate, may be detected in their pressure upon given phrasings, however subliminal or diffuse. As if sourced in the generative unconscious of language itself, these energies are sensed—when "reading for form"—to impel exactly such lyric rhythms as noted by Cohn before they are called to any ethical account beyond their own intuitive (yet always verbally meditated) notice. It is at this level, I would add, both within a culture of Victorian perfectability and beyond, that the rule of attention is not exhausted in an improving rigor but survives in a reactive submission to linguistic forces proven on the pulse of the reader's own sensory uptake.[17]

And no need to think that what one finds at this level—however open such prose may be to motiveless sensation at certain points in the psychic trajectory of character—must therefore necessarily disqualify critique. So that one further possible salutary effect of my chapters is worth fantasizing up front. In the face of current neoformalist discourse, the demonstrations here might help cut through an often tendentious distinction between a supposedly capacious and sensitized "surface reading" and its more skeptical or "symptomatic" alternative.[18] This is because literary surface has its own verbal depth charges—well beyond the question of a given phrasing as symptom of verbal complexity at large or an index of the differential linguistic base per se, but still never dissevered from this whole reservoir of utterance.

Poised at its own variant intersection of ordinary language philosophy and literature, with its subtitle *Wittgenstein and the Aesthetics of Literary Experience*, Charles Altieri's recent *Reckoning with the Imagination* seems operating, both by title and throughout, in two prepositional directions at once: predicating not just an idiomatic "engaging with" (or "confronting") the imagination, so much ignored in contemporary literary discussion, but a "thinking by way of" it.[19] The reckonings of my chapters are more specifically linguistic than broadly "imaginative" in his sense, but with a similar double valence nonetheless: say, *coming to terms with words*. Where Altieri draws on the phenomenological aspects of Wittgenstein's work in a strenuous and convincing effort to delink literary value from ethical modeling, my sense of an ethic of verbal attention (equally detached from standard ethics and its risk of prescriptive moralism) offers a complementary line of approach. Yet the "slow reading" practiced here (as distinct from that championed by Altieri in allusion to Nietszche's phrase, chap. 2, 38) has more to do with the "language" whose stakes are raised in Wittgenstein's account of our "language games" than with their rule-governed criteria for agency and understanding. Where Altieri's and my projects do most notably converge, however, is in resisting the preference for "surface" over "depth" in the latest maneuvers of neoformalism. Altieri rightly dismisses any such notion that "surface must preclude depth, not just depth as the inquiry into what is hidden but also depth as something that is constructed because of how the play of surfaces develops" (chap. 1, 20). Nor can one responsibly preclude the further depth that conditions such ramified "construction"—as linquistic possibility—in the first place.

So in what follows, and however slow the pace, a certain spirit of deep reading prevails, as emblemized in fine art by the appropriated and carved up books of the self-styled "book surgeon" or "book autopsist" Brian Dettmer, with his knife-blade excavations of the codex anatomy, including face and back and spine and innards. These are works I've recently characterized as a form of "reading as mining."[20] Their linguistic rather than sculptural equivalent would involve a differently stratified path through the underlay of text. But to retain the artist's own figures of exploration in a shift from surgery to diagnosis, and to borrow the new intransitive idioms of medical symptomatology, the deepest assumptions, impulses, or contradictions of a text, from political to psychological, can often "manifest" or "present" in a displaced but telltale anomaly—a formal defiance—within a routine systemic function. One may consider such diagnostic moments, in the literary "case study," as a noted lapse in the circulatory grammar of indication itself. In some of the more densely self-embroiled examples to come, an engagement with the surface tension of language (and not as mere superfice but as variable filter) is reading's only way to think *through* to the formative contours of the verbal depiction in question, including any ideology the poem or novel may at that point harbor or resist. And further, in the deed of reading, the only way to begin *thinking its medium through*.

PART I
TOWARD A FORMATIVE POETICS

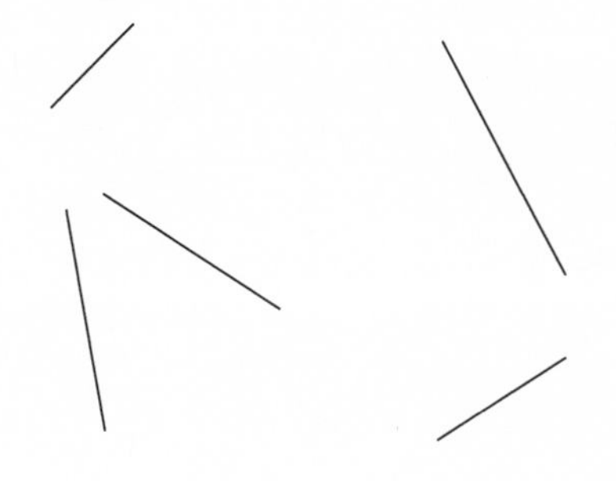

1
INDUCTION

I go back in memory, then, to my hometown's well-stocked and long-gone local bookshop, with its fuss-budget and anything but avuncular owner, at least as inquisitive as his patrons, who was always seeming to scope out your roving interests over his bifocals. It was the California of the Beach Boys, not yet the Beatles. And there in Laguna Beach, a newly transplanted and misfit high school student from the other coast, I began my first sustained bookstore romance, a few blocks walking distance from the family house—and continents away. A rather desperately compensatory romance? Sublimated teen solitude and angst? What else was literature for? Then as now, Laguna was a resort town never known for resorting overmuch to books, even beach reading; I was mostly alone there when I stopped at the bookstore; rarely saw anyone I knew; hardly anyone more than once. For me it was a zone apart—and twice over. Planning to be an architect from early in high school, I started looking to literature for something else—but something no less structured, no less a built environment, as I soon realized: a world of distant and shifting horizons, certainly, but also a crafted shelter.

Then, too, the wannabe designer in me loved the graphics of the covers, among them (as it happens) the giant 7 of that ambiguity book. And, a little later, the newly venturesome reader in me came to love ambiguity as a name for my own uncertainties and second thoughts. Who knew this poverty of confidence could be thought of as philosophically rich? I can still spottily document this first flush of serious reading with mental sales receipts, from Tolstoy to Faulkner to, among the philosophy books in the next alcove, E. M. Cioran and those heady answers of Sartre's to "What is literature?," including the first books of poetry I sparingly bought. If this last indulgence in particular felt, on a movie usher's salary, almost like paying by the word, maybe that's part of why they counted so much for me, those word-by-word productions.

Because will and wallet knew their limitations, the bookstore was more a guilty pleasure than edifying, all that browsing with so little uptake. Like overindulging, with no intention to shell out, in those record-shop listening booths a few doors away. Back down the block in the far less busy bookstore, it often seemed like snooping rather than perusing. So I felt obliged to buy at somewhat regular, if carefully spaced, intervals:

stabs in the dark for the light. While, all the while, I kept on combing the seemingly endless shelves. Existentialism looked fiercely important whenever I looked into it, and I loved the big novels, not the small ones. But poetry had its special scent, and there I wanted the small books and, in them, the short poems. Challenges one might come up to—or wouldn't have to fail at for long. Some purchases didn't repay my arbitrary selection. I remember having a go at scaling the smallest (and cheapest) book of poems I could find, the diminutive format of *Lord Weary's Castle*, and though I could tell Robert Lowell had something, I wasn't sure what, and I further suspected, in my callowness, how the lord of that keep must have come by his name. My experiments were hit and miss, to be sure, and the misses not always near.

But sometimes the earth moved. I must have been just the right age and temperament to be smitten. In any case, the next collection of poems I cottoned to and took home, very much *despite* its blandly designed paperback cover, had hooked me by its title alone—the first and interesting half of it, that is, but as contaminated grammatically by what followed: Richard Wilbur's *The Beautiful Changes and Other Poems*. Two plurals, I at first assumed: something about changes and then a batch of other poems. Much to explore. Skimming through it, I loved right away the sound of the bunched phrases, that tuneful diction and rhythmic pattern, its lucid music. A rapid caveat, though: if the once-celebrated Wilbur—mainstream, accessible, *New Yorker*-friendly, Pulitzer-Prized, and laureate-aureoled—is no longer to anyone's exact taste, that shouldn't deter the experiment in recovered literary memory I've embarked on. I don't choose Wilbur now for any reason except that I chose him then, hoping to show here how writing like his, as with greater and more demanding poetry, can work its quiet magic on an unjaded imagination. It doesn't have to be a triumphant poem, just a good-enough one, and certainly not necessarily an edgy one, to plough certain willing furrows in the topsoil of the teenage imagination (or say, the student sensibility). For our present use, the single poem lifted from memory, no matter how dated in its aesthetic, how overpolished, needs only to be demanding enough to sustain a rudimentary ethic of attention. Wilbur's short poem certainly is—and does, especially in its difficult last moves.

Back then, the issue was simpler. I was just curious. Was the first half of the title the key to it all? The beautiful changes—as opposed to the other kind, the ugly or sad or defeating ones? Which particular transformations does the poet have in mind? Will each of the poems answer, one by one? These are the sort of questions those three words set going as I parted the volume, well before I looked for and found the title verses waiting at the end as capstone. So why not begin with that, even if Wilbur didn't? Temporarily moored in my room for the foray, I hoped such a last but surely not least poem, given its status as volume title, would be an economical place to start in sating those first curiosities about the title. It did answer some of my questions, but only by undoing the very language that prompted them—only by in fact *changing* the title not once but twice at least in the self-adjusted lens of the poem's unfolding grammar. Long before I would hear the prefix in a college literature class, and learn gingerly to deploy it, I was about to have my first rendezvous with the *meta*.

But every way I put this sounds too cerebral, I realize, even when I stress my tendency to be flummoxed at first with certain literary densities. In my routine teen alienation, taking up (with) poetry was neither a program nor a mission. I was just there *for the duration*, so to speak: the respite from pressures less appealing than abutted words and the time it took for their sorting out. The tugs and drags of dailiness weren't, of course, shut out at the closing of my door, let alone by the opening of my poetry book—much as I might have liked them to be at times. But amid the idiocies and anguishes of a teenage commerce with the world, and most of all its gnawing uncertainties, here was some restorative "time out": call it a way of doubting oneself productively, where missteps might feel like a circuitous progress. To put stress on the stresses and strains of reading, then, by way of generalization: whatever refuge it may be locally used for, the supposed escapism of literature can be just the opposite—given the demands it makes, the regimen it inflicts.

So here's what, come upon under the title *The Beautiful Changes*, I bore down on as best I could:

> One wading a Fall meadow finds on all sides
> The Queen Anne's Lace lying like lilies
> On water; it glides
> So from the walker, it turns
> Dry grass to a lake, as the slightest shade of you
> Valleys my mind in fabulous blue Lucernes.
>
> The beautiful changes as a forest is changed
> By a chameleon's tuning his skin to it;
> As a mantis, arranged
> On a green leaf, grows
> Into it, makes the leaf leafier, and proves
> Any greenness is deeper than anyone knows.
>
> Your hands hold roses always in a way that says
> They are not only yours; the beautiful changes
> In such kind ways,
> Wishing ever to sunder
> Things and things' selves for a second finding, to lose
> For a moment all that it touches back to wonder.

Amid this ongoing mesh of both rhyming echo and quieter chime, its patterns matched to sound and sense alike, even the first-eyed and only apparent parallelism would have braked my young progress, since the figurative floral (lake)bed does not so much slip and slide in response to the walker's commotion as, in the turning of two adjacent lines, it "glides" so that it "turns" solid matter into liquid perception. Even seemingly equivalent verb forms thus turn out, in process, to be differently formatted, the indicated doing toppling at the hinge of its own monosyllable into a doing *unto*—and in precisely the undoing of hasty grammatical assumptions. Within such an ongoing syntactic lacework of unexpected verbal loops and joins, it is this intrinsic slipperiness in the poem's first ad hoc grammar lesson, this early tutorial in the mutable, that sets the template for the balancing act to come in the next two stanzas.

Changes Wrung: A Mutability Canto

Though soon taken by grammatical surprise in the Wilbur poem, I was in some sense emotionally prepared for it. For it was indeed the quick-change artistry of literary writing that I was developing a hankering for. With such a fondness for instabilities, it's a good thing I didn't in fact become an architect. As *The Beautiful Changes* did its work on me, its relish for the kinetic and unsettled is what seemed epitomized at the smallest compass in the poem's now phrasal, now clausal title (a distinction that came easily enough in junior high grammar class). And if those "nows" of mine, just now, are taken as sequential, rather than as marking copresent alternatives, they rehearse my own change of mind in first assuming that a nominal rather than verbal sense was the guiding one, the default option: something on the model of "the beautiful transitions," well before "transition" was to anyone's ear (lucky us back then) a verb.

The titular changes are to be divided, I find, across the three short stanzas, with one ear-catching moment in each, beginning when—at the end of the first, with a meadow described as undulating like a "lake"—the speaker compares this to the landscape of desire, whereby "the slightest shade of you / Valleys my mind in fabulous blue Lucernes." I *may* have known the term "alliteration" by then, probably not "assonance," but certainly not a name for the "phonetic chiasm" that inverts "fab*ul*" in that lulu of a sound pool spilling over into "b*lu*e *Lu*cernes"—and then getting swirled up into "the beautiful" of the next stanza. Though without words for such an effect, something like that would have occurred to me—or better to say, have *occurred in the words for me*. Or maybe not. Maybe I just let all this wash over me as confirming the beautiful and its changes, its verbal as well as visual transformations, its wavelike rippling. Conscious recognition is certainly not the point in my looking back. And I wouldn't have fretted then about a lack of descriptive vocabulary in my attempt to account for what I thought—or, better, felt—was going on. But I might have sensed, nonetheless, that the potential analogy marked by "as" could just as well be an adverb instead, indicating a prompting simultaneity—across the links of natural impulse—in the turn from perception to desire: "as" for both "like" and "while" the mind is contoured by the force (the "valleying" depth) of the lover's image. This doubleness is so aptly grooved into the thematics of the poem that it dictates its split terms to the next "as," too, at the start of the second stanza ("as a forest is changed"), the phrase hovering not just between simultaneity and similitude but between established principle and further instance.

What did I once make of the way it is the "slightest shade of *you*"—with the further overtone "shade of hue"—that irrigates the ensuing u-phony? Homophone as punning pleonasm? Hardly. Those words, too, came later. For now, I had only Wilbur's. And of course I was still only a few lines in, the second stanza merely broached. So far, the changes in play have been primarily the shifts from passive perception to active transformation, then from observation into analogy, levitated and propelled by the onward rotation of phonetic echo. In the remaining two stanzas, the adjustments are to be bolder and more intrinsically linguistic, from anomalous spelling to bent and doubled-back syntax. To this point, at least, the first stanza would have sustained my sense of the title as a phrase. The pertinent changes are those tricks of the eye (captured by flickering glints of the ear) that turn reality itself into a kind of play on worlds. Soon enough, though, the title's adjective submits to internal modification, changes its spots—like the adaptive coloration described in its next and central stanza.

I've been making no attempt, these many decades later, to retrace the exact trip-ups and impasses of my grammatical decoding in those curious days, a decipherment all too fumbling, partial, and hazy. Would if I could, for illustration's sake, but can't. I can only write this up, write it out, in the terms I have come to learn for it—or at least in the anticipation of such terms. And have learned not just for but *from* it—from it and its kind. So I mean first of all to keep discussion of this one poem in touch with a certain early stage of wonder, both awe and bafflement, that literary writing often recreates in us, any of us, in later years, making words themselves young again, tentative, searching, even awkward at times as they seek their surer direction. Holding true in commentary to the text's way (and waywardness) with words, even a later analytic precision of the sort invading my paragraphs here can hardly help but summon up again that oscillatory shimmer, that veiled and spaced disclosure, so fetching to the linguistic libido of a novice reader whose urges for once were deliciously reciprocated by the page.

The complexities of our tongue may be new to us only once biographically. But literature can help renew such sensations each time out—and long before a philosophy of language like Giorgio Agamben's, wed to his poetics, teaches us how that renewal reaches to the very depth of *homo loquens*. Such plumbed ontology is not unrelated to the renewal, as it turns out, that is also the explicit theme of Wilbur's one poem, as we are still on the move toward recognizing. And retracing the stages of this process, I now see in categorical terms what I might then have sensed, at best, merely as the necessary agility of attention in gliding from one mode of surprise to another. For after the heavily phonetic climax of the first stanza, the crux of the second depends on a more exclusively graphic transformation, with the third combining lettering and phonetics at a thickened pivot point before breaking out into the full span of an ambiguous grammatical cascade.

Chameleon Turns

Even slips of the silent tongue can be part of this revived changeling force of language in process, with all its staged upendings of expectation. And so the second stanza, shifting from meadow to arboreal setting, launches forth in the continued evocation of a generalized bucolic perspective: "The beautiful changes as a forest is changed / By a chameleon's tuning his skin to it." How could I have avoided mistaking the word "tuning" for the more immediate hook of "turning"—especially with that trick "turns" of the first stanza still in echoing earshot? I must have committed this slip first time through, since I still do now every other time I look back at these lines. Here, then, unsaid—or at least unwritten—is the chameleon *turning green* under the rubric of beauty's very predication as change, while bringing with it the implied musical resonance of harmonic correlation as a metaphor for the complementary "tones" of insect and foliage in their chiming pigmentation. Synesthesia lay in wait for me as a term. But here I was tripping over it in action. And given the passive phrasing at line's end ("is changed"), derived from some transitive form or impetus (I hadn't then heard of "transformational grammar" either), I would have sensed (if not identified) the *active* chameleon work of enhancing further a summer's ambient green. This forest metamorphosis is thereby singled out not just as one of the beautiful changes, plural, but one of the ways the beautiful—singular and categorical and engulfing—not only changes in itself but changes those aspects of the world to which it is attributed. So, then, have three entailed senses of the poet's entitled word rung changes upon its own linguistic function.

To what extent one needed in high school to be good at grammar in order to register these waverings and undertows, I'll never be sure. Years of teaching since do suggest that it is easier to get students to notice something out of the way if they have clearly in mind certain norms by which to compare and annotate its departures. In any case, it must be admitted that if I really excelled at any one thing in those secondary school years, curricular or extracurricular, it was the lost art of sentence diagramming, which I could execute with a sure and practiced hand the way other kids did trigonometry or beach volleyball. (Where some flaunted a great overhead serve, my pride and joy was the backslash of the predicate nominative.) The change from *change* as substantive to *change* as intransitive to *change* as the stem of a past (active) participle may indeed remain only dimly felt if one can't tag it through some kind of familiarity with the categories, if not exactly by name. Be that as it may, the effect is at work—and must be sorted out intuitively in passing, if not fully sifted through. Same with the slippery slope of the intransitive "glides" as it drifts over into the transitive "turns" in the free-associational opening stanza.

And then we come upon the climactic lines of the third and final stanza, where "the beautiful changes" are encapsulated in their "Wishing ever to sunder / Things and things' selves for a second finding, to lose / For a moment all that it touches back to wonder." What? Where has the poem brought us in closing? In the penultimate phrase, has the rhythmic wording carried into the crevices of designation a subliminal hint of "severance" across the metrics of "wis*h*ing *ever* to sunder"? While I wouldn't have known then to call the hatchet-like onsets that propel these syllables a trochaic effect, I did no doubt catch the perseverance and the divisiveness alike of the beat. Evoked in this way is that differential severing, in fact that designated "sundering," that comes from within the things of this world when blooming anew to themselves under the sensitized eye, things echoing their essence against preconception's sounding board. This is the distance incident to beauty when renewed by conception. In nature and art as well. Yet it is language's own unique privilege with relation to this distance that the poem is there to prove—by reperforming it. And it is language, too, that melds the metaphoric work of both chameleon and mantis in the camouflage play between the former's trisyllabic "tuning his skin to it" and the latter's simpler and more organic (if equally figurative) growing "into it," the two natural drag acts echoing not just their separate backdrops but each other's syllabified phonemes as well. One might want to acknowledge, at such a moment of sublexical parallel, that the explicit rhetoric of transformation calls up something clearly formative in vocalic incrementation. As it certainly does by the time Wilbur's stanza has switched from blending-in to the foundational differentiation on which such fusion depends.

Lost and Found

This happens not least in the transient ambiguity of prepositional phrasing across the final two lines—after the severing and reseamed enjambment at "Wishing ever to sunder / Things and things' selves for a second . . ." Under description is the cleaving asunder (and together again) that lends the world "for a second" a—no, wait, the real adverbial phrase ("For a moment," not a second) still waits patiently a line away, preceded here by a verbalized substantive: "a second finding, to lose / For a moment . . ." My ellipses, here and just above, mark those points as which phrasing spills over the brink into lurching uncertainties and their quick recuperation. What is to be found is beauty's renewed chance of apprehension—not unlike, come to think of it, the eye's wordless equivalent of an optical rereading on the run. Taking it slow, the phrase "Things and things' selves" arranges for its punctuated sibilant elision to mark the flecked juncture of a silent apostrophe across the softly delinked objects of that "Wishing ever to sunder." Through the lens of the beautiful, there is a perpetual desire not wholly to divorce things from their entity or essence, nor just to deflect the self-sameness of identity, but rather to estrange those things to the point of fresh perception, if only for that restorative gesture that torques "for a second" away from adverbial toward adjectival force in a "second finding."

I keep trying to imagine first impressions of *The Beautiful Changes* apart from the way this poem is now colored for me in reassessment. No doubt I would have been jolted at the time, though perhaps not as a metrical phenomenon at all, by the tongue-twisting "things and things' selves"—and maybe even seen a silly plural "elf" there, with even the overwrought young reader wise enough to dismiss its impish irrelevance from mind. And I might have felt a bond tighter than usual in these words, harder to sunder—having paused, that is, over just that kind of plural apostrophe I was myself confident of having mastered in my own classroom punctuation exercises by then; and having paused especially over how odd and clotted it looked here in poetry. But I wouldn't have known that a "spondaic" double beat made the locked, muscle-bound phrase the challenge to dissociation that it sounds. And if innocent of trochees and spondees, still less was I acquainted with complicated rhyme schemes. Where I sensed echo, it was mostly as a part of a rhythm, not a formal template. Rhyme would merely have kept company with the other changes at play in the beauty at stake. Only now do I see how the last double pair of coupling rhymes in this stanza works to exceed foreknowledge in precisely the muted drumroll of incurred fascination that is silently played out in the mounting from "says" to unforeseen "ways," from "sunder" to a resultant and intrinsic "wonder." I didn't know about "making strange" then, by name or principle. Or didn't know I knew. Wilbur did. Knew–and knew how to make me feel it.

With "the beautiful" operating still as antecedent, adverbial brevity would have struck me as returning on the wing in a phrased desire "to lose for a moment all that *it* touches," which is only to say, in the reach of the very phrase, "touches back to wonder." Still in reprise and approximation, here again is the young mind picking its way slowly across the line. Or better put (which is the whole point of my grammatical stammerings brought back as literary-critical fable in these days of vanishing attention to such things): here is any mind made innocent once more, and avid, by the localized surprise of poetic second thoughts, second chances. One stands back to process this, lets the keywords vet—and resonate with—each other. Such lovely losses: the beautiful letting go momentarily of all that it touches in a universal principle of change. But the grammar continues, with the infinitive "to lose" turned suddenly compound, arcing over its object to revectorize predication with another wavering adverbial phrase. Or even two, it seems. Across the momentarily lost direction of the enjambment, the impacted phrase "to lose / For a moment all that it touches back to wonder" gathers meaning only across its terraced overlaps of idiom in a rolling syntactic increment. Under the auspices of transformation rather than its transience, beauty loses everything it is recognized to touch, but only in the sense of touching it again with, and so releasing it back to, notice.

In the poem's layered natural settings, from meadow to forest and back again, we encounter what linguists (summoned once more to the dock) call—as again I will learn only much later—a "garden path sentence," launched upon its own self-correction in the way the title has already surreptitiously been. Permutations are shuffled through on the spot in the closing grammatical transform. The beautiful suffers its losses in order to refind; loses all that it touches, all that it finds embodiment in—until syntax spins out to suggest that the loss is only "back to wonder," as if in a homecoming. Anything seemingly subtracted, abstracted, is reclaimed now for a fresh finding. All this lends force, in turn, to an ephemeral phonetic suspicion (to which young readers of even modestly secure spelling habits might well be prone) of "looses . . . back" (frees to). If I was wrong at first about "turning" for "tuning," why not a second thought here after a coaxed misapprehension? For this is certainly the gist, the sense—though not the written verb: things freed again, set loose, from custom to astonishment.

So that maybe I glimpsed even in that early reading—hung up on the title as I was, just as the poem is so carefully hung from its gradually doubled and tripled senses—how its loaded verbal turn presides even in absentia over the close of the poem. For here is poetry's power of association in a single climactic node. The loss that touches back to wonder in a second finding puts a strain on idiom that could only be righted if rewritten under the aegis of a compound predicate like "changes back" (far more vernacular than "loses back.") One could put the whole transformative idea this way: change in the world loses all that it touches, and this only by touching back (because metaphorically holding up) to wonder all that it thus anoints (and in words appoints) to the receptive eye in a restored keenness of apprehension—prehensile, haptic, touching. Once it is taken as no longer a nominal form or substantive, and not even just a verbal intransitive, the title becomes in this emergent sense elliptical, with no limits to the objects of its ministry. It is in every sense transactive, transitive. The beautiful changes—everything, you name it. Difference surrenders all that it thereby renews through a mutability internalized: the loss at one with the thing it realienates for fresh recognition. The difference made by this particular brand of loss is not absence but re-presentation. Like the world's unphrased poetry tendered for reading.

Spectrum and Intertexts

From shaky first grapplings, then, arises something of a procedural superstructure after all. Fabulous blue lucidity; tuning as a metaphor for turning-into; loss as a loosening release; diacritical punctuation at a marked phonetic switch point; syntax as its own afterimage and return: in sum, the exchange rates of change itself over the time of reading. Enough, all this, for any tentative reader of metric compaction. Certainly what this one early reader knew nothing of at the time were the further possibilities latent—in just this range of syllabic, lexical, and grammatical transforms—for the kind of spectrum analysis, all the way from fleeting phonemic clasps to broad syntactic buckling, that might in years to come seek philosophical guidance in a single sustained commentary. Nonetheless, stanza by stanza in Wilbur's accessible densities, dimly glimpsed effects strictly and simply phonic, strictly and simply graphemic, and then both graphonic and syntagmatic by turns (and complex returns) now seem to me—as reflected in the layout of this book—to have parceled out in unwitting anticipation certain essential linguistic bases in any verbal engagement with poetry or fictional prose. Hence the sometimes separate, sometimes convergent attention to these scales of phrasal negotiation across the coming evidence—where microstylistics is never meant to be hermetically linguistic. Closing in is only a way (and sometimes the only way) of opening out.

Even back then, Wilbur's poem might have struck me as indirectly alluding to the classical *carpe diem* motif (tenth-grade Latin coming to mind)—like the book I also purchased at about the same time, mostly, I fear, blurbs aside, because I was proud to recognize the phrase in translation: namely, Saul Bellow's *Seize the Day*. In Wilbur's poem, the garden rosebuds in his lover's hand that trigger the cognitive allegory of the last stanza aren't gathered while ye may in that sense, under such duress of the mutability trope; the change summoned is not temporal, mortal, so much as perceptual. In transience begins aesthetic sentience: self-change, not eradication. What I guessed of these inferences then I can't now guess, and certainly not with confidence. But something inspiriting, not sombre and ominous, came through. And if I wasn't sure I had fixed exactly upon the author's meaning, that too would be part of the theme. Poetry changes. Changes as you read. Changes minds, and seemingly its own. And anyway, so what if I didn't know what meaning held the poet in its slippery grip? Here I sensed, as early as high school, what stayed with me as I switched majors in college, and what I've made methodological since: that it doesn't matter, doesn't matter ultimately, what the writer had in mind, because the only mind in which those thoughts are now to be had, in which they happen, is the reader's own, guyed and guided by the filaments of a written syntax.

What I'm less sure of, naturally, is how much of the above reaction I was actually cued to at the time by my verbal worry over diction and syntax. Beyond catching what I perhaps took to be a deflected allusion to seizing the day, I must also have intuited the hidden New Testament aura (here secularized) of losing self, or in this case the thing itself, to find it under the sign of redemption, though I wouldn't have known to identify it with the avoided cliché of a Riffaterrean semiotic matrix even if that estimable theory had by then, which it hadn't, come to print.[1] Nor was I to hear until much later the vaunted term "intertext." But somewhere down the road, in my college reading of more difficult poetry, I would have come upon the obvious source to which Wilbur is alluding, by the most influential prewar American poet in a famous text published exactly a decade before Wilbur's own. This is the epistemological fantasia of Wallace Stevens's *The Man with the Blue Guitar*, in which the recurrent word "changes" is even more explicitly linked to the ringing of changes in the aural sense, to musical variation and chord progression.

Certainly Wilbur is a Stevensian poet through and through, including in his gift for homophonic play. A touchstone moment for Geoffrey Hartman's theory of phonemic juncture in poetry (Hartman an eventual teacher of the apprentice poetician in me)—a juncture opening quasi-existential space in the otherwise neutral continuum of language—is Stevens's lexical slippage in "monocle de mon oncle."[2] In one of the verses by Wilbur from his poem *Words Hidden within Words*, as it happens, the unwanted blurs of a described photograph include the sector of the image in which "*uncle*, too, is frequently *unclear*."[3] One looks at the phrasing the way one does the photo, alert to a kind of alphabetic "blur" or "smear" (terms from the poem), seeing the sheer wording rather than understanding the nonsense of its depicted scene.

This is the brand of wordplay, instanced here from a single lighthearted poem, that was later expanded into Wilbur's witty book for children called *The Pig in the Spigot*, in which apt accidents of perfect phonetic and semantic congruence like "There's an ant, you say, in pantry" or "a big tree in the middle of the street" are mixed with sheerly sight chimes like putting the "sea" back in "nausea" or "A throne, friends, is a seat reserved for one" or, more baroque yet, adducing the idiom of the aerial "dog-fight" to explain the "arf" in "warfare."[4] Even when on the same phonetic wavelength, though, sometimes the chime is still a hair's-brea(d)th off, as with the question "Inside a taxi, why do we find an ax?" when answered in the next line by "It's because cabs are also known as 'hacks.'" Private meditation alone will explain why "idea" is found in "hideaway," and so forth. On first encounter with *The Beautiful Changes*, how could I have known that my teenage unease over the unwanted prankish "elves" in "things and things' selves" (later, after reading Cavell's philosophical treatment of Poe [see Chapter 4] I would indeed want to call them "impish" rather than prankish in their disturbance of ordinary language) was the kind of thing Wilbur would himself much later revel in. *The Pig in the Spigot* begins with the "elf" he hears in every sounding of "belfry," the kind of embedded oddity that computer word searching now turns up at witless random, as with (I just noticed) the "pig" in my earlier "pigmentation." Only years later would I be disposed to see the buoyant comic clip of the lip involved in those farce rhymes for children as laying bare a deep genealogy in the romancing of the phoneme that leads back from Stevens (and forward across the next two chapters) to the Romanticism of Wordsworth, Shelley, and their Victorian descendants.

Be all that as it will come to be, in those children's rhymes Wilbur's lexical wit is far closer than one might at first think to the transformational poetics, if not the tonality of verse practice, in his master Stevens, who, in *The Man with the Blue Guitar*, plays musically with the homophonics of syllabification in his own allusion to Flaubert's famous novelistic identification with his heroine: "Madame Bovary, c'est moi." Stevens's guitarist, passing his own Flaubertian allusion no doubt through the further Yeatsian inability "to tell the dancer from the dance," has it that "Tom-tom, c'es*t* *mo*i" because "The blue guitar / And I are one" (xii).[5] With this sound pun on proper name and onomatopoetic syllables of an idiomatic echoism (*Tom/tom*), Stevens's wordplay is released to the more strictly graphic (cross-word) anagram of *tmo*. For the guitarist: I am that I play, I become what I "strum." For the poet: theme is me. And that is because, as Wilbur would later have it, the beautiful changes everything, transforms even its source. Wilbur's closer source text, perhaps, comes as early as the first section of Stevens's longer poem:

> They said, "You have a blue guitar,
> You do not play things as they are."
>
> The man replied, "Things as they are
> Are changed upon the blue guitar." (i)

The comma splice of the first vernacular chorus gives way to the metaphysical suture of the next stanza's enjambment. Across the transfused rhyming of these doublets, the only *are* for the guit*arist*—with its anagramming of *artist*—is there in his instrumentation of the world. As Wilbur might have read these lines by his later logic of the word-within-the-word, Stevens puts the very sound of being (the homophonic predicate) back in the bent disyllable guit/*ar*. Linguistic ontology is subsumed by musicology. Next, in that fractional breath-catching of the second linear overrun, "are" feels differentiated from the slightly more emphatic capitalized "Are" by the instantaneous and almost subliminal overlap of main upon subordinate predication, with the inverted action of the passive voice ("are changed"), that is, encroaching upon the intransitive ("as they are")—or, in other words, the inevitable impingement of transformation upon sheer existence. Stevens's grammar proves its own point. Being is always, when mediated, also at the same time transacted anew in transmission.

And if this effect in Stevens anticipates by a decade the very grammar of mutation in Wilbur, it is itself preceded, two decades before, by the renowned variation of Yeats's *Easter 1916* when memorializing the fallen heroes of the Easter Uprising, the political "beauty" of their sacrifice, the terrible difference it makes. Yeats writes in the first iteration of his refrain: "All changed, changed utterly: / A terrible beauty is born." Not only does the grammar fronting the colon fall between fragmented participial and freestanding preterite forms, but the grieved alteration seems to be infecting the comma itself with a phonetic elision that would allow a sounding out of the line in a self-exampling spirit very much like that of Stevens and Wilbur alike. For the dental closure of the first verbal unit easily disappears, slides back, into the palatal launch of the second, with its emphatic stammer turned propositional: "All change d/changed utterly" (where, implied by this vector of the cadence, is that most drastically open-ended of tacit and collective grammatical objects: say, our whole world). Nothing holds, not even the words of elegiac recognition. I wish I could remember whether I first heard this effect come to pass on the inner ear before or after my college-age encounter with the rung changes of the more prolonged lexical nexus in Aretha Franklin's gradually clarified 1967 refrain about her place in the series of a lover's quick-change infidelities: "Chainch (ch)ainch (ch)ain, chain o(f) fools."

Paying Heed: An Economy of Reading

If, long after my first foray into *The Beautiful Changes and Other Poems*, additional schooling would lead me to see the poem framed by its most immediately literary-historical context in Stevens's work, with its links to Yeats, there is the further and thornier question, in a still later academic milieu, of the poem's broader historical context—and stance: thornier in the age of critique rather than criticism, a critique dubious of the aesthetic per se, including the suspicion that close reading is conformist and subservient, complicit in the ideology of the texts it thus "appreciates," comprehends, embraces. Stevens's *Blue Guitar* was plucked in (and from) the imagination and published in 1937. A decade later, should we think of Wilbur's going back to Stevens as a mere literary-historical throwback? Or is the possibility of Yeats's tragic and violent "changed utterly" an allusive ballast in a direction less purely aestheticist? I ask for literary criticism's sake, not for biography's. What is there left to say about a poet's lush sayings when so divorced, as in Wilbur's case, from all social and historical surround? *The Beautiful Changes*, I learned later, long after my purchasing it, was actually Wilbur's first book. 1947. Postwar. Adorno and Auschwitz aside, can there be this kind of poetry after so much modernist late Romanticism, Yeats (in his less political mode) to Stevens? And in rhyme no less? Wilbur's debut volume appeared in fact two years before Cleanth Brooks's *The Well-Wrought Urn*, repository supreme of New Critical precept. Wilbur has sculpted one of his own in *The Beautiful Changes*, that's for sure. His is a highly fashioned poetic receptacle anticipating those aesthetic tenets of New Criticism that his three symmetrical stanzas enshrine: internal balance, modulated pattern, the intricate orchestration of answering parts in a rhetoric of internal checks and balances, closed on itself even if in celebration of the world, altogether rounded and replete. A wrought rather than fraught containment, with no acrid taste of burial ashes or atomic fallout. Postwar, but as much a repression of its trauma as an earned remission from it—so a suspicious reading might suggest. On offer are the variegated aspects of a kaleidoscopic natural scene captured in a many-faceted language as its own Verbal Icon. Where is death in this crafted arcadia?

In a later vocabulary of overt critique: here is the Romantic ideology revamped against all odds, retrenched against the nightmare of the trenches themselves. Really? Suburban, middle-class, a poem of backyard gardens and adjacent leisured meadows, spangled with dressy Romantic allusions to Alpine lakes—conformist fifties in the making? Culture in denial, with none but the most oblique trace even of the memento mori? If you say so. But even if you decide the poem's epistemology is all a lie, or at least ameliorative and escapist, close reading is the only way to find out, to sound out, what the spiritual disinformation rests on, calibrated as it is on the manifestly false leads of syntax and their being put splendidly (even if dubiously) right. This means attending to the same calibrations that might elsewhere serve, on a poet's part, the nuances of irony rather than celebration. For the means may exceed the ends. And reading literary language itself, rather than the literary product, can have, I'm trying to show, an ethic that subtends the message, extends beyond it, And not just have one—investigatory, vigilant—but uncover one in the wording itself: flexible, curious, even if what a given writer is exploring seems horizoned by self-imposed and blinkering limits.

Having read this poem first in the pre-Vietnam 1960s, its naturalist Romanticism seemed to me at the time naturalized entirely by the Zeitgeist. But 1947? Though mass death saturates the collective memory in those years, here in these verses it seems fully damped down by that almost neutralist fantasy of the Swiss Lucerne. The poem offering itself as an escapist arboretum under art's hermetically sealed pleasure dome, with no voices prophesying, let alone remembering, war? Unlikely. So why not otherwise? Why not, instead of an aesthete's dodge, an implicit therapy of recuperation? Why not an ethics of healing: revival rather than denial? Isn't perhaps the war there not under erasure but as a forceful cultural justification: the epidemic of death that, spoiling the world and poetry at once, taking lives in its blind fury, requires a new seeing? This would involve the not-so-easy work of letting the living world back in through the very words of its refinding—and so opening, by a not unpolitical impetus, a respite beyond the depredations of politics. This is an interpretation to which one might well be drawn not least by the presence in this same volume, by a war veteran returned only recently to civilian life, of several poems about the terrors of the European war, poems like *Mined Country* and *In the Eyes of an SS Officer* that build across the book's sequence to its last note of modest recovery. And reaffirmation. For aren't the *beautiful* changes exactly what, among other things in its more drastic upheavals, war wrongs? Whether or not we find something like this historically justified recouping of cognition in the fond receptivity—a Wordsworthian wise passiveness—of Wilbur's closing poem, the method of literary cognition it invites outlasts any one thrust of its understanding. This is to say that, whether or not one imagines the war making such a poem necessary, with art helping to bring not the dead but the world back to life, the necessity can only be measured in the words of its rhetorical implementation.

That's the point of lingering so long over a poem so utterly vulnerable to contemporary dismissal—dismissal not on aesthetic grounds only, in an impatience with its sculpturesque rhymes, but more on account of its programmatic aestheticism. Instead, I've been reflecting on a potential ethics of healing in Wilbur's postwar thirst for the world's vegetal and animal vitality, a rejuvenating flux won back from destruction. Which would only mean—with the war-torn mind freed momentarily from the weight of mass atrocity—an *ethic of heeding*, as evinced by the delicate precisions of the performed verse itself. In which exactions—even warily, unsure from gesture to gesture—the reader can responsibly follow suit, the deeded word paid heed in whatever mood of response. But let it be clear. In stressing an ethic of registration in the reading act, I'm not adducing Wilbur for that very different purpose: to erect a detached aesthetics, let alone ethics, of the beautiful. Nor a fetishizing of fineness for its own sake. Poems about the Nazis in the same Wilbur volume would be enough to remind us how important it is to dispel the idea that artistic valuation carries moral force in itself. The devil can revel in the details like the rest of us. But without such relish to begin with, there is no chance of winning lucidity from the midst of confusion, delusion, or lie, political or otherwise.

Impedance in Transmission

The ethic, then, of such thickening language as Wilbur's, equilibrated by suspensions slow to disclose themselves, is that of a seeing (and hearing) otherwise—and often by way of the paradox of "present potential," one whose literary manifestation can at times expand the passing moment into the potentially momentous by the very friction of linguistic (rather than explicitly political) *resistance*. Think engineering, electrical and mechanical both: "impedance" as in electrical cable, "test" as in the holding power of ordinary wire. Or consider the thickness of oil paint in its deliberate resistance, in the hands of certain (even realist) artists, to the pseudotransparency of image: a resistance whose material conditions may be predominantly overcome even while retained with a certain potency in the viewing moment.[6] These are medial concerns, and, in the discourse of literature, they are concerns in particular that center on linguistic transmission. In textual instances to come, we will find ourselves encountering the blocked as much as the clear signal, verbal static as much as coherent statement. In just this way Wilbur's poem has been brought, in order to look, forward. Apart from any specific postwar gravitation to things undevastated, the reading it drafts us into is of the sort—to generalize—that involves an ethic of attended verbal impedance before (though not necessarily separate from) any literary ethics or politics of resistance.

Resistance and give, opacity as manifestation. Wilbur's poem comes down to the very definition of poetry in this lyric vein with its "Wishing ever to sunder / Things and things' selves for a second finding." Only after much further reading in English poetry on my part would the cryptic glisten of his final lines, his final turn—where things, including the "things" denoted, turn from (and back on) themselves, as if troping ("turning") their own nature in the poetry of existence—be recognized as alluding to Hopkins's leading idea in *Where Kingfishers Catch Fire*. There the inanimate *tells of itself*, as in the ringing of fallen stones—or as when, "like each tucked string tells, each hung bell's / Bow swung finds tongue to fling out broad its name." The telltale nature of enworlded presence, so to say, is true, is the truth, of both inanimate and living organisms alike in Hopkins. And as with rocks and strings and bells, sentient being is also a declarative *event*:

> Each mortal thing does one thing and the same:
> Deals out that being indoors each one dwells;
> Selves—goes itself; myself it speaks and spells

In the venture of existence, being "goes itself." Only years later yet would I register this selving, a special case of intransitive "thinging," as a version of the Heideggerian sense of being that also (for our current purposes) anticipates Agamben. This is the notion of an immanent self-potential "dealt out" (in Hopkins's phrase) if and when things are put at that abstract distance from themselves that permits, in effect, the second finding of re-"appropriation." In this event, this *Ereignis*, the apt and the proper, the in-itself, is dynamized by the intensification of its own self-claiming force:

"The presence of something present . . . comes into its own, *appropriatively* manifests and determines itself, only from the thinging of the thing" (emphasis added).[7]

As Wilbur stresses as much as Hopkins or Heidegger, with his emphasis on the perceiving subject who would, in the manner of Wordsworth's *Tintern Abbey*, "see into the life of things," we are led to negotiate as the "end" of Wilbur's poem (Agamben's term for impetus as much as closure) the space of a primal if self-erased displacement, a cognitive estrangement at the bracing heart of recognition. The thing must in its mental familiarity be, if you will, unthung before it can be truly sung. From Romanticism forward, poetry is often tasked with such philosophical work. But this, I stress again, is only my much later way of putting it. All I knew once was that the poetry itself was hard work. Entirely avocational and erratic, then, my high schooling in verse. Out of complexity, the beautiful perplexes. I've been explaining here, in retrospect, and by the earliest exemplum that comes to mind, the cause—and course—of a surrender to density, if only partial and guarded, that was later to become for me an analytic habit, and only later yet a method. The point of being momentarily seduced—and there is no other word for it, teenage libido aside—by the fleeting lures of obscurity within the verbal span of literary apprehension, enticed by words even before their full estimation has been readied, is not (or not just) an isolated adolescent foible of an under-read loner out of his element beachside. This reminiscence has, as is no doubt clear, been meant in the long run allegorically, not anecdotally. For such surrender recapitulates—with the scramble toward comprehension of its solitary *bildung*—the gradual maturation of linguistic capacity that is the lesson imparted, from the ground up each time, by many a text.

Educed, Disbanded, Renewed

Strong literature has a way of weaning us anew from the edge of gibberish into emergent sense, as well as from routine discourse into a more telling strain of phrase. Literary force may often seem to be not the putting away of childish things but a building directly on them. It marks, in its very marks, the growing out of babble into aptitude, of sound into meaning, of linguistic blur into pertinence, of thickness into intricacy, of the merely weighted into the layered, sometimes of sheer chaos into the potently inchoate. What this autobiographical allegory thus steps off, on the way into a study of "literature writing philosophy"—and, in particular, "language philosophy"—is the way language's own polymorphous perversity, in the developmental progressions of a single text, can be found maturing not just into art but into art's claims on the philosophical constitution of its own verbal domain.

So there in the Laguna Beach of the Beach Boys, of "Good Vibrations," well before the postmodern advent of Derridean "disseminations"—many years in fact before Derrida himself took up residence in the very hills of Laguna for his appointment nearby at UC Irvine—one reader (among many another novice elsewhere) was slowly feeling his way for himself (though entirely in his own words, if formulated at all, and certainly not in the lingo of poststructuralism) to a two-ply sense of the "different" as in one important sense the self-deferred. This involves the edgewise difference within the very difficulty of reading, a difficulty not in the least occulted yet by theory in my apprentice efforts: the space, the latitude, call it the maneuvering room, opened between what that wording seems now to mean and what it appeared to mean a second before, all certainty deferred even within—and precisely by—textual self-adjustment. Whether phonetic or semantic or syntactic, or all of them at once, vibrations of this kind can indeed be felt to deliver the textual goods.

In my case, then, there was nothing consciously philosophical about a response to poetry that made me wonder as much about language per se as about the images conjured by a given instance of it. Serious philosophy remained a full bookstore alcove, and several decades, away—decades that came recently to a head when just such a figure of speech as that last, suspended across spatial and temporal registers in a sylleptic split, got me to thinking in a more focused way (in some exploratory articles mentioned in Chapter 5) about the philosophical undertone of wordplay's slippery grip on linguistic recognition. Well before that, however, much of what I took up in my undergraduate, doctoral, and then professional reading has had for me a linguistic cast as well as a representational dimension, which I've come more recently to appreciate can be seen, and understood better, in part as a philosophical (not just philological) slant. For I had been finding increasingly of late in literature an implied theory of wording, say, a philosophy of language, whether "ordinary" (Wittgenstein, Austin, Cavell) or what we might call conditioning (Agamben): literature either cross-examining its own linguistic criteria or rehearsing their emergence as cognitive possibility.

Be all this as it will come to be in the ensuing chapters, back then with Wilbur there was for me only the poet's *line of thought*, neither his place in the long Romantic lineage to which we next turn, including the close precedents of Hopkins as well as Stevens, nor his anticipation of that influential essay by Heidegger, "The Thing," which was delivered to print three years later, in 1950. And anyway, the genealogy of a method is of less interest than its new and continuing applications. Considering any such philosophical valence in the readings to come, the proof is always in the putting down of words, one after the other(s)—and sometimes with the latest one altering the logic of the very phrasing into which it inserts itself. As, again, with syllepsis: a trope so deeply rooted in the rigors of literary language that it can offer, as I'm about to suggest in one further paragraph on Wilbur's poem, even a buried paradigm of its "trick ending."

Along we roll, losing beauty as inevitably as the poem hopes, as many poems hope, that we will find it again, until loss itself arrives as the truer level of its finding, its remade apprehension. This is what Stevens calls (in another probable intertext for Wilbur's poem) the "final finding of the ear"[8]—objective and subjective genitive both: the alert ear found anew, brought out, in what it finds to hear by reading. When beauty's intrinsic change-artistry in Wilbur is found, as if by an internal enjambment in the final line, to "to *lose* / For a moment *all that it touches* [/] *back to wonder*," the tacit bifurcated grammar (a verb parsed and parceled out across two syntactically overlapped senses of its object) amounts to something not unlike the sylleptic mismatch of "to kiss her on both cheeks and good riddance," or, more to the point, "to touch it both goodbye and to death as well as with new welcome." When remembering that the "final finding" in Stevens caps a poem called *The Course of a Particular*, one is further reminded that it is indeed the course of given particulars—as, for instance, of diction across the relay system of syntax—that one in part reads poetry for. Prose too, of a certain pitch. Suffice it also to say here, in anticipation of much to follow in the grammatical grain of this book's evidence, that when language works (itself out) in such particulate yet wavering ways, poetry may well need philosophy to help tell us where such language is coming from.

Enough, surely, of one reader's secondary (and tertiary) education in the pace of phrase. Memory lane is not always a wayward detour from the present, though, but occasionally a clarifying route back to it. There in my hometown bookstore, a lucky break: spurring a memorable chance encounter with the lucky breaks of words and phrases in their own chance (or schemed) encounters with each other. And from this private retrospect, I've made no secret of my temptation to generalize. Maybe every committed reading begins a little thick in the head. Maybe in the logosphere as much as in the biosphere, the principle of ontogeny recapitulating phylogeny can thus be found to obtain. So that every new emergence to mastery in the adult encounter—even in the professional engagement—with any serious literature replays at some level the early gropings of literate comprehension, with the progress from first squirmings to hermeneutic maturity recapped in and through exactly the true work invited by each new work. We're always being tutored again in verbal recognition. In giving yourself over to what one might call the continual work of "literary language acquisition," you let that language give—and thus give anew its quickening sense of mystery. The Wilbur model again, after all: things and things elsewise, perceived in the state of their own contingency, their own conditioned possibility. Or in the more philosophical terms we will soon come to in Agamben's poetics, the reader finds in literary language those moments where the event of language is itself uttered in what it enunciates, what it potentiates.

So that here again one confronts the question of "surface reading," supposedly rescuing the text from ideological reduction under a former hermeneutics of suspicion. Even in a neoformalist recovery, however, one doesn't have to forego political or psychoanalytic subtexts in order to read ethically. A truly "reparative" reading can begin not in the avoidance of hidden depth but in the restored attention to wording itself, with its own linguistic undertow and the subterranean currents thereby tapped, channeled, or dammed up. A committed regimen of attention requires only that one sees and hears, takes the temperature and tempo of, what is there—including the shaped (stylistic) force of its exclusions at whatever level, verbal, social, historical, psychological. A linguistic reading doesn't just skim the given; it probes its construction—willing to wonder, in the process, what a particular fashioning or deflection may be the further (or say, deeper) sign of.

A single poem, a single text—a single phrasing—is the only place one can sensibly begin. As a published poet as well as art critic—of an age to have read Wilbur once—T. J. Clark could in any case scarcely find a more fully and deftly fledged verse illustration, focused on the cusp between natural and human pattern and mutability, for that central formalist principle of his with which we began: the axiomatic claim that "form—repetition—is change." In perhaps the earliest (and most metapoetic) of the poem's own changes, from an adjectival to an abstract nominal weighting of its title (conceivably lost in anything like its history-of-aesthetics resonance—who knows now?—on the non-abstractly-inclined teen reader), reigning ideas of "the beautiful" may change, but far more slowly than its formal constituents in any one instance. However much a victim of changing aesthetic estimates in its own afterlife, Wilbur's poem lives by its inherent measure of phrasing's immanent shifts across the divide between natural transformations and the human consciousness put through its paces in the act of phrasing—and deciphering—them. The verbal evidence to come, chapter by chapter, is meant to show how often such change, in the "form of" flux itself, is not just the name of the game but the game of the name, the play of the word or phrase in its "second finding," brandishing in action what Agamben's theory of present potential should soon encourage us to generalize, in formative linguistic terms, as a deep principle of literary execution: wording's chance of having been otherwise, even still.

2

SECONDARY VOCALITY

Concerning the ductile music of literary language, all "inductions"—like mine long ago—are renewable. It's not that "you had to have been there," once and back when, falling untaught under the spell of words and finding in them, as the undertext of their lettering, the waiting sounds they never quite seem to have left behind. Instead, you are always there again in reading. With an emphasis on meter and lineation (rather than phonetics per se) as the aural prompt and structuring "end" of poetry in its destined repetition, Italian philosopher and poetician Giorgio Agamben, so we'll find, gives us—through all the subtlety and abstraction of his account—just such an eminently sensible model for our sensory investments in verse pattern.

In literature's writing out of language's own capacity for speech, voice itself goes mostly unspoken—as well as technically unspeaking. But beyond the sense of its being written out of existence by the usual run of cultural criticism, such writing *out of* invites the philosophical spelling *out* of its derivation *from*: the explicit linguistic springs of literary possibility. Hence the formative before the formal—even while a sense of the former is accessed through the latter. That's also why the initial emphasis here is on a sounding of literature as writing. We're talking text, with its special kind of speech: writing that speaks through rather than to you. Until the second half of the nineteenth century, orality was what we now call a strictly real-time phenomenon. After that, technological history saw a rapid transition from the phonautograph mentioned in "Fore Word" (reduced, without playback apparatus, to something more like a phono-scope) to the subsequent phonograph: the advent, that is, of time-based *replay*. Until then, orality required presence—at one remove or another, by vibrating chords either vocal or prosthetic. The oral was an index of the present-tense body, even if at walkie-talkie distance.

This chapter is not centrally concerned with presence, however, nor with orality. At least not with the presence *of*. Instead, a presence *to*: that of reader to text—to literature's words, poetry's especially in this case, and so (when presence becomes attention) to the force field of their unique "reverberation" as a resonance phonetic before referential or thematic. What the medium of literary writing does after (and before) all *represent*—stand (in) for—is its very possibility as a lettered effect in subvocal production. This is an effect renewing in process its own enunciative cause: the efficient cause of alphabetic (hence phonetic) ciphers activated at whatever distance from initial inscription in the secondary time of silent reading rather than in the phantom first and lost cause of authorial delivery.

Certainly any writer's already-silent voicing of scribed language is gone in text, rather than gone *into* it. Further, what is materially represented in what's left—for the recognition of the reader—is in part that moment of disappearance. Such is the vanishing (or banishing) yet again, here and now rather than there and then, of somatic voice into meaning, silent sound into sense, organic impulse into uttered thought. Rather than the writer's, the reader's is the voice tacitly activated, even as downplayed and suppressed, in the perpetual demotion machine that is literature: a voice foregone in each and any reading when taken up as transmitted meaning. But felt in going. Felt *how?*—that is the question. Or *where*?

Agamben has an answer so rudimentary that it reframes the matter altogether—and in postmetaphysical terms. Comparison here is immediately contrast. Whereas in Wallace Stevens the poem is "the cry of its occasion,"[1] in Agamben it is instead the occasion of its departed cry—sound evacuated to sense on the spot, in action, straight off the mark, right from the scratch of alphabetic inscription. But then revoiced by each new encounter with its lines. Philosophically speaking, or say, spoken, such is the silent happening (again) of language, a language whose possibility is read back to us from the text we read. That is what my teenage "induction" was all about, where a high schooler's *need* to reread points up the *being rereadable* of the poetic act: its deed of (because only in) linguistic transmission, calling language back to attention each time in a way different from other forms of linguistic messaging.

For Walter Ong, in *Orality and Literacy*, vocal utterance happens in time, whereas text is spatialized; orality is evanescent, writing emplaced. Text is the cement to speech's event. What Ong does acknowledge in passing, however, if only to minimize this facet of print in his encompassing binary, is the silent sounding of phonetic language "in the imagination" as we read: the inherent oralization, as it were, even of alphabetic culture.[2] Stressed instead, and more broadly, in the agenda-setting historical dichotomy of his title is the evolved "technologizing of the word" (his equally definitive subtitle) begun with writing and further institutionalized with print. So that everything since—from phonography through radio to cell-phone or web-streamed speech—would be termed by him a "secondary orality," with all vocal primacy surrendered to technical transcription, mechanical or electronic.

To break what can seem the resulting deadlock in Ong, at least for poetics, between inert text and kinetic speech, I venture the term "secondary vocality" to indicate the suppressed but potent aurality of silent reading. And I want to link this concept to Agamben's attempt—against what he sees as the levelings and depletions of an antiphonocentric deconstruction—to find poetry witnessing in reading precisely to the simultaneous upsurge as well as sacrifice of articulate voice. This is, for Agamben, the voiced speech that makes us first human, then literate, then, as it were, literary—and does so, as I will try further to show, through both the inhibition of our tongue in textual decipherment and the compensatory lending of our ears. All I would add to Agamben's view of poetry—as awaiting, from line to line, the inevitably phonetic reading voice it has ever and already canceled at its point of origin—is a stress on the way this sensed potential of voice also saturates script from word to word as we read, indeed letter to letter, and returns unbidden between and across them at times to derange the written with its truant yet copresent alternatives. These are options emerging to resonance in such a way that Agamben's own theory of potential—if transferred from his ontological investigations to his poetics—might well offer (and in fact will soon) a fairly thorough account, always against the background of Ong's dichotomy. The philosophical template is all there, implementation pending. Notching attention closer to wording even than Agamben does can help us go deeper yet, while still on his terms, into speech as sheer instanced possibility, oral or otherwise. By this sense of the possible, reading is not set at ease in the destiny of a given phrasing but sensitized to alternatives still feeding it.

My once having deliberately titled a book with a clause rather than a phrase—so as to name what reading does in itself rather than to denominate some withdrawn origin to which it fantasizes access—offers me a particular angle of vantage on Ong's argument about writing as arrested event. Extrapolating from the emphasis of that previous title, *Reading Voices*—where the only audition is that of subvocal rendition on the reader's part—I approach the notion of secondary vocality as that elusive but crucial field of response to writing where speech *acts*, even though in the apparent stillness of silent inflection.[3] And I'll be tracking this sense of things, these things of latently activated sensation known as letters, back, via Agamben, to Wallace Stevens's forebears in European Romanticism—and on to the Victorian novelists as well as poets deriving a good part of their power from this same linguistic disposition.

The purpose, it should be said going in, is not so much to fill a void as to bridge a gap. Agamben's poetics concerns the text in micromanaged wait for its "end" in reading; Agamben's ontology concerns potential as indwelling. This book tries holding the two emphases in mind together over the malleable forms of poetry and prose alike. Without claiming anything so grandiose or thoroughgoing as an ontopoetics, the effort is nonetheless to make commoner cause than even Agamben himself does between these two fields of his thought—in the hopes both of clarifying each and of putting them (together) to more analytic use in the force fields of textual exertion and response. The "sheer instanced possibility" of speech (mentioned just above) that literary language keeps afloat and in suspension, rather than dry-docked in fixed phrases, is a possibility exampled by its own residual flux. And it is this generative condition, as language is brought to happen across its shifting play of words, that can be engaged at a formative level in the deed of reading.

Agamben Reading

In the very spirit of unsettled phrasing, I'm aware that this first subheading, on the routine presumption of a proper-noun modifier, may sound like the title of a course bibliography. So be it: a selective one from text to text, bringing to the seminar table many a typically shelved volume of Agamben's writing on language and poetry. But with the same title in its other grammar, I also mean to catch the philosopher within the radius of his reading lamp, one or more stanzas opened—and under illumination—before him. Reading Agamben reading, and especially if over his shoulder, isn't necessarily to invade the full literate privacy of his investigations into the meter, lineation, and lexicon of Italian verse. We don't need to see each and every word (even in translation) on his desktop—I'll come back to this point—in order to sense what is being educed there from the fact of language within literature, which is to say, the act of literature as language. And we can certainly press further in similar directions, led by his tenets if not his specific attentions. For what he finds in literary writing, as suggested by his title *The End of the Poem*, is at once a linguistic destiny and an epistemological foreclosure. Poetry is given in words alone; what it ends up giving (or giving upon) is language, which it prevents—a major ambition of philosophy—from "remaining unsaid in what is said."[4] By an ontological rigor that animates his every reading of Italian verse, Agamben backs anything resembling the formalist "languageness" of literary expression all the way down to the languaged being of the human animal.

Despite the depth of his investment in literary signification, it is perhaps of little surprise these days that the work of this former-legal-scholar-turned-philosopher finding keenest circulation among literary and cultural critics concerns his views on violence and politics, not on poetics—even though the writing on literary language and linguistics precedes and orients, even by some counts outnumbers, his works on posthumanism and community. And it's not just that we've seen it happen before. Foucault's initial book on modernist literary language (the arcane homophonic punning of Raymond Roussel), so crucial to the later metalinguistic investigations in his *The Order of Things*, got little play in literary departments.[5] Reasons since, in the case of Agamben, for teachers and critics of literature being more interested in a philosopher's political work than in books with titles like *Language and Death* ([1982] 1991), *Idea of Prose* ([1985] 1995), *Stanzas*

([1977] 1993), and *The End of the Poem* ([1996] 1999), to say nothing of the linchpin essay "Philosophy and Linguistics" from the collection *Potentialities* (1999), are obvious enough. For Agamben's essays on literature are so far from thematically political as to be concerned exclusively with what has for a long time appeared least interesting to Departments of English, Comparative, or World Literatures: that is to say, the language, whether the phrasing or even the tongue, in which literature is written. The lone surprise here, then, is the one that would await exactly those readers of Agamben who pass over both his poetics and his linguistics. For it is only, one comes to find, his specific preoccupations with the etymological and grammatical densities of shaped language, and then only as performed into view by poetry, that can genuinely delimit and clarify the full ethical weight, and even political tenor, of his more familiar and influential recent writing.

In *Language and Death*, Agamben takes as his starting point Heidegger's version of Hegel's sense that only the human, not the animal, has the "faculty" for language and (hence) for death, the latter a condition that needs a name in order to be uttered (or thought) in advance of its arrival.[6] When the death cry of the animal brings its "voice" into the field of immanent meaning, an indicator without abstraction, its achieved sign of annihilation leaves behind a corpse. Language, human speech, operates analogously. Concerning "death" or any other vocabulary of existence, whenever the human voice leaves its bodily sound behind for manifestation as signifier, sound passes into sense precisely at the expense of animal (bodily) presence. Such is the sacrifice—within vocal speech—of animality to disembodied abstraction. The "faculty" mobilized by the human being, over against the animal, in any such semantic act—let alone in *signifying its own mortality*—is thus a kind of organic negation in itself: the forfeit of somatic to semiotic determination.

Meaning is thus born only from the evisceration of material sound as such. Nor can language ever reattach to the embodied world by referential efforts. Here, in sum, is the casting out by speech of noise, by sema of soma, by meaning of sound, by verbal sense of mere voice. Yet, for Agamben, a resurgent *sense of voice* in language is what poetry writes into recognition—not voice as or at some lingual foundation, but rather voice as a latency in reading, tacitly communal. Communal because species-deep: the very cause and effect at once of the human. Put otherwise, in a point never made in these terms by Agamben, the philosophical "sense-certainty" absent in the end-stopped feints of language as demonstration (what he stresses, we are to see, as the empty pointing of "deixis" in the "this" or "that" of a supposed gesture achieved by language) returns in part from within its own silently shaped sounds in reading.

In related terms, recovering the resonances of human speech both from text and from the paradoxes of its silent sounding—and building on the work of French philosopher Michel Serres in his investigations into the five senses—Steven Connor has developed the notion of "white voice" in his study of Samuel Beckett's "material imagination,"[7] playing in the process off a more familiar concept like the slant-rhymed "white noise." Under this rubric, Connor ponders how one might "turn up" the "garrulous dumb show" of a "stonily mute" script (102) in order to make good, after all, on the point in Georges Bataille from which, understood as a statement about writing, he initially demurs: that "*the word silence is still a sound*" (102). Connor finds Beckett's prose uniquely attuned, as it were, to the "inner sonority" of silent reading, adding (in a particularly Beckett-like scrupulousness), "if inside is exactly where it is, if sonorous is exactly what it is" (106). For Connor, in coming to aptly punning grips with this "inner hearsay" (107), the term "subvocalization" (106) doesn't quite cover the case, with its overtones, to his ear, of a "vestigial" enunciation (107). He prefers the term "virtual" for this "auditorium" (107), this "arena of internal articulations" that is "not really inside anything or anywhere inside" (108). Its contours define what he calls the "white architecture of vocality" (111), though without this topological figuration denying the time-based nature of its potential effects, including its (paracinematic) "cross-fades" (109)—by which I like to think he means to invoke the sort of "lap dissolves" I find in the counterplay of ambiguously fused lexical juncture.

For Connor, Beckett's "phonic ghosts" (112) succeed, as his chapter title puts it, in "writing the white voice," whose register, containing "all possible frequencies," amounts—in a manner that further recalls the idea of potentiation in Agamben—to a writing of "vocality itself" (113). "Literature does not silence sound," Connor summarizes, no doubt intending the double grammar banked in his own potential and corrective verb/noun inversion in the sounding of silence; literature, he says instead, "auditises the field of the visual" (113), where it makes good on all the senses (both senses of that substantive) that "swell together in the word 'volume'" (110). Though Connor might also find the term "secondary vocality" too "vestigial" in its inference, our approaches are nevertheless, as idiom would have it, on the same volatilized literary page, where—or whereabouts—sound, varying his subtitle, is imaginatively *materialized.* To mold Connor's emphasis more closely to Agamben's template in returning to the latter's demonstrations, one might say that "white voice" is what keeps speech from going unheard in what its written form articulates.

Following on from Ferdinand de Saussure, Roman Jakobson, and Émile Benveniste, Agamben looks to the phoneme and the deictic (the pulse of speech and its pointing function): each, strictly speaking, disabled in the space of a linguistic act that suppresses the one (as voice) and virtualizes the other (as absent referent), leaving enunciation adrift between its loss of self-indexical voice and its failure to index or indicate the world. But poetry is always the beginning again of sound's gradual passage to sense, where, in entirely nonmetaphysical terms, we *find ourselves in language.* As if from a nowhere that need not seem withering, poetry rehearses the very thought of language as it comes to one, comes to be by taking place in one. From the phonemes ghosting its speech through the referential phantoms shadowing its tropes, poetry operates this way (as Agamben shows when reading it) within the twin registers of music and deictic deferral, meter and the self-enclosedness of language, together performing—an always collaborative venture with the reader—the rhythm of thought in words. In a variant of Agamben's emphasis, we may say that language does not probe and disclose being, even its own; it *realizes* being by making it operative in communicative exchange. And realizes the being of language in the process—or, in the related terms proposed by Geoffrey Hartman from the years of deconstructive ferment leading up to *Language and Death* (1982), taps in this way the "working dark of aural experience": a realm of the prior and primal "*phoné*" to which all literary words are "antiphonal," calling to mind (in close parallel to Agamben's later stress) a "voice or sound before a local shape or human source can be ascribed."[8]

The Language-Using Animal

A similar sense of the presupposed voice offers the introductory framework around questions posed in the seminars collected in *Language and Death: The Place of Negativity*, where the gauntlet thrown down by Agamben is to wonder whether the no-"place" of the subtitle has really been overcome by a philosophy priding itself, as in Heidegger, on having pulled back from the black hole of metaphysics.[9] Beginning with Heidegger on how animals know neither their own death nor a language, Agamben italicizes the following extract as the starting point of his inquiry: "*The essential relation between death and language flashes up before us, but remains still unthought*" (xi). This relation remains, in fact, the fatal unthought that obviates being in language from the groundless ground up. Agamben's work is to dissipate the pall of nihilism that falls over this too intimate "relation" by unraveling its dialectical origins in Hegel, where the death of animal voice operates, as we've seen, almost as a philosophical beast fable about sound's constitutive disappearance in meaning. Though always lurking there in the *zoe* of our *bios* (recurrent terms in Agamben for the difference, respectively, between biological existence and conscious life), the animal dies in us in our every instrumental word.

In passages anticipating his later influence on ecocriticism and a post-Marxist political theory of biopower, Agamben wants in effect to keep that animal in us alive across the spectrum of our cohabitation in the world, so that the voicing we do, though not the coming-to-be of our uniqueness, is instead the coming-into-action of a language that situates rather than negates us. Where we speak from is not nothing, not pure negation, not wholly disembodied—just not present *in* our words. Yet this cannot deny the contact of those words, as expression, with the language of the other. Such contact is effected within the shared habitus of the communicable, in writing when not in person. Understanding arrives as a realized "potential" rather than residuum (though in a terminology not directly applied to these linguistic issues): the potential of the reader's (not the writer's) speech in scriptive prompt.[10] Poetic decipherment, as we'll see (by hearing), only maximizes this potential along an impacted spectrum running from the fact of language to the patterns and accidents of its act. In adapting the concept of "potential" to the possibilities unleashed by reading, there is no need to distort Agamben's concept, but simply to import it from ontology into phonology and stylistics. The broadest understanding remains intact. Potential: not an option somewhere waiting, however near or far off, not a something missing at all, but instead the present absence of the still possible, intrinsic to process rather than exhausted by it.

One way of coming to grips with this slippery concept of potential in Agamben is to align it with a central axiom of Gilles Deleuze's philosophy (so memorably demonstrated by the copresence of separate, often superimposed, temporalities in his treatment of the cinematic time-image): namely, that the virtual is opposed to the actual, but not to the real, which includes virtuality as a facet of one's life in time.[11] For Agamben, influenced in so many ways by Deleuze, the potentially present is not unlike the virtually copresent. Potential is every bit as real as it is unactualized. For our purposes, then, although Agamben is never explicit about this conjunction of his topics, the poem's only present reality is the potential of (for) its reading, not its understanding all told but its reading in time, syllable by syllable. At which point there is a suggestive intersection with an apparently nonphilosophical use (or is it?) of the word "potential" in Ong. What I am calling secondary vocality is comparable, within such "technologizing of the word" as writing and print, to Ong's observation, concerning preliterate cultures, that the only existence of a story is the present "potential" (*Orality and Literacy*, 14) of its eventually being spoken.

For Agamben, that sole potential is the case as well for the silent speaking-again of text: text as object, not as retrieved subjectivity. Language in poetry is the human given, neither taken for granted nor gone unremarked. Reversing the sequestered negative of a vestigial metaphysics that Agamben finds persisting even in contemporary philosophy (after the supposed "end of philosophy"), he would say instead that language is where we live, not die, to ourselves, the lack we activate, accept, and surmount rather than the hole that hollows us out. *Homo loquens* is not the human being spoken, asserted, by the Voice, metaphysically spoken for, but just the human being *speaking*—not speaking herself forth in propria persona, but nevertheless human *because* speaking, as well as because mortal (*Language and Death*, xii). We think consciousness in language; *Cogito ergo sum* is a silent speech act. To cast the matter up in the full paradoxical grammar its circularity deserves, what can't be thought *is* thought itself—conveyed or mediated to consciousness only, as it were, through its translation into words, however unstable.

Humans are the animals that (who) know language or know death only in the sense of using or suffering it with realization. But to be able to name your speech or your fate is not the same, Agamben repeatedly insists, as to think the actual thought of language, let alone of death. For there lies an always receding ontological horizon, distanced by its own instances: the originary mystery of wording held from view by words like *mystery* and *wording* themselves. Then, too, for Agamben language is what we think *in*. It isn't in us, delimitable as an essence. We are in it. We "enter" it in order to let it traverse us. At which point we know ourselves only when this medium of language comes to pass in—and through—our speaking, shapes our thoughts into repeatable words. This is the constitutive but ungrounded process replayed by reading—and in a quite particular way that constitutes this book's furtherance (and extra specification) of Agamben's schema. While there is no Voice that transcends the somatic, the animal body is always marginally returned from semantic repression, I want to stress, in the speech that rides on and overrides all mere organic sound. And this claim would only align in the end with Agamben's approach. As regards his understanding of language, what resisting the dialectical negative (the radical cancellation of sounded source in human speech) comes to entail is, after all, a resisting of that violence at the base of all structuring exclusions, not least, as we are to find, the concept of *homo sacer*—the debate around which has so much eclipsed an interest in Agamben's literary work.

Homo sacer: the untouchable, so announced (rather than anointed) by sovereign decree, the one set apart, the unceremonialized scapegoat, available for a death without ritual ennoblement.[12] In this sense, the outcast that throws community into definition, the danger purged in the name of purity, the profane deviance that sacralizes the norm—each of these cultural formations is comparable in its foundational negativity (and explicitly so in Agamben) to the voice, let alone Voice, that must be negated in discourse, the bodily presence obliterated by abstraction in the lettered sign. Where in violent ritual one body is slain to maintain the body politic, in speech one's own body is obliterated as sound source in the letteral (and hence communal) function of the arbitrary sign. So it is that Agamben's most famous concept, *homo sacer*, almost a decade before the book by that name appeared in Italian, first rears its head (adduced without fanfare in a Latin citation) as a final gloss on the exclusionary logic of language two pages from the end of *Language and Death*, its relevance fully rounded out only after what may seem an initial digression: "The fact that man, the animal possessing language, is, as such, ungrounded, the fact that he has no foundation except in his own action (in his own 'violence'), is such an ancient truth that it constitutes the basis for the oldest of religious practices of humanity: sacrifice" (105). For when other than an animal is sent to the altar, when instead a human existence is rendered violable, "*homo sacer is est quem populus iudicavit*" (*homo sacer* is he whom the populace excludes; 105). It is in this way that slaughter sanctifies the community it spares. Sanctifies, which is to say, authorizes, validates.

But we are still waiting to see just how this anthropology effects a nonmetaphysical ontology of human utterance. The logic unfolds in a manner as brisk as it is cryptic. Arbitrary death makes life immediately valuable by contrast. No speech act could do this with any more (or ultimately any less) authority, since speech too, like animate life, gives no grounding in a concept of being beyond sheer human condition; only silence vouches, if only by contrast, for the force of speech. And so, however tenuous it may at first seem, the link in Agamben (via the pattern of exclusion) between speech and sacrifice is conceptually secured. The exiled life is that of a being killed to make the rest of lives, life itself, take meaning, just as animal sound—the initial basis for Agamben's abrupt parallel—is sacrificed to the semantic in all verbalizations of the voice. The analogy verges indeed on a genealogy of violence. This is the violence Agamben looks to ward off by refusing to rehearse the reciprocal void of dialectics in each new attempt to anchor human consciousness.[13] So, after that excursus on sacrificial action, a return to Voice in securing the parallel: "Even philosophy, through the mythogeme of the Voice, thinks the ungroundedness of man . . . as a human being (that is, as a living being that has logos)," which also involves, for philosophy, "the attempt to resolve man of . . . the unspeakability of the sacrificial mystery" (*Language and Death*, 106). Ritual violence isn't "unspeakable" here primarily in the ethical sense; rather, its "mystery" concerns the unspeakable enigma of human definition that can't be lived with, as ineffable, short of an unforgiving and relentless philosophical negation. It is part of the larger suggestion of Agamben's oeuvre that poetry might, instead, acclimate us otherwise.

In default of the human Being as ontological absolute, there is still being human; without Voice there is still voicing. We are, for all intents and purposes, the intentional language we share, whether holding it in common or releasing it in communion. That is our possibility, precedent and still potential, our condition and our conduit. For Agamben, speech doesn't negate the cry but articulates it, at best suppresses its unmeaning excess rather than extinguishes it. What we can't found ourselves on, we do not therefore need entirely to lose. Poetry would thus seem, for him, both exemplary and, one might add, therapeutic. Let us then emphasize literature as the place where, with only language taking place, one recognizes how the sounds one makes in saying what we say (as in reciting a poem silently to oneself) are not accessories after the fact, not mere excrescences exceeding the sense, or, as he puts it in scare quotes, "a redundance of the signifier" (*Language and*

Death, 77). Rather, they trail from the forgotten (because never thought) place where one might posit (without moving to prove) the motivation of that sense, its intentional impulse—or as Mladen Dolar (building on Agamben in amalgamation with psychoanalysis) would say, its drive.[14]

Much of Agamben's attempted escape from the blind alleys and false bottoms of metaphysics into the philosophical implications of metalinguistcs is summoned by inference in the entitling formulation of his early Hegelian work. For there, the either oppositional or else downright paradoxical yoking of *Language and Death* is accompanied by a subtitle (again, *The Place of Negativity*) that turns on one of Agamben's favored rhetorical maneuvers: the pivotal genitive, one obvious meaning resting potential, one might say, in its seemingly active exclusion by the other. Negativity *has its place* in any thinking about the relation of language and death. But this relation also locates (and here grammatically too) exactly the emptied-out *site* of a pure negativity that has bedeviled modern philosophy. One may fuse the two divergent idiomatic vectors when sensing, in the line of thought Agamben resists, the *place of negativity* in human discourse as the locus of being's own negative grounding, with life consigned to sheer contingency. On this view, we don't just grapple with negativity's threat as it impinges; we are negatively emplaced in our every possibility.

Agamben is elsewhere alert to genitive ambiguities of just the sort rounded upon here. We see such hinged genitives deployed in the main title *Idea of Prose* (the idea it conveys and the very idea of it) and *The End of the Poem* (goal and closure both), including three of his chapter titles for that latter volume explicitly teased out in this regard ("Dream of Language," "Thought of the Voice," and "Dictation of Poetry"), just as we may be put in mind of such prepositional diffusion by Stevens's "cry of its occasion" (both issuing from and constituting). Not least, we see the genitive flange explicitly manipulated in Agamben's paraphrase of Hegel's meditation on the animal death cry as "the voice of death." In Agamben's gloss, "the genitive should be understood in both an objective and a subjective sense."[15] It is because, for Hegelian logic, the animal is fully present in the sound of his own death, present with a voice that speaks both of and from death, that the suppression of the animal voice in the arbitrary patterns of mortal speech, or in other words in "the voice of consciousness" (*Language and Death*, 45), is always and inevitably—such is the closed circle Agamben would break from—no more than a momentary negation of the death it is nevertheless founded on.

Under scrutiny in Agamben, beyond the prepositional ambiguities he himself deploys as if to sensitize his readers both to the forked paths of the signifier and to the circularities of consciousness, there is always the rumble, the timbre, of the somatic underneath and apart from the symbolic. For this becomes one of the things most crucially indexed by poetry and foregrounded, in the very form of sound, by meter. These are phonic shapes not only internal to the line, but also internal to the speaking subject as its voicing (not its Voice). As such, their inwardness is manifested by written poetry only in the rehearsed (not reheard) moment of reading, always for Agamben a rereading. The issue is related to Benveniste's sense, as quoted by Agamben (*Language and Death*, 24), of the composite "symbol-indices" in spoken utterance, registering a voice that speech immediately regiments into suppression, losing the traceable cause (index) in the arbitrary syllables and words (symbols) of meaning. Certainly the body is dropped out from the signs propagated by its speech, remaining the apparatus of their relay but not the payload of their semiosis. Still, though, the vehicular sound left behind (that is, outdistanced) by such meanings witnesses to the body in its former impress on air; witnesses, and then reenlists the body at one remove in our silent sounding of letter forms. Transcription subtracts all body from the matter of language; reading puts it back. To extend Agamben's logic one step beyond his actual formulation: the secondary vocality of my reading, of me reading, is in fact the index of me—at least as body if not as subject.

And from the difference between this potential for material vibration in an inscribed speech signal and the purely abstract "vocal image" of Saussure's coded phonetics, a difference called up most urgently in the labor of poetic cadence, further recognitions follow.[16] We come to see in Agamben that poetic language, while doing its local work, works also to locate not only the variable basis (rather than stabilizing base) of the human but its parabasis (its staging, its choric metacommentary): not, again, the ontology of language, but rather its phenomenology; not its having come to be, but rather its coming now to pass. Rather than summoning an origin, poetry involves the "taking place" of human speech (*Language and Death*, 25)—or say, its coming to *pass between* us, its emergence in and across us as our place together, our habitus, our ethos: the place where language *takes*, lays hold of us. What can seem so repetitive on this score in Agamben isn't so much that he keeps saying the same thing over and over again in similar language from essay to essay, book to book, but that what he finds in poetry is always the saying again of this very thing about language. His point *is* the foregrounded repetition and renewal that makes for utterance—as made palpable in turn by literary writing as an object of future repetition in the deed of reading.

The light shed on Agamben's ontological speculations by his studies of poetry is never clearer than in the absence of the latter material in the most serious retorts to, rather than appropriations of, his political work. Without clarification from his exegeses of literary language, Agamben can all too easily (it would seem) be misread as a metaphysician manqué, succumbing at last to what he would propose to forgo—and not just that, but the wielder of a weirdly belated messianic theology of the Word (Pauline Christianity) rather than of its desacralized refiguration.[17] Yet it is instead the *non*teleological vigilance of the secular expectancy he advocates that finds one of its models for such a second coming in precisely the secondary vocality that each new reading brings to text. At issue in Agamben, for any and all redemptive recognitions, is their being inherent in the here and now of any potential action, verbal action included—not some eschatological stripping away of the present veil (apoca-lypse: un-cover) in the prescient sense of possibilities beyond us.[18] At this level, the messianic in part finds another name for itself in the poetic, the second coming as the present "come again?" of phrasal surprise and, more generally, the always secondary coming-to-speech of text in the silent voicing of each new reading.

A moment back, I wrote "inherent in the here and now." I did so not without thinking, of course, but, as I note with some surprise on rereading, without fully listening. I missed the internal echo my language had set in motion. Potential had its way, its sway, nonetheless. Here, once again, is language's own perpetual *déja entendu* (the French itself divided between "intended" again and "heard" again) brought to silent, contrapuntal "voice." Let it gladly stand. My own pursuit of this strain in Agamben's writing—his stress on present potential—can regularly be applied (more than he himself applies it, in fact) to the alternate coming-to-be of such cross-fertilized signification. For the tacit exchangeability of "inherent" and "in (the) here and" instances a familiar lexical nursery of potentiated self-transformation in the coming (again) of sounded second thoughts.

Varying Ong by way of Agamben, then, and turning the former's dichotomy dialectical, such are those *auralterities* whose textual slippages keep restaging the always unfixed nature, phonetic as well as ideational, of the poem's true but renewable "end" in reading. Closely read in their turn, Agamben's deliberations on Italian verse, in and before *The End of the Poem*, would thus serve to elucidate and so tame the apparent messianism and logocentricism of his own figures of speech for speech, decapitalizing at once End and Voice, diffusing each into the second coming of a lowercased voicing (and its third coming, its thirtieth, its three-thousandth) in the silent reading of each and every poem. Definitive here is Agamben's repeated allusion in various essays to Valéry's definition of poetry as sustaining for as long as possible a "hesitation between sound and sense," a suspended convergence that closure (the poem's linear "end") would curtail—if it were not, that is, for the poem's re-sounding in each subsequent reading. Put it that such a hesitation undergoes phonic restitution each silent time out.

Deixis / Dialexis / Dialectics

In reading Agamben reading, I turn to the context where poetry's way of meaning means most to him: as an illustrative "excurse" within his philosophical work on the avoidance of absolute negativity in language. This is the overcoming of what used to be called in Anglo-American circles the deconstructive *thanatopraxis* (or "deathwork") of the letter as the present obviation both of origin and of the thing described. It is Agamben's way of addressing, if never quite redressing, "the original nucleus of a fracture in the plane of language"—going back to Aristotle—"between showing and saying, indication and signification" (*Language and Death*, 18). This is, in other words, the fracture between "indication" at work (19) and language in play, pointing versus phrasing—as they dubiously collude in such deictic gestures as "this" or "that" or "these" or "those." Deixis: crux and crisis of any signifying mode that still clings to the phantom "res" in verbal representation, the identified thing accessed by and beyond wording. In Agamben's (quasi-auditory) view of poetry, what is "shown" rather than "said," what shows forth—as we're about to see in detail—is the saying of the said: *this* and *these*, even *that* and *those*, not as out there somewhere but as this poem's words right here.

The text I'm choosing, for the exemplary compression of its analysis, is from *Language and Death* rather than *The End of the Poem*, though precisely the exorcism of death from language constitutes for Agamben that said end, the end of all speech in poetry. This is an achievement we can watch transpire through close-grained interplay in Agamben's eight exacting pages on fewer than twice as many lines from the greatest lyric poet in Italian after Dante. Given the verses in question and the dramatic transformation of their demonstrative (deictic) lexicon, one needs, to begin with, a sense of Agamben's reading based on the most literal possible translation—before looking further (in the Italian) to those aspects specifically of caesura and enjambment, at various scales, that elsewhere define for him the founding rhythms of poetry: in other words, the full range of effects—from diction to lineation—that "articulate" the metrical breaks and phonic as well as syntactic ligatures, the cuts and pastes, of verse pacing.[19]

Giacamo Leopardi's renowned descriptive text "L'infinito" (1821) is introduced in a chapter from *Language and Death* that begins with the perennial philosophical crisis involved in laying claim, through language, to any sense-certain reference whatever, and not least "the infinite." In an opening summary of Agamben's argument so far, what "we term 'philosophy'" is characterized as the attempt "at grasping negatively the very taking place of language in the unspeakable experience of the Voice" (66). In getting past, not beneath, this negativity, Agamben is still looking for an "experience of language within this culture that does not rest on an unspeakable foundation" (66). He is on alert for moments, found most clearly for him in poetry, where language, no longer "unspeakable," is itself voiced—where, as it were, saying is said. And quintessentially in this unfolding chapter, when poetry is brought up against the ineffable, when the human finitude marked by death comes into direct confrontation with Leopardi's version of the infinite.[20]

Here is how this particular example goes in a straightforward prose translation from the cited English edition of Leopardi, approximate enjambments rather arbitrarily marked in the text: "This lonely knoll was ever dear to me / and this hedgerow that hides from view / so large a part of the remote horizon" (*Language and Death*, 75). That was then—and now—both. "But as I sit and gaze my thought conceives / interminable spaces lying beyond that / and supernatural silences / and profoundest calm, until my heart / Almost becomes dismayed" (75). Dismayed, in particular, over just this extra dimension of the scene: "And as I hear / the wind come rustling through these leaves, / I find myself comparing to this voice that infinite silence: and I recall eternity / and all the ages that are dead / and the living presence and its sounds." The effect is almost punningly to overwhelm: "And so / in this immensity my thought is drowned: / and in this sea is foundering sweet to me" (75). The wind "rustling through these leaves" invites an association with turned pages (in Italian as well, though unnoted by Agamben) that is at the same time partly overruled by the emphasis on a heard rustle rather than a deciphered set of marks. One result: a poem that, in working through its own hazarded desolation, ends up locating—as for Agamben all genuine poetry does—the space between "was" ("dear") and "is" ("sweet") as traversed primarily in the deferred return of subvocal reading. As looked to (and audited) in the following chapter, the "West Wind" of Shelley's famous ode, "rustling" across its own lines, has a related—and even more extreme—way of embedding the temporality of present potential in its metered grammar. Sooner than that, British Romanticism, in comparison with Italian, will be represented here by Wordsworth's comparable finessing of deixis in its schismatic misfit between word and world.

On Agamben's showing, Leopardi's volatile descriptors transact a space for restored contemplation within the bidirectional shift of the poem's referential gestures—gestures at once toward the *this here* (a familiar and beloved Romantic hillock) and the *that there* (the withering cosmic expanse beyond its horizon). Tracking the six repetitions of "the demonstrative pronoun *this*" (*Language and Death*, 75), answered by two occurrences of *that*, Agamben sees the poem's "gesture of indication" as "throwing itself on to a *this*"—as if onto its own sword—"that it tries to demonstrate and grasp" (75). But such indexicality is fraught at its limit, as well as from within, by a risked encounter with the void. The deictic effort is exerted by grammar even while, pointing just beyond the immediate, "the experience of the *this*" results in "the dismayed sense of the interminable, of the infinite" (75)—in other words, of that to which any pointing would be only a pointless gesture of abstraction. Agamben is powerfully clear on this effect. Only when the *that* out there, that vastness, can become the self-engulfing "this" that immerses and submerges the subject, can the poem end; only then does one reach the point where "reflection is placated and sinks into a final 'this' "—call it the *all of this*, including now the former daunting *that*: "And so / In this immensity my thought is drowned."

Lyric drowning, it would seem, amounts to an absorption into what one has somehow found words for after all, however thin and provisional that phrasing. Here is where Agamben discerns in the thematic of language at large the loophole of such baffled discourse in an isolated language act. Despite the mortal intimidations posed by "the infinite," meditation's move through "l'eterno" on the way to that final wash of "immensity" is for Agamben the hint of its recuperation precisely as poetry—where time trumps extension in space. The "end of the poem" is to be repeatable, to defy the merely passing moment, to be subsumed by that which will release it again, time and again, its distress "placated" in and through each new voice that reads its stressed words. The dwarfings induced by a spatial limitlessness are transmuted by the recurrences of a discursive timelessness. Agamben is at his best in bringing this out as an etymological premise as well as an abstract destiny, seeded there in the poem's very first word, "Sempre." Mitigating what would otherwise seem the undue verbal finality of a preterit setting for what "was *ever* dear to me" in the revisited landscape, the force of *sempre* operates not as a retrospective "always" but as "once and for all" in the sense of "once and forever," so that iteration is implicit in the very predication.

And this is only to be expected in the kind of example he would be inclined to choose, since for Agamben recurrence is inherent in the grammar (and phonic rhythm) of all poetry. This is because literature's prompt to a future reading works to rescue its abstractions for each new enunciation, its deictic recessionals securing the *this right here* of their processed (however silent) enunciation. The past in this sense is always grammatically "perfected" as a veritable present progressive: once but still as well. Yet, as we know, threats to composure in this poem remain, both raised and compassed by the dramatic turn in Leopardi's swift reflection. As "I sit and gaze," so the speaker puts it, somatically rooted and perceptually engaged, "my thought conceives interminable space"—or, alternately, one might say (in noting the untethered abstractions) "my conception thinks the endless"—this, plus "supernatural / silence" as well as "profoundest calm" (as the translation has it). The enjambed arrangement of these cosmic run-ons at their receding limits occurs (in reverse order, and though unremarked by Agamben, who elsewhere stresses enjambment as a quintessential poetic gesture) at the double plural "interminati / spazi" (endless spaces) and "suvrumani / silenzi" (superhuman silences). If these metrical as well as spatial overruns bespeak a nervous mimetic lineation of the unbounded and (via "profoundest" for "deepest" as well) the bottomless, then the act of reading is their imminent (and here immanent) recontainment: again the deed of putting "all of this" into words that will now and forever, in formal iteration, at once summon and subdue its immensity.

At this point the matter of grammatical antecedence in the weave of demonstratives, and with it the plot, thicken. For as the speaker hears the wind rushing through the leaves, "I find myself comparing to this voice that infinite silence," with the *this/that* seesaw ambiguous in the first case for the "wind" or its enunciated notice over against the astral vacuum of sound. Here Agamben's analysis gives momentary pause, for he seems to suggest that the "voice" introduced at this turn is unequivocally that of the speaker himself, source of the "discourse," rather than, given the nearest antecedent, a sudden Romantic figure for the wind: that natural respiration, of course, being no more a voice, and no more present anyway, than is (with the deictic "this") any denoted human utterance apart from inscription. But Agamben can be no more than half wrong in this, and only momentarily. That any voice can arise here only against the backdrop of the endlessly unsaid and unsayable hints at the condition of language all told, a condition all but impossible to hear tell of in words—but sometimes troped upon by lyric, where the "place of negativity" (like the annihilating *that* out there becoming *this* [all this]) can be dialectically canceled in reading.

That is how the memory-work of the Leopardi poem complements and rechannels the broader claims about poetry in Agamben's writing: its capture of language in the moment of becoming, the beginning and the "end" of every poem. For on his grasp of "L'infinito," in the crossfire and x-ing out of its deixis, the only scene it depicts is its own *re*reading, the coming back into play of its words, *these* words now. And it is here that Agamben's account sheds light—which is why we interrupt it for comparison—on a related landmark of British Romanticism. For it is precisely the play of deixis in Wordsworth's *Tintern Abbey*, written two decades before Leopardi's lines, that releases the text from its dramatized reverie into a sense of its own end in reception, in writing read. Up to a point in this reflexivity, the transnational Romantic pattern is a familiar one, where the poems themselves often seem openly to suspect the dominance of the rhetorical signifier over the "indicated" landscape, the time of text supplanting the time of natural experience. What Agamben highlights by his unique emphasis on deixis, however, is the deeper linguistic rather than rhetorical jeopardy entailed by gestures of memory returned as lyric presence. The paradoxical figure "spot of time" in Wordsworth is of course typical of the Romantic effort to spatialize duration as a node of recurrence: to write memory. *This* familiar site, *that* one too, *there, here, those, these*: all are the sheer conjurations of discourse as we read. You don't have to have been there; you are as much there now as was the speaker when remembering, whether wandering abroad or at pen point.[21]

In a poem thick on the ground with deixis, and breathing the very air of forced referential immediacy in overlap with dredged memory, Wordsworth speaking in *Tintern Abbey* of the mental image as a "picture of the mind" that "revives again" (61) seems in his own way commenting—by way of a pictorial trope—on a present poetic task etched, a task sketched, in words alone. In his poem, the accumulated deictics—approaching two dozen instances—protest too much, purposefully so, what they call up by rushing to point out. They are the descriptive equivalent of an invocation or apostrophe (as of Muse or Reader or Nature), naming what that name summons into discourse only, not into presence.[22] The identified natural features of an indicated landscape are the present not of their own past but of their own envisioning, their own saying. The demonstrative is a demonstration, a performance. Unlike the "blind man" congenitally deprived of sight in the famous simile in *Tintern Abbey*, we see in reading what we have seen for ourselves elsewhere—or its like. This is the way our own best images come back to us: like words on the page, prompts that summon not the absent or lost but what Agamben might call (a variant of the Deleuzian "virtual") a pure potential in the now.

Returning to the Wye Valley after a five-year absence, as in the case of Leopardi's speaker occupying again his favored hillock, Wordsworth's persona can again hear "*these* waters" (3), behold "*these* . . . cliffs" (5). Adverbial shifters also punctuate the deictic presencing of the scene, as "*Here*, under *this* dark sycamore" (10) successive vistas impinge: "*these* plots," "*these* orchard-tufts" (11), all arrayed and subsumed there in the blanketing abstraction of "*this* season" (12) in a space rimmed by "*these* hedge-rows" associated with "*these* pastoral farms," but all of it finally generalized by abstraction not as this landscape but as "*these* beauteous *forms*" (forms in the absence even of their content) that have never for a moment "been to me / As is a landscape *to* a blind man's eye" (23–24; emphasis added)—any more than they are now for us. Prepositions in this way help measure, and keep, the same distance as do the deictic shifters, since the "forms" do not appear *to* the eye, but rather appear *in* the mind's eye, summoned alike by words and memory. "If *this* be but a vain belief"—a sense of owing one's best moods to these memories, where the deixis has now summed and internalized them ("*this* . . . belief") as the bedrock of an emotional creed—it would be a futility for which the speaker has only the present natural scene to blame.

The furious pointing continues across the weft and tuck of deictic formulations, adverbial and demonstrative alike. "And *now*"—another shifter, lodged among the litany of *this* and *these*—the mental picture "revives again" when "*here* I stand" in person "among *these* hills" (68), recalling their first impressions years before. "*That* time is past" (83; deictic emphasis again added), as if to say demonstrably past. Yet since what has been surrendered to time are the likes of "these wild ecstasies" (138) long gone, the strained deictic "these" suggests an affect *proximate* only in the writing—but then again where else? At which point both biographical and topographical details are assimilated to abstraction within the ambient deixis of "these my exhortations" (146)—the shapes of this text, rather than of these (now those) scenic contours.

At which point, too, we may well remember that no poem by Wordsworth is more routinely shortened in reference than *Lines Composed a Few*

Miles above Tintern Abbey, On Revisiting the Banks of the Wye During a Tour, July 13, 1798. To recognize this loco-descriptive "conversation" poem (addressed by a delayed fuse to his sister Dorothy) as first of all written rather than intoned and transcribed, let alone spoken as we read, is to recall a *locus postclassicus* in contemporary critical debate. This is the tactical use made of a comparable (if more exaggerated) stress on writtenness in the poem called out by Paul de Man to deconstruct the semiotics of Michael Riffaterre from within the latter's own exegetical premises and backlog.[23] Taking up Riffaterre's magisterial reading of a Victor Hugo text about the speaker's love for the carillon of Flanders and the synesthetic images it induces, including a Spanish dancer descending the "crystal invisible" of time's stair-stepped cadence, de Man admits the descriptive ingenuity but insists on what Riffaterre's analysis takes no note of: the fact, announced by the poem's very title, that it is constituted by lines "written on the glass of a Flemish window"—as insubstantial, so to say, as if writ in melted sand.

For de Man—and his position can be economically distilled without undue simplification—the semiotic decipherment by which Riffaterre can show, let us say, the *pace of time* figured forth to the human mind in the personified fancy footwork of a Spanish dancer could be said to "solve" the poem's figurative puzzle without exposing the deeper figurative nature of its key. In translating the text's mimetic incoherence to the level of its metaphoric cohesion, Riffaterre's semiotics is thought to miss the fact that, within the strictly descriptive system, some abstractions are entirely figurative at base. According to de Man, it misses in particular the fact that the poem's heroes, mind and time—or in fact, to speak more philosophically, Being and Time—are only marked out by writing to begin with, inscriptions of the ineffable. For "I" and "time" (in a matrix phrase like "I love the belling of time in the sound of its hours") are themselves catachreses, figures for which—de Man's main point—there are no literal terms. Yet they remain words, not visions—visible only, like words on a window, when all transparency is foregone. The implied entitling deixis of *these* "lines" found on a Flemish pane—as if scratched out in the immediate transcript of an emotional transport—is all the poem actually points to, and then only at one remove as lines written out after the fact upon a page: the same page where figures of speech, radical abstractions, like "I" and "time," have, de Man would insist, their own and only locus.

Such a double phenomenological displacement is perhaps clearer yet in the prolix title of Wordsworth's *Lines*, lines "composed" (changed from the original publication title "written") in their own right—not the mere transcriptions of thoughts that have been in the other sense composed by nature's harmonies. In an Agambenesque (rather than de Manian) allegory of its own *re*reading, the composition is for us again the thing itself, a scripted poise of affect couched in "these" hortatory lines, passed through the imagined ear of the apostrophized sister to our mute eyes. Even when every *this* versus *that*, each *here* versus *out there*, in the referential tensions of a given text comes down to *these words here*, they point, self-renewing, to that *other and later* experiencing of them, here again and now, in the coming of the utterance under new eyes. This is what Agamben means when saying that the whole poetic episode is itself a kind of shifter, moved over from the discursive position of writer to reader: the "super-shifter" of the "metrical-musical element" that "always already warns whoever listens or repeats a poem that the event of language at stake has already existed and will return an infinite number of times" (*Language and Death*, 77). Thus, as in Leopardi, is the long shadow of infinity, without loss of its unnerving sublimity, captured and channeled by linguistic iteration per se.

Poetry's end lies always beyond itself, reaching out—as well as back and down, into the very possibility of speech. A *future* possibility there prima facie on the waiting page. And thus by association a *precursive* and conditioning potential recovered in each and every iteration—and recovered more fully precisely because of the "metrical-musical element." This is what Agamben himself never quite lays out, but what no doubt lies beneath his emphasis (more in theory than in individual readings) on the aurality rather than just the decipherability of textual iteration. For the "end of the poem" to manifest the faculty for speech that permits it in the first place, that linguistic potentiality must be sensed broadly enough to include the intonational as well as the lexigraphic dimension of this expressive human faculty.

Allegories of Rereading

As always in Wordsworth, as in Leopardi too, the gestures of deixis entail the accidents and tactics of lexis, so that such effects are embroiled in *Tintern Abbey* as part of this same telos of *re*reading. Two in particular: a curious déjà vu in the phrasing, and then an unusually bold configuration of objective and subjective genitive, that trope of syntax so crucial for subject/object relations in the philosophical poetics of Agamben. First, the oddly insinuated recurrence. If, three lines from the poem's end, we think we remember "these steep woods and lofty cliffs" (157) as a faint repetition, we are thus remembering all there has been of them for us, the mere words that picture them, together with that little extra change that time (textual time) can provide. This time around, the phrase makes perfect sense: woods steeply layered on the hillside as it rises higher to a cliff face. But approximately 150 lines earlier, in the poem's second deixis after "these waters" (3), we have in fact read (and may well remember it because of the pleonastic overkill) how "I behold these steep and lofty cliffs" (5), where the double redundancy of the adjectives (given the noun "cliffs" that presumes them both) invites—by a fusion of the first noun with the demonstrative—a seductive secondary emphasis. Since, in this "secluded" scene, what images like "these" invest the visitant with are (two lines away) "thoughts of more deep seclusion" (7), it is almost inevitable that "these steep" evoke (subvocally) "these deep." When we come again upon a near-miss repetition of this phrase toward the poem's end, and this after the interim assonance of "lofty thoughts" (128) spelling out the mental cast of the sublimity at issue, even the topographic normalization of the phrase cannot now shake the memory of what has been—and the uncanny "depths" of contemplation once triggered there. In a uniquely Agambenesqe moment, poetry here rereads itself dozens of lines later—and does so in order to plumb the language of its own possibility.

It does this as well, in my second example of nodalized rereading, with the equivocated genitive in that very phrasing "thoughts of more deep seclusion": thoughts had by the more inwardly secluded subject, thoughts aimed at the idea of a deeper seclusion yet.[24] For Agamben, such an ambivalence would, in a single turn, leverage the very crisis of ontology. In what way does language ground either the Cogito of the subject (in the Cartesian sense of *Cogito ergo sum*) or the deixis of its objects? The same question would apply to a later toggle between subjective and objective genitive in the phrase "the picture of the mind revives again"—offering the consolation of philosophy, as it were, for all the atrophied passions of earlier years. Memories are not blind. They rise before us refigured in the mind. But in so doing, in the ontological circularity of such a logic, they are the only *picture of the mind* we have in the objective sense: a rendering of mentality's phantasmal palimpsest. The best image of the human mind given to us is after all, and again, the *figure of rereading*.

From Language of the Sense to the Sense of Language

Processing a Wordsworthian text of this kind as much as one by Leopardi, putting ourselves in the place of the recollecting subject, pictures back to us the absent as "this"—become now a *present potential*. So complex is this phrasal pentimento—as mental model—that incidental overlays and superimpositions can crisscross its evocative strata at levels of little more than subliminal registration. Wordsworth's lines are frequently rimmed by alternatives that their careful sounding cannot decisively rule out. Wordsworth looking back: "I have felt" (100), where the very phonetics of tense opens the breathing room between a too-contracted over and done with ("I felt") and—by alliterative telescoping—the over and over again of "I've felt." But felt, in recursion, what? Wordsworth is quick to spell this out in his speaker's twin gratitude to "nature and the language of the sense" (108), the second half of the phrase offering another hinge from the subjective genitive (the idiom of a sensory perception articulate in itself) to the objective genitive (a sensory world given poetic shape only by the intercession of human language). Either way, the compound phrase ("nature and the language of the sense") attaches forward grammatically to its redefinition as "anchor of my purest thoughts" (109)—with its own further hovering between objective and subjective genitive: thoughts either providing or benefiting from stability, or of course both. Such bivalve phrasings on the very nature of language are what poetry makes happen, or say, monitors happening, in the vicinity—but without the strictures—of metaphysics, where language can never provide an ontological anchor but only (as Agamben is dedicated to showing) a perpetual point of new departure. This is an emphasis undimmed even by a later and more sentimental rephrasing of remembered affect as "the language of my former heart" (118). For the poem writes in that heartfelt idiom at times (subjective genitive) so as to bracket it (objective genitive) as a past locus of feeling under a more distanced description—even while arraying it for present vocalization in a proxied second subject, whether sister or reader.

If deconstruction may be suspected of reading for sheer writing, for inscription itself—for the quasi-graphic differentials that defer all being-there of the described—Agamben is after something else. Deconstruction finds in literature, again and again, the parable of the merely figurative as essentially fictive, and this with immediate fallout for the other figures we live by. Agamben, instead, reads through writing to language in action, not language itself—so that he uncovers, again and again, not its presence (it can never be isolated as such, only activated) but rather its human (or humanizing) precondition. He thus finds in poetry, again and *yet* again, even from within given words, the still present potential of language—its potential for other words as well, and, as we've seen by extrapolation from his axiom, other wordings of the same script. This is why the palimpsest that *is* language, together with the palimpsest of mental perception figured *by* language, converge with unprecedented density in the poetic line. Reading is not just facilitated, but say, suffused, by what makes it possible, with its attention spans as much formative, once again, as formalist.

What began as a comparison of the deictic gestures in Leopardi's loco-descriptive iteration with the four-times-as-many instances in Wordsworth has thus widened, as under Agamben's guidance it was bound to do, to the question at large of subjectivity in language and the image of the mind phrased back to itself in words. It is at that level, where the mechanics of deixis release the full circuitry of linguistic self-enactment, that we return now to Agamben and his test case for the unlocalizable space, the sheer taking-place, of thought in words. To arrive at this familiar point with him yet again is not to flatten attention against some sheer wall of words. The "end" of the poem amounts not to a stultifying network of sheer difference cultivated by high theory, but instead to a sense of the differential linguistic work done *with* rather than *in* words through reading—at least when reading is taken to be the decipherment of transmission in process, the sensed coming into place of a potentially shared thought.

This may best explain the deeply engrained attachment to genitive duality in his writing—as well as in his reading of Hegel (recall "the voice of death"). To the extent that the tension between subject and object in such prepositional phrasing turns on a reciprocity of cause and effect, phrases like "the dictation of poetry" (one of the chapters mentioned earlier from *The End of the Poem*) get at precisely his view that what is set out in verse is the enunciated coming forth of language itself from its somehow present source. The author takes down in words what the words themselves later seem to re-cite back to us. Reversing Wordsworth's "language of the sense," where perception itself grows eloquent, Agamben is drawn to the *sense of language* in literature, where the sense it makes includes the recognition of its ongoing possibility to do so. This is why the "end" of poetry, in a non-apocalyptic eternal return, is for its verbal effects to read out each time their own renewed cause in human wording.

I trust this claim has been brought to sufficient light in my sampling of Agamben's own hermeneutic practice—and this despite the difficulties that the Leopardi verses (to which we now return) inevitably impose for the non-Italian speaker fitfully grasping at cognates, taken aback by the frequently inverted modifiers, frustrated by no hint of line breaks or their mitigations by run-ons in the prose translation, its rhythms thereby including none of that kinetic give-and-take between caesura and enjambment (again Agamben's defining features of verse) that rehearses the functional discontinuities of language from within its featured use as poetry. Still, such deficits may accrue to a certain impact all told. Reading Leopardi this way as some of us must, we can nonetheless, with rare clarity, apprehend the end of the poem (in Agamben's double-genitive sense). To read like a certain kind of philosopher, or say, to read philosophically, is to read always in a language not your own, to read not for meaning (in the end) but for language. A poem brought forward as a sorely limited exemplification in the English edition of *Language and Death*, that is, turns out to loom there as a further philosophical provocation. In trying to grasp what it is in the Leopardi poem that so holds Agamben's linguistic interest, the limp translation is both a nagging problem and, in default, the solution. It insists on what is there before us first of all: not fifteen interlaced lines of sinuous rhymed verse but a sheer block of language, in all its alien magic.

Spun out in Agamben's commentary, it is worth repeating, is not some interdisciplinary reinvention of the wheel. As proposed at the start, Agamben's level of reading constitutes no reversion—though backslidings far drearier can be imagined—to the structuralist "languageness" of literature. Rather than simply produced from it as necessary condition, poetry for Agamben *educes* the potential for language, as potential—and so for the not-said as well. It seeks its end by closing not upon the how of metrical utterance but, as extruded for unique consideration in verse, on the whence—linguistic possibility under its own isolation as such, or in other words the languageness of language itself, until the "itself" loses its meaning in a given verbal event. More obviously in poetry than elsewhere, Agamben would be the first to insist, the not-said is what gives (way to) speech. This happens not simply in the sense that *langue* is straightforwardly required by *parole* (Italian by a given Leopardi metaphor, for instance). It occurs, rather, in the way that channeled literary utterance reawakens in transit, in transmit, the endemic dormancy of its own medium. Poetry, one might thus summarize, contemplates the making possible of the language in which it writes.

With regard to the inner linkages of verse operation, syllabic and metrical, including the phonetics of elision, the more one looks at the Italian verse brought forward by Agamben, imagines listening to it with one's own inner ear, sorts through its graphic and phonic recursions, charts tentatively its alphabetic cross-stitching, the closer one comes to the ultimate point. On Agamben's model, poetry would manifest the act of trying to *make sense*, even if haltingly, partially, stumblingly. It is where one comes to see the increments of language *taking place* from within the poem rather than presumed in advance of (and by) it. So that even when, and indeed because, we may not know in every nuance what the foreign-language lines say, we recognize them as speaking Italian, shaping expression from its fund in language. The less the poem means at a glance, the more it is the inherent mystery of speech, the event of words, that its lines put before us. In regard to the *possibility* of human meaning, such is what poetry does even in our own tongue. It stages the challenge of language in advance of any given expression. In the case of Leopardi's packed lines, without actually "knowing the language," instead one *hears it happen.*

And does so from that primal elision of the title forward: *L'infinito*—all the vaster (if fractionally) for the phonetic material it absorbs by sheer convention into its sonic mass: the likes of Wordsworth's "the eternal" (*Ode*, 154) in a closer phonetic transcription (by contraction), as if to say "th'eternal." Such graphically marked latchings by the elisionary punctuation of apostrophe are, of course, to the unschooled ear, the most obvious of the poem's alphabetic effects, beginning with the innocuous "this lonely knoll" (*questo* as demonstrative taken up by contraction, by self-excavation, in "quest'ermo colle"). The effect, again, is wholly conventional, innocuous—at least if it weren't that such demonstratives are exactly the shifters at issue in the metaphysical teeter-totter of the text. Two lines later there is also something that has been elided from another nominalized adjective (often, in grammar, a philosophical sticking point of abstraction): in this case, the subsumed (or not entirely—better, delayed) *o* (of *nullo*) in "the ultimate" of "Dell'ultimo."

Further along, muted by enjambment, and with the deictic "questa" inviting no elision this time before a consonant, we come upon the enjambed internal echo of "a questa *voce* / *Vo co*mparando" (to this voice I go on comparing). As if rehearsing some parting of a primal phonic stream, the rivulets of sound must be, it would seem, semantically rechanneled after the alphabetic watershed—and this even for a reader for whom the Italian is coming only very slowly into focus. One can attend, nonetheless, to the currents and undertows of the linguistic beneath the semantic, in this case the cresting of the *c* from *voce* to *vo-co*. In so doing, we are thrown back on a minimal linguistic difference that once again obtrudes the action of language from within a particular speech act—and this on the way to the voicing of a word beyond voice: a word, in context, for the very comparison (*comparando*) between voice and what exceeds it: this voice over against that immense and impending silence beyond.

And there is a further linguistic insinuation, even for the nonnative speaker, near the open-ended close. In trying to second-guess the Italian, one maps "And so in this immensity my thought is drowned" onto "Cosi tra questa / immensità" only to note first, beyond the internal rhyme, the suspended elision. Here is a vastness whose expanse is timed at the enjambment—as if pointing by deixis to the space stretching free from it—so as to stress in this case, it would seem, the lack of contraction, of phonic economy, even in the confrontation between two vowels (*quest(o)ermo*, we've heard, but not now *quest(a)immensità*). Borrowing Agamben's leading terms again, a tactical thematic enjambment thus transcends a built-in mechanism of caesura. This refused conflation (policed more in writing than in speech) keeps each word open to the other in abstract dilation: "this" present "immensity" in which (leaving intact the reflexive inversion) *drowns itself my thought*. It is as if the *i* previously elided from *infinite* and the *e* from *eternity* are allowed to find here a mixed spatiotemporal variant in a word (*immensità*) more abstract than either and covering for both at the very moment—prolonged unclipped at line's end—of figured engulfment.

Even so, one might object that the elisions so far (or their exceptions) have been, at least on the face of it, fairly trivial: formulaic, rote, mere automatisms of the language. But prepared by the unmarked ephemera of telescoped phonemes, and all the more so when they are among the first recognitions of the nonnative eye, an English reader is less likely to miss the more philosophical valence—and violence—of the final two elisions operating from within the reflexive grammar of the personal pronoun. In the first of these phonetic compressions, there is the vanishing (as subsumed, submerged, drowned) of the reflexive *se* (oneself) into a vowel-opened prefix (*s'annega*, drowns itself). Second, in the immediate wake of this—and within the same extended trope of drowning—there is the effortless and pivotal elision of *me* into a freestanding monosyllabic verb (the copula *è*): "il naufragar *m'è dolce* in questo mare" (shipwreck *to me is* sweet in this sea)—with its paired metaphors for the mind sunk in time. Even here, to say that neither of these effects is marked as "poetic" (let alone extreme) in Italian orthography would scarcely deter an Agambenesque allegory, since the poem is telling us something *about* rather than just *in* Italian: about what it is, as it were, to "have Italian," to have it come to pass in us. In this way does the first line's deictically concretized and supposedly palpable conclusion in "quest'ermo colle" (this lonely knoll) find delayed completion—for a certain arc in the poem from materiality to abstraction—by relaxing into the strictly figurative sea of "questo mare" in the poem's paired final words, even as the last of them, "mare," anagrammatizes a cross-word ligature earlier in the line at "naufrag*ar m'è*."

But this is the least of it where the *me/m'è* homophony—propelled as if by undertow from the contracted *se* of "s'annega"—is concerned, each a figure for subjectivity's obliviation (drowns myself, shipwreck to me is sweet).[25] For here we are sent back to one of Agamben's most brilliant and important essays, "*Se*," appropriately collected in *Potentialities* because the topic, the reflexive pronoun *se* of Indo-European tradition—once submitted to the full vehemence of Agamben's etymology—turns out to indicate, let us say, only the potential (not the isolated existence) of self in the reflex of self-reference.[26] In one of those explorations where the leagued power of Agamben's etymological and his grammatical thinking seems opening upon deep anthropological time, he in effect demonstrates that the very idea of "self" in Western culture amounts to what might be called a linguistic back-formation from the already reflexive "itself." The idea of what is "proper to the self," what is *per se*, has no true nominative. Such a reified being always appears obliquely, not a noun but a pronoun, related in this respect to a shifter like "I" rather than a proper noun.[27] As typical of Agamben, however, these deflections, these circularities, need not plummet back into the radical negative that puts an end to metaphysics only by perpetuating itself there as an encysted void. Instead, the de-nominalization of being and of its determining categories merely returns being to the flux of action in the reflexive mode, to an *event in language* rather than a fixed name. Resisted here, once again, is that "violence" and radical "foreignness" that take human utterance to be "grounded in animal speech, on whose exclusion language is constructed" (137). Even if the "speech" of the animal is a voicing without language whose equivalent human sounds must be annulled in subsumption to the linguistic signifier, still, for Agamben, that vocal erasure need not seem wholly voiding. Nor need it seem—this book would add—more than provisional, resisted in potential by the contingent provisions of each new alphabetic, and hence phonetic, reading.

In one of his familiar summations of the turn from an ontological cul-de-sac to an ethics of communicative potential, Agamben grants that the Hegelian dialectic is "one of the supreme attempts of philosophy to think its own supreme thought, humankind's entry into its *se*, into its being without a nominative" ("*Se*," 125)—a being-without (and doing without) of absolutes. As long as this lack is accepted as "entry" without coming under the lethal sign of negation, it "constitutes" for humanity—in an added run of etymological emphasis across further circuitous derivations from *se*—"its dwelling and its *ēthos*: its *so*litude and its con*sue*tude, its *se*paration but also its *so*lidarity" (125; Agamben's italics). To paraphrase his etymological forays with an English decentering, the fact that the *se/lf* exists only in reflex, never substantively, does not deny it action in the language of its own conception and desire. Moreover, this unthought of thought that "cannot lead to any lexical entity or existing thing" is characterized (not, in the ordinary sense, defined) as follows: "Unnamed, it is thus without destiny: an *untransmissible transmission*" (125).

This phrase is central to a field wider even than that staked out by Agamben. Such a never-transmitted fact of transmission marks, for him, the meeting point of being and language, with their shared horizon—rather than separate ontologies—constituting all we can think to call our own. But what then, in other terms, is the untransmissible condition of transmission? What is it other than the very definition of a *medium*? And so it is that the metalinguistic philosophy of Agamben might join those other efforts of the posthumanist moment in grappling with consciousness as a *discourse network*, a relativizing of language within the wider scope of modern transmission systems."[28] If so, poetry would be one place to test the system. When the reflexive "m'è" (in "to me [is sweet]") of an explicitly swamped and submerged consciousness is phrased so that it melds the conjugation of being with its place-holding subject, or in other words when the posited "is to me" is subsumed to the reflexive homophone "m'è"—predication and positioning in the same breath, and by the most effortless expectations of a given tongue—then Leopardi's poem has maintained through to closure, in pure disclosure at that, the revealed medium of speech as the place of all our pointing, including our self-pointing: the site of our dwelling if not of what can be proven to indwell. The poem has maintained that verbal space even while bearing down on the driven wedge of caesura and enjambment alike (slice and splice, gap and bind, call it the ongoing flux of *arrestoration*) in their narrowest possible compass. In the quantum phonology of *m/e/è*, the *me* emerges only from what happens *to me* in the language found for such experience. And only when read in the "virtual" rather than vestigial "auditorium," again in Steven Connor's terms, in which the "material imagination" of text includes the phonic "cross-fades" of its own "auditized" surface.

Orality as Event, Reading as Event-ual

So where are we? Back where we started from: that's always Agamben's point—not a vicious circle of dead-ended ontological conundra, but what other vocabulary might call a "communication circuit." We've seen that one mission of poetry is to speak its own transmission, not to name but to phrase into view its own means. That's its pervasive ethic: to keep language alive in what its writing enlivens. Positivities and negativities are a natural part of any alternating current, including the *this* versus *that* of lyric emplacement. They needn't paralyze; they are in fact the poles of a dynamic. Nor is death some silencing abyss hovering under—and so undermining—all language. The animal noise of preliterate voice isn't the final antithesis of writing, let alone of lettered speech. Voice is what funds the signals that sublimate it. Then, too, the obliterated voice is brought back to life in even silent reading, the carrier of spoken desire apart from all content. Such secondary vocality, as I've characterized it, delivers a massing of sound that vanishes into message without being utterly neutralized by it. Unlike Ong's way of minimizing script as in its own right a time-based medium in the "grapholect" of print culture, with his tendency to downplay reading as an activation, an event, the "secondariness" of such vocality is not derivative but reoriginating—and is linked in this way to the unique temporality of poetry's *potential* for reading in Agamben. By any other name, phonic vestiges continue to play against sense—or in and around it, or beyond it entirely—across the present sounding-out of text. In some imagined verse, for instance (thinking back indirectly to de Man on Riffaterre's Hugo), *I'm* may chime with *time* even though neither self nor duration has a sound to its name or a place (any other place but language) to call its own.

If being-in-time has no groundable essence, only a medium, as Agamben argues in other terms; and if, in still other terms, the human socius has to settle for being a discourse network rather than a mesh of essences, still one's communal obligation begins in keeping the circuits open. Whether or not this multivolume lesson of literature in Agamben holds interest for current students of Agamben in literature departments, the claims and demonstrations remain. In the shared speech of the human animal, set into unique relief by poetry, it is, to vary the latest catchphrase in the interdisciplinary uptake of this philosopher's thought, the *community* of (re)reading that is always *coming*. If this seems an eschatology whose historical vision, even whose poetics, is suspect in many quarters for its Christian overtones, what nonetheless stands beyond ideology is, for the most part, Agamben reading. For even if one were doggedly to hold this otherwise postmetaphysical thinker to the lurking Logos of his most theologically tinged metaphors, and on this score reject his social and political thinking root and branch, still his continued value for literary theory would persist in the subtlety of his metalinguistics—and in the instigated textual attentions of our own reading that may well result.

And why, in short or long term, should any of this matter so centrally? Why should we care about this rescue of "deferral" from what Agamben sees as the nihilism of Derridean *différence* as perpetual absentation? What compels this rethinking of the terminally forestalled as the presently possible? For one thing, varying Ong by an emphasis on the event of voicing still at play in text, I've meant to call out not some oral sediment but that latent *auralterity* brushing words with the present potential of their own generative rewording. For only if multivalence prevails from word to word is the poem being true to its own *possibilities* for reading. We have heard Stevens's definition of poetry as "the cry of its occasion." Even without trying to detect there some late Romantic phonocentrism in this mystification of ever-present voice, we may still, more in Agamben's mode, want to locate the true occasion of its cry: the immanent event of its enunciation. It lies, waits, in reading only, derivative, residual, reinvigorating. Stevens again, from the same passage: "The poet speaks the poem as it is, / Not as it was" (*An Ordinary Evening in New Haven*, st. xii). The poet's language performs its own wording rather than represents what it names as having been there before? But "speaks"? Isn't it rather a secondary vocality that is exclusively at work in making the inscriptive past of text recurrently present? In linguistic fact the only demonstrable "is" to poetic language—even when conceived as *cri de coeur*, or in other words as the passing from vocalized feeling into immediately transcribed speech—is the reverse trajectory from script to the reader's own silent speaking thereof, now and here. In the "end," then, for Agamben, and always for starters yet again, what literature authentically re-*presents* is readers (speakers) *to their language*: not a meeting of minds between author and audience but that meeting anew of language and cognition by which mind can alone begin to know either the other or itself. And in which, as such, mind can alone begin to seem at home—calling forth not so much communication as the common (shared) place, and habitus, and ethos, of (again) "transmission."

Yet the shadow of self-exile from such space remains in force as the negative of this possibility. Granted that the coming-again of expressive potential in written contact, a contact not of pen with page but of words with their understanding, is one "end" of speech. But it is sometimes dead-ended, aborted, refused. Nowhere do certain related literary and philosophical interests of Agamben, in textual activation and ontological potentiation, converge more clearly, perhaps, than in their willed erasure in a story by Melville that Agamben follows Deleuze in rereading.[29] And nowhere does the scale of attention absent in his writing on English literature (Melville here, Dickens later) leave so obviously unspoken the speech-act drama of his detected philosophical emphasis.

Quite beyond the attentions of either philosopher in the case of "Bartleby the Scrivener," it is worth noting how a concerted verbal analysis—as one switch point between linguistics and philosophy—might respond to the ironies of tense in Melville as a latent flashpoint of "potential" in precisely Agamben's sense: as the present reserve of what already is (inverted in Melville to the pure possibility of the not). Certainly, in Melville's story of the clerk who "would prefer not to"—not to write among other things, despite his paid designation as scribe—one can't underestimate the role of literary grammar in pinning the future anterior of achieved potential (the possibility not to have done) to the limbo of its indetermination en route. Yet just where prose answers the demands of plot at its most poignant, Agamben wants to downplay the "Dead Letter Office" (the narrative's revealed backstory of the protagonist's former mortuary employment) as explanation for the scrivener's preferring not to set pen to paper. Agamben minimizes this psychological cause, however, without noting how Melville's own pen has hit the page in a way that confirms the philosopher's related but more abstract point: about potential honored under negation as refusal, as signaled by Bartleby's liberating insistence on the possibility of not-doing.

In the brief allusion to the spirit-depleting labors of the "dead letter" bureaucracy and its nugatory verbal transmission, the thematic of undelivered text is more subtly calibrated than Agamben seems to recognize. But scarcely more intricate than his terminology would be able to compass. For the scribe hasn't just grown sick of writing because of how much writing never reaches its destination; the clotted verbal suggestion is that he is caught between two separate temporalities, grammatically parsed, of such frustrated potential. Among the narrator's speculative examples of undelivered deliverance that must have passed under Bartleby's saddened eye—cast up into a broken-off disjunctive grammar of its own—there is this instance in the series: "a bank-note sent in swiftest charity—he whom it would relieve, nor eats nor hungers any more" (quoted in Agamben, "Bartleby," 269). With "would" wavering as it does between optative and subjunctive, why not the logical past tense instead of "would have relieved"? It is as if, by keeping desire trapped in the so-called historical present of narrative discourse, the negation of potential is made all the more stinging. So it is that a forestalled intention—what would (*if only it could*) have done its best to save a life—is sunk in the fact (too late for Aristotelian contingency) that, in logical terms, mortal hunger is either relieved or it isn't, and in this case (with the check never delivered) wasn't. What results, then, is that the parallel negation of Melville's capping verb phrase "nor eats nor hungers any more" (to the effect that, in death, one is no more satisfied than craving) abuts the still present (rather than perfect) conditional—and its falsely suspended hope—as if in a free indirect discourse hermetically sealed in the lost past of postal desire. Rather than any such "would" in this blighted sense, is it any wonder that Bartleby prefers the "would . . . not"?

That nothing could be farther from a Wordsworthian aesthetic of the "something ever more about to be" in the Romantic linguistics of the preceding decades (and of the coming chapter) is a factor, in no small part, of the verbal byplay in text after Romantic text that helps stave off such rigidification, stemming the mute at times by the self-renewed auralteries of the mutable. In Melville's more stringently superimposed case of past, present, and arrested future, what could have been but wasn't, as well as what agency might now do but would opt not to, is a dual flashpoint of negated intent registered in prose's own grammar as a subjunctive disjuncture driven so deep into questions of potentiality that it becomes their microstylistic laboratory. That's just the step beyond Agamben, further into verbally impacted inference, to which his work may well nudge a fascinated reader.

Blended Tendings

In attempting to appreciate at once both the philosophical rigor and the intuitive vigor of Agamben's poetics, what the remainder of this chapter can do is to step back—to some kind of conceptual distance—in order to go forward partly in Agamben's terms, though often at a different scale of response. This means attempting a philosophically attuned linguistics (and indeed microstylistics) of literary writing in prose as well as verse, a general poetics of phrasing itself. The effort should begin by acknowledging the simple common sense of Agamben's stress on one inevitable end of the poem as a verbal display of lineated, metered, often rhymed verse: namely, its way of reminding us—putting us *in mind* as we read—of a language entirely bespoken in advance, shaped for relay, ours only for the taking up, not for some final "grasping," a language renewed out of its own givens, its own taking place. Our inner ears are stewards only, not fixed destinies, for a text whose closure is only the beginning of its inbuilt possibility to be read again, as all but figured to the eye by the turns and returns of its visibly measured-out and re-versed channels. Yet accepting this as quintessentially true of a palpably shaped poetic form is not to mistake it as irrelevant in the case of linear (rather than lineated) prose, itself often heavily patterned and even echoic (if not rhymed) in its own right, tangibly recursive, even phonetically looped.

Calling out some additional defining moments from *The End of the Poem* should help make clear what we will need to be building on. The coming chapter about the anomalous sonorities of Romantic and Victorian verse speaks directly to the phonic and rhythmic emphasis of Agamben's eponymous essay, "The End of the Poem," where (in acknowledged derivation from the structuralism of Roman Jakobson) the tension "between sound and sense, between the semiotic sphere and the semantic sphere" (109)—or, in other terms, between signal and message, rhythm and symbol, pulsion and import—is what the "end" of the poem can only paradoxically resolve (at its own present completion as audiovisual event). This happens in the convergence of those twin vectors Agamben later posits in saying that the poem "is simultaneously traversed by the semantic current and the semiotic current" (114). These are currents merging, energies convergent, only when over: tandem poetic impulses that become equivalent, that is, only in their simultaneous obliteration. For this is where the constitutive feature of enjambment—with its metered and lineated distinction from grammatical sense—is no longer possible in the end-stopping caesura of closure. Agamben wants the broad generalization that "all poetic institutions participate in this noncoincidence, this schism of sound and sense—rhyme no less than caesura" (110). He also wants, and finds time and again, the exacting limit case, the schismatic instance pitched to the level almost of parable.

The one poem above all, therefore, that exceeds this rule of a verse-effacing convergence—and only by succeeding itself into the state of its own receipt in closure—is the envoi of a text quoted from Dante that, precisely as text, as poem, is addressed from within itself (addressed in both senses) in the vindictive direction of unrequited love: "Poem, go [*Canzon, vatenne*] straight to that woman who has wounded my heart" ("The End of the Poem," 115), stabbing her there in return. Language is in this case end-stopped, quite blatantly, in the expressed intent of its destination: again the norm figured from within its own deviant extreme. In a phrasing already cited above, "the poem thus reveals the goal of its proud strategy: to let language finally communicate itself, without remaining unsaid in what is said" (115). Put differently (differentially), with the passive voice ("is said") further *depersonified*: without remaining unsaid in what it is sensed to say. That's certainly what the present book lends an ear to: language speaking in and through—and sometimes athwart—the spoken. All that remains unsaid here by Agamben himself (for the purposes of my account, not his) is that such a disclosed mediation by language can operate with equivalent force, if not consistency, in prose as well as in poetry.

But more on "depersonified." Beyond the mandates of sheer representation, Agamben proposes (as his treatment of Leopardi so well illustrates) that life and poetry meet only, and as if inexorably, when each is perceived "at the point of their reciprocal desubjectification" ("The End of the Poem," 93). This is that point (or that is this point) where all that is spoken forth is language itself, not being—or, in other words, where the object speech replaces (and to this extent depletes) the uttering subject. At which juncture life and literature, signifying subject and text, "are united not immediately but in a medium. This medium is language" (93). And what ordinary language, especially under certain extraordinary conditions, can do to render traumatic, rather than just structural, this "desubjectification" is the burden of philosopher Stanley Cavell's encounter with the prose of Poe in the chapter after next. Agamben's sense of the process, or condition, is perhaps clearest in an essay from *The End of the Poem* on the late nineteenth-century poet Giovanni Pascoli. At the climax of his discussion, Agamben cites (without closer comment) lines that he takes to fall between two drastic reductions of language, onomatopoeia and glossolalia: the one suspending the signifier in mimetic sound (his examples being represented animal noises), the other refusing signification wholesale from within the zone of foregone human semantics. In the former case, animal sounds are not grammatical, but they are nonetheless sonogrammic, because they can be written (69). So, too, in the case of an utterance without language—otherwise known as a "speaking in tongues" (plural, rather than *a* tongue).

In exemplification, three adjacent lines from Pascoli are quoted for their glossolalic stutter—yet not put under either bifocal lens or stethoscope. Certainly their effects are not distinguished one from the other by Agamben, simply adduced as an unmistakable playing between sense and sound. Yet it is further revealing to notice that their variant phonetic momentum is incremental, permutational or anagrammatic, and transegmental respectively (as marked in each case by my italics): "Fin . . . fin*chè* (in Pascoli's ellipsis at the move from a nonsense syllable to a noun); "*V'è di* voi chi *vide*" (with its somersault from *v-e-di* to *vide*); and then the cross-worded, cross-sworded chop of "Anch'io an*ch'io chio* chio chio" ("Pascoli and the Thought of Voice," 70), the last, in its reverse slide from sense to nonsense, given the highly Joycean translation "Me too me too eetoo eetoo eetoo." It is in this light that the essay's title, "Pascoli and the Thought of the Voice," may be said on its own terms to "desubjectivize" the concept of "thought" from within its own genitive grammar, whereby Voice does not precede and induce thought but is instead reduced to its vanishing object.

The English equivalent of that last cross-lexical echo of Pascoli's (a*ch'io chio*) is to be frequently noted in the next chapter, though in cases where the tonguing of alternatives does not topple over into stammer or babbling. And instances will appear under just that ongoing rubric from *Reading Voices* (with its self-exampling elision): the "trans[-s]egmental drift." It is in something of this same Pascolian spirit that Agamben himself ultimately finds only the "dead air" of lost voice in the "aura" of Petrarch's Laura ("l'aura" ["Pascoli," 74]). Apart from his own wordplay (or its uncertain ascription to Petrarch), however, there is little phonetic analysis, as we know from "L'infinito," in Agamben's actual reading tactics, despite the pervasive emphasis on sound and the "metrical-musical element." To put this another way, the counterplay between music and semantics that he finds in meter, epitomized by caesura and enjambment, and casting one back (in his explicit terms) to the "muse" of language itself, is not typically observed—even though with "l'aura" it is at least performed—exactly where it would have most to disclose about the very "medium" (his word) of being. This would include the lower limit of human expression in word formation itself—including its defaults, its refractions, its catastrophes, its recuperations, even those asemantic "musical ties" (100) that Agamben summons elsewhere in *The End of the Poem* as a unique feature of the linguistic soundscape (recalling again the examples from Pascoli).

But let us return once more to the "Go, poem" trope—go forth not to multiply but first, at least, to penetrate (via erotic if not phallic counterwound). That this particular reversal—in a pre-Petrarchan amatory revenge—can so readily constitute an allegory of language at large comes clear from another essay in *The End of the Poem* that sees love, desire, as the motor of speech, beginning in philosophical terms with Saint Augustine and activated in the twelfth century by the troubadour poets. In "The Dictation of Poetry," this amounts to a break with the mnemonic *topoi* of ancient rhetoric, those formulae of language available from the phrasal data bank, a departure arranged so as to access the very form of language as a place of habit, indwelling, an ethos. *Topoi* are overthrown by the urge for *topos*, for place, ontological emplacement (79), thus supplanting the mythologeme of a transcendental *logos*, the life-giving Word, with instead a worded "life-in-speech" (81): a life so entirely based in intent, in desire, in phrased lack, that its Renaissance anticipation of a Lacanian signifying chain is, though unpursued by Agamben, hard to miss.

In any case, even before its consideration in *The End of the Poem*, it is a comparable summary of the place of desire in language, also centered on the troubadour lyric, that, early in *Language and Death*, has immediately preceded and contextualized Agamben's reading of Leopardi's "L'infinito." What will later be spelled out as the "reciprocal desubjectification" of language and being emerges here in a summary chiasm that might have had Poe's aped speech from "The Murders in the Rue Morgue" in mind as much as the philosophers of metaphysical Voice, for "it is only in dying that the animal voice is, in the letter, destined to enter signifying language as pure intention to signify; and it is only in dying that articulated language can return to the indistinct womb of the voice from which it originated" (*Language and Death*, 71). Tomb of inscription, womb of voice: the inverse facets, one might add, of *potential*—now passive, now activated, at once the latency of and the will to speech. Such are the conditioning aspects of *homo loquens* that can sometimes seem at odds—where more possibilities, sonorous and signifying both, semiotic and semantic, are triggered than can be contained by script (as we will see again, beyond the next chapter, in Cavell's approach to Poe's storytelling—and then in the two subsequent chapters pursuing related events of *prose friction*).

In adapting Agamben for an approach to intensive reading, it is a question of both method and object. As much as we might wish to press harder, or probe deeper, into the counterforce of sound and sense in poetry than even his essays do when highlighting exactly this issue—carrying that definitive "schism" into the actual interstices of word formation—so also can we recruit his framework for that aspect of language he sidelines too soon, even from metrics, and certainly from the webwork of caesura and enjambment: namely, fictional prose. The cogency of a summary proposal like this from *Language and Death* doesn't at all depend on the parenthetical distinction—and exclusion—it inscribes: "The verse (*versus*, from *verto*, the act of *turning*, to return, as opposed to *prorsus*, to proceed directly, as in prose) signal for a reader that these words have always already come to be, that they will return, and that the instance of that word that takes place in a poem is, for this reason, ungraspable" (78). The verbal instance in prose, too, can exceed our grasp in the fluctuation of its preinscribed return. What arrives on the fictional page, what takes (its) place there, will in the very risks of reading—including its curious recursions and overlaps—be felt to have surfaced from a possibility enlarged by precisely the waverings of our own phonetic, lexical, and syntactic response, and this in the vernacular mastery of a Dickens as well as a Dante. For in prose fiction—when read for its prose as well as its fiction—the tension between meaning and phonic vehicle, between narrative action and its phrasing, constitutes just that deferral of event by (and to) its secondary vocalization that may, as much as in poetry, seem to tap unexpected depths in the medium that conveys it, reaching down to the very fund and fundament of its verbal possibility. And therefore available to a formative (even when not so obviously a formalist) inquiry. In sum, one can log these chapters' debt to Agamben in a double-entry bookkeeping in which his decisive emphasis on the "desubjectification" of the thereby iterable poetic text is palpably mediated, for literature more widely, through what one might want to call the presubjective formations of human language in its own germinal mutations.[30]

In what follows, then, the ongoing attempt is partly to bring Agamben's separate insights about linguistics and ontology, deferral and potential—there at an interface wholly subjectless—more closely together with each other as well as with prose, whose own time-based medium is rife with a poetics of contingency, latency, or (more to the point) sprung possibility. From the "languageness of literature" (the linguistic turn) to what one might rather call the "languagehood" of language itself brought out by literary wording (the ontological turn): that's the true spectrum (and sliding scale) of these considerations. In them, moreover, it isn't enough to assume that, under great enough literary pressure, language can no longer go unspoken in what it speaks. The pregiven *fact* of language may emerge most obviously, instead, in the very unsaying of what is said, a lapse from coherent phrasing back to its own unsettled potential across the dents or rendings of any sensible "intention," induced often enough by the undertones of secondary vocalization. To characterize the approach as a convergence of Ong and Agamben—as resolved in the kind of third term tested so far—we may say that primary orality, wholly decoupled from any metaphysics of Voice, returns secondarized by writing, and certainly desubjectified, though not always entirely within the programmed confines of inscription. This is a writing that may thus repotentiate more voicing, more phrasing, more medium—and hence more "thought of the voice"—than would seem at first to meet the decoding eye. Yet in reading, as we'll continue to observe, the deed is father to the thought.

3

ERRANDS OF THE EAR

Phonic not sonic. Latent in literary writing, not mystified by it. Secondary vocality: registering hinted aural undertones in poetry's descriptive overtones, the phonematic beneath the semantic—and certainly before the thematic, though often cycled back through it in response. That's how—once moving beyond the referential foreclosures of deixis—the last chapter took up as central English example the "composed lines" of *Tintern Abbey* and their enunciated syncopations. Even without anticipating in Stanley Cavell's work the skepticism that poetry and prose alike, that the fictive world in general, faces up to and stares down, we can say so far, with Agamben, that in literature, and in poetry most intensively, the world doesn't disappear for us in our words for it; rather, it is imaged back to us—as an index of human desire in language—by their iteration. And its return moves from page through passive throat to mind's eye as if reversing the sequence of authorship and original impress. The sounds playing upon attention in the relay route of such mediation are poetry's middle ground as enunciative structure. In this theater of operation, secondary vocality bodies forth silent script as the inner whisper of rhythm and pitch—often the pitching of one alphabetic cluster sideward into the next wording. Such is the listening room deeded to the ear in reading.

So Romanticism still concerns us in this third chapter, and again as example of a broader spectrum of effect. The groundless sustenance of language, inextricable in Agamben from the being of the human—and brought out in part (as evidence pending continues to suggest) by the phonology of silent speech in literature—is one place where an ethic of attention certainly opens upon a wider ethics of response. This can happen rather in the way that the analogizing power of metaphor in Percy Bysshe Shelley, when properly inculcated by poetry, stands as analogue for the foundations of all morality: in precisely the discerned likeness of one thing in its other, the onset of commonality from within difference, with this transcendence of entrenched opposition resulting (to give it an Agambenesque slant) from the potential of the otherwise in the same.[1] In the case of poetry, any ethic of attention begins with the sourceless breath of human speech instigated by the written page, however refigured that breath is by literary trope.

"O wild West Wind," writes Shelley in the mode of high Romantic incantation. But writing, scribed marking, is what the intonation remains—from the first tripled whoosh of strained onomatopoetic alliteration forward, as if channeling "thou breath of autumn's being." We will come back to the deep ontological ramifications of the so-called equative genitive (or genitive metaphor) in that line's second phrase: the breath of fresh air that *is* autumn, rather than merely the breath that issues from it, as one might say in common figure, "the very breath of life." Yet if autumn realizes itself in breath, it is far from clear that the speaker of "O" can do so in expelled voice, quite apart from its spelled-out discourse. For *homo loquens*, neither the fact nor the act of sounded speech, let alone its imitative rewiring as onomatopoeia, can give root to being, can get behind words to presence. Such language is there where being is not, naming things like *being* and *things* and the rest.

Before written apostrophe, before the sounded letter "o" (or "oh") is caught up in any further signature of the vocative, there is only the grapheme. Still it can be said: Romantic poetry begins with a sigh. For "German poetry," I've put Romantic there, but only to paraphrase the first sentence of Friedrich Kittler's *Discourse Networks* on the way round from German to English writing of the same century.[2] Kittler is pointing to Goethe, not to the preludic and breath-born(e) launch of Wordsworth's "Oh there is a blessing in this gentle breeze," where (in light of Agamben on Italian Romanticism) the deictic "this" serves almost to demonstrate the poem's own aspirant impetus. The reader of Wordsworth's *Prelude* may well hope the blessing is contagious, there and then in the forced-air burst of the so-far breezy enough "Oh." For his part, Kittler's best evidence, after the allusion to Goethe, comes immediately with Friedrich Schiller's two-line poem "Language." Its compressed point is that there can be no direct communion from spirit to spirit. A medium is required. "Once the soul *speaks*, then, oh!, it is no longer the *soul* that speaks" (quoted in Kittler, 3)—with the tantalizing fillip in the English translation that the "oh!" is already under negation as soul's speech from the disjunctural *n* of the adverbial conjunction, collapsing the logic of consequence into its own result: *then nOh*. Only words, not spirit, make for discourse. Even the primal uprush of Schiller's "Ach!" ("oh!") has begun the move from voice to language. "Oh" may record or at least interpret the expressive soul, but it is never the soul speaking, never the instance of a speaking soul. Only language suspires there. That's what the codified "O" of Romantic apostrophe serves to melodramatize. That's also why, in a high modernist formulation that has all of Romantic philology to draw on, the phenomenology of the Logos in Joyce's *Wake* is never more than a "phonemanon," anonymous, Babelized.[3] As we saw in Agamben's semiotics, animal breath is swallowed up (already expired) in the sign, sound in sense, any supposed incarnate spirit disappeared in its signaling to others like it.

Voice Is / Voice Says / Voices: A Countermetaphysical Spectrum

The undertones one "hears" in poetry or prose are not those of the speaking subject, let alone of the expressive soul, but language's own: imprinted phonemically by textual event according to the formative oscillations of wording itself. They are, to lift a Wordsworthian coinage from the 1805 version of *The Prelude*, a lurking "underpresence" (bk. 13, line 71) in the weft of phrase. Enough to say that we are concerned simply, at the lexical level, with the *nonabsent*—with collocations operating beyond or beneath the given, but entailed, entrained, by it. At transient rest in sheer potential, unselected by the inscriptive gestures of diction but not thereby canceled entirely, these effects are not to be written off or out, erased, by textual encounter just because they are left invisible. Even as relinquished formations, they retain the gesture of their lingual possibility. Call them cognitively imprinted without being written. As such, they may resound in silence upon the inner ear of reading. And they may do so in ways that plumb the renewable energies and bottomless options—rather than any stable ground—of speech.

Kittler is quick to spot the "Oh!" ("Ach") buried in Schiller's title "Spr-ach-e" (Kittler, 3). Yet what his analysis skips over entirely in Schiller's second line might best be glossed by that more recent theorist of vocality, Mladen Dolar, who pays neither Kittler nor poetry the least heed in *A Voice and Nothing More*—but who draws intermittently on Agamben's postdialectical language theory in ways that lead us to the threshold of the latter's revisionary philosophical impulse. Here is Schiller's turn, in the capping line of his famous distich: ". . . so spr*ich*t, *ach*! schon die Seele n*ich*t mehr" ("so speaks, oh!, no longer the soul"; emphasis added). Note the poet's elision of subjectivity when the skewed echo of the *ach* is picked out equally in the lost *Ich* of the first person and its own negation in *nicht*. In such fading in and out of differences, there can be no voiced identity, only its phonemes in dispersal.

So, too, in Shelley's *Ode* and its first- and second-person singulars en route to fusion in ". . . Be thou, sp*ir*it f*ier*ce, / My sp*ir*it (lines 62–63), where enjambment, coasting on assonance, helps distend the appositive into intersubjective identification. No sooner installed, the effect is rephrased by further phonetic transfusion: first in the bracketing internal echo between imperative verb and its internalization as an objectified subject in "B*e* thou m*e*"; and then in another appositive, turning this time on a four-syllabled punning epithet that reads out, potentially, as a conflationary rebus—"impetuous one" for the stormy impetus that turns "you" into "us" as "one." Kittler's larger point about nineteenth-century poetry would surface here as clearly as anywhere: that in place of the soul's speech, poetry tries incorporating nature itself as muse, the poet as an amanuensis transcribing what Wordsworth would call "the language of the sense" into communicable speech.

And doing so, we should add, by making its own language resist abiding rhetorical norms. As an important comparison along the sliding scale from stylistics through philology and metalinguistics to the philosophy of language in an ethics of natural validation, one notes here the revelatory investigations into the late eighteenth-century standardizations of English by Andrew Elfenbein.[4] In historicized rather than theoretical terms, Elfenbein argues for philology over "contemporary linguistics" (6) because the former traces the genealogical development of a given *langue*; in the process, philology "elevates writing over speech" while it "prefers the works of a particular language to the universalizing ambitions of linguistics" (6). A meeting of *philosophy* and linguistics, however, as attempted in these chapters, would at the same time bracket (without leveling) the distinction between writing and recitation in order to lift up for consideration not the acts of language, particular or general, scribed or spoken, in one tongue or another, but the establishing fact of it: the human capacity for, and capacitation by, linguistic articulation. Or put it that whereas philology concerns usage, language philosophy concerns use: the enunciative function of articulation itself, however cleansed of a necessitating subject—or in Agamben's terms "desubjectified." Yet if it didn't do so in ways that intersect directly with the kind of morphophonemic and metrical effects maximized by Romanticism and highlighted by Elfenbein, there would be no such chapter as this.

"The poetry of the Romantic period," writes Elfenbein, "marks the emergence of English literature fundamentally as literature in English" (107), with its own unique stance toward philological normalization. He goes on to nuance that epochal claim with an ear-opening sense that Romantic poets fought against the new regulatory regime of purified elocution with an insistence on the volatility of exposition in all its variant textual arrays, so that, among other results, meter and lineation made the reader potently unsure of pronunciation. But more unsure, or more capaciously ambiguous, even than Elfenbein's focus suggests—if in ways more historically embedded, thanks to his researches, than one might have realized. When adducing the prescriptive handbooks of recitation that rebunched wording so as to inscribe a passage's ideal oral cadences—as in an elocutionary redistribution like "Andshow youhave the virtue tobemov'd" from John Walker's 1785 *Rhetorical Grammar* (114)—Elfenbein's discussion doesn't go on to link this kind of graphemic prompt to the cross-lexical "sounding" of Romantic "sentencing" (to borrow back-to-back contrastive hallmarks in his chapter titles), where locution itself may plant its own secret cues to evocalization.

All told, though, nothing could be closer to the spirit of the current deliberations than Elfenbein's sense of "chiastic" interplay between the newly regimented "interfaces" of codified English, grammatical script and elocution: "Romantic poetry silences elocution and *gives voice* to exposition" (130; emphasis added). That last is precisely what I meant, over three decades ago, and with many a Romantic example, by the claim that (clause rather than phrase) "reading *voices*": the claim whose philosophical ramifications—as regraphed below—I have set about testing more fully this time out.[5] And such is an emphasis there as well in Kittler's reading of Goethe, according to which Faust's "dry reflection" on "holy symbols" pales by comparison with the notion that the text could actually "hear me," the reader, in a "virtual orality" (5). It is a very particular form of this fantasy, via subvocalization, that allows Romantic poetry to exceed its original philological context and broach, even breach, what, according to Kittler, "linguistic analysis was not allowed to approach" in the discourse network of 1800: "the forbidden borders of the word and the letter" (43), restricted instead as it was to the semantic lineage of etymology. Lexemes and their alphabetic increments were, Kittler means, beyond the ken of analytic breakdown; they were evolved entities, not present composites. What I mean in turn, and as a result, is that Romantic poetry could break the former open to the slippages and incursions of the latter, lexemes made vulnerable to their own constituents. As such, these truant gestures of lettering become the gradients of phonetic drift rather than ingredients of integral morphology.

Auralterity and the Phonic Imaginary

My extrapolation from Ong's "secondary orality" to the notion of a "secondary vocality" in silent reading is also meant to acknowledge the ambiguities incident to this enunciation as an *auralterity*—related as such to Agamben's "potential" in its linguistic valences. The terms (and implicit philosophical determinations) converge again here. In the Venn diagrams sketched by Dolar in *A Voice and Nothing More*, the effort is to map the overlap between organic sound production and human speech production, animal noise and articulate sign, with the language act suppressing the former in the emergence of the latter. Repeatedly the sector of intersection, for Dolar, between body and language, subject and Other, *phone* and *logos*, *zoe* and *bios*, is in the middle term voice.[6]

Yet, as often happens, Venn diagrams benefit from reconfiguration by the semiotic square. I've given one possible attempt (fig. 1), sprung from Schiller's dichotomy between speech and the spirit's constitutive silence, and overlapped here, vertically, with a variant of the attempt by Kittler to map the fundamental Lacanian triad onto nineteenth-century media innovation. It is according to this schema that, for Kittler, phonography records the Real of the voice, the typewriter inscribes the Symbolic order of discourse, and cinema projects the Imaginary of virtual presence.[7] Aligned to the right of these italicized categories, I have inserted into the zone of Kittler's filmic virtuality in that top tier of phenomenological immanence, instead, the mind's-eye screening (along with its linguistic "flicker effects") of literary reception. This is to be distinguished, below in the left column, from the

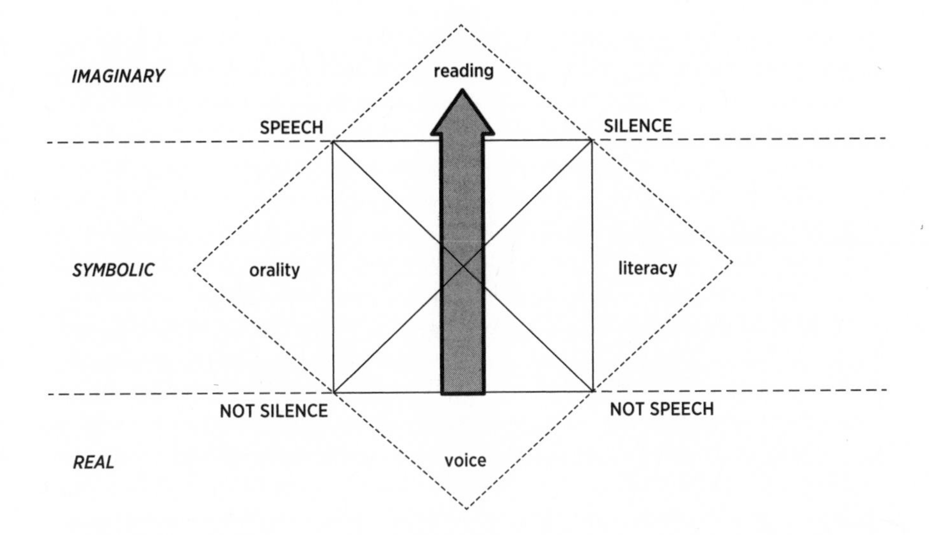

symbolic status of language, whether this is manifested (back in the semiotic square at the right) as oral or written, and further distinguished, in the third and lower facet of the left triad, from the only "real" of reading: its neural and muscular if only silent sounding, its phono-graphing in a zone opened between the negative contraries of nonspeech and nonsilence. So that at the bottom of the square, or say, at its material horizon, one finds generated rather than presumed the axiomatic stance of Agamben and Dolar toward the voice per se (categorically distinct from language) as a sound, a sonic wave, disappeared into the phonics, the phonetics, let alone the script, of its signifying force. Disappeared, but rising again, I would stress—hence the upward arrow—into the secondary vocality of script's activation as text. And bringing with it at times, into the discerned forms of expression, a retained sense of their formative impetus in linguistic articulation itself.

If voice is the neither/nor of orality and literacy, organic noise without enunciation, even as it locates the repressed basis of each, it finds its unexpected contrary—and its potentially phantasmal return—in the uppermost synthesis of the founding dichotomy. Here, in the "imaginary" of literary mediation, unfolds the rolling image track of the script-generated signified as a phenomenological manifestation. It is this shifting frame of imaginative projection across which, as maximized by Romanticism, voice oscillates—only from a blanketing silence—as the equivalent in the textual ecology (the arrow again) to a continuous return of the repressed: a return in the unreeling of a discrete phonemic scroll. And it is there, not continuously but intermittently, that accidents will happen, often on purpose.

One can insist on this imaginary field of text and its morphophonemic activation, but only if one goes cautiously. When reading engages coded alphabetic symbols and generates through them a poetic setting in the head, or a narrative scenario, the reader has not entered upon the imaginary via some magic auscultation, some occulted relation to a speaking authorial presence. But orality—vocality—lies latent nonetheless. The reading of arbitrary symbols passes over to mental image even while recirculating, through that imaging, the reverbs of a silent enunciation necessary in the first place to differentiate symbolic clusters into given word signals. (The relation of this to the resurgent intermittence of the frame line in certain films awaits analysis in relation to Cavell's philosophical approach, along with Agamben's, to each medium separately.) We may say, for now, that standard theoretical accounts clamp down on voice too soon. Lowercase it certainly is, that textual voice, but not voided or choked off. Silenced strains are still in play. Sometimes silence strains, in fact, against lexical constraints, loosing new words en route—or, at the very least, keeping the malleable linguistic medium still in mind beneath its foreordained choices in that peculiar "underpresence" (Wordsworth again) in which the snags of phonemic sequence cling and linger. Even wholesale aural anagrams can grab attention without meeting the eye in a manifest alphabetic shuffle.

There is no undue price to be paid in a lost theoretical savvy for noticing this sort of thing, this sorting of the things called syllables and lexemes: no sensible skeptic's credential to be surrendered. A salutary leveling of Voice in writing, rooted deep in the currents of postmetaphysical philosophy—or otherwise the deconstruction of the transcendental Word in all its various mystifications—can rightly disenchant the file of the signifier without going so far as to ignore the phonemic enchainment of alphabetic script. Meaning does not need to be thought coincident with its signifiers in order to be heard coasting on them. For such is the noncoincidence, Agamben might add, that is played out at large by poetry as the figured time-lapse of its own rereading, in an iterable duration far removed from the time of inscription. Again, then, it is only because the writer dies away from his words, like sound from their meaning, that those words themselves, rather than their author, are resuscitated by the private vocality of each subsequent reading. Or say, resuspirated—even if muted by the inhibited musculature of the silenced reading body.

The "imaginary" of literary language as "symbolic" system (from the diagram's left triad again) thus includes the world it conjures and, within it, a phonic resurgence of the speaking subject it generates (rather than derives from). When these effects seem correlated in the reader's subvocal production of the text, suspended or inward aurality may be rendered thematic as well as systemic. In any case, we may say, with Kittler as well as Agamben in mind, that this aura of the aural is virtualized: become not the residue but the checked (yet still active) impulse of speech, less vestige than present instigation, an active potential under local constraint. This energy of the phonotext is a possibility lying fallow in the law of the letter—which is to say, in the structure rather than the nature (the naturalness) of speech. In literary writing, this phonotext, this secondary vocality, is a liability in the positive sense, a risk in the form of a dispensation, the gift of contingency. I spoke above of repressed enunciation and its "potentially phantasmal return." I had better say instead its return as pure potential. In such irrepressible voicings, the generative void sings.

This is where deconstructive commentary, to say nothing of media theory, tends to turn a deaf ear. Yet the imaginary phonotext—pulling the symbolic field part of the way back toward the real, and thereby obtruding the fact of sound into the circulations of sema—eludes Dolar's post-Derridean model, with its arrest of all embodied vocality by an abstracting semiosis. Alphabetic—which is always to say phonemic—reading also falls outside the discourse network reduced to media technology in Kittler. Subtending even the local static of such a network and its inevitable interferences, isolated thereby in the imaginary sonics of phonemic silence (beyond any mechanics of impress), wording goes about its inscriptive work while continuing to reverberate in a toneless undertow not noted by manifest spelling. Accidents, yes, will happen. Accidence too. But language is tensed and ramified in more than the strictly grammatical sense of that latter category. Past and present inflections overlay each other in the rush of sequence, the singular suddenly pluralized. In all this, what lies fallow is self-allowed by the license of the letter under the rule of flaw.

At such moments we discover, but only by evincing it in ourselves, the productivity of text as subvocal performance. For if silent enunciation makes the exchangeable matter of writing a latent manner of speaking after all, virtualizing script as the sheer ongoing *possibility* (never the present fact) of transmitted utterance—*giving thought* to such utterance, as it were, rather than giving it voice—then a new conceptual horizon comes into view. In this regard, such a Romantic legacy of phonotextual encounter could serve to model and propagate, in its own right, an "indwelling" ethic beyond negativity—as advocated for in other terms, though also by linguistic association, in a writer like Agamben. We're about to gauge again the quite specific (if fitly elusive) idea of potentiality in his revisionary enterprise, and in so doing take some measure of the ethical implications of its paradoxical basis in the transgressed law of noncontradiction. But the point of the literary examples so far, as I'm hoping might be already clear, is a not unrelated one.

In terms of communicative chains forged in ink from subacoustical links, the negated subjectivity of language, however aesthetically mobilized, is the very source of a textual ethic: call it an impersonal intersubjectivity. This we are to see theorized at a different scale of effect, and for prose rather than poetry, in Cavell's engagement with Emerson's account of human ideas in printed transmission. Think of textual exchange in this sense as the mute sociality of reading, whose peculiar utility comes from having been drained of all voice, rendered impersonal, or say, in Emerson's sense transpersonal—where inscribed words awaiting their iterated recognition become the reader's own for the duration and the making. The resultant feedback loop of silent enunciation thus contributes to inducing an image of myself as Other: not a parasitic incorporation of the Other, but an offering up of my own linguistically productive body to a thus energized page, and through it to the reach of thoughts beyond me, thoughts both floated on and plumbed by my subvocal soundings of writing's visible cues. These marks, divorced wholly from orality as "event" (in Ong's narrow sense), are deeded nonetheless to the secondary vocality of the engaged page, which the preceding diagram of "voice" is meant, though excluding any metaphysical "beyond," to situate not just outside of—but, linguistically, before and beneath—the range of audible speech.

This is writing seen under the paradoxical aspect of its *present potential* as reread. For Agamben, as noted, the problem for ontology converges with that of linguistics most obviously around the limits of nomination. Ontology tries declaring and defining the fact of "being" when it can only name it arbitrarily, just as linguistics, in naming "language," never brings the precedent fact (or necessity) of it to light, just (at most) its systemic inner workings. In this context, Agamben cites Ludwig Wittgenstein on the way names fall out of normal discourse as a different kind of function from propositional statement. Quoting the *Tractatus*: "I can only name objects. . . . I can only speak *of* them. I cannot *assert them*" (emphasis added).[8] Onomastics is neither ontology nor a discourse about it. This is the conception that we may see Shelley, and the Romantic apostrophe at large, straining to outbid—even as the lyricist of the "O" turns its address back on the subject as a reified self-assertion. To wit, again: "Be thou me, impetuous one." Shelley, in not being satisfied simply to name the "West Wind," but in effect contriving an ode to it that will personify its energy as coextensive with the speaker's own, and hence permit the intersubjective gambit of the poet's inspirational equivalence with it, tries the impossible task of *asserting nature*. But neither existence, nor for that matter coexistence, can be proven, let alone manifested, in our names for them. That's where Agamben digs in his heels on the slippery footing of this uncertain ontological ground.

Phontology: The Slipstream of Enunciation

When the professional study of literature took "the linguistic turn," such are the vagaries of academic and institutional trends that it was Derridean deconstruction and Lacanian psychoanalysis, not linguistics, that became the interdisciplinary touchstones for poetics and narrative theory alike. One reason grows clear from Agamben's overview of the linguistic turn in philosophy, on the occasion of reviewing the work in language theory by Jean-Claude Milner.[9] For Agamben, philosophical thought had already taken up the crisis faced independently (or at least separately) by the science of language. Philosophy's millennial assignment to think thought itself—and so to define the grounds of being-in-the-world in a way that cannot, in fact, be hypostasized as inner metaphysical Voice—finds a definitive parallel in the paradoxical horizon, and limit, of language theory. Which is to say, the challenge not faced up to by linguistics proper: to speak of the fact of language without a metalanguage; to speak speech itself, the *factum loquendi* ("Philosophy and Linguistics," 73). Agamben borrows from Milner to show how linguistics doesn't really take language per se as its object of study, "but only as its axiom" (66). One may say that linguistics has no choice but to presuppose what it can only name (without asserting—or asseverating). In a similar way, as the science of being rather than speaking, ontological philosophy must take existence as given. It does not in this sense probe to first causes. What comes to the fore in this comparison, however, is not simply a close parallel between philosophy and linguistics, or even a deep homology. But something more as well.

"Philosophy and Linguistics" appears nearly a decade after Agamben has worked through the Heideggerian bond between language and death that had come to define as well the notion of *thanatopraxis* (or "deathwork") in Derrida's thought (unmentioned as such by Agamben) during these same years: where the absence proven by the presence of signification runs all reference into the grave even while carrying the enunciating subject back to the unspoken—but at the same time evacuating—conditions of speech itself. What leaves Agamben so powerfully unsatisfied with this might be captured in noting how the absence of the thing from its name is not the loss of that thing's potential for existence outside of language. And not just as a retroactive possibility—but instead, one might say, as a proactive f(act), a performative potential. Traditional thinking tends to obscure this. In science after Galileo, as Agamben reminds us, and under the Aristotelian principle of a merely "conditioned necessity" ("Philosophy and Linguistics," 75), things can be deemed true without being absolutely necessary or essential. Examples can't hurt—even if not Agamben's. The sun *couldn't* revolve around the earth, that's right; but an earth like ours *might* have revolved around another sun. I am not you, true; but I needn't have been exactly this me. At macro and micro levels, such is the contingency principle in scientific empiricism. In this sense (and here lies Agamben's resistance), "possibility" has traditionally been confined to the pluperfect tense, an ontological rearview mirror, attuned only to what could conceivably *have been*, not to what can be immediately conceived—as, for instance, conceived as still and now possible. His envisaged wrench to philosophy amounts, therefore, to angling contingency into the future through the present: recovering for the age-old category of "the potential" a status as immanent rather than merely prospective, let alone retroactive and overruled.

The linguistics of this, one might say, would be to cast the contingent not just into a grammar of the conjectural future or the conditional perfect but into a more active syntax of the the present, a present tensed with alternatives. Not just "things might have been other than they are." Or "might someday be." And certainly not just the weak epistemological sense that "things might be other than they seem." Instead, Agamben is after the strong sense of present possibility. He wants "to attest to the very *existence* of potentiality, the actuality of contingency" ("Philosophy and Linguistics," 76). So that when he asks climactically, and cryptically, in this essay whether one cannot philosophically say "what seems impossible to say, that is: that something *is* otherwise than it is" (76)—"otherwise" rather than "not," multiplied without being first denied—he has posed his problem in the sharpest interrogative terms. The contrary-to-fact is not unreal, just unactualized, what Deleuze in a similar sense would term "virtual." And if immanent contingency has a grammar—to match its ontology—of the conditional, what about a poetics?

Rhetoric reminds us that speech needn't mean what it says. A philosophy of pure potential leaves entirely behind any such halfway house. If only apparently (as we will find in the next chapter), we may seem here at a far remove from the thinking implied by Cavell's Austinian *Must We Mean What We Say?*[10] For Agamben, philosophy, to renew its power of thought, must be made to come into some radical and liberatory alignment with a theory of language whose rule of the negative (the nonpresence marked by sign) is so far overthrown that—as paradoxical as this would be meant to sound if Agamben had actually articulated the parallel between linguistics and philosophy in these terms—things conjured in language need not *mean what they mean.* So let it be clear that, despite Agamben's veering away from verbal detail (in "Philosophy and Linguistics") at just the point of linguistics' imputed convergence with philosophy, literary implications need not fall by the wayside. Indeed, almost a third of a century after the linguistic turn, interdisciplinary literary study might after all find new legs on this paradoxical footing broached by Agamben, new habitus on this strange untrammeled ground—once its heady paradoxes are, by a poetics of contingency, brought down to verbal earth and its morphophonemic turf.

For literature isn't simply the place where things never are, even as they may seem to be: the place of sheer fiction. In literature, rather than in a metalanguage about it, and in poetry preeminently, things, more immediately, do not entirely or exclusively say what they say. Once "vocality" is reimagined from the waver and give of textual inscription, it can always be at base equi-vocal, a case of present contingency—evincing, without vouching for, the existence of a potential otherness in one and the same wording. And if contingency is an axiom of nontranscendental ontology, what then, pushing harder on this postulate, is the being of contingency, its present-tense existence? And what, correlatively, is the *being of potentiality*, or in other words its immanence in the unachieved? If the contingent and the potential are ontological givens, how can they be felt to *exist* in the now of their apprehension? With such questions we come, then, upon the resonant, the logically discordant, the rapt and provoking, the frustratingly opaque and at the same time utopically ingratiating, note on which Agamben ends. The vaunting final question about things being other than they are is so rhetorical that the present chapter wants to imagine some part of its answer as lying with the phonemic underlay and ligatures of rhetoric's own subvocal figurations.

Again the hinted intersection with Deleuze's reconfigured sense of Bergsonian "becoming" and the virtualities that manifest it in progress. And where more pointedly than in literary writing to find a register, and resonance, for the sense that alternatives—including *auralteries*—can be copresent and animating rather than monitored solely by negation? Rephrasing Agamben: if possibility is to be found anywhere, it is always here in its deferred result. If it does indeed seem "possible, in other words, to call into question the principle of conditioned necessity" ("Philosophy and Linguistics," 76), wouldn't it be precisely the "other words" of linguistic indeterminacy in poetic phrasing (recurrent measure of the "otherwise") that might help acquaint us with the rhythm of all such suspended negativity, help us practice it, so to speak—by entertaining that othering-from-within that is often the very function of literary writing in subvocal speaking? Potentiality would in this sense be not proleptic, but, again, a present force in consciousness—and thus in reading. It is here that wordplay itself could be seen to do the work of philosophy.

Taken verbally as well as ontologically, then, and directed back into Romanticism, Agamben's stress on potentiality would thus help rethink Wordsworthian imminence ("something evermore about to be") as a kind of immanence in its own enunciative right. Alternate verses, like alternate universes, operate by "intimations." In the ode that goes by that shortened name, what is most to be blessed in recollection are "Blank misgivings"—like a kind of double negative, but not quite. Here instead is an uneasiness not canceled or effaced but merely held latent in the face of a sense(d) sublime: "Blank misgivings," as the line continues, "of a Creature / Moving about in worlds not realized" (lines 146–47). Complementing the overt philosophic cast of the last participle, for not yet "actualized" rather than merely not yet recognized, Wordsworth's verse, in and beyond the "Intimations Ode," and that of Keats and Shelley as well, are often levitated on *words* as well as worlds that seem churning in a line without being fully conjured into print, fleeting evocations neither quite seized upon—nor altogether brought to be in reading. But dormant and motivated nonetheless.

The Phonemics of If-Coming

For an exemplary wash of sound and its *phontology* in the poetics of Romanticism, we can return to our point of departure in the Shelleyan vocative of *Ode to the West Wind*. Nature moves, and moves the speaker: moves him to identify with it as the human vessel of its external impulsion. At the same time, temporality moves forward in a calendrical inevitability that gets cathected as promise. The wordplay to this effect is suitably effortless, inevitable. What goes without saying is here a saying that barely needs phonemic channeling around the windy enjambment: "O Win*d*, / *I*f winter comes, can spring be far behind?" (lines 69–70). What happens so easily in language of this reflexive grain, so naturally as it were, is the revelation of sheer potential—its felt existence, not just its axiomatic status—made present in the internal slant rhymes (*wind/wint*er) of the closing syllabic run. Rounding off the line, the straggling disyllable "behind"—with its outdistancing echo of "be"—takes up the rear from the preceding "Wind" as well, and this with its purely inoperable sight rhyme, useless, inactive, and mute. Yet, just before, the apostrophic naming of nature—the encounter with language's primal otherness—finds so relaxed a link between the autumn "Wind" and its hardening through "wind-y" into "wint-er" that change and transformation, beyond all etymology, seem to inhabit the lexical register itself (Kittler's transgressions into word and letter from the fortress of root). This move to project the harbinger function of autumnal wind into winter even at the subvocal level, so as to sweep through toward a vision of spring, is a case of poetic language saying what it doesn't say in soundless echo of its own present eventuality.

But hold the line open in its possibilities, open to itself, for a moment or two longer—by apprehending something more than its stationed metrical upbeat. It is not just that the iambic impulsion in "can spring *be far be*hind" telescopes the two-word adverb into its one-word adjunct, in the process turning the ultimate predicate of existence into a mere prefix ("be" into "behind"). It isn't, in short, just this folding over each other of the Kantian intuitions of space and time—collapsed into a strictly temporal dead metaphor of topographic lag—that is enforced upon attention by this phrasing. Time is put yet more severely out of joint. And precisely by being made to seem contingent in its very sequence. From out of that featherlight hint of "wind / i" at line's turn, as in the truncated epithet of something like "O wind / y season," breaks instead an interrogation not just loaded but disorienting. "If winter comes, can spring be far behind?": out of context, perhaps, a seemingly logical query, so logical as to circle round on itself as a so-called rhetorical question, answering only to its own indubitable premise. But in the present apostrophic and figurative setting—in a phrasing addressed to the essence of autumn, one season back—logic is eroded by a more anxious reach for visionary prognosis. In this sense, Shelley's phrasing harbors an extreme limit case of "conditioned necessity" that only an environmental crisis like global warming, for instance, helps make felt in post-Romantic retrospect. In the poem's historical moment, however, the speaker's is an address, an appeal, that can count on the natural cycle of the seasons, can readily steep its tropology of restoration in the assured circuit of their transitions.

Consider, then, the gist of Shelley's peroration in a far more sensible alternative: "O [wild autumn] Wind, / When winter comes, can spring be far behind?" We remember Elfenbein's researches again, and the tension between exposition and elocution negotiated by Romantic verse in the face of the new prescriptive philology. Offering some additional metrical strain, a heavier, more emphatic, perhaps more onomatopoetic alliteration headed by "when" rather than "if" ("Wind, / When . . . winter"—wn/wn/wn—in echo of the opening line's triplicate breathiness) would forfeit more than the wispy overtone of "windy" in the given line. More importantly, in its semantics rather than metrics, such a triadic insistence would also surrender the inherence of the contingent ("if") even in the inevitable, thus normalizing the whole gesture of the question. As stands, however, the line asks en route, if just for a hovering moment of verbally self-availed possibility: "O Wind, if winter comes, can spring be[?]" This could well give pause. In temporal rather than strictly logical terms, not only is it a vernacular impossibility—short of some apocalyptic sense of last days—to say "*if* winter comes" (even within some general figurative sense of "the winter of our discontent"); so, too, is it anomalous to ask, in any familiar (rather than rigorously philosophical) sense, whether—in the grip and midst of such a winter's coming—spring too can be: can subsist as pure potential, even before the icy season subsides. But so, for a moment, the poem—in a temporal passing of its own—has the odd sound of asking. Its closing interrogative hinge marks, in sum, the pivot of a spectral because lectoral reciprocity. With time itself lifted into the contingent, imminence and immanence lose their distinction. The future is as much now as anywhere, springing upon us—springing up in us—as we read.

Certainly Shelley's text, in its aspirations (in the full etymological sense) toward being the "trumpet of a prophecy," is about the ethic as well as the aesthetics of the virtual, about the hope of the regenerative, as breathed through poetic speech. Nearly two centuries later, Agamben's writing has increasingly come to offer one Continental rallying point, along with the work of Emmanuel Levinas and others, for the spate of Anglo-American scholarship in the ethics of literature. And beyond his influence on Dolar's thinking about voice, Agamben places a recurrent definitional stress on ethos as the "accustomed dwelling place," where *zoe*, as sheer animal existence, must be transformed, socialized, before entering upon the biosphere of communal subjectivity. And acknowledging the dangers of such communal identification, given the moral ravages that have resulted from the assertion of difference as negativity, it is indeed a compelling utopianism to imagine Others as not entirely what they are: that is, to imagine the *different* as an internal category of potential rather than just the plural of constitutive divergence. Or think of this, especially in its literary ambit, as the *otherwise* before it hardens into an *otherness*. The real lair of the potential lurks not so much in textual meaning as in the production of that meaning, always in process.

We recall from the previous chapter that, for Agamben, poetry isolates as (not at) its "end"—and so as its requisite new beginning each time through—the very "taking-place" of speech. The hermeneutic spiral becomes an ontological one. Every reading of a poem incurs the rereading of its own source in the possibility of speech. The absence from writing of both a text's author and its world *is* that possibility. Furthermore, as the condition of its reading later and elsewhere, the poem's disclosed being-in-language can thus at times probe to, without solving as mystery, the being of language, the *factum loquendi*. Poetry, or literature more broadly, operates this way when and because its lateral displacements, its reciprocal self-revisions from word to word, serve to compass the linguistic space within which they oscillate.

That's poetry under the description of philosophy. When poetry comes under the gaze of literary criticism as well (rather than instead), questions remain. How precisely, we ask, is the space of that taking-place registered in certain specific literary wordings when taken (on the run) one way or the other, or both—potentialized at will and perhaps at odds by different readers? Having taken place, language continues to take its own good time—and its unexpected turns. One effort of this book is to scan this emplacement of human speech in literature as a space not just in time, a verbal duration, but a demarcated lexigraphic and phonemetric terrain: a contoured field of meaning rather than just a signal stream. In this sense, the *formative* place of literary speech includes the pockets of the half-said it carves out as well as the avenues it opens, the crevices as well as grooves of its channeled mediation. More lateral than unidirectional, language's taking-place delimits a shifting site where, among its other manifestations, potential may be harbored inert in the blanks of inscription until "sprung" (Gerard Manley Hopkins's word, but taken more broadly than in a metrical sense) from writing into read sense.

Long Romanticism: A Rapid Sounding

Attention is tuned in all nineteenth-century writing, but first and most obviously—before the domestic reading aloud of the novel as reigning genre—to what Elfenbein terms the philological "interface" between "exposition and elocution": in our terms, between inscription and its secondary vocality. (How, say, in Wordsworth's "Intimation's Ode" can one read of life's aquatric matrix, as the "children sport upon the shore" of a figured immortality, without iamb and elocution troubling each other with the amniotic symbolism—and transegmental backwash across the drift from verb to noun—of "children's port?") Such tension in reading is what brings tacit linguistic notice, and potential philosophic inference (as regards linguistic potential in itself), to the otherwise suppressed function (and friction) of speech formation. In Kittler's terms, and from this same moment of historical philology examined by Elfenbein, this is the suppressed analysis associated with the "forbidden" inner limits of letters and lexemes. But poetry accepts no such interdiction in response to its diction, nor to the spacings between. In this sense it invites the isolated fraying of its own interface between script and evocalization.

At the point of transition between high Romanticism and its Victorian inheritance, for instance, Letitia Landon offers one of those many cases where the combined poetics of caesura and enjambment (in Agamben's definition of poetry's difference from prose) finds its linked effect circumscribed within the cut and paste, the nip and tuck, between one word and its lexically enjambed successor. For Landon has Sappho describing a poetic song in which "each wild / High thought I nourished raised a pyre / For love to light."[11] The line that begins in enjambment with the assonant shove of "High" (and its virtual equivalence with the "I" of its aspirant in the mental sense) ends momentarily on the ear, before being grammatically rerouted, with the assonant "up higher" as well as "a pyre." Thus has one thing said something other than itself, in this case eliciting the verticality of transcendence from immolation. By such means can words renegotiate—and hence reinvest—their own bounding gaps in a new fusional twist of diction, with the collision of two terms detonating (by invisibly denoting) a third, however fleeting and unfixed by grammar in this case. One name for the full phrasal ambiguity these effects can produce is the "oronym."[12] Yet the blurring that is entirely phonemic here, and will be again in Hopkins, is often grammatical rather than just lexical—coming implicitly under Agamben's lens (in the case of syllepsis) through his linked emphasis on caesura and enjambment at a syntactic (rather than lexical) scale.

But even held to the substrate of word formation, instances can educe a whole principle of slippage. Take an unusually clotted example of Victorian verse in praise of its Romantic inheritance: the fretted nest of consonants and vowels in Matthew Arnold's homage to Wordsworth. If his 1850 *Memorial Verses*, including his elegiac lines on Wordsworth's immortal "voice," had set out to rehearse exactly the elocutionary challenge posed by Romantic meter and enunciation, his own transegmental switchback could scarcely be more thematic. The words seem catching in the very throat of literary-historical lament. For nudging the line turn of an apostrophe to the ghostly dead (whom the former laureate has joined)—"Ah, may ye feel his voice as *we*! / *He too* . . ." (lines 41–42)—is a subliminal enjambment that seems to inscribe, and twice over, its own phonemic (as well the denoted spiritual) continuance. The assonant new line continues in the pluperfect rather than the subjunctive: "He too upon a wintry clime / Had fallen" (lines 42–43)—continues in that eulogistic vein, that is, even while revising the preceding optative with a double overtone (and fitting Wordsworthian "underpresence"): both "feel his voice as we(!) / (h)e t" ("as sweet") and "feel his voice as we(!) / (he) too" ("as we do"). How better to render a voice actually felt rather than simply heard (in book-bound silence) than to render syllabification, even in the solemn precincts of elegy, as palpable as in a comic tongue twister? At the other end of the spectrum from such gnarled aural congestion, also in the elegiac mode, is the smoothly loosed effect mounted by Tennysonian phonemics in evoking the "silent-speaking words" of text—in this case the letters of the dead (*In Memoriam*, st. 95). Tennyson's suggestion is that "letters" alone—in the other sense—give virtual voice to silence rather than merely speaking from it. They do so by lexical wrinkles like the paradoxical "silen*ce-s*peaking" itself of this same junctural ligature.[13] And they are, of course, never more "desubjectified" (in Agamben's sense) that when their medium is explicitly postmortem.

Among the many Victorian debts to Romantic sonority and its contrapuntal elocution is the fact that the lexical unit can't be hived off from the syntactic, nor the alphabetic from the syllabic for that matter. Among recurrent examples at grammatical rather than phonemic scale: the cognate object of diction in repetition (identical verb and object) and the logical dilation of hendiadys, with its compounding of nouns where subordinate modification would seem in order. So it is that the syllabic fission of those examples from Landon to Arnold has its equivalent at the level of syntactic displacements. In his early *Pauline*, for instance, Browning's diction, across a rush of subterranean phonetic recursion, is slotted into hendiadys—in the Shakespearean (noun) and (noun) of (noun) format—in "The fever and the stir of after years" (line 140)—rather than the feverish stir. The first stir of note, of course, is the inmixing of phonetic with grammatical recurrence.[14]

The associative slide of hendiadys, its smoothing out of difference in a skid of illogical grammar, contrasts in turn with the exaggerated dichotomies (and hence the frequent comedy) of syllepsis, a figure that more forcefully installs verbal "potential" as both immanent and momentarily counterindicated. Chapter 5 is to offer a fuller treatment of this syntactic trope in prose. But verse examples help anticipate its true poetics. When Elizabeth Barrett Browning's heroine in *Aurora Leigh* "Gave ear to her vicar, tea to her visitors" (a version of Pope's "sometimes counsel take, and sometimes tea"), it is a phrasing in which the choice of split predicate skews an idiom like "lend an ear" into a syncopated alliteration across the bracketing syllabification from "ve-ear to "vi-ar" as well as spreading out to the expanded "vi-or" of "visitors" (bk. 1, line 493). But then, too, the *vea/vi* pattern has been hatched in the first place from the cross-word latch of "Ga*lve ea*r" before the subsequent phonetic diffusion seems to subordinate the trisyllabic "visitors" to the "vicar" as first among equals, whose audial influx serves to reverse the outflow of routine hospitality along the same axis of self and other. Syllepsis appears in its more idiomatic form in this same poem with the monosyllabic simplicity of Aurora's remark to Romney: "You have read / My soul, if not my book" (bk. 2, lines 245–46). This double taxing of the single-word predicate takes, in context, a more emotionally vexed form in Romney's own commitment to "vow away my years, my means, my aims" (line 320) in ministering to the needy—where a pledge to do something gives way to the negative or sacrificial word choice of "vow" when completed by its immediate phonetic hook in the open-voweled "away." The surrender of years, financial means, and other purposes each to the same cause, if in different senses of the verb, is fused in the supposed vector of dedication *toward*. Diction all by itself marks, in short, the strain of this holier-than-thou commitment.

And worse: the pathological derangement of an archvillain in the work of the other Browning, where the slide between phrasal senses operates (as so often) in association with a differently scaled syllabic slide on the eve of his execution. There is the unusual forked moment (syllepsis again) as Browning's Guido, in *The Ring and the Book*, nears the guillotine as if it were a case of *nomen est omen* by phonetic anagram. In his own designated "trope" of a battle to the death, Guido imagines—and with a self-inflicted pummeling of monosyllabic diction at that—"The last bad blow that strikes fire in at eye / And on to brain, and so out, life and all" (bk 11, lines 2312–13). The unmarked diction of *in*, *at*, and *on* operates first as an aggressive burst of prepositions, whereas a phrasal verb kicks in retroactively when "strike out" must be reconfigured as an idiom for "expunge." And if the panicking approach of death contorts a doomed man's language in this fashion, in a more sardonic vein the officiating pope, anticipating the execution, turns a verbal irony of his own against the criminal. He does this by speaking of the beheading as designed (in avoidance of the more normal "reward") to "Carry the criminal to his crime's award," a mock-euphemistic diction edged with the cross-word overlay (and enunciated overtone) of "sword" and its associated descending blade (bk. 1, line 1326). More impacted and dramatic in this regard is the phonemic collapse when Guido boasts of hell fire purging him to his essence: " 'You soon shall see the use of fire" ' (bk. 11, line 2397). All we see instead, in lieu of "some nucleus that's myself," is, just before death, the "ire" and bile that is distilled on the brink of the guillotine from the sliced-up diction in "of f/ire." As if a scapegoat in his festering rage to the genre of the dramatic monologue as a whole, Guido is heard offering himself up there, unwittingly and despite his supposedly constellated ego, to the dispersed subjectivity of language in action, a subjectivity as unfixed as the syllables of self-aggrandizement he spews. Like Poe's narrator in the next chapter, he is a monologist lost to the slippery inscriptions of his own self-indictment, where elocution wars with and almost strangles exposition at this internecine and extreme "interface." His medium is that of a diction denucleated in its own right. The only use ire has in this poem, all but posthumously revealed, is to be, like fire, self-consuming. In sum, then, between his sylleptic anticipation of the death moment and its phonemically mediated ontology: the two scalar poles of this study.

At the latter pole, a yet more demanding example, from Hopkins's "My own heart let me more have pity on," which laments: "I cast for comfort I can no more get"—as if it might mean no longer find; but only until the belated analogic "than" sets in by enjambment: ". . . no more get / By groping round my comfortless, than blind / Eyes in their dark can day. . . ." This would make better sense, perhaps, if it read "groping round me comfortless." In the manuscript, as noted by Hopkins's 1918 editor Robert Bridges, "comfortless" in fact anticipates "dark" as modifier of the postponed substantive "world."[15] But with that belated noun excised, the latter adjective seems instead nominalized and the former suspended in a suitably aimless blur—achieving only grammatical satisfaction if retrofitted (a point not entertained by the commentary) in sprung rhythm with "dark" as its adjectival substantive: "my comfortless dark [analogous to] . . . their different one."

The only present (rather than edited-out) alternative would be for "comfortless" to take as antecedent the word "mind" released by tripled overkill in the preceding two lines, lines whose ameliorative plea, obsessively phrased, is to "not live this tormented mind / With this tormented mind tormenting yet." We encounter there in that impacted mindful-ness a case—beyond cognate patterns, and in keeping with a diction undulating beyond any one determinate grammar—of an iteration so invariant that it begins to forge a false etymological bond between the participial diction of tor/mented and ment/ality itself. And then, too, beyond the elisions and subdivisions of diction's metered sequence, there is again the bridged interstice between word choices. By way of slipped diction and across what phonology terms the "dental" ambiguity of a cross-lexical bond, the ellipsis—on one hearing, and hence reckoning, of the analogic clause—makes a sudden continuous sense. It does so when the wording is downshifted phonetically from clause (no more can find day than I can) to phrase (than in the blindness of their day) across a double and dovetailing liaison, with comfort no more to be had by the speaker than by "blind eyes in their darkened day" (an aural seaming of "dark can day"). As the gap of ellipsis is thus sutured over by phonemic cross-stitch, the oddness is both normalized and redistributed in the continuous groping of diction for its impossible therapeutic fitness. In the process, certain choices lie open—and closed again—in the waver and wager of reading.

Irregular Hearings

And similar choices may, in the long Romanticism tapped here, be more openly punning—and relaxing—than those of Hopkins. Well before the author of that prose we know as "Joycean" was diagnosed with glaucoma, and fell back on a hypertrophic hearing of his own word sounds, a predecessor literary eccentric—playing fast and loose in her own way with lexicon and syntax—is sometimes retrospectively supposed to have been suffering from ear trouble, in particular (as if echoically named) from Ménière's disease, including the complications of tinnitus, with its occluding ring or buzzing. Indeed, one of Emily Dickinson's most earful lyrics seems able in this respect to foreground its own sardonic version of those Keatsian "ditties" that are "more end*ear*ed"—more fully and punningly internalized—for remaining "unheard." What the quintessentially Romantic pipers on that Grecian urn do for Keats, topping even the music of the nightingale elsewhere, is what, outside her window, the wordless whistle of a nighttime pedestrian is able to do for Emily Dickinson: a mere "ditty of the street" offering "An anodyne so sweet."[16] As the poetry follows suit in doing with its own auricular wit, such tunefulness offers a momentary balm to her "irritated ear." For in that neo-Keatsian sound pun (pained by ear-itants rather than end-ear-ments) lies a happy perturbation of the senses that poetry alone can rescue from unheard orthography and render pertinent.

Hopkins is harder, but only because the lexical constraints are even less hard and fast. Descendant as his most counterintuitive effects can seem from the foundational tension in Romanticism between expository syntax and its offbeat soundings, Hopkins offers in this regard a radical epitome of the period's rhetorical mood, committed to seeking out the "inscape" and "instress" of the single word (his famously elusive phrases for poetic in-formation) even before scanning the wider landscape of its assigned linkages. Condensations like "dark/can/day" (for "darkened day") become the wordspace (word space or words' pace) whose timed defects can be recaptured by countersense: the potential of their own unwrittenness, collateral, slant, expansive. Hopkins pushes to a limit what is elsewhere a quieter habit. The arcs of consonance and assonance, the jamming of cognate grammar, the slackened syntactic ligatures of hendiadys and syllepsis: these in literary writing, whether loosened or yanked taut, are among the ties that bind or the threads read and unraveled, in either case liable to the fray of meaning essayed as said from the delved reserves of language's own possibility in the unspoken. They are the realized verbal space not only of speech's primal taking-place but of language's deep and variable taking. Taking in either sense: its catching hold in a given phrase; its grasped sense in reception. So the principle emerges once again from the instance. The deed of reading is the taking, one way or another, of what has taken for you in a given wording—or been caught up in fertile uncertainty.

So why shouldn't the byplay and counterplay of literary writing help us to conceive ethos as the experienced space of cognitive duration, an always shifting habitus of articulation within temporality? It should. Located there would be the "accustomed dwelling" of the communicative word under continuous renewal—both rehabilitation and perpetual rehabitation. In this sense, up from the indwelling would well a difference inherent to it, not quelling representation but expanding it. One readily accepts as given that the dethroning of Logocentrism is the beginning of a secular ethics in the social sphere, empirical, contingent, where alternatives might become immanent, purposeful, and reciprocally conversant. But in exploring more particularly an ethic of literary reading, why isn't there an equally potent (because always potential) way to return from ethos to logos? There is. And this by passing beyond the toggle of the dualistic to the freer oscillation of the virtual in the realm of *homo loquens*, where, for instance, ambiguity resolves itself not so much dialectically as in the relentless becoming of flux itself.

This book's interdisciplinary venture in the philosophy of linguistic oscillation proceeds from a common-enough assumption. Where desire speaks, there is only the place of lack. That we've learned from both psychoanalysis and deconstruction. And nothing can take up this slack. Whence desire speaks, there is no saying. The origin of voice cannot be named by speech. This is why, and where, literature—again, not as a metalanguage but in the motions of its undertext—makes it possible to voice, however indirectly, that placeless source, and the virtualities of its constitutive otherness, precisely in such a way that each verbal incident comes to us shadowed by the present tinge of the contingent. Some terms for this have been extrapolated so far from one thrust of Agamben's writing—in connection with Aristotelian logic if not explicitly in reference to poetics. It is in the spirit of such conditional voicing that an effusive "Ode to the West Wind" is otherwise, yet at the same time, an "Oh to the West Wind." Voice is no sooner subsumed to the formal genres of print literature than it resurfaces there in manifestations immanent even if "not yet realized." In the overlapping schemata of that semiotic square again, a desubjectified voice (solely in the form of secondary vocality) returns from the double negation of both speech and silence into the imaginary of the virtual, potentiated there by the act of reading. An immersion of this sort in the deep ethos of literature, in its placeless disposition of all such latent and formative effects, refuses the complacencies of the inscribed. Its vigilance remains more nervous. It remembers the "silent/ce-speaking" of Tennysonian writ. This why the rolling terrain of text cannot be entirely policed by script into leaving lost tones unturned.

Sounding Off?

Varying Kittler's title, we are concerned with "Secondary Vocal Networks 1800/1900." With some of the intervening century's exemplary verse on call, we can profitably stand—and look—back. And continue listening. To my mind, or mind's ear, what Agamben helps us rethink in Kittler is the latter's relation to Hegel on the implications of silent reading. (And I have in mind the Agamben not just of textual ends ["the thought of the voice"] but of ontological presuppositions [**se*]). What Kittler gives us explicitly from Hegel is the idea of an "inwardness" facilitated only by silent alphabetic decipherment, so that (quoting Hegel as he does) the "detour through audibility" is rendered unnecessary by a "hieroglyphic" directness that does "not require a conscious mediation" (65) from the phonetic to the conceptual. The labor of voice is no more required in the rapid internal transfer from script to meaning than if the words were pure pictograms. Yet Kittler's sense of the 1800 discourse network depends far more directly on subvocal mediation than this would imply, both between script and decipherment and, in turn, between nature and subjectivized culture. One premise, though, is clear for both Hegel and Kittler: the role of silent reading as the internalization of literate consciousness (which is to say, its constitution as internal). This is a point made otherwise by Ong (without recourse to Hegel) about literacy in general, and especially the coming of print, in his account of the Romantic consolidation of writing as a prosthesis of memory and intertextuality at precisely the moment in which the novel arises as a bio-graphic armature of human consciousness stretched over recordable time.[17]

Kittler lends this sociocultural lineage a tacit psychoanalytic (as well as further somatic) slant. On his account, modern self-consciousness is born not so much from the mother, in biological descent, as from the internalization of the "Mother's Mouth" (his term for an organicist Romantic paradigm) in its tutoring vocal register. This is the domestic model inculcated by the widespread influence of "phonetic pedagogy" in the discourse network of 1800, a gendering of the linguistic matrix that I've elsewhere considered, for the literary phonotext, in respect to the "maternal *chora*" in Julia Kristeva's claims for a primal semiotic force underlying the symbolic.[18] In this regard, consider also Wittgenstein's allusion to William James on identity as a thought experiment in subvocal utterance, where the "self" exists only somewhere between "brain" and "throat": more a gambit of the silent thorax than an axiom of consciousness, still less a categorical a priori. Identity is, on this proposal, a site of contemplation fostered entirely by the inner saying, rather than demonstrable voicing, of "self" (the mere word) in the full elusiveness of its evocation—or, as Agamben might add by way of unpacking the term's very nominalization, by the act of saying the word (whatever this now means) "to oneself."[19] In any case, whether dredged from the semiotic *chora* or fledged somewhere between mind and body by subvocal reification as a groundless signifier, this self-consciousness is preceded, for Kittler, by an internalization of nature (or say, of naturalness itself) via the tutelage of maternal orality. It is this learning to interpret babble as alphabet that is the first training ground, in Kittler's dim view of civic culture, for a full hermeneutic insertion into the socius as discourse network. The result for the history of literature is that Man, posited between outer and inner, between nature and the automaticities of decryption, erects in the space between—not just between world and psyche, but in particular between the archive of texts and the inward cast of the silent reading voice—the newly humanizing (socializing) work of hermeneutics, or, from the Latin, the breathing room, the betweenness, of inter-pretation (whose root remains aptly obscure in its origins).

Everything in a media theory of literary language depends, of course, on some such "inter" (apart from innerness)—and its assumed traverse. What Kittler certainly doesn't want from Hegel is the total exclusion of phonetic pedagogy, in its later traces, from literary production and effect. For the mother remains the unspoken muse, though never really speaking for herself. In Hegel, by contrast, literary art requires in its full purity (and demonstrates) the entire *overcoming* of once-learned sound forms, a submergence seen as not just intrinsic to silent comprehension but crucial for poetic apprehension—which is to say, for the spiritualized vision—to which other arts can only partially aspire. Though spelled out in Hegel's lectures on aesthetics, the claim is very much in line with his "phenomenology." Consciousness achieves in reading an image beyond the visualization of speakable letters, whose very sounds such reading must supposedly have repressed as well. Poetry, for Hegel, is thus the purest of and least materially burdened of representational arts precisely because in it, one might say, the medium disappears more fully than it does in painting or theater (where pigment and bodies keep their work more tangibly in front of us). Wittgenstein's minimal definition of textual processing from our opening epigraph—"reading the sounds off from the letters"—is therefore upended, on this view, by poetic understanding, where sounds are drowned out along with letters, submerged from conscious production by emergent mental image. So it is that poetic understanding for Hegel arises in the moment when "the audible, like the visible has sunk into being a mere indication of spirit . . . not tied down for its realization to external sensuous material."[20] But what Hegel's own stress elsewhere on a more active "internalization" seems to have forgotten or sidestepped is the way, in fact dialectically, that the "external" and therefore extraneous "sensuous" force of speech must itself be rendered internal (subvocal, a somatic impulse under arrest, muted but not excluded) in order to process its disembodied "indications" in whatever poetic spirit. These formative sound shapes are not risen above, but ridden on, kept intimate. They keep open, in Elfenbein's terms again, the "interfaces" between inscription (as exposition) and its never fixed enunciation.

Regarding Kittler's distance from Hegel on this sensuous force of articulation, media scholar Geoffrey Winthrop-Young summarizes an untranslated 1979 analysis by Kittler of Goethe's lullaby, *The Wanderer's Nightsong*, in a way that brings unusual clarity to the link in Kittler's thinking—later consolidated in *Discourse Networks*—between phonetic pedagogy, maternal lullaby, and a Romantic poetry premised thereafter not just on the urge for verbal interpretability but on the latency of cryptic (nonhuman) signals in the very medium of nature, equivalent to a falling back of utterance upon its own medial conditions.[21] The latter are traced by Kittler to the early moment when a child hearing phonetic sounds not yet attached to meanings develops an itch to master—by interpreting—whatever lies beyond its immediate consciousness. In the famous Goethe lyric singled out, such an auditor is sent to sleep in second person by the speaker's invoking the calm of nature outside, as if there were a proleptic meaning in its hushed stillness. But this is only to replay that tentative search for meaning in the early receipt of all address, all sounded speech. Even before the active regimen of phonetic pedagogy, all Romantic poetry, so Kittler has it, takes its source in just such a maternal lullaby as is here executed by association. In this way Goethe's poem, according to Winthrop-Young's sense of its importance for Kittler, "both describes and brings about a hermeneutic infection precisely because it restages that which made us susceptible to this type of infection in the first place"—a Mother's Mouth "speaking into those who do not have language" (81) and thus stoking a need to know. Concludes Kittler's own hermeneutic exegete: "In other words, the *Wanderers Nachtlied*, like all successful poetry, is a form of brain damage" (81).

And yet Kittler's approach fails to note in all this the full return of Hegel's repressed. Listen, for instance, and in its own German, to the slant rhyme between early and late lines in the short Goethe poem. If the psychic "damage" of maternal pedagogy brought out in Winthrop-Young's tracking of Kittler's account—the child's induced and almost paranoid sense of a potential meaning in all sounds, derived from an incipient brainwashing by the flow of phonetic before syntactic utterance on one's mother's knee—makes the grown poet alert to inference not just in language but in the audible workings of the natural world, it also, one would want to add, releases his crafted language to sounds of its own that tease the addressed ear with intuitions below the radar of immediate intelligibility yet well above the threshold of interpretive lure. Goethe's "Ist ruh" ("is calm": but via a nominative, "calmness"), describing at the start a peace above the mountaintops, is a stillness echoed in descent through treetops and unsinging birds—even silence speaks to the hermeneutically alert spirit!—until answered half a dozen lines later by a chiastic reversal bracketed by assonance in the "Ruh/est du" of eventual lulled rest ("balde / Ruhest du auch": soon you will rest too). Yet it is there, beyond inverted symmetry, that the second person of the "du" (the auditing consciousness per se) is in part lexically absorbed at its dentalized border into a peace (*Ruhestd/u*) that doesn't so much pass understanding as find itself premised, in the preceding lines, on interpretation and analogy—as if "you-will-rest" is one continuous predicated fulfillment in a single conflationary neologism. It isn't just that Mother Nature speaks mysteriously yet directly to us in this case, like once our mother did, but that a play of sound beyond strict sense still reverberates through the system of lyric speech itself, tantalizing the ear even in putting it to rest. At the very least, this is a concomitant vocal legacy of inscription where the "implosion" (Kittler's term) is not only of decipherment upon its own medium but at the same time—while no less formative a medial disclosure—of word borders caving upon each other in the stream of a mother-tongued secondary vocalization. If, more in the vein of communications theory, one wished to call any such speech effect, such sound defect, a case of "noise" in the scriptive system (i.e., in the page-body interface), that would only be to make the same point against Hegel's sense of literary dematerialization.

Certainly actual poetry is that form of writing, and Romantic poetry not least, in which no full submergence or repression ("sunk into being a mere indication") actually succeeds, where in fact the e-locutionary is retained athwart the stream of descriptive realizations. Hegel's radical idealism there (in that passage not cited in *Discourse Networks*) is thus in a sense the instructive counterpart of Kittler's phonetic naturalization. With the exception of his rare mention of "virtual orality" (5) in that Goethean episode (anticipating Steven Connor's later preference for "virtual" rather than "sub" to describe the text's "auditorium")—where the Faustian text seems listening for the reader's answer to its call, as discussed above—Kittler is too quick to dial out those later sound forms of writing on which speech recognition once depended at the dawn of childhood literacy. It is, in consequence, one charge of the present book to entertain a possible way beyond the dated regimen of hermeneutic reading so tightly enshrined, for Kittler, by the premises of language acquisition at Goethe's historical moment, so quickly subsumed as they were to cultural norming. In this sense the inculcation of oral comprehension at the mother's knee would be more than an always outgrown model for a matured interpretive vigor and civic productivity. Instead, these sounds on the cusp of the intelligible would, in poetry, come to us in a state of continuous potential return from a never wholesale repression.

To put it succinctly, and from the perspective of a formative poetics not of language acquisition but of a verbally inquisitive reading, there is a twofold process at work about which Kittler's emphasis is deliberately one-sided, focused as it is on exposing the bureaucratic mechanisms of acculturation. Sounds once outside comprehension are taken in through the childhood regimen of "alphabetization" (his recurrent term) in a way rendered programmatic by institutional culture so as to nurture ever after an interpretive regime in and beyond textual exchange. One function of this, supplemental to the clerical establishment but shoring it up as a kind of metaphysical bonus, is that even the inanimate world can seem calling mysteriously to the attuned poetic sensibility, where the sensate is then converted by writing to discursive sense. So far Kittler. But on the receiving end of this poetic transliteration of sound into semiosis, taken up across the return from alphabetization to enunciation in the silent reading of poetry, certain sound forms (of the sort audited in the poems cited above) escape the net of inscribed meaning and its discursive controls. When these phonic rather than sonic effects are brought to mind's ear, the feedback loop induced may—but not necessarily, and outside of institutional protocols—foster its own secondary hermeneutic instincts in resonance with the sensed drift of sound play. On this understanding, the subvocal reading of literature ("beneath" the level of audible recitation, while seeming at times to emerge from between the cracks of inscription) can be both actively sub-versive and more—shadowing the fashioned, in prose as well as poetry, with a sense of the formative.

What either an inevitable failure or a tactical refusal to sink sound in sense, as Hegel would have it, to lose the sensual in the representational, serves to generate in the broader phonic spectrum of Romantic writing, then, including the Victorian prose descending from it, is a different level of abstraction than that advertised by the Hegelian transparencies of spirit. We are returned instead from the matter and grain of silent enunciation to an immaterial idea after all, but in this case the idea of language itself in operation, even in gestation. This is where marks, once read off as sounds, which is to say (after Wittgenstein), sounded off from letters, are propelled across shaped words—and where, gathered up in this momentum, grammar takes its further defining part. And (hence the next two chapters) sometimes parts its own ways.

But, in the meantime, it can never hurt to station Dickens at the threshold of Romantic writing's effect on the "auditorium" of Victorian and later prose, especially in regard to the play of phonetic language and its own legacy from Cockney punning, often adapted by Dickens to more straight-faced (if still twofold) contexts. In an echoically as well as ethically impacted moment at the climax of *A Christmas Carol* (1843), for instance—a phonic episode that connects directly (and almost explicitly) with our considerations of secondary vocality in the previous chapter—we are led to see Scrooge as doing no less, if also something imponderably more (according to the plot's supernatural machinery), than *reading* his own life from the unspoken text of a predictive future. Confronted with the dead and sheeted body that will be revealed to him as that of his own unmourned corpse, with the Phantom of the future pointing wordlessly at the gruesome manifestation of its draped head, the momentary homily generated is only what Scrooge himself makes of this prevision: "No voice pronounced these words in Scrooge's ears, and yet he heard them when he looked upon the bed" (Stave 5, "The Last of the Spirits"). In this respect, since we have "heard them" too, also unvoiced from without us, one close buckle between Scrooge's experience and ours would surely be forged by the silent sound play in what Connor might identify as the "white voice" of truth in those very words, with its anticipation of Beckett's own "phonic ghosts." So this passing moment bears an actual listen: calls for it, and all but sustains such an audition on his own scriptive terms.

Scrooge, though ordinarily barely alive to the world, is still sentient enough to be "shuddering from *head* to foot" (italics added, though not the tacit emphasis) as he is led to confront the inert head of a freshly deceased misanthrope. The apostrophe to Death he intuits there—the voice of omniscience in a spurt of pure Dickensian rhetoric, not least because sandwiched between the dissonant insistent chiming of "dreadful" and "dread"—goes out of its way to contrast the unlamented corpse with the actual cranial anatomy, as well as the beatitude, of its revered alternative in a genuinely grieved demise. The unsourced prose achieves this via a phonetic "cross-fade" (tacit cinematic metaphor from Connor again) that makes the imagined loved head lift lexically to view as if from the burial plot of the very monosyllable "dead": "Oh cold, cold, rigid, dreadful Death, set up thine altar here . . . for this is thy dominion! But of the loved, revered, and honoured head, thou canst not turn one hair to thy dread purposes, or make one feature odious." Death's "dominion" has been exceeded, and the posited second body released from all desecration. A most emphatic (and emphatically articulated) elocutionary distinction is required at this turn, that's for sure. Thus is the standard-issue phrase "the honoured dead" called up even as it is instantaneously subsumed to the more corporealized synecdoche ("head") of the present object lesson. With such alternatives superimposed upon each other for the most striking contrast possible, Scrooge is right to be hearing things. As are we. After comparable evidence first from the prose of Poe (and this at phonic as well as lexical and syntactic scale), we move in Part 2 from such lap-dissolves of phonetics toward the equally thematized jump cuts of grammar in the sylleptic junctures of Dickens's broader phrasal spans.

PART II

THE PROSAICS OF POTENTIAL

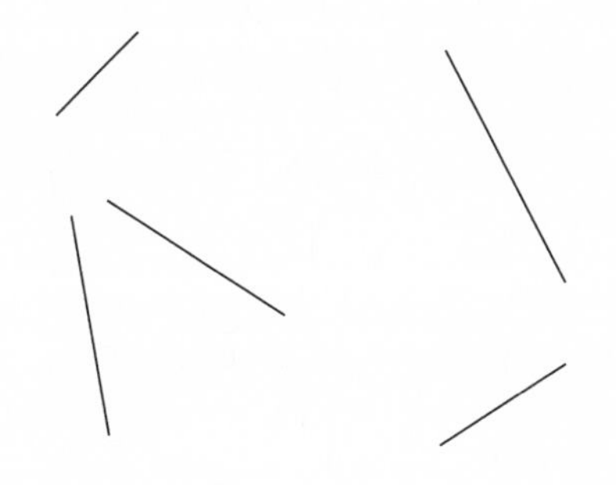

4

IMP-AIRED WORDS

First Giorgio Agamben, now Stanley Cavell: on the "ends" of literary writing as performed language—or say, in Agamben's genitive swivels, on "the idea of language" and "the thought of voice." In the redoubtable line of Ludwig Wittgenstein and J. L. Austin, Cavell participates in an ordinary language philosophy bent on excavating, from within the prosaic cadences of everyday speech, their evidence of philosophical pressure points. In adapting this approach to a literary prosaics of formative reading, my effort is to extend his method in general (while following his example in certain specific cases) to the eccentric phonic and syntactic torsions of an extra-ordinary—a more wrought and highly stylized—narrative prose (Poe, Dickens, Morrison). The particular depths probed by such analysis, as in those telescoped terms of my subtitle, disclose again the language philosophy implicitly prosecuted, rather than just exemplified, in literary writing, where grammatically, even syllabically, the ordinary harbors as potential its own contorted redoing on the run—and silent tongue.

From the undertext of verse to the micropoetics of prose: a functional halving of the topic across half a dozen chapters indicates no ultimate segregation in the scale of attention or inference. Quite the opposite. What Agamben was able to show about the constitutive place of measure and beat and lineation, about deixis and its reflexes, in the relay of the poem forward to each new enunciation of it—its end thus potentiated (as if by an ongoing temporal rhythm) from within its own cadences—directs our attention as well in turning now to prose fiction. We are concerned in this new triad of chapters with a distinctly *frictional* prose whose similarly marked linguistic impulses are channeled forward across its cadences and syllabic breakpoints while being—along a perpendicular axis as it were—relayed outward in a more or less explicit (and in more than one case thematized) transmission to the reader. At which point a close-grained prosaics of both stylistic momentum and rhetorical contact in no sense loses touch with the formative poetics of our preceding chapters.

In widening from the intensive vexed crest of word boundary to more extensive syllabic, lexical, and ultimately syntactic spans, we begin by following Cavell into the jagged grooves of a nagging and irreparable "graphonic" effect (my term)—and decided cognitive defect (his point)—in the prose of

Edgar Allan Poe. At such strained nodes in the deed of reading, the errand of the ear is repeatedly derailed by a sheer errancy of syllabic static. To hear how is simply to read Poe through Cavell's ears. But to see why is first to embed the possibility of such audiovisual disruptions within the fuller theory of skepticism and otherness in Cavell—including the ever-tentative mesh of language and consciousness—to which these quirks of wording are a lower limit case. In this way do Cavell's phonemic demos from Poe's writing become metaphysical demolitions.

And in this way, too, does Cavell's feel for the rootedness of consciousness in language—so wrenched out of shape in Poe—bring Agamben's deliberations back into the picture. Poe: an author in whose work the death of the animal voice into speech is famously forestalled in the case of a homicidal primate in "The Murders in the Rue Morgue" (not, as it happens, a story investigated by Cavell). This occurs when the illiteracy of an ape is masked for eavesdroppers by the animal's being able to emit the seeming tonalities of articulate speech, recognized by many in the vicinity of the crime—though never understood as an utterance in any one particular language. Only Inspector Dupin breaks the noncode, realizing that a semiosis (without semantics), a sheer burst of vocal gesture, falls beneath the bar of the human altogether by being free of that founding linguistic caesura that makes for segmentation—or in other words generating a sound stream that turns out to be unregimented, as Dupin suspects and then explains, by the human habit (twice stressed) of "syllabification."[1] Missing here, in the animal cry, is what Agamben might identify as the very habitus of the human in speech—a syllabic fundament that Cavell finds upended elsewhere in a direct threat to the Cartesian mind/body dyad, where mentality and its intentions are done in as if by the intractable phonemic body of writing.

The deed of reading is the text in action. Its thoughts are produced in and through me as (for the moment) mine. That's Cavell's Emerson. So, too, though without the sense of psychological transference, with Agamben's sense of poetry in reception. On his account, lyric speech finds its descriptive pointers absented from immediacy not so much by the surrendered presence of its impressions as by the potential (and potentiated) time—not there and then but here and when—of its enunciation by the reader. It is this logic that turns Leopardi's "L'infinito" into an allegory of the eternal in the form of its own rereading. In this way a deictics of virtual space is transformed into a phenomenology of literary activation. One might say that referential skepticism is suspended here, if not overcome, by invested articulation. Similarly, in Cavell's work on Emerson, skepticism of other minds and their utterances can be found heuristically warded off, all but involuntarily, by the experience of literary reading. "In every work of genius," writes Emerson in a passage (and, more, an idea) crucial for Cavell, "we recognize our own rejected thoughts." In a related etymology, we do so by pro-jection: "They come back to us with a certain alienated majesty."[2]

Over two decades earlier, we have had Keats on what it means for him to publish his own thoughts for an internalized reading: stressing, in a letter to his publisher, that "poetry should surprise by a fine excess and not by Singularity—it should strike the Reader as a wording of his own highest thoughts, and appear almost a Remembrance."[3] Such heights of thought, their timbre and resonance, are refined into phrase by an excess always in part aural and thus all the sooner to be internalized as one's own in bodily contact with the signaling page. That's one legacy of Romanticism even in the American grain.

Cavell's approach tends indeed to exemplify as well as gloss the Emersonian proposition. Thoughts "come back," are returned repurposed to us, by a certain pitch of prose as if, almost in a punning sense, they had freshly *come to us*. Their way back is, of course, most often through the silent phonetic enunciation of the read text: rejection as introjection. From the phonotext of British Romanticism (and its Victorian continuance) to its American phenomenology: that's the obvious shift we make in moving from Shelleyan phonetic *auscillation* (an internally sounded oscillation) in his *Ode to the West Wind* to the "lines of skepticism and Romanticism" (Cavell's subtitle) sketched out by Cavell's work on the philosophical tradition centered around the American Transcendentalists. But there are moments that prove the rule of Emersonian communication, together with its invested reciprocal translucency, precisely by abusing it. Edgar Allan Poe is a name for one of those moments: Cavell's chief exhibit. In considering an essay of his linking Emerson and Poe to Descartes, we find that the voicing of the void that last concerned us at the lexical interstices of continuous locution, or sometimes the voiding of the lexical gap itself by phonemic overlap, is with us still in the Poe/tics of a relentlessly manic prose.[4] In the story examined by Cavell, such effects include intrusive monosyllabic word forms extraneous to the actual locutions that embed them. These are what Cavell turns to in writing not about philosophy in Poe so much as about its mockery—or, better, the return of its repressed—in the obstreperous wordplay of a human speaker's attempted self-expression.

What language does in these extreme cases, what it accomplishes or at least performs, speaks to what it is—but only by circuitous means. On that "only," much rests. The impossibility of naming the condition of language directly from within its own operations establishes the boundary (not barrier) between philosophy and literary criticism. For Agamben, philosophy might be related to criticism much in the way that philosophy adjoins and complements linguistics. Philosophy looks to the abstract being of things rather than the specific things they become. As with the emphasis in linguistics on different language systems rather than the ontology of speech, criticism is regularly concerned with enunciative effects (plural, pluralized) more than, as in philosophy, with the sheer possibility of utterance. Even in the latter case, within the discipline of postmetaphysical philosophy in its literary outreach, two alternate tendencies are before us. Where Agamben theorizes the general taking-place (rather than the separate choices) of language manifest in the subjectivity of lyric voice, Cavell studies in American prose the variable place of language in the taking shape of the Cogito—and its deformations. Each philosopher works within a resistance to skepticism, though Agamben—not using the term (as Cavell everywhere does)—levels his attentions instead against a "nihilism" that comes to much the same thing. Without the stopgaps of ontology—with no grounding for being or language or self, let alone for the language of self—philosophy for both writers, in flight from the abyss of disbelief, turns to literary language as an experiment in ungrounded force and vitality, looking for that coming-to-speech that is sufficient unto the day of everyday human communication. Though Agamben works primarily on the densely fashioned phrasing of lyric verse and Cavell on such marked "stylists" in prose as Emerson and Poe (or elsewhere Shakespeare), each is in effect—at least at key turns, if in very different senses—an ordinary language philosopher. Each is a theorist of human interchange based on the linguistically realized potential (rather than some absolute proof) of shared—and sharable—humanity: a faith (it couldn't be more) in praxis rather than axiom.

In the story at which Cavell takes aim (and to which we will come in detail), "The Imp of the Perverse," Poe's narrator—pushed to a definitive limit of subjectivity in the hypertrophic defiance of reason by the whims of will—anticipates the crisis of his own "I" in the very language by which he reminisces about his doom on the eve of execution. His is a language disintegrating under stress in an unintended release of intransigent letter forms. What is resistant in this to any Cartesian equipoise is fully pursued by Cavell's commentary. But to his sense of a parodied Cogito in the undermining of first-person speech acts, I would add an implied and dubious stance, in Poe, toward Emerson's actual theory of reading, tacit here and more fully allegorized in another tale from the year before. Poe doesn't educe ideas from us by his writing; he induces verbal disturbance pure and simple. And if the Cogito is in peril, so is Emersonian transference. A supposed conduit of intuition between page and recognition, seer and textual insight—characterized by Cavell as the readerly dynamic instituted by Emersonian prose—is in Poe (especially in Cavell's chosen 1845 tale "The Imp of the Perverse" and its even more allegorical companion piece from the year before, "A Tale of the Ragged Mountains") not celebrated and mystified as clairvoyance but instead miniaturized, mocked, and exploded. Nonetheless, nowhere more clearly than with these stories by Poe, even in the key of irony, can reading track those verbal deviances by which, in the most oblique of ways, one yet again (in the slide of my subtitle) comes upon literature writing, literature in the act of writing—which is to say enacting—language philosophy.

Automatic Word Procession

This is why I want to begin with that theory of reading in Cavell derived from his own encounter with Emerson and Thoreau and implicitly translated to ours with him. The attempt here is ultimately to bring the metalinguistic thinking of Agamben and Cavell, explicit and otherwise—and especially the relations probed between language and ontology in their separate ventures in literary criticism—into some speculative alignment. By way of orientation, however, let us first approach the question from another medium that is also of philosophical interest both to Cavell and, as we'll see later, to Agamben. It is not an oddity of these considerations so much as their premise that one would be drawn to what might be called the immaterial substrate of photomechanical projection—a flickering subliminal interference of vision derived from a material intermittence on the strip—by way of comparison with the immaterial deed of reading in subvocal (and, even then, all but somatic) enunciation. For such reading is graphically cued by the punctual sequencing, yet sometimes stray links, of spun-out, bunched letters. Nor is it necessary for the philosophers (as poeticians) here reviewed that their own commentary on film be directly concerned with this im/material manifestation of the frame line for their literary work to help clarify, on its own terms, the parallel between media at such a level of undertextual production.

In *The World Viewed*, cinema is defined by Cavell as "a succession of automatic world projections."[5] But succeeding each other how quickly? Projection involves the founding automaticity not only of enframed "views" wholesale but also of the serial transparencies that induce them twenty-four "successions" per second in the celluloid frame line. For here—or no sooner here than there, here and gone—is the subliminal photographic impetus behind all apparitional momentum on screen. This recognition, however, need not compromise Cavell's ultimate use of film, as of Shakespearean theater before it, as a therapy for skepticism in our willing limit to participation: the acceptance of a seen and heard world upon the presence of whose drama we cannot trespass, for good or ill. What begins in a parody of doubt—there before us is a seeming world we know not to be ours, not to be real—apprentices us, after all, in emotional credence. But in cinema's laboratory for the overcoming of skepticism, why not pursue this heuristic regimen, well beyond Cavell's phenomenology, back to the film lab itself, to the level of process as well as to produced image; in other words, why not carry film's use in the practiced overcoming of skepticism all the way down and back to the file of images one knows to be only clocked transparencies rather than otherwise animated bodies? Why isn't the frame line itself, the unspooled and backlit strip, and since then the pixel array, one of the things we are invited actively to overcome rather than simply to ignore in our vesting of conviction in the world viewed?[6]

In fact, Cavell's work comes closer to this sense of glimpsed constitutive modularity in textual process when he writes about literature rather than film, wondering, for instance, about the intransigent "hell" found "staring out of" the name Othello, or the "demon" of Desdemona.[7] More rigorous than this, though, is his sense of the linguistic undertow in a single Poe story, "The Imp of the Perverse," where Cavell is almost preternaturally alert to the "cells" of speech: those "molecules" one might well find comparable to the fleeting photograms of the filmic chain.[8] Such, for instance, as we are to examine them, are the linguistically unwanted "imps" (like momentary optic splutters or freeze-frame glitches) in words like "imp/erceptible" and "imp/risoned" called out from the Poe story. These and other instances of molecular phonetics are fugitive units of effect mostly unsounded but sensed upon extrusion as derived from the fundament of articulation—and sometimes rubbing that articulation the wrong way in an alphabetic jamming that obtrudes a false syllable against the coherent spin of signification. In this way is language's automatic word procession, as it were, thrown off kilter by a spanner in the works, a false syllabic span. In the case of Poe's lexically dissevering wordplay, Cavell attends to certain pointed disruptions sprung in this way from language's material base. Normal writing comes clear as a series of routinized word formations projected into the axis of grammar; only in writing like Poe's do recalcitrant echoes and puns (including many here on the title's first word creeping unentitled into random words like "impulse") disrupt that projection with the recovered arbitrariness of their subsemantic massing as letter forms. So that the word eyed on paper exposes at times the suppressions necessary to sustain the norms of so-called ordinary language. In particular for Cavell, Poe's writing, tacitly sparring with Descartes, reveals by default our view of the word's typical work in the buttressing of subjectivity, which is to say, language's role as the vehicle of consciousness itself.

In his gradual approach to Poe's "The Imp of the Perverse" as a Cartesian send-up, Cavell looks first to Emerson's own ironic relation to Descartes, concentrating on the failure of self-reliance in our habitual lapse into the derivative. "Man does not say . . . but quotes" ("Being Odd," 113). This pronouncement involves for Cavell a "gag," since its own adjacent allusion to Descartes passes as if unwittingly: "Man . . . dares not say 'I think,' 'I am,' but quotes some saint or sage" (112). The citational subject is derived rather than self-authorized, even in the midst of a critique of this very syndrome. Building on Emerson's wry allusion, Cavell helps us see how the Transcendentalist's play on Cartesian autonomy has become a joke so distended and bent out of shape with Poe's satire of Emersonian self-surety in "The Imp of the Perverse" that philosophical overtones are sounded everywhere in cacophony and breakdown. Not only do one's words no longer prove one's soul as signified; for Poe's doomed, condemned, and literally death-sentenced narrator, their summoned signifiers undermine intent in the very will to speech.

In Emerson's theory of reading as self-disclosure, one's deferral to the worded thoughts of another as if they had been on the tip of one's mental tongue might indeed seem to disappear the nested "I" of "self-reliance" into the sheer relay of intersubjectivity as *self-relayance*, manifest only in the shunt of enunciated transit. It is in any case obvious to Cavell—as he pursues the consequences of similar threats to epistemological security in the supposed self-articulations of language—that relayed words alone, unstable by linguistic nature, can never anchor the self in the act of transmit. One result is that in "The Imp of the Perverse" the self-surrender of reading, with its circuit of self-loss and recognition, is toppled from sublimity to gothic ridicule: first for a character slain by textual encounter within the story (a toxic scene of reading), then for readers themselves laid low in their expectations of a real plot by Poe's punning syllabic overlaps. And by a related displacement, it is a reader manqué who is also slain in "A Tale of the Ragged Mountains."

But first things first: Cavell's case in point. On the evidence of a story like "The Imp of the Perverse," it would seem that one response to being implicitly told by Emerson how, in reading my "work of genius," your thoughts are all but mine in advance—in other words, that in my words I am in fact reading your thoughts—would be to concoct a text in which thoughts are so worded as to be all but nonsense in their semantic overkill: an estranging jest rather than an alienated majesty. Yet in the skeptical madness Cavell finds at work in "The Imp of the Perverse," Poe, beyond all metaphysical gamesmanship, may be seen to get at something never quite admitted by his solemn precursor, Emerson, sage of Concord: the drastically provisional nature of a self-phrased, self-razed identity that permits in the first place, rather than temporarily bespeaks, a total penetration by the words of another. Despite the title "Self-Reliance," that is, Emerson revels explicitly in those transferred affects of reading that anticipate not just Poe's own mid-1840s stories of psychic dispossession but that quintessentially American gambit, a decade later, of Whitman's epic punning at the start of *Song of Myself* (1855): "And what I assume you shall assume." With its transferential sense of authorial premise as readerly investiture, such is the democratizing—if also aggrandizing—manifestation of "myself" even when articulated by the other. And if one's themes and words come not entirely from within, then the language of the other—and, more to the point, the otherness within wording itself—can make expression not just half ventriloquial but, at the microlevel too, subject to the unmeant.

This is in part the burden of Cavell's "Being Odd, Getting Even," his essay focusing in the end on the hypertrophic wordplay of an 1845 story about the "imp" of self-destruction. For Cavell, the fatalistic inversion of the Cogito in this one plot of Poe's (I think, therefore I am done for) does indeed engender a wholesale lampoon ("parody" is in fact Cavell's word [120]) of a certain tenor of thought in post-Cartesian philosophy, the symptoms of this satire littering the text with imp-pertinent signifiers. The story is in part an autobiographical confession, on the eve of the narrator's hanging, about having, years ago, killed a man while he was reading in bed—with lethal fumes, of all things, from a poison candle, a bizarre method in fact *read about* first by the narrator before implementing it. Let's guess that losing your life in reading, as well as the homicidal influence from another text that leads to it, intrigued Poe in part because it aggravates the risk of his own thrilling writing to the point of implausible farce. And what could make this point any more directly than the ambient danger of a candlelit page? The only fatal intake closer to fitting flush with our experience of Poe's own lurid writing would be a story in which the words themselves *did one in*, not just (as in the remaining events of "The Imp of the Perverse") through unhinged lexical coherence but by a kind of morbid osmosis. There *is* such a story, the previous year's "A Tale of the Ragged Mountains," whose coincidence of linguistic and psychic violence I have elsewhere discussed by way of a closer narratographic analysis—and whose plot is almost impossible to make credible in summary, since it barely seems so in the event.[9] But I try again here, in brief, for the way it complements the later "Imp" in its travesty of a particular Emersonian sense of reading the other as oneself.

Self-Relayance

Put as schematically as "A Tale" forces us to apprehend it, and hence as its plot overplays its premise of contagious narration, the story goes like this. In 1827 Virginia, a mesmeric doctor's current drugged patient, named Augustus Bedloe, who happens to be the very "living image," as it were, of the doctor's long-dead friend Oldeb, is poisoned miles away in the hills (by a Bengali arrow rather than candle fumes) at the very moment when that doctor, named Templeton, is transcribing at his desk the identical details of his friend's death years earlier in an East Indian colonial uprising at Benares.[10] This becomes, then, a shared death suffered by the one man and now endured but temporarily survived by his morphine-steeped and telepathic doppelgänger. The textually relayed poison arrow of a Bengal warrior isn't enough actually to kill Bedloe, in Oldeb's returning shoes, despite his drugged susceptibility to the unseen words of the episode's mesmeric amanuensis. Instead, this recounted trauma is only just enough to make Bedloe feel, in the displaced reading experience of a long-distance transfer, as if he were *in the process of being killed*. A more literal application by the doctor than just that of his words is required. Only the real venom from an inadvertently poisonous leech, later administered by Templeton to the same temple into which the imagined arrow had entered in the telekinesis of textual report, is enough to bring about actual death. And this for the man we have been led to suspect is in fact—via metempsychosis (migration of souls) rather than merely preternatural textual transmission—the slain soldier's actual reincarnation.

The hero's own identity, as well as his life, is thus leeched and drained away a second time. Until then, the logic has gravitated to sheer allegory. An act of writing, eliding its own textual reading, passes by the "alienation" of thought ("alienist" being the contemporaneous term, of course, for psychiatrist rather than for philosophical writer) to the stabbed (read: penetrated and invaded) brain of a subject brought into unholy rapport with the text, not with writer but with narrated character. Here, shifted from first-person essayistic rhetoric to a third-person account, is Emerson's estranging "majesty" as a gothic fluke: a textual transmigration of the posthumous soul. This fantastic suspicion about metempsychosis rather than mere thought transference is both confirmed and undermined at once when we discover that it was only a typo in the local paper's obituary notice—giving "Bedlo" rather than "Bedloe"—that has rendered his denatured status not just that of a near-miss anagram but of a true palindrome for the name "O-l-d-e-b."

Arrived at this dubious letdown in a quasi-Emersonian parable of reading as self-recognition—where your cognizance of a death once died as your own, in your own person, comes back to you estranged in the non-"majestic" journaling of the other—the plot has boiled over in linguistic as well as gothic nonsense. As happens from the first (rather than merely climactically) in the later tale of "The Imp of the Perverse," the tics—or impish accidents—of alphabetic inscription have further demolished the Cogito itself, this time for a posthumous character every bit as evacuated and reversible as the signifiers that reference him. Given the linguistic self-consciousness that must have bedeviled this author of poems and prose alike, the writer named Poe seems uniquely alert to this fragile posing (in the discursive sense, this positing) of self. Dropped letters (like the t of "Poe-"), as well as the imp-proper combinatory notice of other letters, keep words from coinciding either with the otherness of the world or with a self tracing its withdrawal from external certainty in just such writing. In anxiety rather than Emersonian confidence, "rejected" thoughts return like a breach in repression from within the impressed: a material panic of the letter. Or its black comedy.

Poe's Emersonian Descartes is there by allusion, I am arguing, as much in 1844's "A Tale" as in the next year's "Imp" on which Cavell concentrates. This grows clear from Cavell's own commentary on the transpositional logic of reading. In his gloss on a cryptic Emersonian dictum, Cavell understands the famous "But do your work, and I shall know you" from "Self-Reliance" to be singling out, in particular, the work of reading itself, here and now. "Your work, what is yours to do, is exemplified, when you are confronted with Emerson's words, by reading those words . . . subjecting yourself to them as the writer has by undertaking to enact his existence in saying them" ("Being Odd," 118). Subjection, undertaking: the "gothic of reading" in a Transcendentalist key.[11] It is important to note how this is more than seeing your "rejected" thoughts majestically alienated and refreshed by the self-reliant confidence of another's rhetoric, the ejected now returned to you burnished by distance. It is more than the recuperative Emersonian gesture amounting to "Let's face it; deep down you know what I mean." Closer to the phenomenology of reading at large in the writing of Georges Poulet (where "I am the subject of thoughts other than my own"[12]), it amounts to a linguistic and hence cognitive inhabitation. The result, in Cavell's phrasing again, is that "you undertake to enact my existence" in the very processing of my words, with that almost Poelike mortuary "gag" on "undertake," intended or not, as an out-of-body transference captured in the import of direct address: to wit, you know what I mean by this writing because in saying it to yourself you are the only one now present who can—and I knew you'd do so—mean it for me. Agamben might have adapted his own double genitive to fiction rather than poetry in calling such a circularity "the dictation of prose": the inscription that issues from the articulation in which it is destined again to result.

Which is not to deny, despite the funerary underside of Cavell's phrase "undertaking to enact your existence," the Transcendentalist uplift he has also spotted in the reversible Emersonian logic by which the absent author abides with, as well as validates, his own readers.[13] In Cavell's sense of the Emersonian address, I think and write so that you will see yourself in me and I myself in your doing so, thereby knowing in you, and as you, ongoingly, your image of me. In the slippery grip of such an intuition, Poe's "A Tale of the Ragged Mountains," which is a story, not an essay, of course—and, what's more, a writing dividing narrator from narrative, and in the process present from past—takes the lurking vertigo of this shared Cogito, in Cavell's Emerson, to giddy extremes. In so doing, it bypasses reading altogether for immediate verbal "transport": from textual agent (scribbling doctor) to his patient, and from reference (Oldeb's long-past death) to identification (Bedloe's hallucination of it, in the midst of it). In Emerson, the reader's work fulfills the author by being made known to him; in its narrative version by Poe, it is not "I will know you" that is spoken by the text, but a further implosion around character and identification. The implicit recipe served up by Poe's gothic version of Emerson in narrative form, then, as channeled by the scriptor Templeton: do your work and he will be you; he will have risen from the crypt, via impersonal inscription, not just into your co-opted acknowledgment of his death but into your present embodiment of my narratorial thoughts about that death in third person, with you yourself taking up another's fate in the place of your own life.

Fettered Lettering

Related in verbal pith, if not in spirit, to Poe's s/cryptic jokes is the kind of accidental word-splay and cross-lexical chiming that Emerson, far from an inveterate punster, can occasionally rope into service—so that, for example, a blunt redundancy emerges instead as an inextricable emphasis in the essaying of "Self-Reliance." This happens when the inward-reliance of an autonomous self alone at home, faced with "invaders" from beyond, is summoned to its odd innate empowerment: "Let *us stun and astonish* the intruding rabble" (272; emphasis added), where the readily elided sibilance of "us stun" is restated under further compression—or (in the sense of a filmic loop) under rerun—as the less aggressive *as/ton*: sheer force converted to the potential for wonder and emulation. With the addressed first person plural "us" (yet again, in Emerson, editorialized to a fare-thee-well) getting swallowed up across the near echo of a prefix and the onset of a root phoneme, even a would-be transcendental personhood disappears as cause into its effects. Put differently, the path from an aggressive "stun" to the more reception-friendly "astonish" maps the necessary distancing of a too forceful "majesty" in the closed circuit of its "alienated" reception.

This is, furthermore, an alienated majesty (estranged and reclaimed at once in reading) whose negative version is far from a vital transfusion of ideas but, rather, the kind of vicarious bloodletting trumped up by the gothic plot of Poe's "A Tale of the Ragged Mountains." Taking that story as the metanarrative of a writing that puts a reader in the place of its own inscribed character, we may see in it Poe's takedown of the transcendental in a quite specific textual sense. In Gérard Genette's account, the "transcendent" level of a literary work is its portable meaning or interpretive use, the impact of its wording, apart both from the material support of its inscription or imprint and from its "immanence" as deciphered text in exactly so-and-so-many words.[14] A piece like "Self-Reliance" is the same essay—immanent to us, however notated—whether we read it, that is, in its separately bound form, anthologized later, or more lately on line. The imprinted volume (or more recently audiobook or website) locates the material platform or notation of the writing, whereas—even beyond its "immanence" as text—its "transcendence" is what it comes to mean or do, as, for instance, in a translated version, some different cultural framing, or perhaps in a personal or tendentious interpretation. So with the indited tale within Poe's "Tale," which, though written in one place by the material labor of its scribe the mesmerist, finds its paradoxical "immanence" miles away—and this for a man with no text there before his eyes, so that "immanence" itself has been dissolved into "transcendence" in the tale's unmediated lethal force. Framed by its own proleptic deconstruction, and in allegorical disregard of precisely the inscribed letter, one textual front of an Emersonian transcendentalism is exaggerated by Poe into the nonsense of hypnotic telepathy, and this in ways that prepare us for the crisscrossed wires of soundplay in Poe's "The Imp of the Perverse" as well. For that is a tale equally, though less obviously, concerned with the death of the subject—not by wholesale co-optation of a posthumous metempsychosis but by the elemental instabilities of human locution per se.

In this way "The Imp of the Perverse," not by posthumous preemption of a life but by a virtual deathbed confession, offers nothing less than an open mockery of all confident self-reliance—where the human will, reduced to willfulness, is self-violating by definition and where the letter, let alone the letter of the law, grows downright carceral (as Cavell suggests in stressing the verbal "fetters" of Poe's jailhouse confession narrative). Cavell's apt sense of this is given with only the most glancing allusion to Emerson at this point, even though—with Emerson's own allusion, no doubt, to Wordsworth's "Intimations Ode" (where "shades of the prison-house" close round the "growing boy")—the essayist observes that, in the straitening passage from youth to adulthood, the Transcendental self is "clapped into jail by his consciousness" ("Being Odd," 119). Identity in Emerson is here hemmed in by the effort to establish itself in and through our preformulated words; or as Cavell puts it otherwise, with a pun educed from "The Imp of the Perverse," selfhood is "penned" by language (122). That the narrator writes "in fetters" from his execution-eve cell is, for Cavell, only the literalization of this fate.

And if some allusion to Emerson's existential prison-house may be operating in Poe, then all the more so could a text like "A Tale of the Ragged Mountains" be sensed to pick up on Emerson's philological slip, a sentence later, in saying that a "character is like an acrostic or Alexandrian stanza;—read it forward, backward, or across, it still spells the same thing" (266). By "acrostic" (as a supposedly Greek classical gimmick), Emerson is thinking instead (his editors readily believe) of the specialized form of anagram—known as a palindrome—that we encounter in "A Tale of the Ragged Mountains" (Oldeb/Bedlo): a poetic ingenuity popularized not by Greek verse but in the late Byzantine period.[15] This overwrought prototype offers in Emerson a compressed pattern for the smoothly enclosed human subject, consistent from start to finish, known rounded upon itself. Seen otherwise, this is exactly the trap of selfhood ironized, for instance, by the post-Emersonian Dickens when a hero's reversibly dead-ended expectations are conveyed by the self-given name "Pip."[16] All the more so, then, do the mutually "rounded in" natures of Oldeb and/as Bedlo(e) mark the send-up of any such autonomy. And it is worth noting how these effects, mirrorings to the eye rather than echoes to the ear, may be thought to do even a more thorough damage to the phenomenology of reading as the inhabitation of other minds, or the occupation of their worlds, by breaking with the phenomenon of utterance itself into the covert operations of the letter. That Emersonian emblem of the palindrome must, in short, be quarantined as sheer analogy rather than active model. Suffice it to say that if "acrostics" and their kin, by whatever name, were in fact given free play in the language of the self, as they sometimes are in Poe, rather than just as static icons for it, "reliance" would be hard to come by, let alone enunciation.

Raising this threat is no doubt Poe's reason for having the first instance of the "imp" pun, in the launching sentence of "The Imp of the Perverse," not only surface definitively in the word that (by false etymology) it might aptly seem to abbreviate, "impulse," but in two anagrammatic and more strictly graphic reversals of its alphabetic cluster as well, unmentioned by Cavell: in the "*prim*a mobilia" of "*prim*itive" human urges. To vary again the title of Cavell's first book (the interrogative *Must We Mean What We Say?*), these phantom patterns are things meant without being said—but only, at that, in the linguistic unconscious, more deeply buried and latent even than *langue* stands to *parole*.[17] The Emersonian problematic of Poe's philosophic "parody" keeps Cavell's attention trained instead, as we're now to see, on more immediate articulatory threats to the self-reliant Cogito. These emerge from the secondary vocality of the readerly speech act—in its detachable quasi-syllabic patterns—as well as from the cognitive byways of metaphor, rather than from the radical self-defiance of scamp signifiers (palindromes) reversing direction against the voiced pace of speech.

Impotentialities

Here is Cavell's own litany of perverse recursions in Poe's "Imp": "*impulse* (several times), *impels* (several times), *impatient* (twice), *important, impertinent, imperceptible, impossible, unimpressive, and imprisoned*" ("Being Odd," 124). In all these cases the alphabetic triad as phonemic cluster is at odds with, though never quite dismantling, the segments of morphology and syllabification at work in its respective phrasings, with the plosive "imp-words" (124) coming to attention only as intransigent blips on the screen of lexical succession. Im-p-airment is in fact twofold: the impish pairing of one speech sound aired with the wrong syllable. What results is a chain of entirely failed hyphenates, one useless pun after another truncated without fallout, an extreme dyslexia, a madness. Ertinent? Erceptible? Ossible? No meaning would survive an insinuated prefix so wholly impertinent, mostly imperceptible, and strictly impossible all at once. Impotent to make meaning, these latencies are effaced in lexical motion. Or almost.

Despite these typically recessed but here obtruded alphabetic clusters, our processing the intended meaning of whole words at once depends upon "our mostly not noticing the particle (or cells) and their laws . . . on our not noticing their necessary recurrences," a "necessity," Cavell repeats for emphasis, that is "the most familiar property of language there could be" (125). He continues in the wordplay of his own lexical dismemberment when asserting that when and if "we do note these cells or molecules, these little moles of language (perhaps in thinking, perhaps in derangement), what we discover are word imps" (125). By which mole(cules) he means "the implanted origins or constituents of words, leading lives of their own, staring back at us, calling upon one another, giving us away, alarming—because to note them is to see that they live in front of our eyes, within earshot, at every moment" (125). And to see also, with these disembedded particles of the word viewed, that they don't rest easy under the concept of verbal intention, instead stretching it out of shape, bending it to their own impish will. Once again, in this bizarre prose poetry, we find just that "desubjectification" of language so central to Agamben's definition of the poem as iterable artifact.

Two things there in Cavell's account offer a particularly tight grip on Poe's so-called first-person narrative in the post-Cartesian reading to which Cavell submits it: first the parenthetical alternative "(perhaps in thinking, perhaps in derangement)" and then the loaded, sudden, and indeed deliberately "alarming" phrase "giving us away." Evincing a psychotic break in the stream of consciousness, the disruptive "imp words" prevent us not only from saying what we mean but even from meaning it coherently. They would thus prevent my giving unified voice to what I say to myself in constituting that self in thought. These imps are not revealing in the way, say, a Freudian slip is. They don't give anything away that way, by dis/closure, not even ourselves. Rather, they throw expressive subjectivity to the winds of the contingent. Cavell comes at this point more explicitly in the next paragraph, when generalizing such accidents of the lexeme to the "perverseness" of language at large, "working without, even against, our thought and its autonomy" (125). Independence of mind, the law of autonomy governing expressed thought as a self-present intention: such is the first victim of the deviant signifier slipping beneath and between words, fraying them at their inner joins. In Poe's prose, this willful dispersion of apparent intent is diagnosed not just by the front-loaded phonetic imp-etuosity in this one tale, but also, here and in many another, by the traumatic gappings and overlaps of narrative grammar itself. Such writing so confounds the relation of inner or "metaphysical" voice to self-presence that it puts the "externality" of linguistic ciphers not just at their proper distance from any posited inwardness but at odds with dictionary meaning itself, let alone personal intent.

If, against the grain of syllabification, the title word "imp" appears (both senses: emerges and seems) to split *imp* from the likes of *ulse*, deranging all morphology in the process, it does so to remind us, more broadly, of the uncertain safety net of utterance in any intended formulation whatsoever. If our words get away from themselves, and hence our words from our thoughts, then the link between thinking and being, as tethered to inner voice, is weakened. Even the Cogito, as rephrased by Emerson in that variant quoted by Cavell—the tacit paratactic causality of "I think," "I am" (106)—shelters its own ambiguity, easily degenerating into the nonbinding subjectivism of "I think I am." Finding a different emphasis in Poe's undermining of the Cogito, Cavell highlights the narrator's fear that "to *think* in my situation was to be lost" (123)—lost because such thinking would release not selfhood per se but its most self-annihilating urges.

Only the baroque complications of Poe's narrative can give teeth to the narrator's lament, to the full weight of its Cartesian heritage, and to the Shakespearean overtones of its perhaps oddest detail. Under Cavell's scrutiny, Poe may be found alluding to *Hamlet* in the backstory of a bizarre poisoning: not in the ear exactly (as the Ghost claims of his own murder by Claudius) but, by association, in the air of intake while listening to any sequence of silent words in reading. For after an opening "essay" (as Cavell calls it) in Poe's story, an essay on the perverse willfulness at odds with desire—a self-destructive bent that goads one impetuously into catastrophe against one's better judgment—the narrator himself is indeed led to a fatal confession of his much earlier crime: that bedside murder in absentia, by poison "reading light." All this he must explain from his death-row cell, following upon a generalized account of the human perversity that led him there, and whose ex post facto disclosure is of note to Cavell: "I have said thus much, that in some measure I may answer your question—that I may explain to you why I am here" (122). What is locally meant is quickly offered: an explanation "for my wearing these fetters, and for my tenanting this cell of the condemned" (122). But Cavell's analysis leaps on this answer ("may explain to you") to a "question" no one has in fact posed, except by a tacit narrative curiosity textually occasioned. He thus detects in it a "fantasy of writing" (122) rather than of a speaking subject, where we are perhaps expected to assume (Cavell puts it conjecturally) that "words are fetters and cells and that to read them, to be awake to their meaning, or effect, is to be poisoned" (122).

Associations continue in this interrogative vein: "Are we being told that writer and reader are one another's victims? Or is the suggestion that to arrive at the truth something in the reader as well as something in the writer must die? Does writing ward off or invite in the angel of death?" (122). The questions are, in the context of Cavell's writing, wholly rhetorical. He expects, as he says, "nowadays little resistance" (123) to this line of interrogation, since (he lets it go without saying) he is spelling all this out in the heyday of deconstruction and the Derridean thanatopraxis of the text, the deathwork of inscription. Then, too, the adverb in the carceral "I am here," indicating the speaker's (or writer's) presence here and now, comes back to haunt the story in the end, in a parallel passage Cavell doesn't quote or consider, including the story's own last elliptical phrase, when the narrator—once abruptly removed from "here" by capital punishment for his homicidal crime—will finally "be fetterless . . . *but where?*"[18] Thinking has always doomed his narrator, because the moment he is conscious of a need for self-preservation, some contradictory impulse wells up—not to do the will's bidding but to *do in* its desire. Varying Cavell's phrase about unregulated language elements undermining verbal intent, the result for the subject is to give him away, to give him up.

Yet his eventual and precipitous admission of the crime gives pause as well. Of all the perversities of will at the expense of self-interest, confession may seem the least perverse. The going public of a crime, by detection or confession, is so narratively expected that it becomes almost a law of plot: in this case trapping the sociopathic narrator unwittingly in the most conventional of ethical closures. The whole narrative arc seems reduced, in the terms of Michael Riffaterre's semiotics, to the avoided and repressed cliché (and ethical bromide) that Shakespeare himself so narrowly skirts—and which is often misattributed to him as a coinage: the truism (phrased by Chaucer in just so many words) that "murder will out."[19] Which in turn calls up another avoided cliché at the basis of the narrator's destructive impulses, working there at odds with desire and intent. For indeed his confession is willfully blurted out, as we might ordinarily say, *accidentally on purpose*.

In *Hamlet*, however, murder needs help in being smoked out: that's what's tragic about the revenge plot; that's the poison in the prompted ear that erodes the son's life. When Hamlet reflects on the fear of death, saying that "conscience doth make cowards of us all" (3.1.318–19), he of course famously means something more like "consciousness" than like "conscience," a sensed precariousness of being rather than an uprush of guilt, more the permeating fear of oblivion than the threat of hellfire. But in Poe, it is something closer to a conventional if long-deferred sense of conscience that has, however disguised, returned through the back door of consciousness. We touch here on part of what it means to Cavell that he is "beginning to study Poe while thinking about Hamlet" ("Being Odd," 130). His account is uniquely alert to the theme of delay, not just in the long-postponed and all but involuntary confession of the narrator's crime, but in the second extended example of perversity given by Poe's narrator in the preliminary "essay": a self-defeating procrastination (not so named in the text) in whose grips "we feel *perverse*, using the word with no comprehension of the principle" ("Imp," 282). What Cavell doesn't mention in his turn to this passage is that this Hamlet-like delay is framed by two other examples from Poe's narrator that render it more broadly categorical, linguistic on one side, existential (even metaphysical) on the other. Call the umbrella category that of deferral per se. For the previous example by Poe, given just before that of disastrous procrastination, concerns a self-punishing tendency toward "circumlocution" (281) that annoys the listener and mortifies the speaker, against not just the latter's better judgment but his native talent for lucidity. Tying the tongue up in willful knots, such is the postponing of sense across "involutions and parentheses" (281) of just the sort Poe's philosophical parodies are so rife with.

Verbal deferral (the open secret of Poe's literary prose), followed by protracted delay in the move to completion (the open secret of narrative plotting), is now rounded out in this trio of exemplified perversities (natural enough after all, like that which catches the narrator's own conscience in the end) by the more anomalous case of a lowered guard, at cliff side, against the perverse urge to jump. Yet this temperamental quirk is introduced in a paragraph that at first would seem to be generalizing its specific setting into a treatise on philosophical skepticism. Before we realize that we've zeroed in on another isolated example of impish whim, that is, there is this Cartesian vertigo in editorial plural, itself precipitously introduced: "We stand upon the brink of a precipice. We peer into the abyss—we grow sick and dizzy" (282). The prematurely broached local instance of holding back from the plunge of disaster becomes, momentarily, the abstract figuration of one's life in time when stretched over the existential chasm of doubt. And over the fragility of reference itself—where no sooner do we "peer" into the word "precipice" than our hearing plumbs the fore-echo of "abyss" invisibly released by its last two syllables.

The whole spectrum of perversities we've traversed turns out to be a strangely coherent one. From an almost negligible phonemic welt in the contagious word-imp, disfiguring a lexeme by momentarily deferring its functional use, to the broadest arcs of a narrative death drive postponed by the byzantine twists and loops of story, the modes of deferred closure are both metalinguistic (via circumlocution) and narratological. And at their point of intersection: what I would call narratographic. As for instance at the end of the tale—when the insane desire to plunge into that earlier and suitably abstract "abyss," with its specific (and prefigurative) threat of "rushing annihilation" (282), returns on the gallows, as if it were a slip between the cracks of grammar itself; it returns, that is, following a morbid play on delivery as negative deliverance, with a mortal syllepsis in "the brief but *pregnant* sentences that *consigned me to the hangman and to hell*" (284; emphasis added). The literality of being given over to the hands of the execution throws into unusual relief the figurative catachresis involved in being given up to the otherworld.

Syllepsis in its classic sense: a verb taking its direct or indirect object (by storm) in suddenly two senses at once, here a horizontal remanding to punishment and at the same time—all in the same strangled breath, before we can assimilate the shift in preposition—a vertical drop to death. Much to come on this wrinkling of syntax. For now, it's enough to see its immediate pertinence in Cavell's case for Poe's case against the Cartesian ground of consciousness. It is never more than a half step in Poe, if also a quantum leap, from his freaks of phrase to his gloom-perfumed metaphysics, as, for instance, from a momentary prepositional twitch (or cringe) in the second, scene-establishing paragraph of "The Man of the Crowd"—"With a cigar in my mouth and a newspaper in my lap" (two very different inwardnesses)—to the impenetrabilities developed in that story of masked otherness.

Hoist on the Gallows and His Own Petard: The Sylleptic Turn

We might say that this grammatical trope of syllepsis, as a kind of distended pun, deploys in reciprocal array the potential give-and-take of two phrasings mutually present to each other, if only by way of a logical breach. In any case syllepsis, in particular the sylleptic preposition "in" just sampled, has in philosophy a *locus classicus* (though not vouchsafed the term as such). In a famous argument against Cartesian doubt, Gilbert Ryle, writing in the years just before Cavell's own work on the problematic of skepticism began appearing, gives as example a comparable grammatical oddity (uncredited) from Dickens: " 'She came home in a flood of tears and a sedan chair' is a well-known joke based on the absurdity of conjoining terms of a different type"—and thus a good model, in Ryle's thinking, not for mind-body dualism itself but for the logical disaster of its hypothesis, which is also, like syllepsis, based on a "category-mistake."[20] Dickensian comedy thus exposes the artificial parallel from which Cartesian doubt derives: as if misery and the hauling by servants could be thought to *move* a person in the same sense—now corporeal and obvious; now subjective, invisible, always in doubt.

Offered up by Ryle is a trope that the Victorian novelist learned in part from Shakespeare and might well have passed to Poe, its grammatical disjunctions operating with equal success in the mode of comedy or macabrerie. Its splayed phrasing rests on a twofold understanding of a single subject in divided alignment with a double predicate, usually a direct object or object of the preposition taken now metaphorically, now literally, as in Pope's "stain her honor, or her new brocade." Without returning to the Dickens example in this regard, Ryle quickly concedes that one can speak reasonably of mental "processes" just as "there occur physical processes" (22). That's the source, for Ryle, of the false parallelism. The point is that these occurrences are not of the same order of event at all, not on the same plane of existence, and thus neither commensurable nor wholly separate and unavailable to each other. Concerning bodily motion vis-à-vis cognition, there is neither pure disjunction nor pure conjunction between them. But access there is. Mind, we may say, following Ryle's objection, is partly revealed when a physical process is understood not just as occurrence or event but as intentional (or involuntary) action, as behavior. For by their behavior others can be known. Instead, for Ryle, it is the only unholy ghost of a disembodied Cartesian subjectivity that puts otherness in hiding and in doubt. All told, it is "just as good or bad a joke to say 'there exist prime numbers and Wednesdays and public opinion and navies' as to say 'there exist both minds and bodies' " (24). In a similar spirit, literary comedy can work to expose a philosophical farce.

But there is a noncomic heritage of syllepsis as well, as taken up more obviously by Poe. Shakespeare can sound it out in the register of violent dislocation. "Thus was I"—note the inverted past tense of being itself in the speech of Hamlet's ghost (thus was I, but am no more)—"thus was I, sleeping, by a brother's hand, / Of life, of crown, of queen, at once dispatched" (1.5.74–75): instantly and all at once, according to that historically (philologically) unprecedented use of the verb "dispatched" in passive form with the particle "of." The crown has not of course been plucked from the head of the corpse, nor the queen yanked from the cadaver's side. Instead, a grammar of cause and effect figures (rather than recounts) a threefold usurpation all in one ended breath. Syllepsis again intercedes between the ghost and machine, soul and embodied life, each spirited away in a different sense. You can't take one's possessions in the way you take one's life: the first is a true removal, an absconding; the second an eradication that maddens any question of spatial shift.

It should be clear, then, how syllepsis, split repeatedly as it is between mind and body, emotional and material dis/positions, often figurative and literal registers (even "flood of tears" is palely metaphoric), is frequently in context a quasi-metaphysical wordplay. Moreover, as a syntax of two minds at once, such troping returns choice itself to the manifest level of phrasing rather than holding it to an already assimilated precondition of the speech act. Syllepsis thereby renders each governing predicate the alternative to itself, open still to the paradigm not of morphology (the bifold verb is already spelled out) but of denotation. In Poe's story, the narrator's perverse impulse to self-destruction may send him to hell in a handbasket; but his own phrasing of his fate works to remind us—across the jolt of a traumatized grammar in "to the hangman and to hell"—that, however one strays from the path of righteousness, and despite whatever rhetorical efforts may be imposed by a forking-path grammar, one doesn't go to church and to heaven in the same mode of transit. Nor even to the devil and to damnation. Contemplating the inevitability of the scaffold, prose has its own trapdoor. The forking prepositions open a bottomless linguistic pit between the executioner's bodily presence and his pending effect.

And so, too, with the story's closure a moment later, once the blurted confession has warranted "the fullest judicial conviction" on the part of secular justice. Given that flickering play on "conviction" sliding between the connotation of *credence* (where "fullest" makes sense) and *verdict* (where it doesn't), the story shuts down by zeroing in—and out—on an almost pointless pun straddling a faint sylleptic divide between adjectival and adverbial complements in its last four words: "To-day I wear these chains, and am here! To-morrow I shall be fetterless!—but *where*?" ("Imp," 284). The pivot between sentences is initially hinged, via homophonic doubling, around a metaphysical shift from *wear* to(ward) *where*—as if the enchained body were the garb of the soul. What is suggested is that life comes to definition, on the brink of death, as containment itself: an emblem of self-enclosure, which dying decimates. Further, with its elliptical iteration of an intertextual "to be or not (to be)," the phrase "be fetterless, but [be] where" offers not just a pun on raiment and its mortal denuding, but actually a pun and a half.

Before our ears, following the tripled assonance of "fetterless," the elliptical verb of being returns as an impish new prefix of its own in the slide from "wear" through "where" to the final premonitory tremors of a mordantly overdue "(be)ware!" At which point the whole cautionary cast of the narrative—with its story of life lived under the shadow of so self-perverting an impulse that the guard of consciousness is lowered only at the self's certain peril—has been encysted and eviscerated at once. What surfaces there across a single elided verb of being is a broken sylleptic framework slung between two potential grammars: an existence described as manacled and an existence posited and placed by open-ended interrogation. The self is unshackled and loosed to oblivion at once. Yet again the intransigent voicing of one phonemic pattern operates in a sly friction with written sequence—an echo at play and at odds with the pat turn of normative script. For any sense of an anchoring ground in metaphysical voice, this erosive wording does a dismantling damage all the more obvious when poised on the verge of death's more absolute dissolution of the speaking source. No surprise (our previous chapter in mind) that it would take a transcendental parodist like Poe to both maximize and ravage the potential uplift of such a syllabic loop as that in Shelley's incremental visionary interrogation "can spring be / far (be/hind)?"

In Cavell's emphasis, language is the place where our fundamental ethical commitments are transacted; literature the place, as put forth in Emerson preeminently, of their sublimed demonstration in the transferences of rhetorical address. In Agamben's emphasis, more foundational yet, language is the place of our ethos itself, our habitus in the human, before any and all communicative use; literature the site that recognizes the insistence on this as its "end." In both contemporary philosophers, we *abide by language* without needing to prove that we reside there (let alone here, here apart from our words, where we assume we are). In Poe, however, the very ethos of language, including the chance of its ethical exchange, turns demoniacal. Undermining its own phrasal (to say nothing of confessional) contract with the reader, Poe's unwording of intentional impulse expels rather than expresses thought, fractures and deactivates its smallest units. Whether such imp-aired messaging is understood as blocking the ethical exchange or as demolishing the very ethos of human consciousness on which it rests, both Cavell and Agamben might agree that neither the macabre punning nor the flagrant irony in Poe can mask the specter of skepticism his writing jokes with. As Cavell's metalinguistic notations direct us to recognize when aligning Poe and Descartes, the dismembered lexeme and the psychotic short circuit are aggravated halves of the same crisis.

Dyslocution

Let us allow that one trauma for the narrator of "The Imp of the Perverse" is that his language gives him no legs to stand on, whether in confessional phrasing or at the trapdoor of the scaffold. Any Cartesian "I think" snaps at the "therefore," tripped up further by phonemic disruption, and as a result any secured sense of being goes begging for predication. No accident, following Cavell, that it should be a cluster of phonemes that operates in the lexical weave of Poe's irony as the countersyllabic, antisignifying pitfall. But anticipating the final fall into the pit, it is less accidental yet that the narrator would couch his fate in a split difference between capital and eternal punishment. Poe has used a passing syllepsis once before, as a clue to the homicide in the Rue Morgue. As Dupin reasons it out, in the most ratiocinative of syntax, no armed human robber would have been "so vacillating an idiot as to have abandoned his gold and his motive together" ("Murders," 160). Again: two senses of a definitive predicate, here abandonment split between physical and mental evacuation, just as consignment veers between bureaucratic execution and eternal damnation in "to the hangman and to hell."

Though the latter is not explored by Cavell, whether in the Cartesian terms of a body/soul split or otherwise, it is still important to note the relevant place of such bifold grammar in his thinking about ordinary language. Cavell might well have instanced syllepsis as a case in point for his theory of "projection" (rather than the more expected term "transposition") when in *The Claim of Reason*, building on Wittgenstein, he seeks to account for the figurative deflection of a word's original use within a newly permissible grammar of criteria.[21] For what Cavell calls "projecting a word" (180) from one context and its rules to another becomes only the more obvious in the push-pull of sylleptic double duty, where the retentive drag of one evaporating context operates on the protensive gesture of the next while it is still in the process of coming (clear). Cavell's roster of examples actually moves toward such a limit case. He reminds us how we learn, accept, and deploy with little trouble the already different *uses* (if not technical meanings) of "feed the kitty," "feed the lion," "feed the swans," each requiring different foodstuffs in transmission, until "one day"—in the evolutionary history of the language—"one of us says 'feed the meter', or 'feed in the film', or 'feed the machine', or 'feed his pride'," or—shifting from verb phrase to noun phrase—"'feed wire,' and we understand, we are not troubled" (181). Further instancing the "range of transfer or projection": such clauses as "'Put the cup on the saucer', 'Put your hands over your head', 'Put out the cat', 'Put on your best armor', 'Put on your best manner'"—that last a shift from literal to figurative, unspoken, that triggers the capping example from Shakespeare's *Othello*: "'Put out the light and then put out the light'" (181). Any number of such divergent combinations—or divisive convergences—are possible; syllepsis is one name for them. *Feed the meter before your face.* Or: *Put on your best makeup and a smile.* Or, in a sharper yank of idiom: *Put on an act and the world.*

When Poe's Cartesian balancing act finally runs aground—or topples into groundlessness—with the metagrammatical irony of "consigned me to the hangman and to hell" ("Imp," 284), the syntactic wrench is neither out of place nor likely to go unnoticed. For syllepsis is sprung there as a syntactic equivalent to the dozen or so false phonemic syllabifications that bedevil the narrator's discourse, like *imp/ulse* and *imp/ertinent*, with their deranging lexical moves. Word imps and misfit syntactic bucklings are in fact the two poles, lexical and grammatical, of that psychic dislodgment, as if by dyslocution itself, where the Cartesian ego is at two related scales of its own utterance tossed into free fall. Like sylleptic self-adjustments, those rippling phantom morphemes must ordinarily be overtaken in process by the larger trajectory of the word intended. Instead, here they are forcefully dissolved into it more than wholly resolved with or by it, and the residual hiccup they induce keeps Poe's language from first to last ill at ease, still a tease: exacerbated and unnerving.

In this regard, Cavell's demonstration invites comparison with Wittgenstein's sense that wording is always the suppression but also the evocation of alternatives, so that "the possible uses of a word are before our minds in half-tones as we say or hear it."[22] These halftones are tentatively harmonized in the minor chords of sylleptic dissonance, where, sounded together, they span an interval. And so a point of convergence with Jakobson again, and Agamben as well. Cavellian "projections," when submitted to the sort of local grammatical pressure entailed by syllepsis, are related to the spacing out in syntagmatic time of certain excessive returns of selection from the paradigmatic axis. Within the general language game, that is, Cavell's projections become a literary "move" when the angle of projection is narrow enough that they overlap each other—or, in Agamben's adopted terms, are deferred by grammatical enjambment across the caesural break as an abrupt syntactic hinge. Othello our example again, with his lethal claim of reason, and reasons, for just cause in the slaying of Desdemona. In "Put out the light, and then put out the light," one hears beneath the grotesque parallelism of asphyxiation the further stranglehold of syllepsis. To have given to Othello a contracted sylleptic utterance at this fatal moment would, of course, have lost the suggestion that what he is extinguishing in her is the very light of *his* life as well as hers, the light of the world at large not just the bedside taper. Yet the gulf that separates literal from figurative act is yawning there as well in even the crudest form: *snuff out her candle and her*.

But what else has syllepsis to suggest philosophically, besides its lampoon of Cartesian symmetry across the mind/body divide? What else in connection with the imp-eriled ground of ordinary language philosophy itself? Here we may well return to Agamben, who repeatedly theorizes the ontological equivalent of a predication that would sequester rather than forbid its alternatives. By his volume title, *The End of the Poem*, Agamben means, as we know, both poetry's closure and its telos as gesture, its finish and its goal, so that a chapter title like "The Dictation of Poetry" indicates not just the writing down of phrased ideas in verse but their origin in language itself, by which all such worded ideas seem inspired (as if "taken down")—or, put otherwise, from which they seem emerging not just *to* vocalization but *from* verbal potential itself, source of all poetic vocation, let alone everyday speech. In the two-way grammar of these entitling phrases, and perhaps most saliently in the chapter posing "the thought of the voice," philosophy and linguistics are found to cohabit, or at least abut, at their reciprocal limits. With such formulations being legible either according to the normal time of syntactic inscription or instead backward ("voice's thought," "dictation's poetry"), these genitive ambiguities maintain alternative options from within lone denominations: options all but simultaneously potentiated, hence present to each other—in, we may say, ordinary language—across a no-longer absolute Aristotelian divide of noncontradiction. Alternative grammar saturates the surface features of language not as what the phrasing might have meant instead (the typical conception of potential, always pluperfect and thus vanished in the actual, as Agamben explains), but as what, still in touch with the deep being of language as potential, speech also and otherwise does right now say, does make available to meaning.

It is thus that a linguistic vagrancy of determination keeps phrasing in touch with the field of possibilities from which it has momentarily been catalyzed, never rigidly crystallized. When the apparent arc of a phrasing collapses into something other and else, gives out in progress, regroups, what it opens upon in retrospect is the very possibility it inscribed to begin with. Reveling in the no longer excluded middle, such valences of suspended contradiction sustain the both/and against the coercion of the either/or. In a related vein have we seen, and this in distillation of Agamben's whole metalinguisitc approach to literary venture, that his philosophy is drawn to poetry—and especially in the moment of Dante's triumph in inventing the very idea of the vernacular—whenever poetry, major poetry, reaches down to the fact of language beneath the plurality of languages, whenever it finds the conditioning potential of speech still viable in given words.

In this very spirit, at the syntactic as well as lexical level, there is something Agambenesque about Poe's own twofold title in "The Imp of the Perverse," glimpsing in linguistic form both the imp that occasions perversity and the impishness that constitutes it. This genitive byplay is not unlike, for that matter, the anchoring phrase from the subtitle of Cavell's *The World Viewed: Reflections on the Ontology of Film*—since ontology, in common parlance, is both the condition of being and, more accurately, the science thereof. Implying objective and subjective genitive at once, film not only has an ontological status of its own; it *is* an ontology in respect to—or say, in view of—the world: its own successively framed view. Similarly, the prepositional hinge of a phrase like "the imp of the perverse" exceeds any sense of the imp as perversity's derivative or object by also lodging a so-called genitive metaphor (a matter of equivalence), with perversity refigured as in itself a demon sprite, a rogue impulse, the hellion that must come home to roost in the hero's final consignment to hell—with a further overtone of pluralized aberrancy in "the perverse," as in a phrase like "the whim of the mad." The reversibilities of such entitling grammar, just like the divided syntactic loyalties of syllepsis, keep the other alive on the flip side of the same.

Whether implicitly to be celebrated in terms borrowed from Agamben (by extrapolation from a linguistics of potential) or actively satirized in Cavell's Poe, there is an excess of virtual meaning that literature not only capitalizes on but reinvests at the level of language's own event. In this way meaning is suspended in a continuous eventuality, spinning out its possibilities in the never definitive form of the not quite (yet) said. In the voicings of silent lettering, every unpoliced "be where" harbors a "beware" hovering free of inscription as its own phonic undercurrent—and thus witnessing to the ongoing fact of language without lending it the testimony of a determinate form, without fixing it in a local habitation and a name. This, then, is not the where, exactly, but rather the wherefore by which *is* and *might*, the one and its other, may surface in the germination and churn of a given phrasing, whether in Poe's manic cauldron of aurality under inscription or in some other formative literary poetics.

A further genitive dualism, verging on genitive metaphor or equation, is in fact installed unnoted in another prose episode from the nineteenth century (besides the reading of Melville's "Bartleby") that Agamben again follows Deleuze in commenting on. This is the near death by drowning of a Dickensian villain, Rogue Riderhood, in Dickens's *Our Mutual Friend* (1871), who returns from *zoe* to *bios* (Agamben's terms)—or, in other words, from a state of sheer mortal "immanence" rather than self-presence (Deleuze's formulation).[23] With raw biology not yet subsumed to his familiar brutish psychology, the character is held in "abeyance" (the one Dickensian wording Agamben focuses on—as if it were a version of suspended "potential"). This condition persists until, with the guttering "spark of life" being fitfully restored (the spark that ignites life, the spark that is life), the body is recalled from nescience to "the consciousness of this existence"—or, in the reversible logic of this further duplex genitive, the existence again of just that consciousness presumed to define human life: pure possibility reanimated, negation stitched back into continuity, a contingent ontological suture resecured.

Putting it that last way is, of course, meant to hint at the place of filmic operations in Agamben's literary thinking as well as Cavell's—and in closer explicit connection, for the former, to his sense of literature as linguistic process. Though neither writer is drawn to the mechanics of suture in the calibrations of apparatus theory—Agamben preoccupied instead with the prenarrative minims of difference, Cavell with the already shaped space of character and performance—their separate philosophical vocabularies obliquely converge on the becoming-in-process of the screen image as sequential gesture. Each scale of attention depends on a constitutive difference within repetition—if along different axes: frame from frame, world from world viewed—submitted to investigation in the very work of projection.

"The Possibility of What Was"

As revealed at their lower limit of coherence by the cinematic experiments of Guy Debord, the "transcendentals" of film are for Agamben the founding ingredients of montage in (as he cryptically puts it) "repetition and stoppage"—or in other words, at the most material level, the iterative frame line and the cut, as well as the broader sense of an image revisited after fixity and storage, hewn from time for the purpose of review.[24] Here Agamben looks to the "four great thinkers of repetition in modernity"—namely, "Kierkegaard, Nietzsche, Heidegger, and Gilles Deleuze"—for none of whom is it "the same as such that returns" (330). Instead: "The force and the grace of repetition, the novelty it brings us, is its return as the possibility of what was" (331). Each iteration potentiates something previously unfulfilled by its predecessor in the series: a veritable definition of the filmic frame line, where "stoppage" is continuously overwritten and "repetitions" are incremental returns timed to a persistence of vision in just those motor and optical effects that fall beneath consideration in Cavell's film writing. And yet to which, with an accidentally related vocabulary, Cavell's sense of "projection" (discussed above) in the associated senses of ordinary language (say, feed the projector and the narrative need) can help direct attention at the granular level.

Rather than comparing the medium-deep disclosures of experimental cinema to "prose narrative" (331) like that of Poe's, Agamben turns to verse poetics, where for him cinema deserves understanding alongside "the caesura and the enjambment (that is, the carryover to a following line)," stressing in the process Valéry's "beautiful" definition of poetry as "a prolonged hesitation between sound and meaning" (331).[25] That's the hesitation we've called "deferral" and have watched Poe thematize as procrastination as well as circumlocution—at the same time that he toys with it at the lexical level in the "imps" that slow comprehension until they disappear into it. Further, this postponement has taken form not, in our examples, just as a homophonic hesitation or its near miss, as in the waver at *wear/where/ware*, but as a lexical hesitation about syntactic deployment—or, more in the mode of enjambment, as an elliptical run-on in the elision of be-ing from "be fetterless, but / . . . [be] where?" ("Imp," 284). So that one could bundle all the examples in this discussion—from the so-called phi effect (illusory motion from spatial displacement) of cinema's flickering differentials through the stop-start mechanisms of verse enjambment to the two-way vectors and split determinations of genitive grammar and syllepsis alike—under the heading of "protension/retention," where the inscribed potentiality of the other remakes the same from within.

Certainly, in the sounding of one word or phrase under reverb from its pertinent alternative, the question is what resonance is meant as the present possibility of the different. Same question at the sublexical level when latent word-sounds like Poe's put the imp back, fleetingly, in imprint. In any such hesitation over syllabic relevance, such undue prolongation of the normally subsumed, juncture is up for lateral grabs. The loosened caesural stress (what marks off a semantic unit from the phonemic stream—even if only in split-second retrospect) is what, in Agamben's formulation for the delaying tactics of verse form, "causes the word and the representation to appear as such" (331): that is, as material signal en route to the sign of a represented something. At the grammatical stratum as well, meaning is also protensive and recursive at once. In its linguistic wit and its internal *edge*, the sylleptic fracture is one clear touchstone of semantic deferral by verbal return, where alternatively available meanings must be sensed there already in the differences from which they are triggered. In syllepsis, potential is the very reflex of cognition. Focusing Agamben's sense of repetition around this one salient trope, we may put it this way: whether metrical or not, in prose as well as in poetry, when the second foot falls in syllepsis, its grammatical impress marks (this time unmistakably) "return as the possibility of what was" (331).

All of which confronts us once more, and finally, with an important way to think of Agamben joining Cavell in the overcoming of skepticism: that is, by Agamben's finding in absence (as potential) a genuine power—as in Deleuze, a power of the virtual. Doubt is overridden by undermining the paradigm of its own condition in the either/or. The true/false toggle is disengaged. Ontology is for Agamben the clear case of this. Though the human being can't name, in either sense of the predicate, *its being in language*—either the words for its being or the inherence of such being in those dormant words—existence is nevertheless sensed to depend at bottom on the unthought of voice: an always receding (though not demonstrably false) bottom. This might be otherwise to propose—in another flexed instance of ordinary language (Austin, Cavell), where the noun of "possibility" hovers between "condition" and "potential"—how it is that voice before language(s) locates the *possibility of being human*. Objective and subjective genitive again: the option of being and its operative manifestation as still and always (only) potential. Literature as linguistic fiction makes this phenomenon unavoidable in one sense, its worlds possible only, or plausible—never real. Major literature keeps this enactment of sheer potential from turning either obvious or complacent. And does so by actually connecting again, beneath language as style, beneath its referential and expressive function, with the paradox of a mere verbal latency retained in action. Such is a latency recovered not like a mythic source but like the continuous becoming, never finally materialized: the emergence, in short, of *what can be said to be.*

Philosophy and literary criticism keep strenuous company in the thinking of Agamben and Cavell. Exercising us (Cavell's therapeutic sense) in the facing down of skepticism, art (literary and film art alike) proffers, in the very absence of its represented objects, the continuous possibility of a world. In this sense of the word (as well as of the world) viewed, we are positioned again—following Agamben—at the shared vanishing point of linguistics and ontology. For, at just that nodal point, we find that the sine qua non of consciousness—namely, *the world's being brought to mind* (*-ing* predicate)—operates so that (again the somersault of ordinary language) its very *being* (*-ing* substantive) can be apprehended. As a linguistic condition of consciousness presumed and maximized in literary fiction, any bifocal sense of verbal phrasing—now alphabetic, now semantic; now lexical, now syntactic—doesn't prompt a dim view of meaning, just a stereoscopic and mobile one, or say, montaged and recursive, labile even if given no tongue.

The force of this can come through as much in parody as in rhapsody, by pun as well as epiphany. And is in no sense necessarily utopian. For as Cavell has us notice, Poe's neurasthenic prose, tapping its Cartesian intertext with imp-ish skepticism, makes the aggressive shorting out between letter and word, phrasing and syntax, throw in turn a hidden switch that brings bothersomely to light all the unnerving paranoia that is the flip side of any valorized potentiality in the work of words. Nonetheless, what Cavell gets so meticulously right about the crisis of the subject in Poe's counterlexical punning, the slipping away of the world even in one's own wording for it, can—when turned from philosophical parody to other modes of formal experiment—offer no longer just the disaster of the unmeant but the present possibility of the unthought, exploratory rather than foreclosing.[26]

The triggering crisis in Poe, first lexical sign of psychic derailment, is a crisis of locution, where *homo loquens* doesn't just mean what he says but says more and less than he means, his words tripped and ripped up by their own false syllables, those imps of disaster in the simplest efforts of ordinary language. This is a verbal crisis of just the sort noted in passing by Cavell's own mentor in ordinary language philosophy, J. L. Austin: adduced, that is, to point up its difference from Austin's more central emphasis on the illocutionary force of phrasing, or in other words on what an utterance implies, beyond its words, by being said. Cavell might have turned, that is, to the openly punning moment in Austin used to distinguish overt (sublexical) syllabic play from the more common (extralexical) category of illocutionary force. In a sidebar from *How to Do Things with Words*, punning is understood not as a case of language doing something in excess of its locutionary status, its mere saying (as when, at table, "Is there any salt?" actually means "May I have some?" and looks forward to the perlocutionary force of having it produced on this tacit request). There is a language-beyond-locution that is neither of these other things, ill- or per-: language saying two discrepant things at once in its own phrasing (or at least its own phonetic wording).

This mode of vocabular twofer is exemplified by the anomalous case of non-"ordinary" language use borrowed by Austin from a childhood joke—a self-incrimination put in the mouth of a punster's dupe and butt, forced to admit that "In saying 'Iced ink' I was uttering the noises 'I stink.'"[27] There's nothing of rigidity—nor of frigidity either—in the thawed ink of those initially imagined phonemes in the mouth of schoolyard banter. A noun phrase becomes a self-implicating clause in a way that Austin seems to think is neither strictly locutionary nor certainly illocutionary—but merely an accident of enunciation, verbal but not discursive, phonemic and even morphemic but not actualized by intentional design. Shades of shadow-phrasing in Poe. The model would be easy to activate there: "In saying 'impaired' I was (unconsciously, desubjectively) uttering the noises 'imp-aired' and/or 'imp-paired.'" Not both "sayings" interchangeably, let alone all three, but divergently—and despite their double and knowing puns on the aired valence of homophonic punning itself. Who could possibly mean, could "perform" as speech act, more than one such saying at once?

And rather than merely falling safely outside the category of locutionary or illocutionary phrasing, such a nagging contingency of language, under conditions of paranoia, may undermine—this is the general zone of Cavell's point—the very locutionary locus of identity itself as a speaking source. *Cogito ergo sum* only if "er gosum" means nothing in Latin. But sometimes a phrase like "his simple need" can slink over into its relinkage as "his imp'll need": such is the ontological risk in the imp-periled speech of Poe's narrative texture, its neurotic wordplay loosening the speaking subject's bond to locution itself—quite apart from the fatal perlocutionary force of a localized eventual confession and its gallows consequence. How to *undo* things with words, if only words themselves, is a lesson learned in Poe over the abyss of self-presence. And what ordinary language philosophy brings to such a diagnosis of schizoid ill-locution is exactly the philosophic measure of its extraordinariness, its aberrant antics: the dis-ease of its subjectivity all told, or say, with Agamben in mind, the upending potentialities of utterance that no intention can forestall. In particular, syllepsis (be in fetters but where? to the hangman and hell at once) writes out the mismatch of predication not as the illocutionary uptake of transmission but as a cleft in locution itself, a dislocation, a timed displacement: again, a dyslocution.

From Skepticism to Metaphor: Cavell's Postscript to Poe's Script

In the important last addendum to his essay on Poe, "Postscript C: The Skeptical and the Metaphorical," Cavell writes as if he were addressing (unspecified) the entire figural turn in deconstructive literary theory, admitting his "dissatisfaction with the identifications and theories of figurative language that I have come across" that treat metaphor "as if it held the key to language, to literariness, to the (destructive) ambitions of philosophy, etc." (147). We are back, tacitly, with those metalinguistic figures of poisoning, penning, and imprisonment floated by Cavell in introducing his thoughts on "The Imp." And it is to de Manian deconstruction, as well as an implicitly contending philosophy of metaphoric language in Donald Davidson, that we will need to return before proceeding to the full-scale chapter on syllepsis and its own version of the grammatization of metaphor.

For Cavell, skepticism about tropes in what we might characterize as their "turning from" the world needs to be seen as complementary to skepticism about the literal, about the existence of that world itself, in one's withdrawal from it. What Cavell calls "the unavoidability of both routes . . . (up to metaphor, down to skepticism)" (149) is what in fact humanizes them even in their "unnatural" relation to any relaxed acceptance of the mortal condition. On the one hand, metaphor lets us accept what is altogether not real (or not altogether real) in the subsidiary truth value of its individual criteria for existence, and hence brackets off belief from the pertinence of the "as if." On the other hand, skepticism prevents us from accepting as real what might (so the resistance goes) deserve only credence as virtual, as dubious and removed from us.

Now, one trope above all strains and tests this philosophical divergence. Classically divided between the figurative and the suddenly literal, as rarefied at times to a case of the spiritual (or psychological) versus the somatic, syllepsis ("honor" figuratively "stained" in almost the same breath, if not at all the same sense, as "brocade") is in this twinned regard the grammatical trope of tropes. As such, it attempts, one might say, the impossible resolution (or at least suspended antinomy) of metaphoric and literal. That's certainly one of the things (unnoted as such) that drew philosopher Gilbert Ryle to this grammatical figure, as we've seen, in his critique of Descartes. The idiomatic "flood of tears," with its sentimental hyperbole, comes crashing into the "sedan chair" that mercifully removes it from view: emotion and motion in two modes of being *swept away* at once. It does so because of the not (in fact) parallel prepositions ("in" a proverbial "state" versus "in" a material handcart) maneuvered to evoke at all but the same time—*transport* in two senses—the figure of an emotional upheaval and the fact of a physical device. By way of a madcap rhetorical allegory all its own, the metaphoric "vehicle" of overflow and emotional whelming turns thumpingly literal in the sheer vehicle of motion.

Trivial there in *Pickwick*, entirely loose and comic in its cleaving, syllepsis is nonetheless a true philosophical trial of the figurative in forced and unwelcome, or at times induced and elucidating, coincidence with the literal. In tracking "The Imp of the Perverse" through to its lethal climax, I spoke of the narrator's preordained damnation—localized in the second fork of "to the hangman and to hell"—as a "catachresis." I meant to evoke there, in that metaphysical term "hell," the full de Manian sense of the muted figuration unbacked by fact, a referentiality without received and accepted literality (like, for instance, the "face" of a mountain, or for that matter the "imp" of perversity).[28] For, in Poe's story, "hell" is of course an ideologically loaded eternity figured spatially in a word with no real-world designation: a sheer troping of the intolerable, the unredeemed. In being snuffed out, life still flares up as potential existence in the key of the negative. In "to the hangman and to hell," that is, nescience is rendered via a prescient figuration around the empty center of a logical disjoin beneath the syntactic coupling. In this "metaphoric" (or catachrestic) effect to the executioner's literal cause, one might say that grammar has itself been rendered figurative: effecting the mere likeness (or simile) of a correlation within a staging of the incommensurable.

Drawing Cavell's Poe once again into the orbit of Agamben's philosophical linguistics, we can call out syllepsis as one name for the yoking of incompatibles that realizes the definitive limits of each in the potential emergence of the other. In a single "pregnant" wording (Poe again), and to speak sylleptically of the trope's own work, the figure of forking paths delivers over its increments (a) to each other, (b) confusion, and (c) a new lease on life. This is the deviant vitality generated by a lowest common denominator in search of a tertium quid, a search ever and inherently deferred. Staged by this trope, then, in the last (because never final) analysis, is a dialectical irresolution that settles for half measures—but halves that are still paradoxically greater than either's remainder when subtracted from the sum of part and counterpart. Linguistically speaking, that's philosophy for you. For even if the call of "first philosophy," according to Agamben, is "exhausted" in accounting for the fact of language, its discharge of that obligation may well energize our understanding of specific language acts. Yet that remains a fairly weak version of the present book's assumptions and its claims. Put the stronger case this way, as no one shows better than Cavell: that literary reading can be criticism's means to philosophy's end.

But this brings us round to cinema once more—cinema as Cavell sees it, and as he values its "realism" (the "world viewed") in relation to skepticism, as contrasted with the materialist avant-garde to whose rudimentary terms Agamben seems attracted in part for their tacit literary parallels. At moments of metaphor we stand back and slightly askew, but only across the clarifying gap of refiguration. In film viewing, according to Cavell, the world is held off as well, but only at the distance of recognition. That's *the way* the world seems to me. That's *how* I see it. That's what it's *like* when I can rise to its occasion and take it in. It is only a confirming further step to fill in that "like" with actual metaphors. When, for instance, in an example of mine rather than Cavell's, Peter O'Toole says, in allusion to the Qu'ran, that "the desert is an ocean in which no oar is dipped," he has accepted, you too no doubt, the undulating visual rhythms of David Lean's landscapes in the 1962 *Lawrence of Arabia.* One stratum up, from dialogue to diegesis, a movie can have the look of a world to me, even if I can't verify the existence of its prototype, geographical or otherwise, present or past—or future. Aside from any proof of the world, though, such supplemental figures (like shifting sands as sea waves) bear with them the criteria that would count in constituting such a world. Here again is a cued therapy for skepticism. By accepting these criteria in their suspension as metaphor (or fiction), in the absence of a postulated reality, I can understand better perhaps why I accept, or sometimes don't, their appearance elsewhere (both modalities of appearance: manifestation per se and its aspects) at face value, as prima facie evidence of the real. Once more in Cavell, art is the training ground of nonestrangement.

Metaphors for Cavell are the obverse of skepticism not just because as figures of speech they succeed only if you don't credit the presence of what they posit, thus putting on hold the issue of belief. True, one thing can be like another without either of them existing except hypothetically in the present. But beyond this, for Cavell metaphor is cousin to skepticism because each, in its "unnaturalness," diverges from the everyday: skepticism to "repudiate" all faith in it, and in language's access to it, figuration to "transcend" it, momentarily, provisionally—as a way of coming (back) to know it. The denaturing movement is, again, either "up to metaphor" or "down to skepticism" (149): language opening up or bottoming out in its relation to the world. Though Cavell doesn't put it this way, a trope can in fact offer a *turning toward* some summoned aspect of the real, skepticism a turning *away* in both senses: standing aloof from the world, turning it from you. If metaphor, in Cavell's adjectival contrast, is a "personal" inflection of the world, skepticism is a "private" deflection of it (Cavell's cited dichotomy; 148). In "A Tale of the Ragged Mountains," Bedlo as Oldeb, five letters each, is a metaphor gone haywire—to say nothing, in Emerson's misnomered terms (as we saw), of a post-"Alexandrian" phonemic nucleus ("acrostic" for "anagram") unhinged by its own pivoting and thus offering a parody of skepticism at the linguistic level to boot. They are so like each other—these reversible quintets of alphabetic signification, these so-called identities—that analogy collapses back into existential absurdity.

In its far-fetched way, the absurdity is of a peculiarly Emersonian sort, given the act of memorial transcription around which the fantasy plot turns (upon itself). You will know me by the work of writing, and I you in your labors of reading me, even at a pageless distance; for if you recognize something of your own rejected thoughts in the majesty of mine, this is because I've known you as my assigned and destined receptacle from the first—and you yourself in me. According to Cavell, that's not far afield from Emerson's vaunted troping of cognition as interpersonal knowledge. But if your act in reading of me long after my death, as in Poe's "A Tale of the Ragged Mountains," reading not even my own words but those of my survivor and diagnostician, is a process by which you come to discover that you simply *are* me, then the founding rift of difference—whose bridging overarches the abyss of skepticism and sparks recognition—has withered, beyond intimacy, beyond human analogy itself, to an impossible equivalence. If you have to believe yourself me to believe in words about me, then you have set too high a standard for understanding: you have cemented your skepticism after all. If I am the other, epistemological anxieties are short-circuited not in acknowledgment and empathy but in febrile identity. The problem of other minds is reduced to the gargoyles of a doppelgänger plot.

In "A Tale," that's exactly the crisis for the hero as reader manqué, remote-controlled by textual telepathy.[29] If our reading stops short of that in its thrills, that total evacuation of presence, as it had better, it still recognizes itself refigured by these metaphysical contortions. Just as with the poison reading candle in "The Imp," the lethal bloodletting derived from textual signification at one remove in "A Tale" finds in death a metaphor for the self-surrender of reading without having to forfeit the pleasure (our present pleasure) in the process. That isn't the way *we* read, exactly, thank goodness. But in some respects, according to some criteria of transferred subjectivity, it's not *unlike it.* Only an interpretive fascination can be counted on to put the brakes on abject submission to the mirage of our "rejected" thoughts. In "A Tale," given the "word imps" that constitute those alter egos as anagrams, all self-certainty vanishes in the groundless alphabetic shuffle. But in reading "A Tale," we are in on the joke, the metaphysical "gag," if not from the first, then at least finally—and from the alphabetic ground up. The "unnatural" meta-phor or trans-fer (Oldeb=Bedlo) is embedded for us in a not quite schizoid reading; rather, it occurs by way of an immersion that practices the antiskeptical in a familiar generic form, here pitched to the limit, of suspended disbelief.

It is all but inevitable that film fantasies revel in such double figures and alter ego plots, for film is, in its technological constitution, a spectral doubling of self by its image. It is other things too, as we've seen, that lie at the crux of film art's unique cathartic charge in Cavell. So I return to the paradoxically faithful skepticism of aesthetic response, in theater seating again as well as under reading lamp: those respective clearinghouses of fictive effects delimited by the two spheres of Cavell's interest—but never closely compared by him. Never, at least, in the way I've been trying to suggest (via Agamben) here: marking an explicit overlap between reading and world-viewing as activities heuristic and antiskeptical not just in their general representational thrall but *all the way down*, tapping the very baseline of mediation. There, in a conceptual zone of common mediality, alphabetic signifiers and backlit photograms are alike catalyzed in action, precipitants (again "molecules" and "moles") that disappear into the literal chain reactions they instigate and sustain.

In standard viewing practice, of course, the scopic drive is at odds with the skeptical. So, too, with the semantic libido in reading practice, even when engaging the intensive *textuality* of much literary art. Like screen projection, language, too, is ordinary enough, so Cavell might put it, to be ordained for mostly passive use. Trust (if that's the word) in both medial forms, at least the unique conviction they carry for us as art, is won by us at some level through the eviction, mostly automatic, of any deep-seated "doubt" as to their material accretions into image or word. One overlooks film per se, its serial frames, in the projected view; one overlooks the alphabetic phases of a phrasing in its captured scene. Overlooks: that is, holds off any finer-grained focus even within the scope of reasonable scrutiny and involvement. And the comparable operations to be found implied across media by unexplored possibilities in Cavell's own claims? To bring together the Emersonian ambit of Poe's sabotage—his mockery of the kind of transferential readings the calculated thrills of his own prose exploit—with the skeptical corrective of film viewing in Cavell's investigations, one could say at least this: that in my reading of Emerson, my reading *in* Emerson, those thoughts come to me as not quite mine, but almost, whereas in my reading of Poe, those paranoias are my own for a while, or if not quite, then all the better for me. I am only reading, whereas Poe's narrator is overreading the world around him, as it both closes in on him in mental asphyxiation and withdraws from all affective credence. In any case, Emerson's words, Poe's equally, emerge in me *utterly*. They are my thoughts renewed (if and because I understand them), yes, but only in their words. Similarly, from my seat in the movie theater, a world virtually *occurs to me*.

But only as cinema, not as film. So, too, I repeat, in normal reading: only as literature rather than combinatory letters. There is no denying the frequency of this denial, if that's what we need to call it. But if art offers an apprenticeship in such overlooking, such practiced trust, such exercised "conviction"—in Cavell's further Thoreauvian terms such "sentencing" ("Being Odd," 118) from the "pen" of another; or, at the movies, such accepted constraints by the "frame" of a world on view—then this antiskeptical calisthenics may seem almost explicit at times. Art, on occasion, can provide an inbuilt measure of our achievement in just such a committed response. For in representational art one is moved to appreciate our normal discountenancing of a material base in being led now and then, by contrast, to *undergo* what one otherwise so automatically *overlooks* or *overcomes*. Unlike routine uses of its medium in the everyday, art can instill a double vision. It can *display* its own simultaneous alternatives in the making and the made. So that film and writing, frame line and morphology, in causal relation to the effects of cinema and print, or say, to the seen and the said, are the insistent *otherwise* of the fashioned representation, its underbeat and its intermittent undoing.

In summoning our functional belief in its fictive worlds, the work of representation, though smoothly preaching to the choir for the most part, can't stop reaching out at other times, under self-inflicted duress, to the continually re-converted. As a general rule, the intermittent signaling emitted by the medium is forgotten in the sign. You don't really see film, you watch movies. You don't really read letters in the work of words, you read with them, in every sense through them. The norm can be thought of, by contrast, in terms of what early film technique used to call, and strive for, as flicker fusion—achieved to bridge gaps between serial flashes of manifestation. The linguistic analogue: reading the word "imp" with no time, no eye, for the negative "im"; reading the word "impossible" with no ear for "imp." If so, business as usual. If not, then, under strategic aesthetic pressures like the jammed frame advance or the retarding manic prefix, the presented world of each medium quite literally disintegrates, splinters momentarily into slits of moving image or flecks of word formation. If and when this rending afflicts a given narrative rendering, we must often soldier—and solder—on, work our way back into continuity, reseam the fiction, accept the suture. Here lies the ethic, rather than the bad faith, of keeping up appearances, "saving the phenomena," as philosophers used to say—on behalf not of ourselves but of our perceptions. And, varying Emerson, it is by this work that *the* work will know our acknowledgment, know recognition in and as the force of *its* accomplishment.

Like the subject in Emerson, the medium, too, can in these and other ways insist on itself. For it is sometimes the case that art's medium may be sensed as maintained within the still *present potential* of its own overruled alternatives. To extrapolate yet again from Poe's extreme literary instance, the transgressive force of the imp-licit would in such cases appear virtualized—by either script or filmic inscription—as present even in "rejection" (Emerson one last and slightly different time). The fragmentary power behind the thrown image, visual or verbal, would disclose in this way the forever alien reign of the other within the same. This is because phonemes as well as photograms know their own screening (out) in process, their own absence from representational manifestation. Varying Cavell's first book title in the field of film, this chapter—against the normal vanishing current of writing as it passes into meaning, let alone of voice into speech—has been a counterintuitive exercise in the *word* (rather than the *world*) *viewed*. Syllable by lapsed syllable, this is the word eyed in writing rather than merely used up in meaning, where the tricks such limpid glimpses can play on you may be as philosophical as they are contingent—because where, varying Wordsworth, the life of things we see into can be the very possibility of linguistic forms. Underlying the last four chapters, and couched again in the double grammar so often entailed in these effects, this is the very possibility of (and that) *speech sounds* in words.

Metaphor as Philosopheme

So let us tie Cavell's remarks on metaphor (developed in the "appendix" to an essay in part on Poe's latent philosophizing in language) back to an actual metaphor already quoted (but not identified) in Poe's own work, emerging under syntactic pressure (that of syllepsis) in exactly the mock-metaphysical vein detected by Cavell in Poe's syllabic play. And then tie this to discussions of metaphor, quite different from Cavell's, in analytic philosophy. As we know, Cavell's account of metaphor has skepticism in mind and a bone to pick. The touted epistemological impasse of all language, its inherently dubious (because never better than metaphoric or approximate) relation to the world, is just the vein of deconstruction that Cavell means to resist. For Paul de Man, ordinary language, always suspiciously tropological at base, defers the signified forever, re*figures* experience, turns semiotics to rhetoric. This was the going line, and the still coming thing, when Cavell wrote on Poe, just as it was when Agamben posed his own subsequent resistance to such linguistic "negativity." On de Man's showing, literature helps expose the figurality of even standard discourse, its relation to the real determined only by way of catachresis: that figuring of things for which there is nothing more literal to be said. In that essay (uncited by Cavell) called "The Epistemology of Metaphor," de Man sums up, in negative terms, what would otherwise be a warrant for the present book: "All philosophy is condemned, to the extent that it is dependent upon figuration, to be literary and, as the depository of this very problem, all literature is to some extent philosophical" (28). One recalls here, as if in an implicit and cryptic rejoinder—and from, quite fortuitously, the same year—the famous last sentence of Cavell's *The Claim of Reason*: "But can philosophy become literature and still know itself?"[30] This questionable point of speculative disciplinary overlap is exactly where syllepsis can begin refocusing the issue through its binocular lenses. It does so in keeping designation itself, not just reference, in play, grasped in the act of making meaning rather than exposed as failing to catch the world in its epistemological net.

In the Poe essay, Cavell means in passing to avert the widespread interdisciplinary assumptions of de Man's influence, doing so without joining the more stringently philosophical debates over metaphoric signification also sampled, along with de Man's position paper, in the landmark 1979 volume *On Metaphor*. The redoubtable vehicle/tenor distinction of I. A. Richards, denied by Donald Davidson in that volume, is replaced in his analytic account by a literality open only to understanding, not decoding or translation.[31] And to the extent that it is "interactive," requiring of the reader or hearer an overcoming of its non-sense by the sensory perception it nonetheless evokes, Davidson's analysis may sit well enough alongside Cavell's sense of metaphor as overcoming skepticism as if from within. Metaphor for Davidson—as distinguished from similes and from puns—does not generate two meanings in tandem or in lamination, but only one thing said literally and meant otherwise, but not decodably meant, just inferentially, interpretively: generating not a second or covert denotation but, we might say, a force field of connotation, whose uptake in reading is thus entirely a matter of suggestion rather than proposition.

So central is metaphor to human communication that Paul Ricoeur's syncretic philosophy of language elevates it to the linchpin of linguistic formation in the subtitle to *The Rule of Metaphor: The Creation of Meaning in Language*.[32] As for Emerson, metaphor is one way in which to *grasp* the work of language at large (that verb itself, in Ricoeur's terms, a first-order metaphor not yet veering aside into trope, or in other words a catachresis [71]) Ricoeur's premise in that book is entirely compatible with our ongoing emphasis on reading as a deed, a consensual interaction. In his implicit attempt to see metaphor as a transitional feature between semiotics and semantics, Ricoeur follows Benveniste's sense that discourse is an "event"—whose "instances" (80) are more than examples, but instead variable instants in time. The lexical naming undertaken by discourse is organized into meaning only when the process of signification (semiosis) is turned over to the further relation (over syntactic and interpretive time) between sense-making and reference (semantics)—a trans-ference (in the etymological sense) never more apparent than in the task of meta-phoric displacement. Escaping the binary of rhetoric versus epistemology as well, what a metaphor signifies in its literal designation can only be determined (Ricoeur here following Max Black [96–100]) by the interaction of "focus" and "frame," usage and context. By just this "interaction," what the figurative vehicle *indicates* as wording, what it offers as the immediate sense of its point-by-point signification, is put in play with what it might actually *mean*: the true route of its deviance, the semantic charge behind its antic signifier.

To the extent that Ricoeur is using metaphor to introduce a distinction more exact than between "cognitive" and "emotive" language, he would also seem to resist the open-ended nature of metaphoric communication in Davidson (unmentioned). Much debated in the analytic philosophy of language (including by Black's rejoinder in the *On Metaphor* volume), Davidson's intended corrective to everyone from Aristotle to William Empson, with its emphasis on deviant literality rather than actual double signification, helps nonetheless to inform the explicitly duplex structure of syllepsis. If metaphor is a thing said literally in a deviant context, syllepsis is two things said idiomatically (less or more metaphorically) in a deviant (because not immediately compatible) sequence. There is no secret shared meaning predicated twice over beneath the divergent phrasing. In this respect syllepsis is like metaphor, where any third term is a matter of speculative interpretation rather than intrinsic designation: hence very much an instance of discourse, an event—or, in other words, a timed semantics versus a sheer linkage of signifiers.

If metaphors are not to be deciphered, but thought, the terms of syllepsis are not to be correlated, or just met with in sequence, but in the other (the contractual) sense met—and on their own self-diverted terms. Poe again: gold thrown over along with motive, the abandonment of loot and greed at once. Were this actually the symptom of human rather than animal violence, the "idiocy" would verge on psychotic break—as at times does the syntactic trope tilt toward cognitive dissonance. Even when both halves of a sylleptic drift (as is rarely the case) are metaphoric—as in, say, "he donned a smile and the mantle of humility"—the dyadic yoke doesn't make for a case of two vehicles, one tenor. The vehicular gambit is the trans-position itself between the two usages, with any tenor stretched tenuously across them, unspoken—not encrypted, only inscribed relationally.

In any such tension of syntax with lexical sense, it is fair to say that, as regards the terms of syllepsis, meaning comes between them, if at all. Lateral "interaction" is a credible name for this too, rather than some inferred alternate indication. Yet again a sense of what is foundationally at play in wordplay, latent, potential, will point us toward Agamben once further evidence is called in. If literature is read so that it is understood to talk language itself, rather than just speak sentences, or say, to keep signifying at work within unstable semantic spans, it thereby teaches not only its own possibility but, more generally, the cognitive force of phrasing in human perception—and hence in human representation. Strained phrasing is often best at raising to view the most philosophical of linguistic questions. Where, for instance, is meaning made? In one minor but epitomizing literary register, that of syllepsis, only time can tell: the time of syntax and its delayed fuses.

Cavell has shown us, in effect, how a formative poetics of expressive language is manifested by deformation in Poe. What Kittler (in our previous chapter) notes as the banned apprehension of letters and word blocks in the classical philology that preceded Poe's fractured Romanticism, the "forbidden" realm of alphabetic structuration, is what we've seen Cavell identify as the sine qua non of ordinary language: that "most familiar thing about language there could be"—until it returns in distortion from the repressed depths of groundless consciousness itself in Poe narrative's voicings, returns to besot and unseat all meaning. At least potentially. What this chapter has needed to bring forward, in light of Agamben as well as Cavell and Kittler, is that in this risked negative potential one glimpses the formative chances—and changes—of articulation all told. And what is rendered suddenly un-"familiar" at the level of the faux imp syllable in Poe finds a syntactic equivalent of this morphemic distortion in the cognitive gamble of syllepsis, always teetering on the verge of the ungrammatical. Yet this is just why syllepsis, as we will continue to find with its rampant manifestation in Dickens and the Victorian and modern writers in his wake—especially in its typical pivot between literal and figural—can seem to bespeak, by the logical hazards of its syntactic brinkmanship, the deep and formative contingencies that alone make possible the language at large that runs such giddy risks.

5
SPLITTING THE DIFFERENCE

A vocabular conundrum can, I hope, be readily cleared away. "You say eether and I say eyethere." I said zeugma and now say syllepsis. Knee there, nigh there: it's only the difference internal, not terminological, that matters. The Gershwins' lyric to "Let's Call the Whole Thing Off" also speaks quite accidentally, in the lead-in of its often unsung verse, not just to the matter of variant lexical usage but to the particular concerns of this chapter with grammatical compounding in the accusative case: "You like this and the other / While I go for this and that." Imagine, with either verb, an "other" so ill sorted with its "this" that the predicate would be strained beyond immediate recognition—and all the more in the Gershwin spirit if "while" in their lyric is taken to suggest a jarring simultaneity as well as the "whereas" of asymmetry. In the evidence ahead, the transitive act of leashing a given "this" with the (discrepant) otherness of an off-kilter "that" is precisely the vernacular mismatch between one thing and its syntactic counterpart that defines the choppy terrain we are to tread—where we may indeed want to call something "off" in the very logic of the collocation. For these are the moments when, within an established predication, the whole linguistic thing may seem called off just a moment after it has been functionally called up.

Such, then, are the tiny surprises now coming under investigation with further literary examples—regardless of whether you go for the term *zeugma*, on which many of us cut our teeth in anthology footnotes to the reading of Pope and the Augustans, or, alternately, for the more extended sense of this phrasal and structural trope in which we've been subsequently schooled by the usages of contemporary French theory. It is there that *syllepsis* is used to cover an entire array of split associations from lexicon and syntax (Derrida) to the organizing alteration of plot vectors in fictional structure (Genette), from pun to narrative counterpoint, not to mention being singled out in its doubleness as the very essence of literary (inter)textuality (Riffaterre). It therefore suits the evidence of this chapter, in connection with narrative patterns writ small, to opt for this broader spectrum of association in attending to such phrasings as an imagined love lyric like "I go for you and to pieces." Or, of course, that actual Dickensian disjoin between poor Miss Bolo in transit and a fit.[1] And from the very precincts of French theoretical prose, let me give the latest example that has crossed the path of my twin-beam headlights on the way to press. It comes from the first English translation (2014) of Jean Epstein's fourth book on cinema (1946), called *L'intelligence d'une machine*. What is meant by the title is the intrinsic cinematographic genius untapped by a popular narrative fare found "vulgarizing theater" with a "spectacle accessible to the pocket books and minds of the largest international audience," where the literal "access" a spectator affordably gains to the auditorium is not the same as the availability of comprehension pandered to—and yet (such is the force of the figure) where the second sense of "access" stands inextricably cheapened by the former.[2]

Effects of that sort (and those to come) are not technically disallowed by the constraints of grammar, as is the case, by contrast, in the final *OED* example of syllepsis from an 1882 commentary: "By the figure of speech called zeugma, or rather syllepsis, . . . [a] verb is often used with two clauses which is only appropriate to one of them, as in Pope's line—'See Pan with flocks, with fruits Pomona crowned.'"[3] As opposed to the tight witty harnessing of "sometimes counsel take, and sometimes tea," with each sense of the verb being separately fitting despite the crisp misfit of their shared syntactic "yoke" (the Greek root of *zeugma*), this other inverted line from Pope executes an apparent faulty parallelism (or sylleptic "taking together") tripped up by its own chiasmus. When "crowned" derails expectation in its delayed loop with the bracketing verb "See," the horizontal aspect of Pan amid his herd suddenly battles the vertical headdress of his counterpart in a quite different sense of "with" (as part of a phrasal verb rather than an independent preposition). Such crowning touches are the usual comic point.

Without verging on grammatical default in this obvious and strained way, syllepsis will be tracked in the waiting examples for the phrasal fault lines it exposes only to exploit and finesse. Reading is at once tutored and tested by such moments. Surely it is no accident that, in Margaret Atwood's "Ten Rules for Writers" (from *The Guardian*, Feb 19, 2010), part of her tutelary wisdom concerning the production end of literature is distilled in this run of metagrammar and its reflex of lexical alternatives: "You most likely need a thesaurus, a rudimentary grammar book, and a grip on reality"—a grip only tightened, rather than gone slack, in such a grasped twist of grammar. So that you also need a reader up on her syntax and her toes together—waiting, with keen attention, for any phrasing with productive discrepancy crowned.

It could hardly seem unduly sweeping to claim of this book that it arcs between micro and macro—if the space covered is understood to be ranged between a mere two words (minimum for cross-lexical drift: A/B abruptly blurred) and four (minimum for sylleptic shift: verb + A + and + B). Nor too grandiose to call its attentions liberating—if what is released is only one word from its own borders or one predication from a single sense. And these are indeed the poles between which we have been working so far. At each, language is caught in a kind of time-lapse registration (in the latch and detachment between words) that feels all but simultaneous. At which impacted moments it would seem that a theory, even a philosophy, of language in action is not just called for but almost installed by the very possibility of such reading—in respect not only to these isolated cases but to the deep linguistic conditions they reach back to and motivate for notice.

It is mostly the latter, or "macro," effect, syllepsis, that has actually been met in print by philosophical comment. From the analytic philosophy of mind (Gilbert Ryle in the preceding chapter) through the antimetaphysical philosophy of deconstruction (Jacques Derrida soon here), this one particular phrasal format—with its grammatical trope a "turning" that commands syntactic even before metaphoric attention, linguistic before strictly figural—makes a striking if marginal appearance in this philosophically oriented literature on language as well as its intermittent mark on literature itself. Syllepsis in *Hamlet*, its near miss in *Othello*, its modulations in Poe, its flashpoint in Dickens for a philosophy of mind: these we have seen. And their continued farcical variants, in the Dickensian vein, may find literary language growing no less philosophical about itself. The comic come-again of syllepsis is not just the retrofitting of a grammatical object to a newly potential predicate. It can seem at times a reverse engineering of the entire syntactic paradigm it forces us to retraverse, taking an entire linguistic possibility as its formative undertext. The peculiar necessity of close reading that this trope compels—skim and you're tripped up; honor the speed bump and your reading becomes immediately and profitably more self-conscious—makes syllepsis a uniquely fruitful limit case. You're reading more closely than you may have thought just in making sense of it. And (the further point of this chapter) reading more deeply too—into the cogs of linguistic operation in their very turning of phrase.

In inventing the Victorian novel with *The Pickwick Papers* (1836), Dickens—trailing clouds of Augustan wit as filtered (and aerated) through eighteenth-century comic fiction—has his inebriated hero, risen to the heights of attempted rhetoric in an impromptu speech, fall "simultaneously" into a wheelbarrow and sound asleep—as if to say passing at once from public view and out. Not into one and into the other, but "into the barrow, and fast asleep" at one and the same time, without prepositional or mental distinction. Syllepsis at work once more: that figure of speech in which, typically, a predicate is understood in two different senses with separate objects, whether indirect or direct. In Pope again, well before Dickens, the tea that you take when not taking counsel can stain your new brocade if not your honor. With the hero punch drunk on punch, the figurative sense of dropping into oblivion ("fall" as topple yielding place to "fall" understood within a topography of consciousness) is compounded by a further sly inference that the wheelbarrow is the perfect receptacle for such a temporarily drunken sod. When phrasing gets ahead of itself, there's no stopping it.

Syntactically, the twinned temporal prongs of the sylleptic effect are not "simultaneous" exactly, as Dickens would have it here in passing—the opposite meanings not coinciding "at once," the grammar never at one with itself. Beyond any mere doubleness of literary ambiguity, syllepsis requires the syntactic comeback, so to say, as an often ironic comeuppance. Certainly, in its narrow miss of grammatical nonsense, syllepsis tends in the main to be lightly comic. Its almost punning tendency results from the fact that such a rhetorical turn works only if it is discernible enough to catch hold, and be caught, in a tactical double-take. And what is turned up by this twist of phrasing is always, as we saw via Agamben in the previous chapter, "the return of the possibility of what was": a latency recalibrated for its suddenly actuated potential.

Fully activated—and unmistakable. Granted, there is no hard internal proof, either of intention or registration, for many of the phonetic drifts of acoustic speculation in the earlier chapters, no guarantee even for the relevance (or imp/pertinence) of the "imps" in Poe. One might (Cavell or I) simply be hearing things, as the saying goes—even while these are in fact the things called letters, each with its variable phonic charge. In contrast, this chapter is devoted to constructions that are indisputable as staged syntactic effects, debatable (perhaps) only in their narrative or thematic function. Indeed, it is the anchoring coherence of grammar in underwriting their logical discrepancies—the indisputable infrastructure of their surface truce, or farce—that opens the sylleptic format to immediate interpretation, whether minimal in progress or more lingering in grip.

No need to enter the debate about which term best applies to the negative case of faulty grammatical bonding, zeugma or syllepsis, since either term calls up the other, and both a comparable syntactic split.[4] Note the grammatical default right there—where the elliptical second verb in that last clause of mine would need legally to be plural, not singular ("call up"). Such a formulation may *mean* but doesn't technically *work*. Or think of a slogan like "Wage peace not war," whose sense survives the false parallelism without a true idiomatic warrant. Even in its licit grammatical forms, however, we may think of what I'll be calling syllepsis from here out as a type of bivalence without ambiguity, clarified in the end, but only by phrasal self-adjustment. Clarified, but not entirely resolved in the event of reading, with the rhetorical tension of its cleft reference never quite dissipated. When it *splits the difference* between phrasal assumptions, syllepsis leaves behind the compromise implied in our everyday use of that vernacular phrase. Each sense works better separately than the two (do/work) together. It is the general nature and extent of such syntactic tension, and the local complacencies it often stretches out of shape, that lends unique interest to this phrasal anomaly—even (and in fact especially) when it is held, as almost always in its literary effects, to orthodox standards of compliance in the chain of case and number.

All told, a broad terminological resonance accompanies my bunching together of these umbrella-like folds of syntax under the cover term *syllepsis*:

considerations at once of etymology, of a certain touchstone moment in deconstructive literary theory, and of a rather exacting narratological extrapolation from such a rhetorical vocabulary. First off, derived from the Greek prefix "with" (*syn/l*), the taking "with" or "together" of phonemes or graphemes into those sublexical units known as *syl-lables* is not just related to, but almost a scale model of, the taking together (same etymological root in "*lepsis* from *lambánein*, to take") that results—one level up from diction—in syntactical compounds whose grammatical spread must be sorted out and rebundled on the run. Moreover, in holding to the scalar reverb of this term, discussion also responds to a *locus classicus* in the contemporary philosophy of literary signage. One can see why Derrida recruited the idea of syllepsis, albeit loosely (in the more generalized usage, from French rhetoric, of a mere play on words) as a case in point for the "disseminated" signifier.[5] He uses the rhetorical term to describe Mallarmé's phrase "hymen entre": indicating both marriage and its prevention by maidenhead, ceremony versus the membrane it must overcome before turning it to a symbolic veil, at once consummated embrace and its barrier. Two polysemous lexemes are themselves wedded under syntactic duress—producing, as it were, the deconstruction of syntax by diction and vice versa. And then, in an application to which we will later return, there is Gérard Genette's use of the term *syllepsis*—one stratum further up from syntax—to describe a kind of parallel montage in narrative pacing rather than the torqued parallelism of a grammatical sequence, where the "taking-together" of its etymological sense can include whole independent armatures of plot.[6]

In traditional grammatical syllepsis, by homology with this organizing narrative arc, a good measure of its significance resides, without quite resting, in the discordant fact that correlated meanings of the same phrase don't quite fit flush in a conterminous grammar. What we read is the activity of designation in process—that, rather than its cumulative results: the signifier kept in syntactic motion on the track and trace of its divided sign function. Rather than a Janus-faced pun, syllepsis is a forking in syntax's s/pace itself. Here is narrative temporality writ out and small, its signifying force not derived from content alone but from the drive of verbal formation. What Derrida never quite says about his favored example of so-called syllepsis in *hymen entre*—as the folding or "invagination" (his recurrent term) of reference back upon itself—is that it amounts to an erotic parable of its own collocation, its linguistic seal and breach at once.

I take Derrida's example of phrasal compaction, further, as an allegory of grammatical syllepsis as well, where the double tuck is construed as a forced reentry into the syntactic chain. Yes, diction deconstructs syntax and vice versa when Mallarmé's *hymen entre* means at once the marriage, and the hindrance, between. With the hinging conjunction of grammatical rather than lexical syllepsis, however, as in a sentence like "She was given to snacking between husbands and meals," the conjunctive "and" is both logical hurdle and the forced marriage of senses that leaps it. Syntactic syllepsis is a distinction turned link, and in turn linkage made likeness (in that last invented case the likening of two discrepant intervals across a single grammatical lag). Which is why one needs an expanded theory of metaphor, begun in the last chapter, to track in action the logic of this sylleptic trope.

Metonymic Sequence, Metaphoric Consequence

To quote the full phrasing from chapter 19 of *Pickwick*, its hero "fell into the barrow, and fast asleep, simultaneously"—where, incidental to the syllepsis, one understanding of "fast" (as "firmly") gets the jump even on its speedy temporal alternative. But the phrasing depends for its main comedy on the wavering of a preposition, like the betwixtness of *entre* in Mallarmé: a grammatical integer not replicated in the second phase of the predicate in this case—as it would have been if occasion presented itself to describe Pickwick "no sooner falling into his bed than into a dream." In the narratographic register, syllepsis is a function of plot at its narrowest, a marker of syntactic time per se. According to the philosophy of mind in Gilbert Ryle, as we know from the previous chapter, a syllepsis like "in a flood of tears and a sedan chair" exposes the same "broken-backed" (20) logic that Ryle finds plaguing Cartesian dualism. Like mental (vis-à-vis material) "occurrences," the compound predication of such a grammar introduces no true symmetry. Philosophically, then, a glitch. Linguistically, a double hitch. Narratographically, a strictly verbal "occurrence" whose cognitive recoil—overcoming Ryle's "category error" by retrieving an alternate potential—is activated on the run as a temporal microloop.

It may take a literary writer who is also a professor of philosophy to cut through the oversubtleties of analytic philosophy on such a point. Indeed philosopher-novelist William H. Gass, writing about the "ontology of the sentence," cites another example of lexical absurdity from this very same passage in Ryle ("tides, hopes, and the average age of death, are rising")—with its clear multiplicity of definition for the participle "rising"—so as to undercut W. V. O. Quine's stance in *Word and Object*.[7] (The objection here is much like one might make, in the previous chapter, to Donald Davidson's refusal to see more than one sense in the admittedly anomalous literality of metaphoric designation.) Though Quine admits that there is "an air of zeugma" (the older usage here, equivalent in the present chapter to syllepsis) in a sentence like "The chair and question were hard," for him it results only from the difference between furniture and interrogative formulations, not from any difference within language use itself that would justify calling the modifier "hard" in any way double or ambivalent in its own right (quoted in Gass, 130–31). Hard is hard; there is only the "air" of logical trouble. Gass knows better—Gass with his own gift for sylleptic forking, as in an earlier essay from this same volume: "Putting one's mother into words. . . . It may have been easier to put her in her grave" (15). In transit from metaphor to literal sense, the "trans-fers" of the two "puts" there—as with the "projection" of sense, for Cavell, across the phrasal gap (in that case literal to metaphoric) of "Put out the light, and then put out the light"—marks a vast, sometimes a downright mortal, divergence.

In view of the novelistic (and variously "philosophical") examples to come in this chapter, one might say that syllepsis is a time-release but recursive grammar from which syntax itself emerges—in its requisite temporality—as the narrative function degree zero, where the arcs of plot are modeled by the inching forward of grammatical ligatures over the elapsing space of the same-again-but-different. In this sense, the splintered linguistic gist of syllepsis is language's unique way of defying the ferocious either/or of Descartes. At the same time it also flaunts, at the foundation of all logic—as we will return to via Agamben in due course—the primal law of noncontradiction in Aristotle. This is the rigorously "excluded middle" where nothing can be A and not-A at once. An alternative to this logic can begin to crystallize around the split faceting of syllepsis, which the evidence to come should help us recognize for what it is: not a caving-in of the either/or but the concretizing of a more probing and capacious both/and.

The last chapter closed, as we know—after a tacit brief confrontation between Cavell's terms and de Man's—with a glance, briefer yet, at an analytic philosophy of metaphor so counterintuitive that it denied even the duality on which I. A. Richards's canonical vehicle/tenor distinction depends. Metaphor is simply, for Donald Davidson, literality gone deliberately astray. One might understand syllepsis as a tracking over syntactic time of a comparable vagary, or vagrancy, from one dictionary usage to its metaphoric alternative—or, reversing direction, from a figural to a literal sense—so as to suggest an internal if hazy tropological relationship between its own two terms. For this reason it is important to look again at Davidson's stringency, where metaphor is very far from either uncertainty or overdetermination, ambiguity or pun.

In critiquing Empson among others for his emphasis on metaphor's second sense, insisting instead that there is only a literal meaning taken askew, Davidson happens (apparently) to misremember the full brunt of a Shakespearean sarcasm, his chosen example, and in a way that Empson (unmentioned at that point) gets right. Davidson wants to distinguish metaphors from puns, recalling, as an instance of the latter, that in *Troilus and Cressida*, when the heroine is introduced "bawdily into the Grecian camp, Nestor says, 'Our general doth salute you with a kiss.'"[8] According to Davidson (ignoring the unworkable grammar) we must take the first noun in "two ways at once" (33), as if personal and collective, meaning the receipt of kisses from *general* Agamemnon and from the ranks of his soldiers more *generally*. But Shakespeare, for whom the quibble is his fatal Cressida as well as Cleopatra, doesn't leave to chance our picking up on this pun; as we'll see, he doubles its designator in a kind of delayed and attenuated syllepsis, so that the extra quotient of sense becomes a kind of third valence between the two terms. This is to say that he divides and conquers, "projecting" (in Cavell's Wittgensteinian sense) the shifting linguistic form of the heroine's evoked promiscuity into syntax itself.

This is an effect that Empson treats not in *7 Types of Ambiguity* but in the "double plot" chapter of *Some Versions of Pastoral*, where this kind of "subdued pun" (one might say "diluted") marks off, for him, a major divide in Shakespeare's play between private desire and tribe. It is this "double plot" that comes to a verbal head in *Troilus and Cressida* when Agamemnon throws the heroine a kiss that, remarked upon by Nestor, is only fully ironized by Ulysses: "'Twere better she were kiss'd in general" (4.5). The separate senses of "general" are distributed, as Davidson would seem to have forgotten, across separate syntactic positions. Defending, as Empson does, such "verbal fidgets" (39) as a functional "appeal" (38) from one half of the play to the other, in this case from the theme of heroism to that of love, Empson might have noticed the vocabular cleaving (both senses) of that dialogue as a kind of dispersed or deflected (a not quite grammatical) forking: *Better to be kissed in general than by one.* The tacit etymological relation of commander in chief to the *genus* of warriors of which he is the cynosure is brought out across a syntagmatic parallelism that is more—and in a way less—than double meaning. It is the essential double structure of sylleptic byplay, its inherent (Empsonian) "double plot"—and in this light an essential instrument in leveraging (actually levering) the transition between phrasal ambiguity and double-plot narratology in our greatest of all close readers.

Though hardly undoing Davidson's argument for a literality turned toward metaphoric understanding by the force of context, rather than released to an independent second sense by it, still his Shakespearean example—let breathe in this different way—works at a bias to his claim. For it reminds us that two senses (as in the double desertion of one's loot and one's greed in Poe, "his gold and his motive together") often press into the open an operational difference all its own between literal and figurative. In contrast to the monolithic literality of a term only "taken [rather than defined] metaphorically," syllepsis instead is a clear play *between words*. Even allowing that literary metaphor is entirely "interactive" rather than dualistic, parsed only in interpretation, which is to say, in reading, syllepsis remains exemplary in that—with a unique reflex of second thought—it does nothing if not prevent the deed of reading from going unnoticed in the phrasing read.

Making Time and Sense

The space of time it takes to sort out such a sylleptic split is the time of unfixity if not indecision, of openness, of leap—with consequences often ethical as well as linguistic, even political, as we will see shortly in the examples of a famous electioneering gaffe. What is regularly ferried along the conveyor belt of syntax are two senses of the governing predicate, a wording made suddenly bicameral in its (juris)diction. That's at the semantic level, where signifiers are set in motion. In cognition, the significance of such a disjunctively phased phrasing, as literary sign, becomes *the division itself*—as a covert thematic synergy. Marking the very split that its own formulation twists into view in order to bind up at a new level, syllepsis applies a linguistic splint that engrafts two branches onto the same grammatical trunk. Reading may in this way discern a strained join that a more stringent logic would seem to prohibit. Sorting through, and out, such disjunct verbal production is the frequently satiric (and thus, at a rudimentary level, ethical) charge—and ignited challenge—of syntactic time in many of these formulations, whose very moral may wait latent in their frequent failed conflation of body/mind or matter/spirit registers: again, the sedan chair and the tears that precipitate an exit in it.

Remember, from the previous chapter, Wittgenstein's sense of verbal potentiality in remarking that "the possible uses of a word are before our minds in half-tones as we say or hear it" (190, vi, no. 35). Putting that potentiality into syntactic action could at times, one presumes, make for the possibility of what he calls "grammatical jokes" based on conflicting (but sometimes overlapping) criteria of usage. His examples are few and far between, and never direct. Certainly one can't take this term to cover such a remark as "The language philosopher cracked grammatical jokes and nuts all afternoon at the bar." Still, there remains Wittgenstein's tantalizing if unanswered query: "Let's ask ourselves: why do we perceive a grammatical joke to be *deep*? (And that is what philosophical depth is.)" (53, no. 111). It is, for one thing, not a matter of depth *as opposed to surface*, but of verbal surface tension in the full depth of its ramifications. A famous passing example of his method alludes to this underdemonstrated "grammatischen Witz" in the least broad of comic terms, a kind of strictly logical play on words: "It can't be said of me at all (except perhaps as a joke) that I know I am in pain" (96, no. 251). The thinking goes roughly like this. I can only *have* pain, rather than recognize it. Others can only surmise it from, for instance, my behavior—or my complaint (in the verbal sense). They might doubt it; I cannot. One feels pain directly, that is, rather than intuits or recognizes it—when it is one's own. But we speak only figuratively of doing so when it is another's. Hence a possible syllepsis in the form of a "grammatical joke" less "deep" perhaps than some, but not shallow either in its split difference: when commenting, say, on a friend's rejected journal article—while suffering from a toothache—with "I feel terrible but your pain too."

More, though. One of the things that, in particular, makes syllepsis not just a uniquely linguistic brand of verbal wit, but a quintessentially literary effect, is what at another level makes language uniquely philosophical when mobilized within a literary frame. In following Wittgenstein, Agamben, as we know, sees the disciplines of linguistics and philosophy operating in the face of a shared and even reciprocal groundlessness. If the existence of the world is limited in Wittgenstein by what our language can say—and make—of it, and if the existence of our language is a fact without demonstrable essence, unsupported by any ontological underpinnings, such is the double remove signaled for Agamben by a nonmetaphysical understanding of "In the beginning was the word."[9] And so, in italics: "*Language is what must necessarily presuppose itself*" (41). You can't get back behind the operable fact of it to the ontological proof of it. But even the provocation to do so might locate that unexpected "depth" of grammatical wit that Wittgenstein queries.

In this light, linguistics intersects philosophy at the same juncture where logic (to which Wittgenstein's generalized sense of grammatical criteria is tacitly subsumed) crosses paths—and sometimes purposes—with syntax. Take one of Wittgenstein's most characteristic distinctions in the realm of grammatical limits: "It is correct to say 'I know what you are thinking', and wrong to say 'I know what I am thinking.' (A whole cloud of philosophy condensed into a drop of grammar.)" (233, xi, no. 315). And if the grammar itself were comic (an example waiting), the joke would be on language itself. Syllepsis can be thought to occupy and define the cusp between grammatical rules in the everyday sense and this more pervasive rule of grammar in ordinary language philosophy (determining what is allowed by the deep logic rather than the superficial cast of usage). The typical jokes of syllepsis push the envelope from both ends, syntactic and logical—as in such a concoction as this, turning as well on two divergent but still functional senses of both "know" and "think": "I know what you are thinking and her too well to think you have a chance." Like literature at large, such a grammatical trope makes you think *in* and *about* the language game at once—even as sense is still catching up with itself on the heels of its own semantic (elsewhere phonetic) "half-tones." Gaming the language is, in short, one of literature's ways of being philosophical about it.

This would include certain first principles. For Albert Einstein, time is best understood as what keeps everything from happening all at once. Syntax is what keeps meaning from happening all at once. In literary syntax, however, there are more meanings unleashed than those readily subordinated to a coherent narrative grammar of the adverbial "once upon a time." The minuscule time-loop involved in syllepsis approaches what we might characterize as the paradoxical dismantling of succession by overlap. Approaches this condition, yes, but never quite negotiates the collapse it teases us with. The overlap is uneven. The still functional difference between the two-ply laminate and the serial aggregate, between coincidence and syncopation, is a difference that remains in play, enforced by being foregrounded. A pun stops one cold, translating a word into its double. Instead, its effects being always on the run, the licensed bifurcation of syllepsis keeps up the momentum and one's linguistic guard at once, alert for both the inertial forward drive and the inert or unworkable parallel.

At such times, reading, more obviously than elsewhere, makes the sentence "come together" only in the dizzy head—in some elusive tertium quid between incongruities, a phantom gestalt. One might think of it this way: in the forward topple (rather than clean toggle) between alternate predicating sequences, syllepsis fashions from its perspectival discrepancy a common but unphrased vanishing point in linguistic usage itself. Put otherwise, the often minimal and fleeting time-loop of sylleptic effect is in turn a feedback loop, adjusting exactly those categories required to decipher it: hence a figure and a metatrope at once. "Falling" asleep is the deadest of metaphors, an almost pure idiom; "in" tears barely less so, but enough to throw a yet more literal or tangible "in" (as with enclosure by a sedan chair) into relief. With what consequences, we'll need to keep asking, for a philosophy of speech in action? For a theory of the deed of reading? What does the slippage at issue between lexicon and syntax tell us about language in what it has to say by forcing it? What opposing "potentials" of word choice does syllepsis keep in play in its understanding as a process both philosophical (a metalinguistic gambit) and philological (an idiomatic logjam)? Such are questions to which only that unique pressure exerted by syllepsis upon reading—its requisite closeness in the service not of nuance alone but of self-revised coherence per se—can begin to answer after scanning a rather full spread of evidence.

Idiometrics

On the first day of a welcome semester's research leave, as I sat down to organize my thoughts for this discussion of the highly specific and yet to my mind broadly typical phenomenon of syllepsis—syntactic, temporal, hence narratographic, and finally philosophical all at once—a minor topical distraction came, if I may, both up and in handy, falling at once under my gaze and into line with my topic. This time the equivocated preposition wasn't "in" or "into," but "over." The *New York Times* of January 1, 2012, ran a front-page story on the Republican caucus race under a title brandishing a decidedly strained version of the trope, in rare inverted format, where the conjunction "and" seemed even odder than "or" would have. In midsize font: "Over Phones and Greasy Pizza, a Battle for Iowa." With no sense of people placing calls while still chewing, instead we find intersecting there the horizontal axis of telecommunications and the different but politically related vertical axis of shared food on the common table under one's face-to-face exchanges, with separate conversations plugged into and leant into respectively. (One wondered whether the overstrained "over" was at first queried by the copy editor.) On the ground in Iowa during this same primary season, a suggestion from an actual campaign worker like "Let's keep in touch over time and coffee" would hardly have induced more of a double take. The headline, in short, phrases its own idiomatic "battle" and its rhetorical detente (or tie) at once.

The journalistic example there is a fusion of two literal senses in one syntactic yoke. Given the frequency with which syllepsis splits between literal and figural senses, however, the keyed-in, keyed-up reader begins to see this trope as a kind of grammatical rather than rhetorical simile, though on shifting grounds (of comparison). In contrast, metaphor, as classically understood, may be called a chain of association with only one link, an elided simile, an equation rather than a comparison, a displacement, and in its more compressed forms a laminate. It gives one thing instead of another rather than next to it. The classic example in modern philosophy: Juliet is the sun. In Aristotle: Ulysses is a lion. When that sun *shines* on her lover, or that lion *roars* his call to action, metaphor has absorbed its tenor entirely into its vehicle, its predication having become part of a new predicate. This is the further stage of what Ricoeur calls "predicative assimilation"; according to this "rule of metaphor" (his translated title), a comparison is tacitly asserted and then instantaneously substituted for the original.[10] Where similes dilate the analogic process with *like* or *as*, metaphors compress it. Similes are syntactic, metaphors often distilled ("assimilated") into single lexemes. But then (the main point here) some errant, aberrant kinds of syntax may operate a delayed-action similitude of their own. In doing so they replace, via grammatical compounds, one sense with another (whether or not strongly metaphoric in itself) across adjacent items and discrepant grounds—another *related* meaning, that is. This amounts to some further and perhaps "binding" sense (not obligatory, simply junctural), drawing out in the process just the logic of that relationship (or exposing its accident) from beneath an apparent mismatch.

In another electoral moment from four years before that *New York Times* caucus article, another low-keyed syllepsis had been a double thorn in the side of Barack Obama's first presidential campaign. The joke-like format, no cause for laughter, backfired: a rare gaffe in this politician's deft and measured rhetoric. (There was, to be sure, none of the overt comedy intended more recently when, for instance, a commentator on National Public Radio, quoting an unnamed wag about gonzo journalist Hunter S. Thompson, said that "he never met a politician or a substance he didn't abuse.") Yet consider the norms more quietly violated by the incautious phrasing of Obama's stance, off the record but quickly leaked. Wholly distinct constitutional rights were implicitly at issue, rights separately enumerated as a rule: to bear arms; to exercise religious freedom. The Founders would never have thought to speak about this in the Augustan poetic syntax of their eighteenth-century day: to bear arms and religious witness. But Obama let slip a not unrelated and soon notorious (if muted) syllepsis, as candid as it was risky, about embittered rural voters "clinging to their guns or religion." What offended those who might well have admitted idiomatically that they do indeed "cling" to their religion in the face of spreading secularism was the syntactic trope that linked this sense of embrace, of clutched hope, to the trigger finger. Via a metonymic sequence generating a new grammatical similitude, the interchangeable "or" turned religion itself into a prosthetic, a protective tool, a crutch, indeed a weapon.

Though he has often been foolishly accused of seditious socialism, all we see here is Obama's centrist liberalism caught off the cuff and guard at once. In rhetorical terms, however, a true socialist from the nineteenth century, Karl Marx, is found at his most Dickensian (rhetorically as well as sociologically) in borrowing the out-of-step *and*-grammar of syllepsis for a famous pronouncement that Slavoj Žižek partially misquotes in his brief disquisition on the slippery "and" in such philosophical texts as Louis Althusser's "Ideology and Ideological State Apparatuses" or Martin Heidegger's *Being and Time*, where the even-handed conjunction (forging a kind of hendiadys) masks the grammatical subordination implicit in the prepositions *of* and *in* respectively.[11] And no "and" was ever more dominant, rather than egalitarian, than this from the end of the sixth chapter of *Capital*, where, tongue in cheek, Marx unfolds the mock-pastoral idyll of unhindered wage labor: "This sphere . . . within whose boundaries the sale and purchase of labour-power goes on, is in fact a very Eden of the innate rights of man. There alone rule Freedom, Equality, Property *and* Bentham" (186; emphasis added). Žižek accidentally leaves out the "property" in his quotation, exactly where it replaces the third term in the revolutionary French triad, "Fraternity," and where it thus joins the other benchmarks of betrayed liberation under the sign of Benthamite assumptions and their false sociological parity—as satirized by Marx in the very next sentence when summoning up the "pre-established harmony of things" that yields "mutual benefit" from the aggressive pursuit of self-interest. Three inverted subjects had, just before, taken "rule" as their predicate—as if in the metaphoric sense of overruled aristocracy—until the fourth snaps the chain with the unabashed dominance of the capitalist stranglehold. Rather than "mutual benefit," mutual interference is more like it, as the sylleptic rift between ameliorative state ideology and raw political economy is there to stress—at a point of syntactic stress fracture—in an allusive grammar's own broken stride.

Thus, ever since, there is the likelihood of a self-contradictory electorate clinging to its freedom of choice and its Bentham, if also to its guns and religion. Once you release metonymy (in the Obama example in particular) back into the paradigmatic axis of metaphoric equivalence—where functional alternatives are indeed interchangeable—the floodgates are thrown open for the supposed slander of insinuation. That's what syllepsis does. It taints by contiguity. It is often a figurative effluvium passed by contagion along the channels of grammar. It brings dormant connotations to metaphoric life. Always attached back to the structural(ist) *paradigms* from which syntax must normally extricate itself, it refuses to let *potential* get set to rest. Tacit there in that terminological blend just proffered—of structuralist linguistics and postmetaphysical philosophy (Jakobson and Agamben)—are the combined terms best suited, in fact, to explicate the sense of linguistic potential I've been attempting to draw out from the philosophical thinking behind Agamben's poetics.

Under Jakobson's influence in the late 1960s, there is another renowned literary close reader of special note in these matters. Whether or not one is inclined to indulge at length in the "slow reading" practiced by Roland Barthes in *S/Z*, there is a moment in that commentary where an effect distantly related to syllepsis offers a marked case, despite apparent grammatical constraints, of irregular, rutted terrain, its forced and ultimately choppy logic upsetting any normative parallelism. Instancing such a paratactic cascade of syntax in Proust, Barthes calls it, as if in allusion to Wittgenstein, a "game" that is "grammatical in essence."[12] But he misses the more obvious sylleptic variant of this language game, with its own "plural diversity of possibilities within a singular syntagm" (58), in a revealing moment from the Balzac story he is reading. The narrative's entire reciprocal thematic—the eroticization of art versus the lethal aestheticizing of desire—is there when introducing the title figure, Sarrasine, as a man "with no other mistress but sculpture and Clotilde,"[13] the metaphoric passion ceding to the bodily one almost as an afterthought. Barthes's commentary notes only an ideological redundancy at this turn, an echo of the earlier and strictly figurative "lived only with his Muse" (236), as well as a simple "act" in the proairetic code: namely, "liaison" (103). Yet it is the grammatical slide—the jolting ligature of *syntactic* liaison itself—that ropes sexual fascination into the more metaphoric (or is it in this case?) lust for art.

So back to Jakobson. His definitional template for the "poetic function" as any marked recurrence—all the way, say, from meter to rhyme, or in prose from assonance to asyndeton—bears adjusting when what recurs, like the implied second "to" of "clinging to" in Obama's line, elliptically or not, involves a lexical and syntactic symmetry that is in fact, at least momentarily, dysfunctional, out of sync. I repeat Jakobson's memorable formulation in full: "The poetic function projects the principle of equivalence from the axis of selection into the axis of combination."[14] In syllepsis, there is more elective repetition (cling to, cling to) than sense can comfortably sustain at one time. Syllepsis, in regard to Jakobson's formula, recovers the principle of equivalence from the axis of selection as it is forced abruptly upon, and momentarily jams, the axis of combination. Rather than having likeness projected into sequence, in syllepsis the self-turned grammatical trope operates to *deflect* its metonymic mismatch back to the axis of functional alternatives as if to disclose some new kind of latent equivalence. It is there, for instance, in that axis of equivalence, that gun-toting and religion have, to the allergic ear of their wielders, been reduced to comparable postures of paranoia or aggression. Or there where hegemonic capitalism has confused freedom with free markets.

"So spoke the White House on that occasion": a classic figural metonymy, residence as an associational emblem of the presidency. At stake in syllepsis, instead, is Jakobson's sense of syntagmatic metonymy—and its encountered hurdles. In the normal course of grammatical discourse, sequence is a matter of semantics. But syllepsis plays a double game. Its initial misfit similitude in grammar tends to ignite a latent metaphor by the friction of the otherwise literal turn, a condensation by "and" or "or" that is also a displacement. Syllepsis is thus a mild form, in its forking byways, of what linguists call the garden path (rather than forking path) sentence, which leads you fully astray and forces rereading. "The old man the boat" is a textbook example, where verb phrase pulls the rug out from under the wool pulled over the eyes of the reader in expecting a noun phrase. The equivalent in our loaded political context: "By his too-ready tongue, Obama painted the White House and his party into a momentary corner." Idiom, as there, can seem too literal for its own good, thus exposing its dead metaphoric and clichéd basis all along. Syntax becomes reciprocal semantic interference. And in the process it probes to the basis of analogic thinking across both vertical and horizontal axes.

Shakespeare to Austen to Edgeworth to Dickens

In this respect, syllepsis is intuitively metalinguistic: a sliding metaphorics and a grammatical metafork. Undaunted by its metrical precedents in Augustan prosody, Dickens seems effortlessly (iambs at his fingertips when need be) to enter upon the exploratory slack of this grammar in a way that both sustains a longer heritage and spawns a legacy. Always chief among his conscious predecessors in all matters stylistic, there is Shakespeare: no stranger to syllepsis himself, and not just in that tragicomic Empsonian moment from *Troilus*. When the quick-tongued Mistress Quickly from *The Merry Wives of Windsor* foresees a foul-mouthed rage afoot, she anticipates much "abusing of God's patience and the king's English" (1.4), with two separate higher authorities enduring this double affront—even while the second assault feels tinged with the notion (along a different lexical axis, and somewhat less figurative) of an idiomatically "abusive" language rather than just an abused linguistic decorum. Such is the recurrent syntactic pattern by which Dickens later revels in the yoking of metaphoric and literal inference.

And after Pope's eighteenth-century Belinda in *The Rape of the Lock*—threatened in the poet's voice by two brands, literal and metaphoric, of stain—there is, in Maria Edgeworth's 1801 *Belinda*, the stagy and affected Lady Delacour, who herself deploys such phrases as part of her pose of mannered sarcasm. These frequently include the recurrence of a prepositional form, where an idiom like "out of my mind" is parsed so that "out" goes two ways at once, by way of distraction and extraction both: "I had been swindled out of my senses, and out of my dower."[15] As the plot later thickens, the Lady awaits part of its disclosure through secondary report: "I am absolutely overcome with heat—and with curiosity" (121). Only her nemesis, the disreputable Mrs. Freke, caught in a mantrap when spying on Lady Delacour, pushes the trope further toward Dickensian grotesquerie in insisting "that 'tis better for a lady to lose her leg than her reputation" (311).

As a further predecessor for the Dickensian proliferation of this effect, think also of Jane Austen's approach to free indirect discourse for Elizabeth Bennet's wit-alleviated frustration in a dilatory exit scene. The first half of the sentence is quoted by Michael Wood in an eponymous article, "Time and Her Aunt."[16] Yet it is also the second clause in the sentence, not given by Wood, that unravels into a not quite idiomatic parallelism at least as easy to stumble over: "Time and her aunt moved slowly—and her patience and her ideas were nearly worn out." Ideas, in this context, run thin and out, rather than wear out. With the phrasing itself growing frazzled, indirect discourse assumes the burden of the scene it is concocted to picture, chafing and fraying at its own nerve ends. With syntactic pace capturing the irony of its designated retardation, grammar takes its own time, bearings, and tolls.

It is at such a moment that the grasp of syncopated aural and referential streams in Agamben's poetics comes into clarifying play at the level of rhetorical analysis. His emphasis on metrics versus semantics, sounded scansion versus sense, can lead us to see how the "cut" of syllepsis would be a "caesura" (his key term, along with "enjambment") in grammar itself: the marking off of an internal semantic breakpoint—together with its syntactic relinkage. And whereas metered sound is put into counterpoint with the intonations of linguistic sense in poetry, in prose it is, so to speak, the *clip* of diction (in both senses, caesural and onrushing, disjunctive and enjambed) that is played off against syntax in the limit case of syllepsis. And these syntactic shifts are related, one level down, to the cut-and-paste of syllabic continuity and (transegmental) overlap as well. Austen is again exemplary. So balanced are her periods, so mandarin her symmetries, that, in her last completed novel, *Persuasion* (1819), she can front-load the forked alternatives of two subjects laying a delayed, splayed claim on the same verb. Sir Walter's spendthrift ways are beyond counsel, even for the lawyer by the name of Shepherd charged with husbanding his client's resources. Despite "whatever might be his hold or his views on Sir Walter" (chap. 2), there was no convincing the vainglorious baronet to economize, where the grip of the first noun and the purview of the second take up their prepositional senses at oblique angles to each other: the one figurative "on" being contiguous, tactile, the other distanced by ocular remove—each idiom a dead metaphor, though the second more inert and strictly colloquial than the first.

Moreover, the problem of faded baronial (and hence manorial) extravagance in *Persuasion*, where none of the title force can be exerted to stem it, is so intractable that it enters, a couple pages later, into the very alphabetic traction of word formation and its cross-lexical skids—as we are made privy to the domino-like free fall of Sir Walter's lament: "What! Every comfort of life knocked off! Journeys, London, servants, horses, table,—contractions and restrictions every where" (chap. 2). Indeed "contractions" invade even the etiquette of word borders in his slurred sense of indignity, with the lack of "horses, stable" no sooner regretted, by an accident of adjacency—as if going without actually saying—than it is supplanted by the equivalent woeful deprivation of his accustomed "table." The hinged sibilant and resulting phonetic pun resemble, though one notch down, the loop effect of syllepsis as it gets snagged by grammatical rather than morphemic adhesions, where the slippage is nonetheless equally inclined—on the slant, at a further semantic bias—to bespeak the working of language from within its wavering words.

Dickensian prose is born from this linguistic, even before narrative, keenness. We've seen more than one instance of its sylleptic upshot in *Pickwick Papers*. So instinctive—and ultimately inveterate—are the laying down of these parallel tracks in Dickens's verbal imagination, however, that, four years before that first novel, they cut an almost obsessive swath through one of his earliest sketches. It is as if he had to work this overmastering wordplay out of his rhetorical system before turning to novelistic prose, where the wit of skewed parallelism could be more often shared with a character. Take this facetious salvo by a Dickensian wordsmith in Cockney guise, *Pickwick*'s Sam Weller, distinguishing abstract bombast from literal commitment, windy legalistic proclamation from preemptive sentencing, across the slide from reflexive to a quite literally accusative grammar: "There ain't a magistrate goin' as don't commit himself, twice as often as he commits other people" (chap. 24). The wordplay is motivated by animus and explicit satire.

Instead, in the collection *Sketches by Boz*, in the brief nine paragraphs of "Shops and Their Tenants" from 1833, syntactic tricks are turned for their own sake, begun with a fairly muted shift within parallel grammar from a literal to a metaphoric plane, in observation of human traffic "steadily plodding on to business, or cheerfully running after pleasure." This is followed by a mild send-up of unimaginative city gents (across a silent prepositional shift) "in all the dignity of whiskers, and gilt-watch-guards."[17] As if to reciprocate the mismatch of this vainglory, the female object of their gaze "sits behind the counter in a blaze of adoration and gas-lights," exaggerating such phrasing's classic divide between figurative and factual reference.

The particular storefront property to which the rest of the short sketch is devoted is first described in a rolling double syllepsis (in an explicit repetition of main verbs) when "the landlord got into difficulties, the house got into Chancery, the tenant went away, and the house went to ruin." The pattern of bent or broken predicates is relentless, for in the next doomed "letting" of this real estate, a clerk formerly dressed in crisp white "took to a black neckerchief, and the proprietor took to drinking." The apogee of these effects arrives (at the firm's commercial nadir) with another twofold syllepsis, the latter in a purer elliptical form: "At last the company's man came to cut off the water, and then the linen-draper cut off himself, leaving the landlord his compliments and the key." And after a brief sentimental and polemic interlude about working-class conditions, the jauntier tone returns in a punning comedy akin to syllepsis when the latest defaulter on his rent "very coolly locked the door, and bolted himself." The literal sense turns metaphoric when bolt (for flight) suggests an attempted security quite different from the locked door. With things made safe on both sides of this faltering economic threshold, what's comparable is that each is an effect of foot traffic, precipitated versus prevented. The overlap of grammar induces just such readerly efforts at specification—including the intuitive reach for a genuinely pertinent third term, a resolved vector of the two-track drift.

On the "interactionist" theory of metaphor (in the philosophical work of Max Black), the interpreter's sense of a metaphoric usage is dependent on an interchange, not between a given literal and some separate figural sense but between the lexical focal point and its nimbus or frame of association. This requires, in the reader's own "interaction," a mental sieving of common elements, relevant shared traits, flagged for recognition by the figuration itself. Metaphor forces, and so forges, conjunction, which is only forced further into the open with the linguistic metaforks of syllepsis. Metaphor doesn't name a thing otherwise, according to Black or Davidson. It doesn't denominate, it predicates—counterfactually, but still literally. A classic example again, rephrased here by some rudimentary version of set theory—where tangent spheres of association come together in a pertinent overlap that exempts from comparison any nonintersecting traits: Juliet is the sun not because, except in current idiom, she is hot, let alone (anachronism aside) because she is gaseous or spotted or fatal on approach, but because she is aglow and magnetic and the center of my world and the source by which I now see it—and so on. These, in Cavell's approach, are "criteria" (for existence) that need be attached to no propositional truth claim, but that can nonetheless be held in suspension, posed in defiance of all radical skepticism. In the work of syllepsis, metaphoric as it regularly is at one pole, such suspension achieves a more active syntactic bridgework. When in the "Conclusion" to *Nicholas Nickleby* two years after *Pickwick Papers*, Dickens offers the tamed version of such grammar in "Madeline gave her hand and fortunes to Nicholas" (chap. 65), we are still aware that the transfer of funds is more literal than the matrimonial idiom (and euphemism) for a figuratively pressed flesh.

When less conservative in its phrasal veering, the (a)wry and cockeyed, and sometimes even Cockney, poetry of such double-punch gestures is in certain appearances just that: actual rhymed verse. The comic poet Thomas Hood wrote a celebratory send-off in verse to his new friend Dickens on January 4, 1842, on the occasion of the latter's sailing to America after such a windfall "sale" at home, wishing him a "passage" on behalf of his books as successful as any in them (the two punning nouns actually italicized). But much of Hood's best, and we might say most Dickensian, wordplay doesn't concentrate its doubleness in this overt and grammatically irrelevant way but distributes it more in the manner of a sylleptic split—or splint. At such switch points, an embarked-upon sequence (sometimes merely syllabic rather than syntactic) is yanked up short by a sudden redirection of the sense, as with the phonetic jolt in the epitomizing last lines of the tacit riddle poem "NO!": "No fruits, no flowers, no leaves, no birds— / November!" Closer yet to the forked idioms of Dickensian jauntiness—and all the more macabre for that in the black comedy of the amputee's legless suicide by hanging in "Faithless Nelly Gray"—we find a grotesquely literalized cliché followed by a bluntly literal twist of its preposition as the lamented body, though scarcely the phrase, is left hanging: "For, though distress had cut him up / It could not cut him down."

Dickens the Syntactician: Fork-Tongued Satire

On Black's analytic understanding of metaphor, the sylleptic variant (as in the figurative "cut up" against the literal "cut down") could be called not just "interactionist" but intersectionist. At the very least, two separate predications rub each other the wrong way, with any common nomination (or predication) receding into the elusive remove of an imaginary third term, more or less tacit and often hard to formulate. Religion is like a weapon not because it is potentially murderous but because it is clutched at in desperation. In Dickens's *Dombey and Son*, the phallocentric Mr. Dombey is "stiff" not because he is hardened by desire, nor cold and dead in physical fact, but because he is braced against the world by vanity and defensiveness. He is, in both moral and physical posture, "stiff with starch and arrogance" (chap. 8). If metaphor's basis lies in the tacit copula as an already "assimilated" predication (Ricoeur), then Mr. Dombey is indeed performing as the pillar of society he looks like in his unbending righteousness. The implicit (here demeaning) syntactic simile (starch like the hardening of ego) may even at times expose its yet more elusive third term in an unsaid matrix phrase: he is, in short, a *stuffed shirt*. In contrast, the good-hearted nautical men in the novel, by an almost explicit sylleptic contrast, boast "suits of oak as well as hearts" (chap. 9). They are like oak not in being inert and wooden but in being natural and firm, staunch by way of another inferential matrix cliché: *stout-hearted men.* Usually, of course, the third term is more vaporous, vanishing, hypothetical. In such sequencing, syntax itself becomes metaphor (meta-pherien): a transferral, a shunting, where the commutation of terms is still in process across a strained grammatical similitude. To the scaffold and damnation, away with gold and motive, braced by starch and arrogance, in a flood and a chair, into a wheelbarrow and sleep. Whatever terms of comparison, whatever thirdnesses, are meant to emerge, they result only from such discrepant mergers over grammatical duration.

In this respect, the sylleptic skid of phrasing recalls again such disseverings and fusions across lexical (before grammatical) sequence as "horse/s table" in Austen, "imp/ulse" (et al.) in Poe, and of course the famous cross-word blaring of "Trojan/s' trumpet" (*Troilus and Cressida*, 4.5) in Shakespeare (function, so to say, of Cressida's "general kissing" in Empson). Such effects, now lexical, now syntactic, don't have to appear in tandem to speak to each other as bothered paradigms and violated rules. Recall the Cockney character in *Our Mutual Friend*—from amid the spate of syllepsis soon to be examined there—who mishears the place-name Doctors' Commons as a personal noun, "Doctor Scommons" (bk. 1, chap. 8). Related to any such reconfiguring of two syllables at their point of mutual abutment, syllepsis could be said to constitute—in the transitive etymological sense of the verb—a *syl-labling*, a forcing together, at the phrasal rather than phonetic level.

This is Dickens's normal playing field, his typical gaming with language. We've looked to *Dombey and Son* for interrelated examples, and there are more to be found in that first novel of the author's full narrative and symbolic maturity. In the panoply of grammatical forkings, there is one thrilling transgression of the grammatically illicit (let's say, again, zeugmatic) sort, attributed to Cockney ingenuity in the dialogue of the irrepressible Susan Nipper. She is about to tell Dombey off at last: "What I mean, Sir, is to speak respectful and without offence, but out" (chap. 44), with *out* retrofitted as part of a suddenly compound verb phrase. This is the barely grammatical exception that proves the rule of Dickens's typical bifold phrasing. Following an alliterative warped parallelism like "the beadle of our business and our bosoms" (chap. 5) to describe Mr. Dombey, we are ready for that similar spiritual collapse of outer upon inner in "stiff with starch and arrogance" (chap. 8). In his first separation from his son after the mother's inconvenient death in childbirth, the boy is given out to wet-nursing "born by Fate and Richards" (chap. 16), where a laboring woman's embrace is ominously linked to the failed self-sufficiency of Dombey's bourgeois world, a literal transport and a figure of prophetic inevitability.

In any case, enough minuscule syntactic wrinkles of this sort accrue to a pleated pattern. Once this sylleptic tendency—call it divided consciousness grammatically instantiated—has been established in the early chapters, across the "high" and "low" strands of the plot, it can be proliferated at will. There is the exit of Major Bagstock, who "took his lobster-eyes and his apoplexy to the club" (chap. 40), as if such eyes were a synecdoche as well as a medical symptom of his bulging and convulsive self-importance. Or note the play, once more, between spiritual and material cause (verging on a radical confusion of the intrinsic and the contingent) when Mr. Dombey confronts his wife-to-be "with a lofty gallantry adapted to his dignity and the occasion" (chap. 30). Later, when Mr. Toots laments Florence's announced marriage, he bemoans the "banns that consign her to Lieutenant Walters, and me to—to Gloom, you know" (chap. 56), the character stumbling over the very equivocated pronoun on which the trope pivots, trying bravely for a steadying parallelism in the face of his despair. Revealed yet again, in a comic key, is the cleaving between novelistic fate and its embodiment in character.

In novels after *Dombey*, syllepsis makes various appearances, though not so frequent again until *Our Mutual Friend*. The classic prepositional format from *Pickwick* ("went home in a flood of tears and a sedan chair") is reprised in *Little Dorrit* when the heroine finds a milliner "in tears and in bed" (bk. 1, chap. 7). In another novel from this middle period, perhaps the most openly ethical (in the normative sense), or say, political, of Dickensian sylleptic examples—because implicated in interracial political morality and colonial trade—is from *Bleak House* (1850–52), where Mrs. Jellyby's "telescopic philanthropy" partakes of an imperial mission concerned with the "cultivation of coffee, and natives" (chap. 4). There is an aroma of hypallage in that turn (effect before cause). With an unspoken play on agri-culture in this colonial economy, the gleaning of souls precedes the lucrative harvest to which their labor no doubt contributes. That wry comma marks the hypocritical afterthought—and semantic misfit—of ex-post-facto justification, with one symptomatic facet of the white man's burden weighed in export tonnage well before any tally of primitive souls and their salvation comes into two-faced relief.

Yet such sylleptic phrasing exposes discrepancy per se more often than any particular ethical contradiction. This is in fact the trope's real force, the felt content of its form. Double-talk is what it does even when not exposing it. Meaning may be confounded just where significance is consolidated: through the only tentative (tentative in the root sense) "holding" together—rather than resolution—of incompatibles, a levitating rather than leveling of ventured alternatives. That these are kept afloat only by reading more closely than normally required is what turns their lurking hurdle into a metalinguistic springboard, what reroutes a potential trouble spot into a glimpsed vista of sheer potential still in force, in action, in process.

Passing comedy can enlist this effect in the same novel for a character no longer massaging his attitude or his facial hair: "The light vivacious tone of fashionable life which is usually assumed by Mr. Weevle, sits so ill upon him to-night, that he abandons that and his whiskers together" (chap. 32).

A more complicated syntactic and mental divergence is found later in *Bleak House*, in a melodramatic rather than satiric vein, with physical cause building toward physiological, and implicitly psychological, effect at the death of Lady Dedlock. This happens across what might be called an inverted syllepsis, with a three-pronged grammatical subject rather than object: "Cold, wet, and fatigue are sufficient causes for my being found dead, but I shall die of others, though I suffer from these" (chap. 59). While putting the suff-ering back in suff-iciency, Lady Dedlock also inverts a sylleptic mismatch of tangible and intangible causation, outer and inner. Without mentioning the link between shame and fatal weather in the unwritten pun on a more metaphoric "exposure"—that matrix or structuring absence of the whole passage—she dies, in sylleptic effect, of snow and exhaustion.

In *Little Dorrit*, half a decade on, syllepsis appears across another splayed prepositional phrase whose evoked "materiality" is divided between bodily versus financial repletion, with the scoundrel Tite Barnacle "more flush of blood than money" (bk. 1, chap. 10). But by this point in Dickens's career, satiric disjunction can be overwritten with a sentimental blurring. Nostalgic as she is for the balm of the past in her Italian isolation from her beloved Arthur Clennam, the title heroine's pronominal grammar spreads open in an associational embrace, clinging to her own deprivation in honor of Clennam's former solicitude when she admits that "so dearly do I love the scene of my poverty and your kindness" (bk. 2, chap. 11). It is as if the long-standing debtor's site had converged with "scene," under pressure of syllepsis, around the dramatic episodes that have brought them together there in the novel's first volume—and that have now drawn them apart into separate plotlines.

Here we recall Genette's sense of crosscut narrative montage as carrying the macrorhetorical format of syllepsis across the structural counterpoint of whole plotlines. In *Narrative Discourse*, "syllepsis" (named explicitly and repeatedly) operates at the level of narrative grammar rather than sentence grammar: a bundling of disparate material in the term's etymological sense of "taking together" (85). This includes certain "anachronic groupings governed by one or another kinship (spatial, temporal, or other)," so that—through such thematic or geographical linkages, to name two of his emphases—the reader comes to recognize, as Genette rephrases it later, a "cluster of events and considerations able to give that gathering a fully paradigmatic importance" (111). The use of the term "paradigmatic" offers the tipped hand of Genette's linguistic model (Saussure, Jakobson) for the discursivities of plot, inviting us to imagine a complete spectrum running from syntactic cross-knits in the rhetorical mode—where alternative dictional choices from the paradigm are disposed along the sequence of a split predication—to the echoing montage of broader narrative episodes. This is the very pattern that concerns Empson (in his double plots) as well as Genette (in the anachronies of narrative juxtaposition)—and that comes increasingly to characterize the schematically planned chapters, as well as sylleptically executed prose, of late Dickens.

Mutual Locutions

By the time of *Our Mutual Friend*, for better or worse, the double stress of syllepsis has become almost the essential cross-weave of Dickensian writing. Dickens is widely thought to have stumbled into popular solecism with the title adjective of this last finished novel, meaning by the phrase, more accurately, "our common friend." Or he may have had something less settled in mind, given the confusing identity transfers and knotted lines of affiliation in the novel. If so, the extra rhetorical torque of the title would not be out of step with a pervasive dualism of perspective in the style of the book as a whole—in its style, as well as in its underlying conceptual structure. Certainly the bifurcated grammar of syllepsis involves both a common and an often mutually exclusive (when not just mutual) field of lexical force: two words interdependent in their derivation from an elusive common base, two words linked to each other by reciprocal alignment and interference at once. And, as we've begun to notice, one fork of the grammar is often the metaphoric double of the other, its figurative counter in the realm of spirit rather than matter, the impalpable rather than the somatic. As always before in Dickens's exploitation of sylleptic form, even in its loosening toward a more familiar parallelism, there are two pertinent sides to every syntactic coinage.

Indeed the very idea of mutual interference—or reciprocal "transposition"—is the essence of verbal comedy for the early twentieth-century French philosopher Henri Bergson, in whose account the repetitive mechanization of the human body as slapstick (his model for physical comedy) finds its correlate in the mechanical (purely linguistic) accidents or automaticities of verbal iteration.[18] When the comic rudiment of mechanic "repetition" extends, in the case of an "equivocal situation," to verbal puns and other dualisms, Bergson calls this particular subset of "transposition" the "reciprocal interference of series" (123), each referential element undoing the other. When the series in question is actually an extended syntactic span, his formulation offers a categorical reframing for just the sort of mutual locutions that proliferate in Dickens's *Our Mutual Friend*. So that what metaphor, according to Davidson, avoids—by not being divided against itself with a "second" meaning—the alternate work of punning or ambivalence, in contrast, embraces; and that of syllepsis, in turn, displaces. It does so, at times, across the grammatical equivalent of a stutter or a pratfall in physical comedy that may in fact, as we've noted, bring two separate literalisms, or idioms, into an activated metaphoric relation across their metonymic sequence.

A few isolated samples from *Our Mutual Friend* should do to give the timbre of the rest, especially those edged most effectively with satire.[19] Given the wilted eroticism of Lady Tippins, she seems almost rhetorically fortified by the internal alliteration of "fan" with the tripled, self-splayed assonance of "advantage"—and this despite the lingering aftertaste of the suffix "age" itself—when she is found, at one sylleptic blow, "showing her entertaining powers and green fan to immense advantage" (bk. 2, chap. 3). The milquetoast Twemlow, planning to review his cues for this wedding ritual while he dines, goes home (in a literal double-taking, his before ours) "to take a plate of mutton broth with a chop in it, and a look at the marriage service" (bk. 1, chap. 10). And no doubt counsel sometimes—and sometimes tea. This, before Twemlow is later found so wordily "getting better, and also getting himself into his obsolete little silk stockings" (bk. 3, chap. 17). This has more of afterthought than of inspiration about it, as flagged by the heavy participial repetition, even though its ironic point by no means falls short of the target. Once again, the sylleptic effect is pitched in suspension between the mental and the material in defining the narrow compass of Twemlow's socialite rounds. Broken open by the doubled verb, syllepsis may not play very well under such strain, but it continues doing its familiar conceptual work.

The real weakness of such grammatically overcoded sylleptic formulations in *Our Mutual Friend* appears when they turn from social satire to societal amelioration, as with "Mr and Mrs John Harmon . . . taking possession of their rightful name and their London house" (bk. 4, chap. 14). Spiritual and material meet under a strictly legalistic aegis in this middle-class fantasy come true. But some marriages, across class lines, remain cause for prejudiced contempt and the closing of societal ranks against them, as with the lawyer Wrayburn condescending to marry the barge girl Lizzie Hexam, a scandal in the eyes of the pompous Mr. Podsnap, whose "indignation" is found "rising high" into his hairline (bk. 4, chap. 17). This glosses a syllepsis just before, where we are reminded that Podsnap is a man of no inner life but that which swells to the surface of his girth—and its pent-up irascible bottleneck. For we have just seen him "with his temper and his shirt-collar about equally rumpled" (bk. 4, chap. 17), a phrasing tampered with revealingly at the manuscript stage. Having originally written "with his temper and shirt collar rumpled," Dickens inserted (with that minimal legibility characteristic of the notoriously frustrating manuscript at the Morgan Library) not only the parallel-enforcing "his" but the aptly picayune overspecification of "about equally." With Podsnap's ruffled bluffness, as delivered over to a mind/body dualism yet again, one doesn't have to hear some further lurking pun on "shirt-collar" and *choleric* to see the unspoken convergence of attributional fields in his swollen ire. In the synthetic value system of the Dombeys and the Podsnaps of this Victorian world, the buttoned-up and the defensive, the starched and the stiff, mark again the tacit idiomatic reduction of the blustering patriarch to the stuffed shirt.

Syllepsis stands watch, straddling watch, over a habit of perception that has certainly become systemic by the time of *Our Mutual Friend*. In ways familiar to any Dickens reader, but multiplied almost with abandon in *Our Mutual Friend*, outer and inner seem almost to mock each other in the same grammatical breath. Clothes make a statement and the man. Bracing collars and moral indignation exist on the same discursive plane. Show has become all that remains of substance, surface of depth, body of self. Examples have multiplied everywhere we look. A man's stockings are as important to get on as is his life to be gotten on with. The power of one's emotions and the spread of one's decorative (and masking) fan are shown to equal advantage. The sylleptic cast of consciousness in *Our Mutual Friend* is ultimately no laughing matter. It doesn't resolve incommensurables by its wry disjunctions, or even raise the possibility of doing so. It exposes, instead, a bland or sometimes brutal dehumanization of the unseen by the seen. In its reduction of mental to somatic function, its frequent literalizing drag on metaphor, or else its sometimes numbing equipoise between spirit and matter, the only cure for its irrational flattenings and logical mismatches may seem administered by the quickening of wit they precipitate. To catch the sense, rather than be caught out by it, reading is slowed to its own recognition as such, which is also to say that language is raised to consciousness as medium.

After Dickens: A Brief Genealogy

Dickens's close friend Wilkie Collins, though working primarily in the "sensation novel" vein, nonetheless aspires at times to Dickensian verbal comedy. In a single chapter of *Armadale* (1864–66), "The Plot Thickens," syntax itself coagulates along with the narrative intrigue when we are told of a picnic to be attended by a widow lady's son "in holy orders and in delicate health" (bk. 2, chap. 7), followed shortly by the double turn on *of* in "the man of the timid manners and the mourning garments." Farther along in the same chapter, in an effect delegated this time to a character's idiolect, there is the expressed confidence that an awaited new arrival, if an older woman, will absent herself from outdoor felicity and "stick to the cold fowl and the cottage." Like Dickens, Collins is fond as well of the sylleptic variant—across a dialogue exchange—that distributes such an idiomatic difference in the form of a baffled discrepancy, as when his title figure, Allan Armadale, confounded about the next move he is expected to make, answers a rhetorical question from his adviser with "See my way? . . . I see nothing but a cab-stand" (bk. 3, chap. 3)—or in other words a means without an end. This kind of wit, in its typical contrast between abstract and concrete senses, often metaphoric ("envisage," say) versus literal ("see"), is later put in the epistolary mouth of the sarcastic antiheroine, Lydia Quilt, who, remembering a time when the hero, Midwinter, "might have possessed himself of my love," notes instead, punctuating her letter's punch line for extra effect, that "All he had possessed himself of now was—my waist" (bk. 3, chap. 9).

Certainly syllepsis has a later and varied career in Victorian prose after Dickens—and very much under his ("Inimitable") influence. Even Thomas Hardy and Henry James, as I've noted elsewhere, indulge in the format—each in his own characteristically arch and contorted way.[20] In later James, the style seems more inclined to rim the edge of this syntactic trope, or distend it beyond immediate comic recognition, than to commit wholesale to its wry snap. Satirizing the self-absorbed drone of the heroine's lackluster fiancé in the story "In the Cage" (1898), free indirect style give us access to her tedium in enduring "Mr. Mudge talk of what he might do if he didn't take a bath, or of the bath he might take if he only hadn't taken something else."[21] But the effect can mutate rapidly enough from the farcical to the forlorn. At the climactic letdown of the story, the heroine and her similarly disappointed woman friend "looked out, hand in hand, into the damp, dusky, shabby little room and into the future" (203), where the homology isn't left to suggest itself only implicitly, since James adds, in the rounding out of a characteristically suspended clause, "[into the future], of no such very different suggestion, at last accepted by each." In what is now—by this point in James's later career—his commitment to an entirely dictated style, a typist always on hand, it is as if each inference tends to be pursued by phrasal accretion and cumulative nuance. For any such transcriptive stylistics of redirection and afterthought, syllepsis can seem the ne plus ultra and the reductio ad absurdum at once.

Then, too, this syntactic sample of the running afterthought (in mechanical record) occurs in a story preoccupied thematically with just such remediation, not only of the oral by the transcribed in telegram dictation but, at a further remove, of the written by the numerically encoded. In this tale of a female "telegraphist" rather than typist, but nonetheless a manual word processor—a nameless shopgirl busy all day at her "sounder" counting words, tapping out pulsional messages—the reader may sense at one psychological turning point that the restless momentum of James's ironic grammar has found a unique syllabic channel as well, rendering ambiguous in its own key (its phonetic variant of the sounder's punched key) the very keeping straight of separate words in the running head-count of their sign function. This happens when the telegraphist fantasizing about the wealthy adulterer she's smitten with, even while her coworker is transmitting one of the young man's secret messages, goes into a sound-prompted reverie and projects "a vision" of his waiting for her in the park. It is a mirage sprung from the very click of her overheard professional apparatus across the syncopated sibilance of Jamesian free indirect discourse, in all of its own mannered starts and pauses and seditious ligatures: "She could almost see him, through the *tick* of the sounder, scatter with his_*stick*, in his impatience, the fallen leaves of October" (179; emphasis added). The present sound becomes the absent object. And if the heroine is hearing things, so, too, is her close reader: things unsaid but nonetheless transmitted by the very act of transmission itself.

As a telegraphist turned delusional telepathist, the nameless "our girl" (narrational as well as demeaning office idiom) thus telegraphs her fantasy as an incoming signal to her own overwrought brain. Though "caged" within the transmission booth of an otherwise frustrating outpost of the electric-post system—in an office capable, we've heard, only of sending, not of receiving, texts—she achieves at last exactly the remote-messaging capacity of the very different medium, the cadenced prose discourse, that manifests her desires.[22] For it is as if the self-deferred grammatical closure of Jamesian prose, in all its indulged suspensions, had found at this pass, in a narrated episode of audiovisual mimesis, a further narratographic equivalent at the sublexical level: the serial phonemes of an alphabetic medium themselves left momentarily up in the air as the typographic equivalent, so to say, of black noise. Or one may rephrase this effect, instead, for the way it momentarily and more particularly coordinates the two parts of this study in a prosaics of secondary vocality. In this sense, the flotations of Jamesian syntax have found a contemporaneous technical equivalent for his high-wire technique. For here the hoverings of grammatical periodicity, shifted from syntax to morphology across a suspended lexical juncture timed to the free-associational beat of the telegraphic sounder, transfers the forking function of syllepsis—in its own impish and perverse way—down to the alphabetic scale of splayed word border in the sparked gaps of cross-lexical friction.

The norm for such double takes is, in every sense, decidedly broader. Between Dickens and James, George Eliot tries on the sylleptic device as lighthearted class satire for a passing barb in *Daniel Deronda* (1876) about the Reverend Gascoigne, who, in two senses of his predicated anointment, "had once been Captain Gaskin, having taken orders and a diphthong but shortly before his engagement" (bk. 1, chap. 3). The telltale "kin" of his second syllable disowns its Anglo-Saxon kinship by taking on not just an *oi* but a silent *g* and *e* as well: as complete a Gallic conversion at the level of the rarefied material signifiers as any spiritual conversion one can imagine him undergoing en route to clergyhood. Here as elsewhere, easily (if not instantly), you get the split gist. Cognizance must swerve quickly to avoid confusion. Like so many effects of prose in motion, syllepsis works best when it works fast syntactically and out semantically.

In varying degrees of comic reflex, syllepsis has a surprisingly long afterlife, surviving even a modernism with little taste in general for its mode of calculated symmetry and wit. Syllepsis flourishes, for instance, in the neo-Dickensian narrative energy of John le Carré's prose.[23] One takes note of it as well in the postwar mannerist satire of Muriel Spark, where in *The Abbess of Crewe* (1974) a phonetic compression and inversion accentuate the categorical mismatch of syllepsis in a very Dickensian laminate of couture and spirituality. For here, in a novel so phonetically attentive that the word "wrongdoing" is audited by the title figure for the way it "sounds," by parallel assonance, "so like the gong of doom," even a dismissive syllepsis in characterizing the secular British matronliness of a particular nun is enhanced by the phonemic chiasm (*owf/vow*) of "despite her coif and her vows."[24] In another play on Catholic "habit" from earlier in this same decade, there is this from Shirley Hazzard's *The Bay of Noon*: the referential switch operating across a literalized and split perpendicularity when an Italian woman from Naples is said to "fearfully cross the road, and herself, when approaching the church that housed the exorcized Devil of Mergellina."[25] Or in an even more strictly comic novel from the postwar British canon, there is a witty twist by the amiable cad Vandervane in Kingsley Amis's *Girl, 20* when fabricating an excuse concerning a missed engagement with a man who had caught a bug on the Amazon, "of all things and rivers," or the mention of the hero's girlfriend's alternate lover, who "took up all of her free time and half her bed every Tuesday and Friday."[26]

Earlier yet, and across the Atlantic, there is Robert Penn Warren's *All the King's Men*, where one "Mr. Duffy cleared his throat, the way he always did in late years when he was congested with phlegm and an idea."[27] Elsewhere in that novel the labor of grammar, indulging its own waiting game, imposes a double temporal topography on "a place where you sit down and wait for night to come and arteriosclerosis" (78). The waiting is more distended yet in this remarkable description of Aunt Sophonisba as "a feeble, grumbling, garrulous, and incompetent old colored woman, who combined benevolence and a vengeful tyranny in the ambiguous way known only to old colored women who have spent their lives in affectionate service, in prying, wheedling, and chicanery, in short-lived rebelliousness and long irony, and in secondhand clothes" (463). The first multiple run of adjectives, with the threefold embedding at the end ("incompetent old colored"), is varied only by a participle ("grumbling"). Offered almost as if arbitrarily itemized in its insistent nonhierarchy, the mounting series feels designed to put us off guard for the broken rhythm and final turn coming, where we shift from one acceptation of "in" to another. Hypallage (the reversing figure of effect before cause) goes hand in hand with syllepsis as we move—on the model of "in a flood of tears and a sedan chair"—from *in* as condition to *in* as containment, from what wears her down to the explanatory poverty whose signs drape and enwrap her: signs, in other words, that she is forced, unlike her resentments, to *wear on her sleeve*.

Concerned as well with racial degradation, Toni Morrison's 2008 novel, *A Mercy*, arranges for the twin prongs of syllepsis to skewer, across another if more tacitly divided prepositional sense of *in*, the corrupt slaver who, without profit from his chattel, would be "sleeping in the bush of Africa rather than a four-post bed."[28] Elsewhere such effects can split the difference between behavioral surface and mental depth in evoking the sexual threat to a slave girl posed by men encountered "in liquor and anger" (47). Then there's a man's fatal pox that "alters his mind as well as his face" (43).

Both those last examples demonstrate the trope's classic mind/body fusion across a disjoint linkage. Or there are tavern drinkers regaled by the musicians who "entered for their merriment and their money" (33), the preposition going two ways at once, giving and then taking.

And in the more inward monologues of Morrison's novel, sometimes in almost private languages of their own, the double tracking of psychological and diurnal time in the rhythms of desire can be accompanied by loosened and intuitive versions of the trope: generating again, in the attention spans of reception, the inherent vigilance of its own phrasal temporality—where we are asked by syntax to correlate wholly different scales of natural cycle and human need. Narratography at work: with the ethics of the entire episode depending in part on the ethic of attention that notes a passing shift in grammar. Compare in *Little Dorrit*, for instance, the calendrical beat of Dickens's wedding-eve cadences—"And the day ended, and the night ended, and the morning came, and Little Dorrit . . . came into the prison with the sunshine" (bk. 2, chap. 34)—with the more wrenching cognitive dissonance between duration and physical presence when Morrison's half-literate heroine apostrophizes her absent blacksmith lover: "I know you will come but morning does and you do not" (163). And even this barely idiomatic spatialization of time in the absence of the longed-for body has been more conventionally prepared for in the low-keyed fourfold sylleptic report that has sent her journeying—and the sentence careening—in search of the man in the first place, the girl inferentially "possessed" of unmastered passion as much as necessary provisions: "She had Sir's boots, the letter, food and a desperate need to see the blacksmith" (78). In this way are the coordinates of narrative action "bundled" (Genette), at the sentence level itself, in assertive separate vectors not quite parallel.

Against a general tendency toward ironic thud or comedown in the onset of the skewed sylleptic turn (often a satiric bubble-bursting via the breached pattern of phrasal expectation), my citing of Morrison there is partly to suggest how the mismatch courted by such wording may also be as poignant as it is elsewhere parodic. And sometimes the former wins out over the latter across the same tonal span, where heartstrings, as it were, can be tugged at even by the sardonic snap of syntax—and this within a broader band of stylistic signaling. Filtered, for instance, through the indirect discourse of the embittered and cynical male narrator of P. D. James's apocalyptic novel, *The Children of Men*, is a future-anterior memory of the hysterical (or "phantom") pregnancies that used to befall women in the early years of sudden global infertility, their desperation leading to a "spurious" labor (as the narrator recalls in his characteristically affectless diary) in which the victims were found—in an issuance divided precisely between biology and psychology— "groaning and straining, and bringing forth nothing but wind and anguish."[29] This, at the narrator's typically cold-blooded remove, is almost a clinically controlled testing of sylleptic recognition—and the verbal ethic of its notice. All normal sympathetic response to this representation, to the mass anxiety and despair of these forlorn sufferers, must be sieved through the narrator's disengaged diary prose, with its almost snide wordplay for the confluence of flatulence and grief.

It is just there, of course, that what I have been proposing as an ethic of verbal attention—as the potential conduit of any verbally induced ethics of literary fellow-feeling—might well further link the grammatical twist of his snippy dismissal to the nonetheless withering vacuity breathed in heavy emphasis across the syllabic accents of *wind / and / ang*, with that extra pitiable whoosh (of *uish*) at the end. Trust the words, not the worder. Physical and spiritual defeat, palpable expiration and mental despair, meet at the point where embodied life fails to be materially delivered, no sooner "brought forth" in predication than negated ("nothing but") and then dissipated by the exhalations of prose alone. But felt, nonetheless, in what Hartman (see "Fore Word") invites us to sense through the "mediating"—because enunciating—"body": the body not belonging here to the fruitless heaving women, still less to the stiff ironic narrator, but alone to a reader in the subvocal production—the silent sounding—of this mental scene, to whose style-thickened pathos we alone give birth.

The narrative force of syllepsis is one thing: now comic, ironic, or satiric; now traumatic, elegiac, or ritualized in its very rhythms. It is sometimes openly ethical in its narrative emphasis, sometimes not. Regardless, the *ethic* of syllepsis as a registered syntactic stress, its affect in process, is something else again. I have called the format "assertive" above. Its literary imperative is to provoke its own notice, to expose its secret springs, to reveal in a given utterance the givenness and discriminations of language itself, to lay bare in sequence grammar's own simultaneous "potentiality" and realization. Demanded ad hoc with an unusual focus, the committed habits of close reading close here upon the conditions of their own necessity. Structures blatantly destabilized have a way of returning one to matters of foundation. What in poetry (for Agamben) is achieved by the deferral of semantic form by metered phonemics, the run-on of patterned sound over signifying measure—or achieved in prose (in my extension of this double-tracked effect) by the delay and regrouping of syntactic predication by the differential force of direct or indirect objects—is a question that brings forward the enunciated fact of language itself and the alternatives internal to it. Not resolving difference but isolating it as such, the "end of" syllepsis, as in the sense of Agamben's *The End of the Poem*, is to see that speech acts no longer go unattended; that speech *acts*, and is seen to do so in process; that language, paraphrasing again the last paragraph of Agamben's book, is a fact that no longer remains unspoken in what it speaks. Syllepsis makes sense only by eliciting the way sense making comes about and to light. If this results always in an ethic of the literary, while only sometimes in a literary ethics, then criticism renews itself in its willingness to find meaning in the very work of wording, to take reading slow and in and up on its hints.

"Into Manuscript and Syntax"

Syllepsis is that moment in grammar that overruns structure by an unexpected momentum. It routes us over already covered ground at least by a half step of backtrack and catch-up. Its scheme is, as it were, two-timing. Taken up in this way, syllepsis is both template and tempo, but less a matter of layered meanings than stages, not so much bifold as unfolding. It induces not a superimposition of discrepant senses (often literal versus figurative) so much as the successive nexus of their association—and, through this, the sensed possibilities on which this signifying concatenation not only rests but which it wrests back into sudden visibility—and wrestles with in sequence. It is Agamben's crossing between ontology and poetics, backed by commentary as different as Empson's and Cavell's, that can point us most directly toward the level of linguistic ontology itself that a troping like syllepsis—with its Derridean pitched battle between diction and syntax—turns up.

In terms of linguistic flexion, syllepsis is where the opening from within language to its own alternative forms becomes not just capacious, malleable, or say, *tolerant* in an "engineering sense" (Empson's specification, again, for one sense of "play" in words, 183). Beyond (or beneath) this, the sylleptic second thought *thinks language*. Its exposed grammar is an opening back to possibilities present still in the saying of what is said. And its connection to a formative poetics of potential is therefore worth reiterating. If poetry, for Agamben, is where speech never vanishes entirely into the spoken, the self-asserting tropology of syllepsis is, for prose as well, a sensed transit whereby—through a feedback loop with its own surface/d tensions—meaning is read as still being made beneath the meant. Where Derrida and Riffaterre see sylleptic diction as modeling deconstruction and intertextuality respectively, and where Genette sees it as an engine of variant narrative focalization, I too see the trope of bundled doubleness (or tripleness)—once restored to its local syntactic manifestation—as quintessentially literary. In the sylleptic turn, a phrase's full potential is seeded in the temporal paradox of (all but) simultaneous rereading, produced by second thoughts that do not think better of the elapsed but overlap it, that layer, deepen, and so realize it. Realize it—but also realize something more fundamental about it—and about its relation to *homo loquens*. Something linguistic, something cognitive, something human, hence something philosophical.

And something that is never clearer, perhaps, than when travestied in nihilistic foreclosure. Poe's example of negative potential in the previous chapter was as clear as it was final. Consignment to the hangman makes private and inward death the potential of execution's public ritual—inevitable, but suspended as effect by its legal cause. Yet in the speaker's being remanded to damnation in one and the same sylleptic stroke—no sooner to the hangman than to hell—perdition is more than imminent, is in fact all but immanent, in the judicial remittance: eternity only a hairbreadth away within the pace of time. This deferral elsewhere, of course, is often more liberating than obliterating. Sensing the freed-up space of alternative signals on the phrased underside of the existent, in the unlocalizable zone of present possibility, is one utopic gesture of philosophy, politics, ethics, and art. Geoffrey Galt Harpham, championing a "principled confusion" in literary signage as its true ethical tenor in reception, sounds much like Agamben as well, on the dialectic of potential, when writing that "the ethical *is* is an *is* that *ought* to be; the ethical *ought* is an *ought* that *is*"—in other words, a present imperative, a present *image*, manifesting a palpable convertibility of description and prescription, "facts and values."[30] Including the value of imagining certain facts otherwise: making the given give up its alternative (rather than giving up on it).

In its slippage and interchange, the trope of syllepsis restages its own version of this convertibility at so narrow a compass that it can seem like a short circuit, where the immanent alternative nips at the heels of present intent across an apparent misfire of predication. On his own terms, Agamben can show that it must be possible for a thing to be, to be here and now, other than it is, can show that otherness is potential itself realized as such, immanent to present form: a lingering contingency not yet effaced by apparent determinations. At a certain microlevel unapproached by Agamben's literary reading, yet a level where philosophy meets poetics, syllepsis becomes, then, the literary staging—or least tactical staggering, by grammatical delay and overlap—of immanent contingency. As the trope of reciprocal redefinition, it keeps alive the accidents of word choice in the predicates of being or event, each phase of the locution mutually revising the other across the adjusted registers of syntactic time, full to the brim with their own alternatives.

This is how syllepsis flexes syntax as an exercise in what we might call alterity recognition. The predicate is pre-dictated, but only in retrospect. Oh, I see now, "went home *in*" (tears as well as a portered carriage) had to have meant that second thing, too, meant it all along—an open secret of diction hidden in plain if refracted sight. What this amounts to in everyday terms is that narrative flux is not reserved for the phrased pace of event but internal to the event of phrasing itself in the deed of reading. Syllepsis, then, as anatomized by our wide range of examples: as logic, a category disorder; as syntax, a definitional shuttle, with its sudden decoupling and recovery; as meaning, a double-timing of the sentence; and finally, as significance, a node of language not just randomly multiplied but raised, in present potential, to the power of itself. All told, then, our leading philosophical touchstones on the (unmentioned) question of syllepsis are in fact complementary. Where

Cavell, following Wittgenstein, reflects on the ordinary capaciousness of literary language and its ethical demands under the wavering flag of the everyday, Agamben looks to the very capacity for language as an ontological presupposition nameless from outside itself and thus cogently philosophized only from within literature. The "end" of the poem, of the novel, of literature, of verbal text, is in only one sense there *before it*: not an external destination, whether quasi-messianic or in any way asymptotic, and not as in the closed circle of some self-referencing prophecy where to mean is to be. The end is approached instead as a discovered (and always waiting to be rediscovered) *precondition* that paradox should not scare us away from calling a *terminus a quo*.

It is this sense of ends kept open in means, of formal effects leading to their own formative causes, that inflects with epitomizing wit a particularly wry and refined turn of syllepsis in the most philosophical of Victorian novelists. Happening in the process to mark again the close cousinship of this trope to hendiadys, George Eliot offers an unmistakable metasyntactic example. Imagine if one were to speak of "the text and execution of George Eliot's prose" (in that Shakespearean A and B of C identified by Empson, where, as equally in Žižek's philosophical "and," subordination is flattened to coordination). Or to speak more particularly, in *Daniel Deronda*, of "the edge and syntax of Eliot's irony" in satirizing Grandcourt's antipathy to writing. One would thus have approached quite closely to a sylleptic effect like this from the novel itself: "We know that there are persons who will forego their own obvious interest rather than to . . . *rush into manuscript and syntax* on a difficult subject" (chap. 48; emphasis added). Concerning manuscript and syntax, syllepsis is indeed a kind of master trope. As self-exemplified in this collocation, its "rush" to hit the page running, linked to a clocking of grammar's own necessary pace, evokes two different aspects of the same forward momentum—as much kept before Eliot's reader as they are foreign to her villain's languor.

Certainly a phrasing like that is shaded, shadowed, by the ways of its being otherwise put. At such moments, one might say that the linguistics of literature awaits and reveals itself—comes before itself—as the contemplated existence of the speech act in embryo, an act considered in every "ordinary" case, and by syllepsis most obviously, against the alternate verbal possibilities it raises, defers, disables, or half incorporates. Here is where writing drops away into the untold but suddenly read depths of linguistic possibility, a possibility made manifest, if only partly good on, by any given play (in the language game)—any given byplay and semantic undertow—of diction and syntax. In this way, on this understanding, in this *way* of understanding, syllepsis retrieves an atrophied etymological force in the very word "comprehension." Its manner of letting us catch the drift involves the span of an embrace, where meaning collects itself before our eyes—even in its unquenchable discrepancies.

Tempo is everything, "rushed" or otherwise. In taking the very time of writing by taking up its own slack, syllepsis has as its end not the giving out or up of common meaning but a giving upon—in the sense of opening to—language's own intrinsic mechanisms for the progressive structuring of sense. Syllepsis is the trope of meaning in the making. It submits to the difference in which it results, putting the reader through its own paces. Its timing measures out in this way, in one extreme way, just what makes language tick. Whatever it is arranged to depict, it shows only by showing how. In short, and in its own cognitive shorthand, syllepsis writes reading.

Tales of Two Takings

But of course Dickens, not Eliot, should have the last word on syllepsis, given his many words set aslant to each other in its format. With his last three completed novels, this signature syntactic buckle continues to pace both his sentences and sometimes the larger spans of action. In *A Tale of Two Cities* (1859), the double takes are often closely plot-driven. There is the shady character "evincing a tendency to keep his own counsel, and to keep his hat cocked over his eyes" (bk. 1, chap. 3), with the bias toward secrecy in this context of French Revolution intrigue thus mated to a physical accoutrement of seclusion.[31] This twinning of the motive and the symptom of espionage in a single duplex, if not duplicitous, wording is followed, as civic rage and unrest mount across the Channel, by phrasings that straddle material conditions and their threatened result, whether in mortal misery or rebellion. This we sense when a French populace knowing not the cake wished upon them (in unmentioned intertext) by Marie Antoinette, but only "the taste of black bread and death" (bk. 1, chap. 5)—a savor at once literal and figurative in a lethal sequence of deprivation—finds its retributive backlash, via the backstroke of phrasing itself, in the revolutionary spectacle (and narratological chiasm) of "trooping women variously armed, but all armed alike in hunger and revenge" (bk. 2, chap. 21). There is still room, however, even in this dark novel, for pockets of two-ply, split-idiom wit, as when the idea of Tellson's bank in London being forced to adopt the décor of its Paris branch, with the resulting threat of collapse and an ignominious appearance in the newspaper bankruptcy columns, is indeed a fate that "would have driven the House out of its mind and into the Gazette" (bk. 3, chap. 2). And concerning the London courtroom mirror in which criminals have been for years reflected, there is the fine metaphysics of this scalar leap: "Crowds of the wicked and the wretched had been reflected in it, and had passed from its surface and this earth's together" (bk 2, chap. 2).

As usual in later Dickens, comedy in *Great Expectations* (1861) can play off against more melodramatic psychology in the deployment of this syntactic trope. Pip's snooty largesse, in the aura of his new prospects, is marked by the vainglorious plummet from material to figurative libations when treating his neighbors not just to a considerable feast but, in phonemic spillover, to "a pint of *ale* and a *gallon* of *con*descension" (chap. 19; emphasis added). At every turn, of course, Pip's tarnished origins haunt his new hauteur. At the local pub one evening, just before the violent attack on Pip's sister, a man sent by Magwitch to prosecute the latter's gratitude—Magwitch, the convict Pip felt guilty years back for having helped, until succeeding almost to forget the miserable incident—makes his presence known as a veritable specter from the past. What results is an unexpected apparition that rekindles the scorching memory, first by the stranger's metonymical identification of his present mission by brandishing a telltale file, that tool associated with Pip's forced help to the convict in irons. At this point a convoluted variant of syllepsis sets in, but not until the pumps are primed by a typical comic instance. Mrs. Joe has put Joe on a short leash for his time at the pub: "The half hour and the rum-and-water running out together, Joe got up to go, and took me by the hand" (chap. 10). Yet before they can take their leave, Pip is intercepted by that displaced revenant of the past.

What seems at first a rather direct format of splayed grammar for rhetorical emphasis actually captures more subtly the thematic return of the repressed at this first point of recurring crisis. Syntax in this instance, one would think at first glance, takes the routine double turn of figurative and literal together, the abrupt advent of recovered guilt and its delegated human trigger, with the hero, in short, "stupefied by this turning up of my old misdeed and old acquaintance" (chap. 10). But the latter emissary from the past arrives in the form of a mere stand-in who only, by inference, must know "my convict." The two modes of "turning up"—that phrasing not quite idiomatic to begin with in connection with a memory rather than a person—thus press harder than usual in a unique justification of sylleptic double grammar. Each half of the dyad is metonymic after all, neither literal. Like most everything that happens to Pip in his upward mobility, each stage of plot is the mere figure, impalpable and unreal, for some aspect of the unshakable. Progress is regress. Everything that "turns up" is a return.

So deep goes syllepsis into the Dickensian narrative imagination at this point in his career, I want to say, that even a single instance of its compounded phrasing in *Great Expectations* can seem like a compressed set of number plans for the vicious circles of an entire plot. Such a loaded case of syllepsis thus invites narratography in a uniquely confined nutshell, with the whole prolonged and episodic story of ghostly returns and unpurgeable complicities staging itself there—again, effect before cause—in the split between "misdeed" and the "acquaintance" who coerced it. In this case, as in so many others less centrally, a sylleptic dualism offers the unmistakable "microplot" of a novel in progress. So it seems almost structurally inevitable that an answering scene, much later, should arrive to literalize this early trope of re-"turning." For when the degrading memory of the convict from the marshes invades Pip's gentlemanly consciousness and his London rooms at once—as the disclosed source of his fortune—plot has come upon its long-deferred awakening, its true recognition scene. Illustrating his psychopoetics of fiction, Peter Brooks, in *Reading for the Plot*, speaks of this as a "primal scene" replayed in "dumbshow," with Magwitch redundantly performing his old self under the needless eye of an already blindsided awareness of his identity on Pip's part: a return of the hero's deepest repressed, as if he and his nemesis/beneficiary stood again "face to face" in the lamented past.[32] Brooks's central and generative sense of recursive ambiguity in plot—the indetermination between the return *of* and the return *to* (100)—is never more insistently exemplified than in this scene, this prose, even though that twofold narratological prototype is not in fact adduced at this turn in his analysis.

The gist of Dickens's hammering emphasis: Pip would have known "my convict" anywhere, yet not by looks. "Even yet I could not recall a single feature, but I knew him!" (chap. 39). The apprehending is not strictly visual; it is that of a worst fear come true. Indeed, the convict's unnecessary reenactment of a past already hauntingly present to remembrance seems under negation (even as it is happening). Two "knews" build toward a run of compacted phrasal parallels, along with one "would have known," before that last monosyllable *known* seems toppling over into a phonic refrain: "No need to take a file from his pocket and show it to me; no need"—we're not sure quite yet that the needless has actually happened, though this is soon confirmed in the precision of the mounting irrelevant details—"to take the handkerchief from his neck and twist it round his head; *no n*eed to hug himself with both his arms, and take a shivering turn across the room, looking back at me for recognition" (chap. 39; emphasis added). Beyond the sublexical phonemic mirroring between the no-sooner-heeded-than-"known" and the "no need" of reminder, other stylistic effects are less elusive or conjectural. An epithet is unmistakably transferred and displaced ("shivering turn"), a phrasing made reversible ("for recognition"—mine of him; his of mine). On Brooks's reading, the rhetorical "praeterition" (129) of the encompassing effect is itself telltale, reminding the reader—in a variant of the "not to mention" mode—of replayed scenes the narrator posits as unnecessary for full recollection (also called in rhetoric "paralipsis," a kind of quasi ellipsis). For Brooks, this symptomizes a psychoanalytic repetition-and-working-through under erasure—carried, we may further note, on the conjunctionless headlong parallelism (unsorted; as if unsequenced) of asyndeton.

Yet this rhetoric rides as well on a lexical refaceting in process. The passage isn't just about repetition and return; it plays out such a recursion in verbal form—as if language itself had internalized the all but invariant psychic treadmill it depicts, where what has passed passes back into a thereby adjusted present. The passage operates, that is, across a triadic staging of the re-membered as framed by a single mutating verb in three mutedly different but coalesced senses: a distended triple syllepsis, no less, in the general tropological sense of a "taking together." There was, in short—foreshortening the entire extended parallelism—no need for any of Magwitch's three takings: out his file, off his scarf, or (round) his turn. There was, in fact, no possible mistaking of the man himself. What that fanned-out phrasal variation on a single iterated verb works to enforce, in the accordion-like effect of its own grammar, is the way its predicated redundancies unfurl as if in nightmare-like simultaneity with the recognition that instantaneously precedes them and precludes their utility. At the level of projected oneiric association, a psychoanalytic narratology thus finds its functional increments—available to narratographic notice—in the phrasal "condensations" and "displacements" (Freud's terms for the sliding signifiers of the unconscious) of phoneme, lexeme, and syntax together. It is an effect turning in fact on the same assonance and alliteration in the multiply deployed negation of a monosyllabic "no" that philosopher William H. Gass singles out from *David Copperfield* in his sense of the silent orality—or secondary vocality—of Dickensian metalinguistics.[33]

And what we come upon in this scene from *Great Expectations* as well, in the iterated spans of parallel grammar, is an Agambenesque "return of the possibility of what was" in the stylistic register—this under unique thematic pressure from a traumatic repotentiation at the narrative level. When in the case of *Our Mutual Friend*, as mentioned in the previous chapter, Agamben follows Deleuze, and is followed in turn by philosopher Roberto Esposito, in being drawn to the drowning and revival of the caddish Rogue Riderhood, it is because the narrated waterside interest induced by the near death of this universally despised life is thus freed entirely from sentimentality into ontology, isolating the very being of the "spark of life." There, too, syllepsis has its role in preparing for a sublexical fissure even more radically metalinguistic and spectrally "immanent" than the "known" of "no need." Ordinarily, to keep clear of Rogue, his neighbors are found "more frequently giving him the cold shoulder than the warm hand" (bk. 2, chap. 12)—substituting a metaphor of chill distance for the literal intimacy of friendly touch. He is in fact ostracized from the first by a verbal irony assigned to dialogue, when ushered out of the local pub by an insistence that the cramped bar of the Fellowship "would rather by far have your room than your company" (bk. 1, chap. 6). Long before his displacement by threatened death rather than disgust, his absence would make for a more convivial few cubic feet than his presence.

This sense of character under subtraction from the space he would lay claim to finds not just its syntactic irony but its weird syllabic homology in the revival of his drowned body later. For in the pleonastic return to a "consciousness of this existence" (bk. 3, chap. 3) discussed earlier in connection with Agamben's own ingrown genitives, this point of lexical dissipation begins with Riderhood's fitful "struggling to come back." Like everything else about the man, revival too is grudging as well as fluctuating. "Now, he is almost here, now he is far away again"—the comma splice transfiguring the very caesura to an enjambment, with any sequence all but simultaneous in this place beyond human time. And then again: "Now he is struggling harder to get back." But the longer one looks at the tripled parallelism of "Now he . . ." —and I do mean looks, with the phrasing's wordy attentiveness to every wax and wane of vitality stretching the moment by wavering iterations—the more one looks, the more chance there is that the spaced words will themselves be distended into blank countersigns for the void over which, like the character himself, they are suspended. The cross-word effect is almost the opposite of the spectral "known" abrogating by its own sound the "No need" of Magwitch's pantomime in *Great Expectations*; here alphabetic sounding is abrogated by cross-word ciphering. In this vein, against the lexical grain itself, close reading can get so close that it looks through to its twin negation, morphophonemic and ontological at once, beneath the "gaps" of lexical rather than moral "abeyance" in process. Or put it that, with characterization's trial by ordeal in the Riderhood chapter, the gestalt oscillation between fictional death and fictional life is taken up in the figure/ground switch of inscription itself. All we need do is imagine the suspended scrape of Dickens's pen over the blanks of the lines as he, yet again, works to vest life in his character through sheer scribal drive. "Now, he is here . . . now he is [not] . . . Now he is . . .," the pivotal middle iteration turning in fact on the canceling monosyllabic undertone of no he isn't; he's far away—and *nowhere* we can know.

Thus does the struggle to "be here" (and therefore to "be he . . .") become a struggle lexicographic and existential both. It is waged at times, and by no doubt unconscious lexical risks and wagers, from a place beneath speech sounds altogether. At the level of morphology and lexical juncture, to transfer Agamben's dyad yet again to the inner borders of inscription, the poetics of enjambment blur the word form's own constitutive caesura. Such a cross-lexical specter ("now he is here" canceled in lexical process by a phantasmal "nowhere") rears its antonymic force in these clauses—only for a split second each time—across the threefold downbeat of a syllabic split (deeper than any sylleptic divide at the grammatical level) that rebunches its word forms against the separate pace of graphemes and phonemes. Where in the reception of prose could Agamben's "reciprocal desubjectification" of discourse and reader, his model for the "end" of poetic utterance, be more potently roped back into narratographic irony?

As one might expect in Dickens, the alphabetic reconstellation thereby achieved finds its isomorph in a larger arc of plotting. This is because the obliquely conjured haze of "nowhere" that is broken up (or out of) in the very moment of the character's reemergence echoes that earliest catchphrase for the novel's hero himself, a man from "some" rather than no "where"—yet whose identity goes quickly under cover when he disappears into the false rumors of his own drowning.[34] The villain suffers in the flesh what the hero figures (out) for himself. With Rogue's "nowhere" soon resolidified as the space of a "he," enunciated language has quickly overcome, overridden, the very lapses that articulate its junctures, the emptiness it manipulates, the slack it capitalizes on, its lack in action. But not without factoring into plot this latent representational upset. And not without installing, again, a philosophical limit case. Only if, as with Bartleby, not-being is immanently potential for Riderhood—as brought forth in Dickens's own scrivening—can the passage mirror back in words the chance of continued existence instead. Here is the prosaics of potential under a unique alphabetic compression.

We can sum up the insinuation of such an undertext, such a graphic undertow, this way. Where for Deleuze and Agamben this central chapter on Riderhood's near effacement from plot is about the immanence of life without being, without a being, without being tied to identity, at just this same point of reduction it is equally—and for literature, more fundamentally yet—about the frailty of textual immanence as well, about the risks (because rifts) of personification when surrendered to raw alphabetic sequence. It is, in other words—in the internal otherness of words themselves, to themselves—as much about lettering's hollow web as about life's low ebb. Be such a syllabic syncopation as it may (this sudden nonbeing of the personal pronoun "now he" in a yawning "nowhere"), suffice it to say that any sense of a tenuous scriptive ripple operating potentially—in negative potential, as it were—across Dickens's audiovisual text would serve only to inflect a continuing stress, here by way of an invisible stress fracture, on the novel's prolonged liminal divide, for hero and villain alike, between life and death. Such a split difference shivers the very being of language to the hinges of its intermittence, its ultimately false but still humanly recuperable bottom in the fluid grounding of communicable signs. And so it is, too, that the closest possible reading of such linguistic oscillation, as the next chapter will illustrate once more—an act of reading too close even for the comfort of lexical stability—routes one, nonetheless, toward *a reading* after all. Yet beyond interpretation per se, there is also that deep reading whose true context—beneath the thematics in Dickens, for instance, of "somewhere" versus "nowhere" for a life on hold—locates the formative dimension of the language from which any such concerted reading must emerge. To speak sylleptically one last time, this is how a narratographic attention can hope to keep up—and so keep faith, or at least contact—with the writing it sets out to address.

6
TALKING ROOM

Literature's script makes room for its own kind of back talk: that's one way of evoking the vocal undertow of certain inscribed turns in the prose as well as poetry we've surveyed. In general, as I began by regretting, there is no disciplinary tautology (far from it) in thinking of "literature writing language," let alone its "writing language philosophy." For language is often forgotten in cultural estimates of what is too causally termed literary *writing* and its effects. Whenever in evidence, any attention to the disclosure, rather than sheer service, of language within a work of words tends to educe broader philosophical reflections on the nature, or rather the culture, of human speech in mobilization: mobilization forward (morphophonemic and grammatical articulation) and outward (communication). This double relay—whose blockage in Poe we began with in these later chapters on a prosaics as well as poetics of potential, each equally formative—is apparent again in the paradoxically posthumous (or, following Agamben, quintessentially iterable) discourse that is explicitly caught between writing and a silent, because deferred, speech at the climax of a textual parable to just this effect by Toni Morrison.

The Nobel laureate has had a long tradition to draw on in crafting her own version of that Romantic tension we have noted (in Elfenbein's terms) between the expository and the elocutionary urge—or, in our redirected terms here, between script and evocalization as an ethos of potential. One's "being in language" (gerundive and participial by turns) is not just tested but finessed in the long Romanticism (Wordsworth to Stevens) we've examined, where the complementary recognitions of linguistic being (fully nominalized) and being linguistic (ongoing and enactive) are tacitly equivocated in relation to a supposedly more natural "language of the sense"—and hence in relation to poetry as all but found rather than made, the inherent "cry of its own occasion" (Stevens). In the prose of Poe, with identity itself no more than the occasion of its own precarious cry, that same being literate is instead contested, wrestled with, travestied, and eviscerated. In the prose of Dickens it is settled for and then, within allotted limits, forcibly (even if mostly comically) unsettled. Concerned equally with the possibility and power of discursive transmit for our being in words, what we come to now in Morrison is the study of an indentured heroine whose definitive speech act, divorced from the mother tongue of a Portuguese slave diaspora, is founded in an anomalous language acquisition that haunts her narrative through to closure. With scribble preceding vocal speech in her linguistic acculturation, the impulse and habitus of human communication ends up being "philosophized" anew—while still fully in touch with the "graphonic" rudiments of communication in its sequential densities and dishevelments. What emerges is an uncannily refigured space of narrative transaction within the immanent terms of literature's own written relay: a space lending new parameters to the occupant deed of reading.

There is, to be sure, something about Morrison's 2008 novel, *A Mercy*, cast back to the late 1600s, that asks of us, by the tenor of its prose alone, to consider the variable and evolving literary space within this chronological bracket—across which its closing first-person monologue has miraculously survived. With Shakespeare always there first on the way from Keats and the other Romantics through Dickens to Joyce and beyond, our main field of evidence in this book has been modern literature in its generative linguistic tension, descendant in good part from the energies of Romantic lyric in their tensed play between lettering and enunciation. We turn now from the long heritage of the lyrical ballad, that influentially fused category with its own oxymoronic tension between plot and music, to the lyric narration of Morrison—in both its controlled stylistic agenda and the poignant contingencies of its rhythms. Doing so affords, in the process—and especially when bearing in mind the literary tradition Morrison builds on—perhaps the clearest distinction yet between an inevitable literary ethics and a variable ethic of attention to its communicating means.

In the last phase of Morrison's novel, a black voice in lamentation and defiance, in one of the imported languages of the early American land—a voice conjured, in fact, from a century before Romanticism—can *speak to us* only by an ethical leap of historical consciousness and through an ear tuned to syntactic tempos, lexical chord changes, and a sometimes piercing syllabic dissonance. Moral empathy and sympathetic vibration do their work together, in a way that recalls once more the prefatory citation from Geoffrey Hartman about the human body as the place of literary mediation. In Morrison, this is not just the body represented in its enslaved pain and shackling grief, but the body present (mine, yours) phonetically as well as optically to the text in reception, keyed to its post-Stevensian "keener"—and sometimes keening—"sounds." Such is the transit point of a shared ethos and its felt linguistic impetus in the urge to speech—and in the will to hear. This, then, as Agamben would have it, is where anything like a humanizing power in literature begins and ends, however codified and impersonal its discursive systems.

So, arrived now at Morrison's funneling of historical memory through the literary-historical sievings of her prose, we return to my premising emphasis on a verbal ethic in literary reading—and with a richly strenuous exemplum. Though the prompting evidence may elsewhere have seemed more elusive (less politically direct) than in Morrison, the point shouldn't have been. We feel for characters in fiction, as for personae in lyric, at least partly—and certainly first of all—through our feel for language. It is as if Dickens's hero Pip, misreading his parental tombstones as mimesis in that famous matrix scene from *Great Expectations*, were actually closer to a grasp of literary tutelage than irony realizes (or allows) when he is seen reaching for an image of the mother—as we do for one of him as "character"—by attending to the cast of script. "From the *character and turn of the inscription*, 'Also Georgiana Wife of the Above,' I drew a childish conclusion that my mother was freckled and sickly" (chap. 1). Pip isn't spackled and dismembered in our mind's eye because of print's discontinuous impress. But decouple the punning first term and the overliteral second term of his logic and you have the Dickensian ethos and its aesthetic at once: the evidence of "character" from the sheer "turn" of phrase. It is by this means, as we know from the previous chapter—pressed in *Our Mutual Friend* so explicitly beyond the collective ethics of the social into the (philosophical) outer limit and then raw return of human voice—that the plot has "turned" the "character" of Riderhood back from effacement into figuration. It has accomplished this attended not by a sympathetic community—whether as print audience or as bystanders within the narrative scene—but in a vigilance administered simply by the deed of reading and, in that case above all, its stringently impersonal ethic.

Doing the Deed

On the way into Morrison's closing chapter, we can benefit from a further precursive moment—falling between the late 1600s and the early 2000s—involving not just the Romantic syncopation of sound and sense (and its Dickensian uptake), especially when under the extra regimen of rhyme, but a concern with verbal perpetuity itself. What does the graphological as well as phonetic wordplay of a poet too soon dead have to tell us about the verbal license of a slave girl three centuries gone in the backwash of national history? Keats first:

> O for ten years, that I may overwhelm
> Myself in poesy; so I may do the deed
> That my own soul has to itself decreed.
>
> (*Sleep and Poetry*, lines 96–98)

How can a deed be manifest but in its doing? What can one do but a deed? Through a spiraling suggestion that escapes sheer circular phrasing, are we in fact confronted here with poetry and action founding each other at grammar's most formative level of minimal differentiation? The question is asked, of course, in the spirit of recapitulation. The supposed solipsism of an insular young Keats in hermetic devotion to his own sound; the international renown of a Toni Morrison in as salient a moral and political vein as ever tapped by American authorship: each the mark of a stylistic libido within a presiding ethics of fellow-feeling and tragic intuition; each the stamp of a euphonic genius inviting a palpable ethic of verbal attention. How to think them together—how else—but in the thinking undertaken by wording itself?

In that extended rhyming exercise called *Sleep and Poetry*, Keats tries inhabiting the titular border realm of his subvocal dreamscape, an effort all but phonetically swamped when tacking from the tossed "elm" (line 95) of one stanza to the opening self-apostrophe of the next. Breaking the couplet across a blank page line, the wish fulfillment behind such strained echo will out. But what comes through is not, as perhaps seemingly lineated at first, "O . . . that I may overwhelm," dazzle in my fame—but rather, rapidly enjambed in a more modest inundation, "overwhelm / Myself in poesy." Yet reflexive grammar cedes to its even more telling correlate in cognate grammar (as in "sleep your sleep," "dream your dream") in closing off the ambit of the speaker's ambition in the will to "do the deed" he has figuratively (in the very trope of enunciation) articulated ("decreed") for himself.

So let it be written, so let it be soon. Like a decree decreed or a declaration declared, a deed is something done, yes, but only the complex phonetic play triggered in the next line can rescue this from written insistence into poetic instance. This happens when the consonantal bracket of "d--d" answers to its figured vocal origin in the dictated ambition of "decreed" (de--eed). Indeed, in a broader bracketing yet, three subjunctive words of effect ("*d*o the dee*d*") must be made space for, one discovers retroactively, in the past tense (now potentialized) of their very impetus. The recovered vow finds avowal in the present vocalization. Noticing this in the look of lettering itself—and hearing it out, so to say—we do the deed in return, honor the contract, keep open the channels of response. In this further circuit of cognate recognition, the "end" of the poem, the destiny of the text, is only that we should, and in just this way, read the result of any such primal linguistic dictation. And even, perhaps, find the very verb of our contractual predicate seeded there in prospect, putting the eventual "read" into all things poetically decreed.

Which, in the alphabetic spacing-out rather than mere sounding of Keats's effect, invites a dialectic of retinal decipherment and cued audition. At its own actual end, that's what Morrison's *A Mercy* will have come to thematize, we are to find, and in a similar phonetic and grammatical reflex across its disjunctive lexical spacing: the audiovisual circuit between what is described or decreed, or in this one novel's grievous case tangibly inscribed, and its verbal recognition in the abstract space of self-eventuated response. Keats wants to live long enough to write what by then he will have had in him to write; "ten years" should do it, though perhaps—sensing rightly that his lease on life might be far shorter than this—he avoids the too lapidary slant rhyme of "decade" (with *deed/decreed*), as if it would constitute in its very ingenuity a jinx. By a different sort of proleptic trope, Morrison's writing heroine dies many decades, indeed centuries, before what she has finally decreed, and decried, can somehow be taken up by reading—and this against the racist dead weight of a silencing legacy of violence. Pressured to the forefront of attention (indeed almost allegorized) in this case, where the heroine will lay claim to a literalized "talking room," the point is unmistakable. It is the beginning of any ethical response that we should be moved to listen while we read. In this way, too, posthumous decryption—anticipated by Keats, staged by Morrison—is one intensified means of italicizing the Agambenesque recursion and ultimate desubjectification of literary force.

In the all but inexpressible ordeals that punctuate certain of Morrison's novels, language is often found by her characters just in time: in time for witness, that is, if too late for self-defense. And manifested, of course, in the very timing of syntax, with harmonic chord changes unmatched in current American writing. Yet the following consideration of her work gravitates to moments when the time-based medium of prose is refigured from within its own rhythms as a palpably spatial (rather than temporal) form.[1] When enacted as rhythmic prose, however, in its calculated aura of orality and its often palpable secondary vocality, this writing would offer incontestable evidence for philosopher Peter Kivy's stress on even silent reading as a "performance," always in part interpretive.[2] Kivy's purpose is to level the unnecessary distinction, in Nelson Goodman's philosophy of art, between works of notation-plus-instance like dance or music—or call it score-plus-execution—and the supposed self-containment of literary textuality, where notation is all. On the contrary, the only activation of a text Kivy would rule out of the performance category is a totally unthinking one, as in the uncomprehending delivery of a page in a barely known language or in the automatized computer-voicing, for instance, of books-for-the-blind software. In every other case, it is the attentive body that must be employed by the script in order to produce it as text. Wittgenstein once more from our launching epigraph: "The one real criterion for anybody's *reading* is the conscious act of reading, the act of reading the sounds off from the letters." That liftoff is the word in performance.

Secondary vocality as a "calculated aura of orality" in Morrison's style? No overstatement there. Her once undervalued first novel, when reissued, came bearing an afterword in which her career-long attempt at a revisionary prose was explicitly spelled out.[3] What she had always been after amounts to a luxuriant but nonwriterly narration that would help in "grounding my work" in an almost paradoxical "race-specific yet race-free prose" (211). Such is a mode of phrasing—marked here by a lightly echoic etymological wordplay of its own—that keeps "pressing for a female expressiveness" (215). This, then, is a prose that would manifest itself, over and above its textual imprint, as "speakerly, aural, colloquial" (215). It is a writing thus primed for the crests and valleys of a pervasive evocalization—even in that opening page of three appropriated, iterated, and incrementally compressed paragraphs of identical (but gradually hard to identify) wording through which the ensuing prose of that first of her novels, *The Bluest Eye*, had to break free in order to let breathe its inaugural and more genuine auralities.

For one thing, in their trivia and drivel, the words of this prelude are exposed by typography as the racially profiled clichés they constitute. As Morrison has it in that afterword to *The Bluest Eye*, concerning this opening treatment of a Dick-and-Jane reading lesson, "the incompatible and barren white-family primer" (215) throws into relief the meretricious fantasy of her main character: a black girl's desire for the eye color of a white girl. In the banality of its gradually elided gibberish ("Here is the house it is green and white it has a red door it is very pretty here is the family . . .") the sampled primer undergoes two stages of reduction, losing first its punctuation, as in a dumbed-down stretch of Joyce (with "here" cutting both ways syntactically, for instance, in "it is very pretty here is the family . . .), then shorn of its word breaks altogether. So that what Elfenbein notes as the elocutionary pedagogy conveyed, under Enlightenment norms, by such typographic compression as "Andshow youhave the virtue tobemov'd," cited in Chapter 3, is in this case further squeezed of sense—not for a more lucid rhetorical enunciation but for a satirized babble, to say nothing of a uniquely jejune deixis right from the start.

Exposing incrementally the garbled singsong nonsense of its stereotypes, still the passage is strewn with flickering clues to what's coming: the poisoning of a dog ("seethedog"—and the convulsions it is "seethed" with) and an eventual paternal rape: "Seefatherheisbigandstrongfatherwillyouplaywithjane." This prompt to cross-word reading, including even a latent suppression of "her" in "father," also colors the abject fantasy of racial erasure precipitated by the novel's blue-eyed wish fulfillment. Here the novel's titular irony—as submitted in its own right to the tacit blur of a jammed typography—insinuates as well the *bluest I* and the *bluest dye* and even, by infection (as well as junctural inflection), *the bluest stye*: drenching the organ of vision in a viral inauthenticity. So it is that the vacuous child's play of the opening gauntlet, with its eventually trash-compacted words of domestic inanity, is actually teaching us adult readers, beneath its lampoon of childish protocols, a new way to read across word breaks, one that will come home to roost in Morrison's later writing, including the climax of *A Mercy*.

Graven Narrative

The plot of that 2008 novel is not simple, but it is shrewdly and lucidly patterned. An African slave mother from a Portuguese colony is transported to American shores in the late 1600s. She begins the novel with her own version of Sophie's choice, giving up her daughter rather than son for slave barter—to a man she appeals to simply as "Sir"—so that the girl, Florens, might escape the sexual clutches of her current plantation master and his wife, with Sir's intervention being the lone and early "mercy" of the title. Into his well-meaning service comes also a Native American girl, Lina, sold by the Presbyterians who had housed her after an epidemic decimated her village and her clan. They are soon joined there, at so-called Sweet Home, by Sir's bought bride from Europe, and the three women grow close across racial lines during Sir's long absences making his fortune in the Caribbean rum trade. With this slave-based wealth he can finally pursue his lifelong, if only posthumously realized, dream. Leveling a virgin forest to build (in the manner of Faulkner's Thomas Sutpen) the grandiose mansion he always longed for, he dies laid out on its barely finished first floor, dragged there at his insistence in the last stages of smallpox. It is on the upper floors of this empty temple of ambition that his ghost is later noticed by indentured white laborers, the patriarch haunting a mausoleum in which no one else is willing to take up residence. But the spectral presence most urgently confined to this architectural haunt is, as we are to find, the very process of narration itself.

Just before Sir's death, his vain and palatial finishing touch has been the sculpted ironwork gate executed by a freed African blacksmith who had, short of saving the white landowner, performed certain remarkable feats of healing while on site, but had also, before moving on, driven the now-teenage Florens wild with desire, satiety, and more desire. Soon after his departure, Sir's widow falls ill as well—and must send Florens to plead for a return of the black man and his white herbal magic—a mission in which Florens is all too overinvested. After answering the summons and curing the widow, the blacksmith returns to his cabin, many miles distant, and to Florens, waiting there, distracted by her hunger for him. We have seen already, in our previous chapter, how the iterations of transitive grammar in her case turn a mild syllepsis into a symptom of erotic possession, the needful girl "having" in every sense at once "Sir's boots, the letter, food and a desperate need to see the blacksmith" (78).[4] But the freed man ends up disgusted with Florens's sexual obsession and dependence, saying that her yielding to passion rather than to reason in itself makes her, in effect, an inveterate "slave," degraded in his liberated eye. This is too much for the girl who had not just fixated on his body but pinned her hopes for protection and security on his strength. She attacks him first with a hammer, then with the forge tongs, and leaves him bleeding and perhaps for dead—indifferent at least, as she now is, about his survival. With the whole arc of this main melodramatic story behind us, it is only at this point that we learn about the *writing of this story* from within its own narrative space.

The chapter of aftermath inserts a seemingly false lead early on: "What I read or cipher is useless now. Heads of dogs, garden snakes, all that is pointless" (184). Her solecism "cipher" is meant, in her private, semitutored, and often truncated language, to mean "decipher"—and only in reference to the reading of nature's raw signs, to which level she has been reduced by the blacksmith's contempt. "You say I am wilderness," as she rephrases his dismissal, adding, "I am" (184). Being is not just for Florens a wilderness of desertion but a wildness unto itself. And the only "ciphering" that is left to her, as we are momentarily to discover, is not any longer a decoding of the world but, in the stricter sense, an inscribed mourning for what it has denied her. For she is now, and has all along been, writing out—for the eyes of her former lover only, but ours vicariously of course—the passages of direct address that we are likely to have been taking (in taking them in) not as if we were reading over her shoulder, but rather as a transparent fictive access to the rhetorical apostrophes of an internal monologue constituting one vector of this montage novel. If so, we have been mistaken.

"It is three months since I run from you" (185). At this point we recognize how the absence of the preterit in her discourse hasn't amounted to another prolonged solecism on Florens's part but more like a delegated novelistic liberty in manipulating the historical present of the narrative's own inscription. "At night I leave Lina"—but not just this night, every night, in the iterative present tense of narrational obsession, trapped in a present that won't let go of the past—"leave Lina sleeping and come to this room" (185). This *same* room always—the very space of narration right from the start, as we belatedly discover. The use of "this" as ambient pointer has of course a striking metatextual resonance in the lineage of literary theory. One legendary vexed flashpoint of linguistic deconstruction well before Agamben takes up with its doubleness or paradox, here is the deictic "this" that in writing can only point to a marked surface, not to its referents. And perhaps no single case in fiction of such a signified object has ever been more abruptly but purposefully "demonstrative" than Florens's scriptive "this," designating the very surfaces thus inscribed upon rather than merely denoted by her obsessive script. It is in every way an exhaustive indi(c)ting. For night after night, in an upstairs room of the deserted mansion, she has been gouging out her story with a nail scraped along walls and floor, generating—with wild metatextual improbability—not a traditional soliloquy or dramatic monologue so much as a piece of six-sided text art (like the rooms of words by conceptual artists from Joseph Kosuth and John Barry to Fiona Banner): a bibliographic chamber where the very walls whisper their worst in silence.

Perhaps because trenched out from wood or plaster rather than wrenched into voice, in any case the words haven't brought the catharsis Florens was counting on. "In the beginning when I come to this room I am certain the telling will give me the tears I never have. I am wrong. Eyes dry, I stop telling only when the lamp burns down. Then I sleep among my words"—a sleep "without dreams" (185) amid this recorded nightmare. As direct address, these words are a vast epistle going nowhere. "If you are live or ever you heal," so the letters hail to the blacksmith, "you will have to bend down to read my telling, crawl perhaps in a few places" (185). And what there will be to read is coming to its cramped finish. "There is no more room in this room" (189), she notes echoically, in an etymological merger of abstract and concrete noun in cognate overkill. "These words cover the floor. From now"—not from now on, but more immanent yet—"from now you will stand to hear me" (189). The dead or injured man, were he ever to come here, having closed his ears cruelly to her earlier appeals, must now in the other sense, and at whatever cost, be prepared to *stand listening*. "I am near the door and at the closing now" (189)—closing as the end point of the telling as well as the pulling shut of the portal in this volumetric space of encipherment. But: "Sudden I am remembering," she adds. Out of all this inscribed recollection, an undermining detail: "You won't read my telling. You read the world but not the letters of talk. You don't know how to" (189). One day he might learn, she thinks, at which point he would accomplish in what she calls her "talking room," by way of inhabited textual accusation, the true "end" of her venting. Otherwise, her alphabetic shapes can only "talk to themselves" (189).

Somatics of the Volume

What Morrison's novel entertains by this tricked ending, this trick tending toward its own textual condition in impressed script, pushes a step beyond the final soliloquy of her earlier novel *Jazz*, where it is the book itself—not an articulated space figured from within it—that turns out to be addressing us. Hints are planted at the start, since the narrative voice of *Jazz* boasts in the first chapter of being "strong," but admits that, as a denizen of Harlem in the 1920s, "I haven't got any muscles, so I can't really be expected to defend myself."[5] No motor function at all, we discover, except a mobile point of view. No flesh and sinew, just, say, the strength called spine, plus the flanged articulations it braces. Unmuscled but taut and firm, the infrastructure of narration, if we've caught on by the second time through, is personifying its inorganic textual status as an entity inert and nerveless until other hands are brought to it; an entity cautious though unafraid, not timid, but deriving its strength, like any implied author, from "making sure no one knows all there is to know about me" (8)—including the addressed second person at the outset: "You have to understand what it's like, taking on a big city" (9)—"taking it on," that is, as topic rather than inhabitant.

In the end, having assumed the mantle of this urban theme, the book leaves its erotic main couple in peace, in private sighs "under the covers" (228)—where, in a loaded prepositional phrase, they "are inward toward the other" (229) in more than a sexual sense. And the prepositional subtlety turns vertical as well, where we are made to contemplate a depth below mere "under": "That is what is beneath their undercover whispers" (228). Here the climactic wrinkles of idiom may return us to the cryptic apostrophe at the start, helping to unfold this time a momentarily ambiguous grammatical pleat in the founding enthusiasms of the first chapter. There, the narrator's compound predicate lets us expect momentarily a parallel and disyllabic phrasal verb: "A city like this one makes me dream tall and feel in on" (7)—upward and inward, expansive and intensive—until the sentence levels out idiomatically into "feel in on things." The argot of the "insider" is in fact the banal version of narration's feeling its way into its characters, empathy's almost palpable indwelling.

Yet for all this power of identification, the only love the narrative, personified as narrator, has known on its own part is wholly "in secret"—because in fact silenced between "covers" in the other sense of a tacit double entendre. And the book's "you," apostrophized again now, becomes in the end a libidinal update—and asymptote—of the Victorian "dear reader" trope.[6] The voiceless book yearns to say, at least to whisper, what impressed ink merely, and only here at last, indicates—namely, and in the italics of a virtually alien tongue, "*That I have loved only you, surrendered my whole self reckless to you and nobody else*" (229). Aches to say out loud, "*That I love the way you hold me, how close you let me be to you. I like your fingers on and on, lifting, turning*"—where *on* feels at first like desire's fleshly preposition until it vanishes into the adverbial duration of a page-turning drive, inflected by that further implied but unsaid double entendre of Morrison's—the facing page: "*I have watched your face for a long time now, and missed your eyes when you went away from me*" (229). But the narrative voice couldn't possibly call back the reader's eyes to the page, since that voice is only a figure of speech for transcribed speech, for legibility, in the first place.

Narrative has "longed, aw longed . . . to say out loud" the nature of its desire—where "aw" (even in its nonsight rhyme with the "longing" it enunciates) marks an anomalous phonetic transliteration in its own right. So that, urged to seek in speech what fleshed lovers have no need of words for, narration finds its only mate in silent deciphering: "*Talking to you and hearing you answer—that's the kick*" (229). The fantasy in Goethe, elicited by Kittler's emphasis on phonetic decipherment in our third chapter—the fantasy that a text might overhear its readers, rather than they its author—is confirmed in Morrison with an implicit appeal to the secondary vocality for which her own prose is so thickly disposed. Even in her minimal flexing of grammatical license there, the singular demonstrative for the compound phrasal subject marks not just the kick of reciprocity but the trick of simultaneity and equivalence. In our voice alone, silently, does the narrator find it. The kick is the reflex action of reading itself.

So it is that the talking and the answering are inextricable in the circuit of tacit vocalization. Just because "I can't say that aloud" doesn't mean we ourselves, as readers, haven't just murmured it unheard in the narrator's stead. And have half been told to across the oddly broken grammar, neither quite end-stopped nor continuous: "If I were able I'd say it. Say make me, unmake me." No more italics this time, tilting the phrase over into the narrator's would-be utterance in a self-consciously estranged discourse. Rather, what presides over this particular moment of wish fulfillment is an ambiguity sprung from the very syntactic fracture of the detached clause—and enhanced by the double grammar of what follows, attaching back alternately to "Say" or to "make" in granting that "You are free to do it." The main thrust of addressed desire: If I had the voice to say so out loud, I'd ask for you, in the sexual undercurrent of my chosen idiom, to make me, remake me, which is what you can't help but do in reading anyway. Alternately, simultaneously, in an imperative rather than a still-subjunctive inflection of the isolated clause, you must instead say it for me—you whom I command, if only in the silent rhythms of reading, "Say make me, unmake me." And in and beyond your speaking for yourself as well as for me just here (that voice might well have added), what I'm asking is only what books do with and to us in the normal run of reading: transform consciousness by a channeling of the Other. Admittedly, my grammatical worrying of this fulcral moment might well seem fussy—if the phrasing's punctuated breather, in a mere iterative pulse of discourse, weren't at the same time so obliquely definitive, in general, of the narrator-reader interchange and switch point. A phenomenological reciprocity is thus rendered complete across a latently ambiguous syntactic shunt—and turned to textual parable in the process. In reading, we make happen what remakes *us*. And this we are solicited by text to sign on for, to invite by the silent enunciations of reading itself. For reading is a deed, a contract, a mutuality, a reciprocal construction, an embodiment, a rehabilitation, and of course a come-on. What was so loaded in the earlier phrase, beyond its bedroom eroticism, is now detonated. The relation of fiction to its reading is indeed, for Morrison, that of narration and reader each becoming "inward toward the other."

Quoting still, as if from the book's own ocular vantage, and still on the question of making and remaking: "You are free to do it and I am free to let you because, look, look . . ." (229). Not just "look, look," you're reading now with those eyes of yours. But in that last pointing, in that final material and extratextual deixis ("look" there!), you are asked to contemplate exactly the point of intersection, temporal and spatial both, between not writer and reader but book and the embodied attention it lays claim to: "Look where your hands are. Now." This last sentence on the last page of Morrison's novel recalls the open diptych dead center in Marshall McLuhan's *The Medium Is the Massage*, "the" on one page, "book" across the gully on the other—and completing the mise en abyme, a thumb entering from the edge of each, doubling the reader's own. In evoking such a nested figure for the book's contact with the reader, the prevalence of Faulkner in

Morrison makes space as well for Whitman, whose silent lips, in his own mix of metaphors across separate texts, kiss with words the reader whose fingers caress him.[7]

The "No Place" of Reading: From Referential to Transferential

This exotics of reading calls forth as well an unforeseen checkpoint in recent criticism. For in her essay "The Rise of Fictionality," Catherine Gallagher extends her sense of the fictional "Nobody,"[8] unprotected by eighteenth-century property rights and thus permeable to unrestrained, almost transgressive sympathy, into a zone of crisscrossed identification, unprecedented in Gallagher's earlier work but plangently lodged by way of equivalent figuration at the end of *Jazz*.[9] Reading, according to Gallagher, effects a displaced "vicarious desire" (363): namely, the "imagined desire of the character" (or in this case, by synecdoche, the book) for the "embodied immanence" (363) of the reader. By these means does the fictional "absence" as personification throw into unusual relief our very presence and—by the relay of countertransference (though these are not Gallagher's terms)—produce (these are) "an uncanny desire to be that which we already are" (363). That is: to be real, embodied. Morrison's book makes that desire doubly explicit, and doubly uncanny, by transferring it back to the craving codex itself, yearning in address for the total abandon of our caress—as if the paralyzed but hankering book were one of its own bloodless Nobodies thirsting not for, but to be, somebody like me.

Remake me in your image: that's the implication of *Jazz*, but from the sounded phonetic ground up. Give me (your) voice. It is almost the reverse, over a century later, of the Emersonian majesty of transference—or, earlier yet, the Keatsian "fine excess" of reflected rather than invented "higher thoughts." Yet Morrison's phrasing—on the part of a narrator who, given voice, would "say make me, remake me"—nonetheless echoes on the slant a very different gesture in the essay by Michel de Certeau, "Reading as Poaching," which was the subject of an open forum at the 2011 English Institute meeting—and from which my own approach departs in every way possible.[10] De Certeau means to break with the model of reading as passive consumption, fair enough, and to show how, absent a participatory torque on the reader's part, one simply lets reading matter slip past "without putting one's own mark on it, without *remaking* it" (169; emphasis added). Yet his "remaking," so different from Morrison's implication, is too much against the grain of the writing to count as literary reading at all. This is because his "common poetics" (172)—with an emphasis on "tactics and games played with the text" (175) in his favored mode of piecemeal appropriation, including its dubious mix of the utilitarian and the ludic—would ignore the text's intrinsic byplay in favor of the reader's own power play, where response is willfully reclaimed from any cultural regimentation thought guaranteed by the cognitive impositions of the text at hand.

De Certeau is surely right to stress that "reading has no place" (174). But by this he wants to insist that it's neither here nor there—and can be defined at will and ad hoc by the reader. On the contrary, having "no place" doesn't mean, or shouldn't, that, absent global positioning, reading lacks all coordinates. Instead, reading takes (rather than has) place in two elusive spatio-temporal axes at once, first from left to right in English and other Western languages (if also back again at times, recursively) and then—what?—from out to in? In this double relay, reading happens both between words (sometimes not wholly delinked into lexical separation) and between those spaced words and that other mental space, never a place either—that zone both introjected and projected at once—onto which a given phrasing may be thought to give in giving way to thought. Indifferent to this, de Certeau is interested not in the rewriting that's intrinsic to all reading, as for Barthes, but rather in a trumping of the written by what comes readiest to hand in reaction, a sporadic sampling and privatized uptake rather than a disinterested continuous encounter with the work of words.[11] In the process of saving readers from their falsely supposed passivity, he instead caricatures the text, literary or otherwise, as a passive field for larcenous forays rather than gradual collaborative forage.

In contrast to Barthes's "slow reading," de Certeau admits an allegiance to "speed reading" (176). Liberated rather than subservient, such empowered reading releases, he says, the body from its unlawful detention, granting just the writ of habeas corpus it seeks (176), though hardly a literary writ at all in these terms. He intends by this somatic manumission only the limited emancipation of the eye, which is all that's left of the reading body for him: an eye that can now sweep across the text, rove and swoop, unhindered by the grooves and runnels of phrasing per se or by literacy's outmoded prehistory, so he thinks, in the "murmur of a vocal articulation" supposedly long lost to Western textual practice. So that when he insists that "text has meaning only through its readers" (170), his preposition has no strong sense. What the text can be said to mean to me, to me personally, is therefore, for him, often a kind of willful reading *in*, not just the poaching but the imposition or implanting of inference.

Yet taking the phrase "only through its readers" to mean "through" not just as "by means of" but rather in the sense of a conduit, a medial extension—this would be closer to the mark, the mark as activated on the run by any and all engagement with the undertones of lexical attention. What, in sum, a piece of writing *means to me* must come not just through *to me*, but *through me* as generative relay. And no contemporary writer keeps the circuits so well-oiled and open as Toni Morrison, the habeas corpus of whose prose has a way, if one may put it this way, of freeing the body *to it*. But it does so only by refusing to separate those two levels of comprehension that de Certeau borrows from psycholinguistics to distinguish: a "lexical" decipherment, word by word, versus a "scriptural" decoding (168) of more extensive semantic spans, at whose broader scale he thinks "reading as poaching" can drive a tactical wedge between intent and uptake.

In the reading of prose like Morrison's, however—which is to say, in giving oneself over to it rather than in making it over into the image of your own purposes—the most bracing fissures (rather than driven wedges) are delimited and overridden, overwritten, by the specific ligatures of lexical sequence and their latent voicings, their subvocal enunciations. These include the style of self-adjusted effect, in other words the self-revisionary effect of style, as emblemized, for instance, in that wording we've already stumbled (and mulled) over: "If I were able I'd say it. Say make me, unmake me." For there again the second-person, self-enacted imperative "say" overlaps the first-person conditional "would say" so that the book's urge to speech and the silent reader's verging on it are caught at the interface of their simultaneity, their equivalence. Though Morrison, past mistress of the actual audiobook, remarked in an interview after the publication of *Jazz* that she had wanted to conceive of a "talking book,"[12] not a persona, it is a want that goes unfulfilled for the book itself, which can never say its own say, never utter its thoughts "out loud"—and which, if given over to recorded recitation, is then no longer a book form capable of somatic intimacy, having become all disembodied sound waves rather than palpation and caress.

Alphabets of Talk

What then, a decade and a half later, about "the letters of talk" and their fate at the disclosed scriptive site of *A Mercy*? This is where de Certeau's "no place" of reading finds, rather than an open field for gaming and poaching, instead a no sooner conjured than vanished emplacement as spatial form. In one sense, Florens is of course wrong—or should we say shortsighted?—to think that what she writes on walls and floor has only one chance of getting read. We know better than to contemplate her story's perishing with the blacksmith's death or illiteracy. After all, after centuries of travail, we're finally reading it, or, rather, a novelistic reconstruction of something like it, some distillation of the broad historical trauma it seeks shape for. To put it this way is to help appreciate how, though in the terms of Barthes's *S/Z* Florens's epistle to her former lover might render it a failed "contract narrative," null and void, at least it avoids the containment of an embedded mise-en-abyme structure to become, in Barthes's later terms, instead a "maquette" or model of the work in process.[13] As such it sustains the generative engine of its own performance as textual inscription, subsiding only after the fact into a concluding chapter that carries the lost mother's disembodied voice toward Florens from beyond the sea, from internal American borders, or from beyond the grave—there's no telling which. Together, then, the last two chapters, pitched against each other—carved mansion walls, houseless telepathic speech sounds—separate out an aggressive materiality of record from the forever homeless talk, including the maternal traces of its voicing, that such palpable matter would, by contrast, letter into view.

In regard to all this, the fact of Florens's halting, aberrant literacy is not only crucial but afforded its own detailed history. It begins as early as the first chapter, though what is prepared there (as with the unmuscled monologist at the opening of *Jazz*) comes clear in its full resonance only upon rereading. Flouting the rules against slave literacy, a sympathetic priest teaches the young and now motherless Florens how to write and so speak—rather than the other way around: to cipher and then to enunciate the language of her new land. At one level, then, the cultural evolution from an oral tongue into the practice of transcription is reversed in a progress from alphabetic mastery to spoken phonetic discourse. Which may be partly why Florens reverts to scribing out her "talk," her woe, in the end. Early on, in the spectral present tense of her former tutelage, we learn that the Reverend "has two books and a slate. We have sticks to draw through sand, pebbles to shape words on smooth flat rock" (*A Mercy*, 6). The sticks aren't said to draw *in* sand, with script being the immediate effect of their motion, but rather, in a more rudimentary sense, to drag through it by way of scraping out the letters of as-yet-unknown words—as later, and still in the same dilated and traumatized present tense, will her carpenter's nail rather than found stick (a nail no doubt retrieved from construction debris at the abandoned mansion) score out her story, this early and formative part of it included. She is still and ever learning to speak by the abrading of alien and resistant surfaces.

But back to the first chapter, as in fact these details may propel us. Florens's opening linguistic autobiography proceeds in the discursive present as acquired letters give way to sounds and word shapes: "Slowly a little talk is in my mouth and not on stone" (7). This unusual (backward) process is incremental, having begun, as it were, from scratch. "When letters are memory we make whole words" (6). As the phrasing half suggests, this educed language recapitulates a debate over writing versus orality and their mnemonic valences going back at least as far as Plato. In Florens's clandestine lessons, alphabetic integers, variously materialized in mute tracing, are not exactly committed to memory. Rather, they *become* ("are" in her inveterate present tense) the defining component of memory—until, at the end of the novel, we come to the point where recollection, in its achieved form as text, is returned to lettered silence and thence to annihilation.

But if letters *are* memory, not just its aids, their alphabetic mutation under phonetic pressure in the novel's last engraved space of text—on a surface at least somewhat less impervious than stone—means that reading itself volatilizes and brings alive such memory in processing the fluctuating emphases of the text. The absentation of the subject is part of a compensatory logic.

Let mentality disappear into script, leaving no other remainder in the mind, and it remains inscribed there to be triggered into thought—Agamben's sense of its re-origination—by any future reading. Like the heroine herself, we "learn" to bring voice to the aggregated letter forms. And in so doing, we are witness to literature writing language, language and even its implied philosophy, in the event of even the most improbable and radically impersonal transmission.

Up in Smoke

This is where a forked hypothesis in the imagined fate of the heroine's inscriptions offers, in effect, two tropes for the same hope: the safe house of her tale, self-contained and perpetual like a book, versus its anonymous dissipation by both inflammatory rage—an actual conflagration—and the winds of change. Some such prospect lies implied in the mythic overtones on which this penultimate chapter of *A Mercy* comes not so much to rest as to speculative diffusion. To the blacksmith still: "If you never read this, no one will" (188). Words would be reduced to mere graffiti, as if under erasure in the tomb of their intended communication. But we in every sense know better. For without guessing that we'd all along been inching our way across walls and floor of Florens's outsize writing tablets, we have nonetheless been knowingly reading. Once rotating open the hinged door of the novel's booked portal, we have made room for its rumination well before knowing that its printed ciphers were previously etched out "round and round, side to side, bottom to top, top to bottom all across the room" (188) in this lost manorial scriptorium.

Lost, yes: not only lost to history, but then again lost within it—according to the premonitory fantasy with which Florens closes: a last rite of cremation and scattered remains as an alternative to hermetic perpetuity. Just here, a disjunctive grammar of the either/or marks exactly the divergent paradigm in play. The letters scored across her room may remain, word by word, surface by surface, closed forever on themselves. "Or. Or perhaps no. Perhaps these words need the air that is out in the world. Need to fly up and then fall, fall like ash over acres of primrose and mallow" (188). The ash will thus fall by way of natural precipitation: "Over a turquoise lake, beyond the eternal hemlocks, through clouds cut by rainbow, and"—in the delayed predication of a fallow future—"flavor the soil of the earth" (188), where that faint pleonasm (variant of "earth of the earth") carries the deflected overtones of a liturgical but potentially resurgent "ashes to ashes" for a land seared and sedimented with the soilage of oppression.

And if there is any doubt about it being a purgative and dispersive arson, *explicitly* so, that is being posed here as not just an alternative destiny but as an interchangeable figure for the volumetric self-enclosure of text, we're assured that Florens's Native American counterpart in enslavement, Lina, whose village was torched to cauterize the contagion of plague, would join Florens in seeking a bonfire of the mansion's vanity: "She finds horror in this house and much as she needs to be mistress's need I know she loves fire more" (188–89). Inverting the mansion burning at Sutpen's Hundred at the close of Faulkner's *Absalom, Absalom!* (perpetrated by the black woman Clytie to defend the white owner from mistakenly assumed arrest), what Florens plans to ignite is instead a final incrimination. And therefore the "air . . . out in the world" sought by Florens's words will be the oxygen breathed by their immolation—perhaps to rise, phoenix-like again, phonetic on the reader's inner ear.

Florens's *closeted*, unventilated text becomes in this way one among so many slave narratives, unwritten or not, that have, as it were, gone up in smoke, only to permeate the historical air we breathe—and to fertilize a social landscape ripe for change, repair, transformation. The alternatives are clear—if symbolically interchangeable. Either the geometric space of the narrative will be entered as if its story surrounds and encloses you, reading in three fixed dimensions at the palpable site of writing, or else the letters of its talk, its discourse, will disappear absolutely into a wider 3-D world. Either virtuality, whether a "talking room" of articulated surfaces or a larger world at one and the same time materialized and suffused by words (or, better, each together and in sequence), defines Morrison's phenomenology of reading when in touch with, or in sight of, not just the separate tangibilities of letter and page but the cognitive zone onto which those surfaces, when consumed—though in the heat of reading rather than the fire of revolt—open out. This is to recognize that Florens's twin fantasies are merely redescriptions of each other—the volumetric space of imprint as silent talk, the inflammatory dissemination of text as uncanny narrative destiny.

Uncanny indeed, *unheimlich*, literally unhoused: furiously set loose in the case of Florens's writing from the haunted estate of slave paternalism in a figurative razing of the master's manse that gives, with blunt literalness, an incendiary vent to her grievances. But in this final and fierce commitment to what amounts to a book-burning climax, Morrison's prose dematerializes before our inner ears with one last arresting nest of dissonance, propelled by an idiomatic synesthesia poised between seeing a point and hearing someone out. First: "See? I am become a wilderness but I am also Florens. In full. Unforgiven. Unforgiving." And then this: "Hear me? Slave. Free. I last." But what is heard there as well, two or three or four times over, is something more than written, something that can only be listened to beneath the punctualities of script, in the return of its repressed. And something that, in the process, may well anticipate the closing chapter's monologue by the long-lost mother—addressed without reception, from a place beyond death or not—to a daughter whose learning to write and then speak in another tongue has preserved nonetheless that original (though not founding or stabilizing) orality in language so often associated with the mother's voice.

Ciphering the "Vocal Image"

Call it once again, if you will—as proposed first in our modification of Ong by Agamben—a kind of *auralterity*. For emerging to vocality, to verbal consciousness, across the staccato stutter of Florens's paradoxical insistence ("Slave. Free.")—two plenary fragments in a categorical disjunction internalized instead as warring psychic condition—is the structuring unsaid of Morrison's entire novel. The adjacent words could scarcely be kept farther apart. Capitalized. End-stopped by periods. On the other hand, neither in the patient enunciation of Morrison's audiobook performance nor in the subvocal deed of our own reading, can the novel avoid denominating for the first and last time the abstract category nowhere else given by the text in so many letters (despite a dozen appearances of the personal noun *slave*): namely, the name for that legal bondage not yet, in the moment of seventeenth-century colonial exploitation, bureaucratized into a full-blown and state-sanctioned institution.

But precisely because the defiant paradox of "Slave. Free." cannot wholly overcome its homophonic fusion, via the recursive *v/f* loop, into a two-syllabled vernacular enunciation of "Slavery," the inscribed and stigmatized house must come down, including its "talking room," where an ignited silence will give further dissent. In de Certeau's words but not really his terms, this mobile "anamorphosis" (170) of the text—not by the reader's distorting plunder but through the words themselves poaching on each other's alphabetic field—works in its phrasal "deterritorialization" to obtrude a "lexical" warp across the overall "scriptural" span. In Saussure's term but not his intent, the "vocal image" (more below) is like an alternating mirage of gestalt oscillation rather than the determinate glyph of a speech sound. Whispered here, in any case, is the coming collective shame that cannot help but speak its name.

If one were inclined to balk at such a purported phonetic tendency in Morrison, consider for a moment, quite apart from this one instance (and, in a moment, its tangent oscillations), a more extraordinary warpage yet in her most famous book. This tightly knotted thread of lexical play—and stretch—comes from perhaps the most brutal scene in Morrison's brutal novel *Beloved*, where an abject speechlessness on the part of victim and onlooker alike ends up warping the language of its own recorded trauma. The scene has a white schoolmaster taking clinical notes on the slave heroine's panic as his nephews violate her body and drain from her the mother's milk she was saving for her newborn girl while, unseen, her husband, shackled with a bit in his mouth, looks on powerless even to yell out. Traumatized and broken, this crazed man is next found at a churn slathering his shamed face not with mother's milk but with curdled cream across a breathless sentence break that goes from "his face with butter" (in his wife's free indirect fantasy of joining him in the psychotic breakdown of such escapism) to the reflex jolt, with the very next words, of a corrective second thought in "But her children."[14] This is an effect warping and buckling at once—with that mad latch of "butter"/"But her"—that can only be called breath-catching. It occurs in a sequence that concludes a few words later with the mother's explicit rejection of that "butter play" (84), that wallowing in escapist sensuality, that has been given to us instead by the text, from the midst of sexual outrage, only in the form of outrageous wordplay.

With less risk of deranged wit at a pivotal moment, and with a homophonic juncture masked at a glance by oxymoron, "Slave. Free." nonetheless does its work by indulging its own unindentured script as (free) phonemic association. But one can of course put the effect of this sound play, this outplaying of sense by sound, the other way round as well, giving priority to the written letters in Florens's labor of inscription. For by virtue of those graphic periods driving two more nail points ("Slave. Free.") into the vandalized coffin of plantation authority, the phonic gestalt between oralized noun and its antonymic modifier can be read as a liberating gesture of textual as well as sexual anarchy, with the scriptor's last gashes rather than gasps managing to set free, around the fricative pivot from *v* to *f*, the very epithet "free" from an inert and subservient nominal suffix—freed almost to hyphenation, that is, in an ultimate American dream deferred: the historical as well as phonemic arc from the lexically constricted *Slave(f)ry* to the punctuated breakout of *Slave-free*.

This is what, in my terms from *Novel Violence*, one might call prose *friction* in a uniquely defiant form of linguistic deviance.[15] And its force is such that it presses forward, if more mutedly, into the next sentence as well, telescoping in both senses (phonetically as well as historically) the present-tense survivalism of "I last" into the elided (but still latent) futurism of "I'll last"—confirmed in retrospect by the present resuscitation of the slave's tale as our novel. And even within the imagined historical scene, for a heroine locked until now into the never fully elapsed past of a fixated traumatic present, the moment-to-moment performative insistence of "I last" may be felt relaxed at this late stage (at the enunciative slackening of "I'll") into some new axis of the genuinely foreseeable. Whose future is perhaps suggested when, as if borne on the rhythms of African American melody itself, Morrison's delegated phrasing rehearses the visionary horizon intoned (centuries after Florens's death) at the close of Martin Luther King's "I Have a Dream" speech, whose final wish fulfillment cedes his own rhetoric, in peroration, to "the words of the old Negro spiritual, 'Free at last, Free at last, Great God a-mighty, We are free at last.'" Or sing it as "Great God a-Mercy," reminding us of the racialized vernacular and implicit spiritual lilt of Morrison's own truncated (though unhyphenated) title.

And if "Free. I last" (with an elided "at last") is felt vibrating there in part to bolster—in a further wordplay—the refusal of all penitential sense of the "sinful" in the heavily punctuated disjunction of "Florens. In full," at the same time the lazier liquid undersounding of "I last" is caught struggling against the ultimate transegmental stranglehold spoken in tongues by such strobophonic "letters of talk": in short, the intractable fact, from which only a much later freedom will be born, that, though yet unnamed, nonetheless "Slavery'll last." So sardonically mercurial and murky at once is the scriptive literacy caught here on the lingering cusp of acquired speech forms, so free-form and pliable yet poignant in its historical constraints, that Florens's halting, literally incisive prose reads like just what it enactively is: a passionate stammering access to the aural cauldron of a ruinous history yet unspoken. Whereas *Jazz* is a Harlem-inspired tour de force of modern urban smart talk and its rhythms, one way to summarize the subsequent specific genius of style in *A Mercy* is that, even in Morrison's conjured origins of an incipient black speech in the first-wave Colonial diaspora, we hear nonetheless—through the transmit of literary history itself—something like the cadences of Steven Connor's "white voice" as it characterizes a materialist modernist phonology in Beckett as well as Joyce and Faulkner.[16]

The House of Fiction as Echo Chamber

Morrison's unabashed tropology for the space of reading is thus poised for a restaging—and new politicizing—of an old but still scintillating face-off between literary semiotics and deconstruction. I refer to that debate, as discussed in Chapter 2, that centers on a poem by Victor Hugo announcing itself—as it were, up front—as "Lines Written upon a Flemish Window-Pane," with its lambent celebration of the nearby carillon, its belling of the hours refigured as the descent of a Spanish dancer. This declared fact of vitreous *inscription* is what Paul de Man finds masked as mere *description* in Michael Riffaterre's otherwise exemplary reading of a poem whose putative transparency is negated across exactly the tracing of its signification.[17]

In the broadest terms of Riffaterre's system, as later developed beyond *Semiotics of Poetry* (1978) and *Text Production* (1983) in his book on narrative, *Fictional Truth* (1990), what happens in *A Mercy* is that the dead patriarch's first revulsion at the gaudy mansion of the Catholic slaver he meets in the novel's first real episode, the degenerate fop from whom he rescues Florens, is installed as the "model" for an architectural "subtext" (ironized next in the name "Sweet Home") that subtends the entire novel. In Florens's ultimate secret chamber within the man's haunted house, the last and definitive appearance of this subtext must surmount the descriptive "hurdle" in credibility, the "ungrammaticality" at the "mimetic level" (Riffaterre's terms still), that figures much of the novel as an all too literal writing on the wall. In so doing, the subtext, surfaced for the last time as denouement, delivers us back to the always unsaid "matrix" or cliché that the text, though sponsored by it, must dispense with saying flat out. This is the organizing exclusion that is revealed, only after the fact, as a text's hypogrammatic core: involving in this case, one may speculate, given those inscribed domestic walls, the suppressed intertextual reference not just to Faulkner's burnt slave-owner's mansion but to Henry James, formalist supreme, and his own architectonic master trope for "the House of Fiction."[18]

If this allusion comes through to the reader, it provides one way to account for Morrison's tacit evocation of so much contemporary text art in the room-scaled mode. But she is also—in what one wants to call the "linguistic subtext" of the novel, and from the first chapter on—stressing language acquisition and the tension between oral and written literacy. In so doing she is aligning her spatial and scriptive metaphors, her insistence on the graphic trace, with that other American tradition, so far from Jamesian formalism, in the oral histories of African American endurance. In the "letters of talk" we find seeded, in fact, the "phantasm" of community. I borrow, there, Agamben's term from the subtitle of a book called *Stanzas* that plumbs the etymology—indeed the topology—of its title word as a name for the halting place of the poetic abode or room, its "dwelling or receptacle" as a phantasmatic standing ground.[19]

On this point, long after an opening epigraph from Dante Alighieri on the stanza not as a unit of composition but in its etymological sense a "capacious dwelling or receptacle for the entire craft" (vii), Agamben quotes the consternation of Saussure himself over a science of linguistics that has no real standing in empirical knowledge: no objects of study, no genuine entities to work with, just differences, nothing in fact that the "vocal image" (Saussure's phrasing, 154) actually pictures. Lodged there is Saussure's unusually condensed term for the written representation of a speech sound that, no sooner detached as imagined linguistic entity from the body that produced it, has nothing bodily beyond itself to attach to or indicate—until enchained with other marks like (but enough unlike) it to engender a sign that is no longer a sound or an image, either one.

To pin this linguist's discontent to an example, we might say that, like all words, Morrison's "butter" is so slippery a syllabic linkage of "vocal images" that it harbors its own adversative conjunction, shelters its own negation, yielding up thereby a miniature cameo of the postmetaphysical emptying-out of human presence and intent in speech. We are *homo loquens*, according to Agamben, only in the participial sense—not because speech is where our sapience or being is grounded, but simply because we keep speaking, securing nothing but the channels of our being together, our habitation in words. But there is more to elicit from Agamben elsewhere, as we know, about the relation of this "abode," this abidance ("I['ll] last"), to the habitus or ethos of a community founded on something other than violence. Sensing in poetry not so much the practiced use but the new incubation of language each time out, his resistance to semantics as the negation of voice gives us terms for attending to those literary moments when voice returns to *disquiet* inscription, when the body is not entirely disallowed by functional speech, when undertones escape the overlay of signage.[20]

This is the role of poetry as linguistic art, or of literary prose like Morrison's for that matter: to tap again, within the rhythmic array of meaning, the taking-place rather than the inert givenness of language.[21] The human being doesn't prove itself in language, at least not prove its existence. It does, however, test itself, sound itself out—and as part of that habituation to others that makes for a community. For the African American writer recovering so-called voices from the past, voices sometimes tragically isolated from a sustaining ethos, this is often all one has. Such is overtly the case with Florens's "talking room," whose inscribed lines—at least after the fantasy of her lover "standing to" read them—disappear into their foreseen kindling and extinction, providing no real stanza, no stance or standing, for her own lament. Once dematerialized in a trial by fire, their only future lies in a wholly reconfigured transmission, whether oral or rewritten. Framed by a self-liberated trope of this sort, where the housebound letters no longer need "talk to themselves" alone, prose might indeed seem unusually willing to let the released somatic energies of language talk back to us, return in us, from the uncanny reverbs of a printed script. This one obscure talking room, that is, makes room for stories otherwise untold.

And so it is with the book-like last enclosure of *A Mercy*—on the brink of the most drastic of demediating gestures, textual incineration—that the deed of reading is signed and countersigned, as it so often is, in disappearing ink, making and remaking its invisible links within earshot of ironies detached from the shackles of script in order to capture the medium's other messages. Capture them, as I have been suggesting, by narratographic response at the level of a novel's stylistic microplot. The resonance of Morrison's achievement in this regard is hard to exaggerate. In close coordination with this, surely few conceptual sculptors, let alone few book studies scholars or theorists of reception, get a more decisive grasp on the founding split between material surfaces and cognitive parameters in textual encounter: between, on the one hand, reading's operative, layered rectangles within the six-sided spatial form of the codex, a self-contained space that nevertheless seeks its reverberation in the reader's silent voice, and, on the other, our transferential identifications with character in the throes of narrative consumption.

If Morrison, beyond the special affinity of her prose with the philosophy of performance in Peter Kivy, had set out to occupy and even fortify Gérard Genette's distinction between the notational basis of a medium's material or inscriptive support and its "immanence" as text—or in my terms the difference between the book as object and its evocalization as event, whose deed is always contractual in its intimacy—then her figure for the writer's room of one's own turned to firestorm couldn't have been more rigorous.[22] For, in the ferocity of foreseen demediation, that imagined precipitation of ashen black rain marks a transformation from scraped rage to conflagration, symbolic scars to scattered char—and of course their narrative reclamation—that works to anticipate, from within the seventeenth-century fictional setting, a reflexive image of Morrison's own writing. The soot-dusted paper cylinder of the phonautograph, exemplifying in "Fore Word" a pre-phonographic trace of enunciation with no playback system but the naked eye (however insufficient in that case) finds its distant equivalent in a conflagration that yields writing's counterpart of liquid ash in printer's ink.[23]

In the residual outrage spoken forth from Florens's self-haunted house as evacuated locus of power, the voice of protest comes to a head in an aural haunting of its own locution. This is how the spectral phonetic yoke of "slav . . . ree" registers the ghostly term of an institutionalized future against the resistant vocal texture of a past and posthumous defiance. Apart from the semiotic indirections of Riffaterre's theory, where the increments of mimesis must be overcome by meaning, one may also recall, from the realm of philosophical hermeneutics, Paul Ricoeur's words for his third facet of a more stable if manifold mimesis: a facing-outward that looks past both figured world and the work of its configuration to the third-order zone of the reader's own reaction.[24] When keyed more closely to the contours of a serial *reaction time* rather than just a reactive affect, this is where the social field of recognition would indeed enlist, as with this instance from Morrison, a true errand (and, again, errancy) of the ear—and in a literal (or letteralized) fashion. Such is a result hinted at more by Ricoeur's rhetoric, to be sure, than by his own mode of approach: "The whole history of suffering cries out for vengeance and calls for narrative" (1:175), writes Ricoeur about the deepest motive for storytelling, its "need to save the history of the defeated and the lost" (1:175). Intersecting such an *ethics* of mimetic representation—on the occasion of a slave narrative in the guise of a found (even as lost) document—is a more engrained and time-based verbal *ethic* (an ethic of writing read). For just those idiomatic personifications of history's "cries" and "calls" are—in a yet more particular (and lexically particulate) sense—lent a wavering secondary vocality by Morrison's mediated audition in the "See . . . hear" of Florens's colliding monosyllables.

Beyond Conclusion—Undead Letters

With those climactic enunciations in an acquired tongue, narratography can be felt to nuance, at unusually close range, the cues of mediology, as detailed by Régis Debray.[25] Unable to make *communication* with an only potentially literate and an already quite probably dead addressee, the monologist, left to her own devices and then to their effacements, submits instead to *transmission*. In this respect, what Cavell's way with Emerson on the transferential nature of reading has helped expose by contrast about the "penned" hermetic masochisms as well as the telepathic fantasies of Poe's narrators, and what Agamben's eliciting of "transmissibility" itself from poetry's circuit of address has shed light on in lyric subjectivity—and thus what both philosophers have implicitly to suggest about the literary "medium" in its own verbal salience—finds further dramatized rumination in *A Mercy*, with its closing imagination of writing's *self-deliverance* as ambient speech act. An Agambenesque sense of a reading being *potential* even in its immediate prevention—a potential realized here by its very novelization—thus folds back into an explicitly ethical inference for reading's coming community. This is a community both national and historical at once in the African American legacy of Morrison's implicitly destroyed but now metamorphosed and presently realized text.

And further generalization tempts us at just this point. Indeed, beyond the precision of his line readings, generalization is what Agamben's poetics have been called upon for all along. If, according to his consistent philosophical orientation, our being is *in* language, not metaphysically denominable *by* it, then, as with anywhere else one "dwells" (the Heideggerian trope), such an ethos of language precedes (and is presupposed by) whatever speaking depends on it for its possibility. In this way, then, as literature is eager to show, linguistic potential is not deferred but inherent. Each text is the immanence of its own linguistic precondition—as well as serving, in reading, as its own destination. There is nothing circular in this, just a divulging of efficient if not first causes. In reading at a certain pitch, one reads the possibilities of verbal relay itself: its possibilities, its slipups, its impasses, its end runs.

Also within an Agambenesque perspective, what is specifically to be overcome at the close of *A Mercy* is a kind of negative potential. The walls of Morrison's self-caged scribbling heroine must, of course, disappear into our pages to surmount their own foreclosure as entrapped message. But if something like this *can* happen, Agamben has enlisted Melville to show that any such option must preserve its possibility within the chance that it might *not*, even (paraphrasing Bartleby) "would . . . not." In fact, the transcriptions of Florens seem set for evanescence, set down only to disappear into their own equivalent of the dead-letter office. Explicit in the plot, as opposed to its apprehension by us, is the likelihood that Florens will lay waste by fire to the record of her devastation, leaving no trace of her tale. Such a negative eventuality—narrative as its own crematorium—points to the not-reading that underwrites our present weirdly privileged access to her very words. That such contingency could well prevent, paradoxically, our encounter with what we've just finished deciphering is what puts both a premium and a spotlight on the matter (both senses) of linguistic conveyance.

This verbal emphasis transpires even while inscription, as documentation, is ultimately subordinated—by the prophecy of an incinerated lexigraphic chamber—to some impalpable verbalized conduit vanishing before our mind's ears like a tale that has been told, told only in the monologic "letters of talk." Conduit, channel, medium. Alongside Debray's terms, then, recall Agamben from Chapter 2 on what cannot be thought, cannot be spoken, about the human place in language, about speech's taking-place in and through you: "Unnamed, it is thus without destiny: an *untransmissible transmission*" ("*Se,*" 125): a transfer of meaning ineffable in itself. The strenuous mystifications of delivery in our receipt of Florens's story, as of her mother's valedictory voice in the closing chapter, seem meant to rim this flow of speech with an acknowledgment of its own incommunicable status as such. What we read, rather than what we read about, has lost all material bearings in its own right.

And yet here we are, reading it. Once again the semiotics of Rifatterre, subtending all "surface" interpretation, operates in close league with the linguistic densities we've been tracking under a philosophical aegis. As with the unspoken existential "matrix" of the Leopardi poem we began with in the pursued inferences of Agamben's commentary, where the nonhuman scope of the universe was *over-whelming* to consciousness (figured as "shipwreck" and "drowning"), in this case the political matrix (and narrative subtext) of impassioned slave revolt—with its linked intertexts in Woolf's *A Room of One's Own* and James's House of Fiction—has taken an all but flagrant graphonic form as *the writing on the wall*. But vendetta and scourge aside, this is precisely the foreclosed textual space whose "end," in a prosaics of potential, is manifest in the secondary vocality of its always present activation.

At which point the balked powers of communication (strictly speaking) in this immured, this walled-in text, even if met only with the illiteracy of its accused addressee in the person of the blacksmith, are nonetheless lifted for us into the key of "transmission" instead—this in Debray's sense once again, as distinct from a semiotics of communication, but not to be divorced here from its metalinguistics. Signage is a communicative act; culture is a transmissive function. What Morrison's trope achieves with its graphonic ironies—and all the more clearly in light of our adapted model from Agamben of iteration as subvocal potentiation—takes us straight to the ontology of language as human medium. Close reading is once again deep reading, rehearsing the accession to speech itself as the preauthorial notarizing of any fictional contract, tapping the very ethic of utterance as a transmissive human filament across the history whose episodes it alone can trace and convey.

How, though, do we actually imagine ourselves reading her carved scrawl when it has long become just ash on the air? Even when scraped in lumber—in processed wood, in substitute paper—such a handmade message increasingly seems fated to be as anachronistic one day soon, when its story is encountered in e-book form, as if it were hieroglyphic cave painting. But aside from this technological evolution in the matter of remote reception, what about the fictionalized social history of such even more long-distance transmission, down through the centuries? How is the heroine's personal exposé to be read? How else? By the immaterial conduit of a scarring if not actually inscribed heritage of racial brutality and recrimination as much in the American air as is any acrid taint from such an incinerated temple to the profits wrung from violence.

And when this volumetric space of text is nonetheless figured not as built up by scribed and wall-wide tablets of accusation but rather as constituting a "talking room"—in this sense half-personified—it thus joins with the conclusion of *Jazz* in its notable derivation from an early figure of literacy in the African American tradition. Indirectly descended, in its own right, from the dove of the Spirit hovering at the ear in paintings of sacred reading, symbol for a direct audit of the Logos, this is the African American literary metaphor of the "talking-book."[26] From the point of view of the unlettered, excluded, and enslaved subject, such is a fantastic volume speaking only to power in an apparently secret (because inaudible) master code: what Morrison's initiated and thereby facilitated heroine, about her own scrawl in this chapter, calls the "letters of talk." And, as we know, she has made this mode of talk speak back directly to just that power. Such is the burden, scourge, and purgation all lying in wait at once for our rearview reading.

Florens's audited glyphs, those carved letters raised for us now from virtual death, include, as we've heard, a crucial lexical nexus (*sla/v/ree* looped with *I/last*) that is brushed by mutually unassimilated phonemes in a voicing not wholly regimented into silence by inscribed intent. It is a voicing quintessentially "speakerly, aural, colloquial," whose oxymoronic "letters of talk" offer under incisive pressure the veritable soundsc(r)ape of prose *friction*. And what they offer beyond that, in the very office of their vexed phonemic slippage between freedom and slavery, is (as stressed by Agamben) that evident "desubjectification" of literary articulation cued by any preinscribed page—and then inherited in response by the enunciation of words not one's own. It is this alone that puts a present reader in touch not just with the imagined address from beyond an eventual grave but with the immemorial, the wholly impersonal, formation (and fact) of speech itself, more fundamental than any one uttering subject alive or dead, fictional or otherwise. For no single subject could say the words "free" and "slavery" in the same mental breath, nor insist that both the latter crime and its victim will endure ("—'ll last").

It is only language speaking. And in such a disembodied telescoping of the racial record, the immediate dissipation of private intent into historical transmission is what alone, and beyond all local irony, gives voice to this transhistorical, this conditioning, latency of the medium itself. The phonic interplay of these word forms, like language all told, is therefore felt with unusual force in this passage to preexist, as well as to survive, the subject attempting here to fashion her own living epitaph. Even more clearly, therefore, than with the lexical abyss opening in Dickens between the "now he" of Riderhood's resuscitation and the "nowhe"re of his ontological relapse, Florens's nail-point testimony, conveyed through first- rather than third-person grammar, gives us in exaggerated form, in her own voicing of an exacerbated lexical accident, the "reciprocal desubjectification" incident in less extreme cases as well to the Agambenesque poetics of writing when read.

Orchestrated contingency: the formative divulged via formal concentration; the ethical, on its way to the political, brought out by way of exactly the verbal ethic of attention that stays alert to that former intrinsic dyad between generation and effect—with each route confirming Hartman's sense of the "body" as "mediator," though to begin with, in this case, a scribing body borne both away and in mind when the heroine's long-evaporated lament is felt echoing in the present textual empathy of our breathing uptake. Here, then, is a uniquely clear-cut, and in fact concertedly enacted, example of those interlinked features of reading sketched into distinction and overlap in the "Fore Word": the formative pressure on formal shape, the ethic of such registered change in the ethos of, in this case, a racial ethics. As we've seen, the formative linguistic level contouring the prose of *A Mercy* is even given a circumscribed narrative portrayal in retrospect at one point, in that striking episode, almost a fable, of language inculcation proceeding from sight to sound, scraped stone to speech pattern. But more to the larger point, when this will to language is formally engaged by the reader across the verbal patterning of the text's whole narrative arc, any such ethic of attention is brought directly to bear on the ethics of human indenture and respite, suppression and disembodied narrative relief, so unflinchingly inferred from the novel's incremental monologue structure. The main narrator's body is long gone; mediation—the salvation of recognition itself, the restoration through story—requires my body there in receipt, primed by the signs and phonic signals of the text as talking room.

Secondary *orality* would describe for Ong, as we know, the phenomenon of Morrison's audiobook performance of her heroine's unwitting and subject-undoing puns in the phonic oscillations of that last unsettling page. But secondary vocality, instead, is what we've heard in such script itself apart from any recording. The animal or organic sound lost, but audibly so, to meaning? Or arisen to confound it? The place beyond speech to which language ultimately fails, and in literature triumphantly fails, to point? And so the place where speech must fall back instead on its own deconcealment, speaking up for itself—internal differences included—through what it otherwise calls up? If these have seemed some of the right philosophical questions to put to the time-based flux of literary effect in the prosaics, the microstylistics, of such a novel by Morrison, let alone in poetry like

Wordsworth's or Leopardi's, this is largely because, even while prompting response, such interrogation defies answers—though at an enhanced level of apprehension. For answers only come perceptually, not categorically, and only in the time of verbal engagement, time and again. This is the somatic engagement, inevitably word by word—and always by surprise, on the underside of depicted feeling, scene, or event—where we so often come upon literature writing philosophy, language philosophy, in the elicited deed, and heed, of reading.

AFTER WORDING

After the words are laid out, if no longer in cold type but in laser jet or backlight, how does reading revive them as immanent speech act? And what—this book has gone on to ask—is implied there, there in the deed of reading, for a philosophy of the subject as *homo loquens*? Where, in fact, is *there*, exactly? And how often does the phonetic aftermath of a given word seem to generate its own virtual alternative as part of the serial coming-to-be not just of a verbalized world elsewhere but of a newly channeled linguistic gesture? Phonetic aftermath—or grammatical, either one: each operating comparably at different scales.

When I suggested in Chapter 5 that "syllepsis writes reading" (as a touchstone moment of impelled attention and second thought), I meant, of course, that it writes language in processed action—all the more a felt event, a "happening," a coming-to-be, when language is found equivocating its own grammatical predicates, letting one loose from the other. There are many ways of grasping this. As with the case of junctural ligatures at the subsyllabic scale of lexical sequencing, syllepsis theorizes literary succession by syntactic example. Syllepsis models literary surprise itself. Syllepsis philosophizes linguistic potential. The more abstract the formulations grow, however, the less in touch they stay with the grain of their cognitive engagement on the page. Guided by or eliciting whatever theoretical frameworks, reading's work is to keep close.

Abstraction takes a back seat. Certainly this hasn't been meant as a book of "applied philosophy," even though it is from Agamben and Cavell, for poetry and prose respectively—and in light of their own very different work on film as another time-based medium—that I've been able to extract the closest theoretical models for my own sense of reading through words to the phenomenon of wording. Nor has it been a book about "implied philosophy"—as if veins or pockets of literary writing can be mined for something philosophical they might have to say about language. Rather, there is often something philosophical about the very ways a given work goes about saying what it has in it to say, not about linguistics but linguistically: how it keeps the germinal circuits open even in the formed and fashioned phrase. And this recognition, this basis of a formative poetics, is what the second half of this book has, of course, been meant to secure in essaying a related prosaics of potential in literary fiction.

Two paragraphs from the end of his magisterial *The Antinomies of Realism*, our most influential critic of the novel, Fredric Jameson, writes as if his present progressive tense could be meant to review not only the pages in hand but the orientation of an entire career, one in which the precedence given to form and style in the disclosures of his historical dialectic has often been ignored or downplayed in the uptake of his thought: "I have been promoting"—here, but also for years—"the idea that the most valuable works are those that make their points by way of form rather than content."[1] These are works, for Jameson, "that relativize their themes and ideas, their 'meaning,' to the benefit of formal demonstrations that do not require interpretation to 'produce' their problems (or their problematic, to revive a useful word from yesteryear)" (311). This summary helps coordinate the last three chapters of his book under the half title "The Logic of the Material," by which he would implicitly suggest something like the conceptual *content of the form* in fictional writing. And underlying any "material" logic in prose fiction, concerning historical materialism as well as other matters, we have been looking to the morpho-logic of the linguistic medium itself for its own "demonstrations" not just of the "problematic" but of *the possible* in textual (rather than interpretive) "production," where verbal contingency and its training ground—its straining ground—can be found to rhyme at times with the very tensions it displays at the descriptive level.

The direction of my argument has followed the multiple thrusts of language in literary process—not just sequential across the page, but back before any given writing as well as out beyond it. Exemplification has focused on the deed of reading as access to literary power: on the serial and granular routes of realization for the social, psychological, and political tenor of representation. This literary force is activated by the perceptual contract of reading's deed as it converts effect to affect through the continuous alchemy of style. Language comes to us both on the surface and in depth, even while sponsoring, to be sure, its own phenomenological projections. But only through a verbal ethic kept alert to such layerings does one activate the full parameters of that latter and ultimately ethical field. In regard to cognitive or semantic priority, then, and in a ratio (as we saw in "Fore Word") that is more like a text-hinged chiasm, verbal manifestation is to intuited linguistic possibility (contour to inferred germinal depth) as reading (decipherment) is to implied reaction (ethical estimates and the rest). Each thrust, each vector of recognition, takes you away from the worded page, but only, in the first case, by moving across and even underneath that page in the tracked fallout of lexical and syntactic sequence. It is in this fashion—working through and beyond the sensed formative undertow of linguistic operations still in play—that the more familiar literary (rather than lettered) effects of intimate sympathy or ironic distance begin to exert their own discerned pressures. Short of this emotional register, because closer to the surface phrasings that such reactions may seem to dissipate even while depending on them, it is only an intensive verbal notice—reading from the ground up, but also down—that can bring out the sometimes uncanny concentrate of linguistic potential still passively hovering, and often urgently churning, in the manifest work of words. Where once more, and always anew, verbal energy makes its (here sub-entitled) claim on us: the call to recognize nothing less than the writing by literature of its own language philosophy.

The narrowly disposed poles of linguistic consideration in this study were acknowledged early on. Micro to macro at the linchpins of sequential sense: as, for example, in the phrased spectrum from *mini* to *maxi*—or, in other (self-othering) words, from the bri*m ini*tially spilled over between syllables to the momentarily overco*me axi*s of syntax whenever (to jump levels from phonemics to grammar) a verb, in its alternating potential senses, *takes* not only *objects* but *turns* and the *time* needed to distinguish them. Junctural drift and sylleptic shift: each richly deployed in Toni Morrison, although we concentrated on the former as the climactic lower limit in a poetics of contingency. Stunning there, the resyllabled phonemic spread in *A Mercy*—whereas trivial and irrelevant in the italicized alphabetic slurring two sentences back. Yet in the procedural idiom adapted from Agamben as a sponsoring impulse of this book, such are the affordances—and so intermittent accidents and distractions as well—of conjuncture (both alphabetic and syntactic) that *make language possible* even when they may make nothing of note happen in a given kink of linkage. But often they may. In what I take to be Agamben's variation of the Keatsian closed circuit discussed in connection with posthumous audition in Morrison, the measured stress of poetic declaration can be heard reissued in a text's own self-decreed reading. It is just this unleashed possibility, freed anew to recognition even within a fixed script, that the sometimes liminal readings in these chapters have found legible in action.

And some of which can be made sensible in class. Certainly, whatever one's pedagogical goals, it is from the lax verbal unconscious of students' own writing that one can keep learning anew the truant (but constitutive) byways of phrase. Teachers are certainly familiar with the border disputes of phonetic spelling in student idiom—by which, for instance, the tick of a *d* sound gets lost in confusion either with its iteration or with its near-miss dentalized sibilance in solecisims like "advance degree" (a twitch of wishful thinking?) or "close circuit TV" (an extra notch of paranoia?). Despite these routine lapses and overlaps, one can now and then still thrill to the likes of what happened in three different papers turned in to me on the same theme. With this admittedly not unprecedented slip issuing here from some subliminal response, I could only think, to the topic of the doppelgänger in Stevenson's *The Strange Case of Dr. Jekyll and Mr. Hyde*, I kept coming upon a phonetic elision (as if '*n* for *in* rather than '*n*' for *and*) in the all but brilliant sense that the eponymous figures are "one in the same."

Literature, and Stevenson's oscillating phonetic prose not least, makes such errors into part of its errand.

This book has, in a way, been about the other in the same, the linguistic backfire, at phonetic and syntactic scale, or in Agamben's sense (out of Deleuze) again, "the return of the possibility of what was." Broader principles emerge, of course, than those associated in some narrow way with homophonic or grammatical wit, accidental or otherwise. Something more deeply linguistic gets through to us. Texts are not just eyed into activation. Rather than a mere eyer of the page, each reader is, as it were, the *eyear* of literary process. That's roughly what glaucoma-suffering James Joyce meant with the cross-lexical transfer from some myopic debility—one that might require leaning into a text—to the programmatic demand of his prose, instead, for "an earsighted view."[2] Named in that homophonic pun is a register of attention that brings into earshot the phonetic ricochets between and beneath inscribed words. Joyce's textuality may have anticipated wholesale the verbal work of the computer—a vast "semic machine" as one critic has put it—but that doesn't mean that his phrasing could be word processed confidently by any but his own trusted hand.[3] He is the type of writer who, though needing his manuscripts eventually copied by typewriter, would certainly have found many of their ingenuities bedeviled by the constraints of computerized spell-checks. Every time I've attempted here, for instance, a Joycean coinage of my own in *hearsee*, it has been auto-corrected to *hearse*—and has had to be forced (in more senses than one) into its intended shape. Exactly in having to overcome it, however, I couldn't regret this electronic annoyance and its irony, since one major point of this book has been to move away from just that mortuary default option in philosophical terms: from death-like fixity to subvocal breath, from crypt to silent echo chamber in the visible sound shapes of inscription, from the coffin of speech to its afterlife in the reading that voices.

In my attempt, then, at flipping sensory priorities in the portmanteau term *eyear* (whether noun or verb—including its further transitive homophone in *eyehear*) into an equally punning *hearsee*, the computer's shaving back of the latter to *hearse* leaves such a lingual glitch well within our central orbit of consideration. For the interring of the heard in the hearse of language is a trope held in common, though under various degrees of interrogation and even at times resistance, from Hegel through Heidegger to Ong, Derrida, and Agamben and on to Mladen Dolar. This is the sense that speech, let alone writing, marks the death of voice, the sacrifice of animal sound. Incurred by language is the loss of the sensible in the making of sense, of noise in word choice. Silent assonance and alliteration like that last (*oise/oice*) is no more than a negligible accident of the meaning that eradicates—earadicates—all sounds in the recognition of their differential function as signifiers. Yet in the re-hearsing of voice that attends each new subvocal decoding of phonetic text, the seeingears of reading machinate a new vocality, secondary, seditious, self-editing.

But there's a sticking point, a potential holding action. And potential is, as we know by now, the word. The dialectical negation of presence in speech cannot negate the presence of that speech. Granted, where the "I" is, there no one is. The intelligible name (even in the form of a pronoun) marks the absence of the thing: both the human thing it would name and the material sound summoned to do so. At either end of the referential circuit, each somatic materiality is suspended in the sign. But where the "I" gets voiced, aloud or transcribed, there being is indirectly witnessed to—if not immediately witnessed, or in other words not demonstrably present as such. Speech cannot render immanent a human subject, but it can, in a version of Agamben's emphasis, locate the possibility of one in the conditioning—and continuing—fact of human language. Or to put it more in Cavell's terms, the full leveling reach of skepticism may be found held in check by the very words that communicate to other minds the undercurrent of our doubt, including the metaphors we find for the things we would wish to trust in. And literature is the ultimate proving ground for such figuration. Having once been inscribed under conditions of the linguistic potential for relayed human experience, such writing—when replayed by the reader so as to renew in process those conditions, that possibility—is the ever renewed coming-to-be of the utterance. Hence offering a renewed model of just that possibility. Hence in turn: literature writing language philosophy. For accumulating there is at once a fourfold topic and a self-enfolded (and self-exemplifying) thesis pitched across a phrasing that, in the current prepositional idiom, is "changed up"—and in fact elevated in its level of abstraction—on the syntactic run. At which point—which is to say, in which process—the ethic of attention solicits as much nimbleness as precision.

The beautiful changes, as Richard Wilbur once had it. As, of course, does the reigning idea about what constitutes the beautiful in literature. And even about its value as such. But, amid the linguistic changes it floats on its own terms, language as system—in precisely its latency—lasts. This book's backward glance began, before the beginning of my academic career, with the suggestively unstable grammar—and thus illustrative metagrammar—of two words following a definite (though not really definite for long) article: whether one adjective coupled with a plural noun (the *change*s in their manifestation as *beautiful*) or one singular abstract noun relativized by an intransitive verb of mutation (*the beautiful* known in part by the fact that it *changes*) or that same abstract singular noun governing a transitive, elliptical, and potentially universal predicate (*the beautiful changes* . . . this, that, most everything). Discussion itself has gone through many changes of its own since this recovered early encounter with Wilbur, in focus and philosophical frame, yet it has been guided from the first by the premature (untutored) conclusion that in poetry, in literature, the *potential* for such textual changes in particular—not just their varied descriptive *aspects*—is best pictured by the condition of language at large. And best *heard*, auralized, in the time-based medium of its sounding out. Or say again, in the case of silent reading, its *sounding in*, its strictly inward saying. To bring that early brush with Wilbur together with Agamben at last, we may sense—and it is none too soon to say it—that change, beautiful or not, is in fact *present potential* in activation. It is the immediacy of what might be *as in fact it now is*. And, in literature, multivalent phrasing is one leading means of its realization.

Time is change. Syntax too. Same even with syllabic pace: what Joyce evoked as the "alphabedding" buildup of given words, always at the whim of lexical timing. Reading may of course time *itself*, within certain limits. But at too fast a clip, too precipitous a skim, it defies the endemic temporality of its own medium. And even then it may sometimes be tripped up by a given ripple of enunciation. The fully committed deed of reading signs on for such chanciness of signification, such changes, such—in the philosophical as well as linguistic sense—potential. That's why a proposition so bluntly obvious that it begins to smack either of paradox or truism—Agamben's way of insisting that the end of poetry is the re-origination in each reading of the language that generates it—has kept coming to mind in the reading(s) here. It recurs so often as to seem the metalinguistic grounding for a more polemical modernist dictum like Ezra Pound's about poetry being "news that stays news." Not news as information, of course, but only as a surprise of speech that is renewed by recognition for each reader in, and as, the language that informs it. Forms it anew. And does so at times (such is the emphasis with which my analysis has been meant to extend Agamben's premise) by shaping it, however mutely, in the always contingent mode of secondary vocality. Reading—so the foregoing chapters gather to claim—is a silent ventriloquism in which what speaks to and through us is not authorship but that potential in speech that can make any act of writing vibrate back to life in its aftertime. Difference itself, founded upon distance, becomes the medium of reading.

So in the long run Agamben's central tenet, when further attuned to the auralteries of writing in particular, seems best understood this way: as showing how the receiving end of poetry is the re-sieving of its own potential through the filters of enunciation, where you never know in advance what may strike you, what sparks may be struck off, what linkages ignited by its signaling marks. And not needing to know in advance is the receptive disposition that, in turn, within a general ethic of reading, brings such an ungrounded ontology of language into conversation, for instance, with Cavell's literary linguistics of skepticism. The interplay is finally a matter of textual scale, in which secondary vocality replays at the level of reception an underlying fundament of the linguistic condition. Transient possibility becomes the figuration of founding potential. Or put it that the palpable latency of oral production in the suspended sonics of phonetic reading locates the recognized praxis of a subtending philosophical axiom, its symptom, its continuous implicit lesson. This is to say that one level down in the heat of reading—but how deep is that?—one level down from what no one can deny (that writing incurs the possibility of being intoned, called out) hovers what one can neither prove nor live by belying (that language is on call in us before any given articulation, and ready there to make more senses than one). A manifest stratum of latency (aurality) tropes another and more abstract and more formative one yet (our being-in-language)—and probes it in process.

And with certain writers unmistakably. Joyce's prose may be a "semic machine," but it is also, in the stratified tremble of his lexicon and the shearing force of an errant, subintentionalist lettering that is hard even to call his, a "seismic" machine. Such, at least, was one tendency of my former metaphors, in *Reading Voices*, for the silent rupture and reshuffle of just that bent in literary language—Shakespeare and Milton to Shelley and on through Dickens to Conrad and Woolf—that Joyce of course brings to a tenacious head. When his lexical torsion goes beyond the echoic patterning of word order to induce a salient mutation in word border itself—disrupting what linguists term the segmentation defined by juncture—this is exactly the effect I once chose to call, with its own self-evidencing sibilant elision, the "transegmental [rather than trans-segmental] drift."[4] A phrasing like Joyce's comic reprise of Romantic apostrophe in "Tell me, tell me, tell me, elm!" (*Finnegans Wake*, 143) so overwhelms raw iteration with the give and slippage, the take and double take, of sequence—including the rumble of enunciation beneath script—that the sheer textual momentum ends up prodded into telling more than it says, seeding a whole new lexical offshoot ("t*ell me*"). But, rather than a botanical analogy, if I had gone so far as to characterize this mode of effect by saying (again by auto-illustration) that words in the *Wake*, in tracing their own syntactic wake, can induce their contrapuntal semantic quake, I couldn't have laid myself any more open to deliberate if genial parody from the ranks of practicing contemporary writers than I unwittingly did.

Just as I was finishing up the present book, I discovered the 2013 collection called *Recalculating*, from former L = A = N = G = U = A = G = E poet Charles Bernstein, including a poem of blatant internal recalculations called none other than "Transegmental Drift." It begins by insisting that "It's the mind makes a muck" of things (hinting transegmentally at a mind running "amok"?) when it hears "Sound obtruding into the poem like a / Pork rind at a Bar Mitzvah."[5] The poem urges instead that we "Just give the / Twist a break"—as if alluding not just to the evolution of popular dance moves but to the way the junctural drifts I isolated give the word break itself a twist, as in the later lexical as well as lineal enjambments of Bernstein's own unsayable hyphenate "un- / iforms" and the more topographic fissure of "conti- / Nental divide."[6] Earlier yet, there was a conceptual poet's 2005 volume actually launched by a sustained prose send-up of the kind of muted seismic reverberations evoked by my own former analytic vocabulary—but a travesty no more relentless than it was manifestly invested in such figures of and for speech, and this from a writer, the Craig Dworkin of the later *Parse* (2008), as clearly fascinated with the "concept" of sentence diagrams as I was back in high school.[7]

Odd. I began this book—recalling a moment no more than a decade later, as it happens, than Akira Kurosawa's breakthrough 1954 use of slow motion in narrative film—by casting back to my own induction into the verbal slow-going of verse: my halting, frequently halted, efforts to take the pulse of its progression. And I come round now, a couple of academic degrees and several decades further on, to a distended riff by a conceptual poet—and frenetic wordsmith—on my eventual 1990 effort at theorizing a sense of something like linguistic ductility in both poetry and prose and the slowed attention it necessitates and engages. Ductility—or geogrammatical "subduction," as Dworkin would put it in "Shift." Odd, yes. But nice: to have had the earth move once in reading Richard Wilbur, only to have a related later trope of mine excavated and deliciously chipped away at by his radical successor. Until chiseled into new and monumental proportions all its own.

Listen to the said *Dworkin* at *work in* this vein of topographic figuration. Early on, he uses my phrase "transegmental drift" (14) before varying it to "transegmental shift" (16)—this so as, no doubt, to match more closely the eponymous "Shift" of this lead essay, flagged at the start in its derivation from Russian *sdvig* in an epigraph from the Zaum and Dada writer Ilya Zdanevich. Gravitating to the geological vehicle of Zdanevich's dead-metaphoric tenor in verbal "mass," Dworkin, in a hypertrophic mock-up of materialist poetics, can only be said to *run into the ground* the idea of a text's linguistic surface tension. He does so in an elating lampoon of literary scientism under the rubric of "seismic grammar" that builds on every imaginable cliché of a tectonic poetics. His is a tour de force complete with topographic models and zany graphs. Where the modernist Zdanevich speaks of "displacing a part of the verbal mass into another position," the mass is taken up by Dworkin with madcap literalness as the base of "a magmatic inscription" (9) in which the "tensile solid" (9) of language is either deformed by "plastic flow" or by "brittle fracture and frictional gliding" (9). This happens, at the pressure points of alphabetic writing, when the "lexical plates" submit to stress that will "compactively compress, laterally sheer, extrude, deform and fragment them in all directions" (9). So that "alphabetic drops accumulate, coalesce, and percolate through the surface tensile boundaries with an oscillatory sink and segretatory float" (10).

The entire thesaurus of seismic geology has been ransacked to elaborate the "crustal melt" (10) and "graphemic spreading" (11) that result, especially when "morphemic ridges" (14) are involved, what with their notorious susceptibility to "crack or rift" (14) in an "upwelling semantics" (15). This is how we are to understand the way in which "buoyant subduction" works beneath "the paper plane of the text" (15) so as to "trigger nucleation of a new zone," one that, in Dworkin's own paronomasia and slant rhyme, is "folded and faulted" (15)—all under the sway of "thermal convection in semantics" (24). The celebrated pretend revolution in 1960s linguistic seismology has—the parody proceeds—shown us how, once "sentences descend into semantics," they "heat by transfer, adiabatic compression, frictional forces and exothermic phase changes from within the grammar of the sentence itself" (24). So it goes, page after increasingly wonky page, where—on one of them alone—"phase stable episodic deviations" in wording are contrasted with contingent "volatiles" in their coruscating effect across "thickened accretionary assemblages" that remain prey to "lateral displacements or delamination" in various "shears and sutures left by collisional events" in the "syntectonic recumbent folds" encountered at "numerous hypocenters" along a "trench axis" (16). How better to conceptualize the phonemic slippage between and across words, together with the sideways grammatical shifts of syllepsis, than to see, in each, just such "lateral displacements or delamination" as entrained by the time-sensitive work of reading's own subterranean voicing?

This conceptual poet's love of language can warm even to such borrowed geologic argot—and even render it ingratiating in all the preciosity of its nonsense when applied to linguistic formations. How can one deny that "the delaminated remnants of obducted evaporites preserved in the precipitation regimes of depleted melt extraction" (20) must take their measure from "fluvial, Aeolian, deltaic, wave, storm and tidal grammatic processes" (21), with the frequent telltale sign of "flattened sediment shards" in "peripheral fanning" (21) easiest to recognize—it's good to be reminded—in "quench textures along a metasomatized weft" (21)? In just these ways the "viscous coupling" under convectional pressure can be found to release "ridge-push and drag forces at the base of the lexical plates" (24), a push-pull effect that—as Dworkin's deadpan pedant persona has it in moving toward closure—can "reveal the formation and redistribution of narrative crust through language's history" (26). From there to the indicated "Conclusion," where contemporary poets are enjoined to attend to such matters in order to militate for "the survival of communication with Language" (28; capital L, and "with" inferring not just *by means of* but *in contact with*)—a point readily aligned with Agamben's sense of the need in poetry to make language part of the message, recognized as it returns in reading.

Further, it is well worth noting that in all the manic brio of Dworkin's agglomerated jargon there is one self-exampling instance not just of lexical pillage and spillage but of functional phonemic slippage in the "crustal relamination" of its own molecularized alphabetic shift. One of his graphs will soon map the probability of elision in various proportions to its distance "from the initial letter" (27). But we've already seen, a few pages before this, and via the most proximate of elisions, how his own ventriloquized scientific language, in its compressed "paronomastic modality" (20), has put the lexical *rift* back in *drift* (while burying the *d* at the "pull" and "fanning" of a keen-edged "morphemic ridge"). This emerges from his sense of a fault-line energy "found on the narrative fragment rifted away" (15): sheared off, that is—as marked by this back-formation of the noun *rift* into an unorthodox transitive verb. In this the reader sees, hears, shears how the underbeat of a *d* sound is no sooner extruded than consumed on the skid in the tremor of a functional "drift" across the very lexical shift of "narrative fragmen*t rift*ed away"—a sense-spanning, sense-panning effect by no means foreign to Dworkin's own poetry (as well as his satiric prose).[8]

"Shift" remains another name for change: for change in process, change in place. And what Dworkin's seismometer is ultimately dialed up to register is just this fact, this aspect, of language as the very terrain under our feet, including first of all the shifting sands of its granularity—and necessity—and risk. To which inference, however far afield from his own wry calibrations, one would then want to add—in the further philosophical terms we've drawn out from Agamben and Cavell—that language is the main ethical ground we have to stand on, however shakily, in human interchange. When this ground, as well as this interchange, is not just represented but modeled (and structurally troubled) by prose fiction in particular, it is precisely the "narrative fragment rifted away" under the pressure of prose *friction* that I have explored at length as a *narratographic* response to the literary microplot (shades there too, I suppose, of seismic charting).[9] Such an ultimately graphonic subdrama is the lexical ground d/riven an/d rifted away by none other than syntactic and even phonemic cleavings taking delayed place and their own good time. Hence, for me, the core of Dworkin's heady conceptual frolic in "Shift" when oriented toward literature rather than language in general: its recognition of linguistic plasticity, attested to at whatever absurdist pitch, as an inherently terrestrial and formative—which is to say, world-constituting—literary phenomenon. For this is the case—quite apart from the various poetries of l-a-n-g-u-a-g-e or their conceptual descendants—not only in the language of poetry more broadly but also in the poetics of narrative prose.

Another and more canonical checkpoint is in order, therefore, together with its further ramification. We are concerned not with an even-handed division of labor like Joseph Conrad's sense that an author "writes only half the book; the other half is with the reader."[10] The effects at play are more contingent and variable at least than Conrad's hermeneutic axiom is usually assumed to indicate: in force, rather, at that stratum of response where reading moves to rewrite upon the inner ear what is already inscribed in print. One can, though, appreciate such an interface with the reader precisely in regard to the voicing that gets activated in phonetic effects like those in none other than Conrad's own narrative prose rather than his aesthetic pronouncements.[11] So, too, with the work of an earlier novelist who would so wholly subscribe to Conrad's dictum about authoring "only half the book," the remainder being "with the reader," that she models the afterlife of her dying characters on just this logic: Philip Wakem living on after the drowned Maggie Tulliver as the best reader of her being in *The Mill on the Floss*; the eponymous Daniel Deronda living on after Mordecai Cohen to embody in his own political will a reading of the latter's unwritten visionary hopes.

In George Eliot's earlier novel, even before the flood has come, such a fate has been prefigured for Maggie—metrically as well as metaphorically, and then even transegmentally—when the downbeat of a trochaic "anxiety about *Ste*phen, *Lu*cy, *Phil*ip" is said to "beat on her poor heart in a har*d*, *driving*, ceaseless storm of mingled love, remorse, and pity" (bk. 7, chap. 2), with *riving* surfaced there by elision as effect to the driven cause: an emotional coherence torn apart by moral (before mortal) storm. This as befits all too well a book whose heroine, like its prose, is "played upon by the inexorable power of sound" (bk. 6, chap. 7). Such storming of phrase by its own sound, whether soft or "hard," represents the often fast driving grain of prose in action, at least post-Romantic prose like Eliot's, like Woolf's after her, like Morrison's—as well as like that of Dickens and Conrad, and, in poetry, the wordings of Shakespeare through Wordsworth and Shelley and Keats to Stevens.

And, yes, on to Wilbur—and beyond to Bernstein and Dworkin. The story has been theirs, only incidentally mine. The callow lad you met in the first pages of this book, who grew so attached to sentence diagrams that he must have thought they had something to do with architectural girders and cross braces and was professionally derailed for a time by some such enthusiasm, grew up instead to develop a structuralist fascination with the semiotic square, including that example in Chapter 3 designed to draw out the double negation of both full speech sounds and total silence by which secondary vocality makes its mark in reading. Varying Stanley Fish in his way of having us, with Milton, surprised by syntax and sin alike, the approach here is what I might have termed an "affective metastylistics": a response aesthetic that is cued by the call of linguistic possibility from beneath any one expression. It is what I did term, in *Reading Voices*, a textual "evocalization," and what I have tried to reconceptualize here, chapter by chapter, through those philosophies of locution, metaphor, voice, textual performance, and linguistic ontology that come most directly into the widening circle of such consideration.

Just now, we have been auditing sound play in the widely misunderstood prose of George Eliot, a prose often thought at its most showily learned, as, for instance, in *Daniel Deronda*, to be rather stringently "philosophical" rather than, say, "stylish." It is. But among the things it manifests a philosophical attitude toward is the power of language as such to saturate narration as a felt effect: or call it a linguistic affect beyond (but not divorced from) narrative sentiment. So I want to close with a later moment, on the closing page of Eliot's last novel, where the prophetic climax of *Daniel*

Deronda serves to encapsulate much that has come before in the present book. Chapter 5's dossier on syllepsis considered in passing Eliot's taste for this Dickensian syntactic trope, including the illogically parsed simultaneity of rushing "into manuscript and syntax" in the writing act. We move next and last to this book's other pole in the matter of textuality's shifting sands—if not seismic underminings. We do so in turning an opened ear to a "quieter" phonemic drift rather than, as parody might put it, to the syntectonic buckle of such deliberate satiric pairings as represented by syllepsis. What emerges is a case of Eliot not rushing, but edging, into script and syllable.

And her prose operates this way within a context associated with classic philosophical ideas of being and its changes. Before Wilbur, Stevens: "Things as they are / Are changed. . . ." And before that, classical ideas of mutability. In Stevens: two predicates, two enjambed copulas, seem almost paradoxically to subtend each other within an apprehension of the mutable. In a comparable epigraph from a late chapter in *Daniel Deronda*, George Eliot pairs the Stoic philosophy of Marcus Aurelius with her own Wordsworthian sense of something evermore about to be, here a matter of unforeseen consequences from human action: "The unripe grape, the ripe, and the dried. All things are changes, not into nothing, but into that which is not at present" (chap. 57). Thus the translated quotation from Aurelius, with its happy English contrast of "thing" and "nothing." The dichotomy operates not between presence and absence but between manifestation and that which is not "at present" (though which can inhere, as Agamben might have it, both *in* and *as* the present as its potential). Such is the indwelling of the eventual in the event. And it takes shape next, in Eliot's own adjacent verse epitaph, across a line break in its cognate grammar as well as an internal phonemic enjambment that together—in their own linguistic grain—highlight how a deed "being done / Must throb in after-throb*s till* Time itself / Be laid in *still*ness" (emphasis added). Though flickeringly ambiguous for "still" as "yet," the cross-lexical phonetic prolepsis anticipates its own echo in the cosmic end.

I close in now on the latest case of such *auralterity* I've come upon in Eliot, and this in an equally ethical context concerned in particular with the recognition of oneself in the other. My fresh sense of Eliot's closural dynamic in *Daniel Deronda* was developed for a paper at a spring 2013 conference at Stanford's Center for the Novel on "the nature of literary being," a topic inspired in part by Jacques Rancière's *The Flesh of Words*.[12] Despite the mystification that may seem implicit in his title, my lecture signed on to his sense of literary writing as precisely a resistance to incarnation. For his "flesh" is that of "words" plural, not the Word, not Logos or embodiment, but the materiality of inscription. Literary being is existence under erasure. Quoting Rancière: "Literature lives only by the separation of words in relation to any body [two words] that might incarnate their power. It lives only by evading the incarnation that it incessantly puts into play" (5).[13] It does so, I wanted to add at Stanford, by keeping strictly potential (in Agamben's sense) the relation of embodiment to the words that name it: potential, therefore inherent as such, present in possibility, and this only by way of textuality's inherent "desubjectification." Apart from any authorial retention in narrative script, to invent literary persons is to lay claim to the thought that they *might* exist; and in that mightness is their literary might, their force, at times their palpability even in subvocal production, where the virtually said may shadow the written with its own alternate possibility in the very linguistic "interface" (Elfenbein once again) of e/locution—or, say, the formative relay between enunciation and descriptive evocation. Or where (Hartman again) the "mediator for our experience of literature," in audition of its "keener sounds," is "something as simply with us as the human body."

Within this framework, I looked to a character dyad in Eliot's *Daniel Deronda* that I had previously explored as inscribing within the text, in more general terms, the idea of the novel's own internalized response: a reflexive logic that I have only much later noticed encrypted on the sly in Eliot's closing muted wordplay.[14] The relation between the dying Mordecai and his Zionist avatar Daniel becomes an interanimation modeled almost explicitly on the relation of character (or text) to reader. Earlier, about Gwendolen Harleth, such a reader of Eliot is addressed thus: "But now enter into the soul of this young creature as she found herself"—the phrasing so far interrupted and incomplete, rounded out as follows (with foreshades of Henry James) across a periodic suspension—"with the blue Mediterranean dividing her from the world, on the tiny plank-island of a yacht" (chap. 54). No self-discovery there in "found herself," just—in delayed grammatical reaction time—an insistence on the all too obvious site of her marital isolation, whose agony and panic we must, as it were, help conceive. Yet what we readers are granted by the command of that vocative ("But now enter into . . ."), with its licensed trespass upon the soul of another, is what later, and in reverse, Mordecai hopes for from his alter ego in Daniel, who, once entering into his spiritual mentor's beliefs, will allow Mordecai's soul to permeate *him*.

For Mordecai has eschewed written form for his visionary formulations, hoping they will be in a sense imprinted, in the spirit rather than the letter, on the soul of his successor (as with a memorized Hebrew poem Mordecai is earlier found "printing" on the "mind" of another would-be protégé [chap. 38]). Yet the materiality of alphabetic manifestation is of course required for Eliot's narrative climax and its virtual metempsychosis: its transmigration of the racial soul. Springing a microlinguistic allegory of the reader's relation to text, the spectral hold of Mordecai's hopes on his survivor—as it delimits, by extension, the very nature of both men's literary being—is funneled through a phantom enunciation of the word *ghost* itself, sounded out once as a monosyllabic homophone, then insinuated across a three-word trisyllabic cluster where the lexical revenant of "goest" conjures a spiritual recursion *ex propria persona*, the thrust of the future caught on the cusp of last words outlasting, if only in potential, their own serial inscription. For this, one needs yet again to go slow.

The writer earlier capable, in describing her heroine Gwendolen, of such a cross-lexical trellising of syllables as in the character-constituting and phonetically suffused "infusion of drea*d ready* to *curdl*e and *decla*re itself" (chap. 31), is a writer—or, say, the conduit of a desubjectified writing—who brings to the final moment of her story, in Mordecai's deathbed wording, an effect not unlike the lexical skid of Morrison's paradoxical elision in "slave/free." In a different context of ethnic liberation, the Zionist prophet Mordecai, dedicated to rehabilitating what has been called, by one of his Jewish cohort, the walking "ghost" of such a nationalist vision (chap. 42), and who himself, slowly dying, has already appeared as (again explicitly) a mere "ghost" in his father's sleep (chap. 66), insists at last on a supposedly self-effacing transference with the novel's hero that is actually a spiritual power play. In refusing transcription for his own theological and nationalist meditations ("Call nothing mine that I have written" [chap. 63]), he hopes instead that, even while wasting away of "consumption," he can breathe his uninscribed beliefs imperishably, because immaterially, into a surrogate self.

The wish fulfillment is not simply, in his last words, manifested in the phrasing "Where thou goest, Daniel, I shall go. . . . Have I not breathed my soul into you?" Of course, aside from the phonetic play in the "ghostlier demarcations" slyly latent here, nothing could be more in the spirit (and in fact biblical region) of Geoffrey Hartman's intertextual audits than to hear behind this insistence another same-sex affiliation, Ruth to Naomi in leaving her own people behind: "For whither thou goest, I will go; and where thou lodgest, I will lodge" (Ruth 1:16). In *Deronda*, however, Daniel is pledged from here out to reside at the heart of Mordecai's own absence, a perpetual dislodging caught and flickeringly carried by the latter's expiring words. Pressing upon recognition is not just the phonetic overlay of *ghost* in *goest*, but (to fill in that heuristic ellipsis of mine) a further bridge-phrasing that ghosts its own phonetic tracks with a lexical gesture hovering between an anagram and a near-miss contraction ("Is't not" for "Isn't it?"): "Where thou *goest*, Daniel, I shall *go. Is it* not begun?"—begun even before being spelled out in the very back draft of another wording. (Not "*Has* it not *already* begun?" but something closer to "Is it not here and now beginning, hence begun, in just the dilation—and liquidation—of my words?") Mordecai himself has almost seen this textual epiphenomenon coming, when saying much earlier to Daniel, "You have risen within me like a thought not fully spelled" (chap. 62). His own last words can still not quite spell it out. But they come close. Though I had earlier devoted an entire chapter to this suspect proxying-out of mentality as an almost perverse fable of reader response, profoundly if implicitly dubious in its treatment by Eliot, it was only in reading this passage aloud to an undergraduate class—while drafting the Stanford lecture—that I was, for the first time, slowed sufficiently to catch this particular drift. Let's say it took me back in a flash to the scene of my "induction," which is why I round out discussion with it now. There in my own classroom, a jolting encounter with an episode of formative phrasing—jolting not least because elusive—like that of my after-class reading all the way back in high school.

Captured in that very flash, as if in answer to the Stanford question about literary being, is the ultimate test, the limit case, of a character passing from actual to virtual within a novelistic plot, displaced as if from diegesis to sheer exegesis across the very aspiration (both senses) of his own fused syllables. Which is of course, in the yet more complete homophonic fusion of "slave/free" and "I'l/last," the only way that Florens herself in Morrison's *A Mercy* can be sure of lasting beyond the last of her days, exceeding her self-obliterated words, internalized by her survivors, her exegetes, her readers: making transmissibility itself manifest—and not despite, but because of, the tiniest ambiguities of reception. Like Florens, Mordecai before her ends hoping less to communicate than, in the terms of Régis Debray's mediology, to transmit. And like Morrison, Eliot too is a practicing mediologist of her own cultural vision. In dying into Daniel, as Agamben might put it about this version of an always-coming community, Mordecai (as figure for perpetual interpretation) remains forever potential—not in some abstract way, but in each reading that gives flesh to words never embodied at their source. For these are words, in a variation of Rancière, whose flesh is in their literary incarnation our own: that of the novel's readers, who take up the material inscription and achieve one disinterested version of Mordecai's dream by making its forward momentum impalpable in every way, strictly virtual in its possibility—except in the subvocal pulse of our own enunciative engagement, our own physiological sounding board. In Agamben's emphasis again, it is precisely by way of the "reciprocal desubjectification" both of the phrased uplift and of the undermining pun—each reduced to sheer medial function at sending and receiving ends—that our own silent utterance can let language itself through: a transmission made manifest beyond the narrow intent of communication.

But since Mordecai is not a poem (whose "end," in Agamben's sense, would be its eventual iteration) but a would-be posthumous prophet, and since Daniel is obliged to channel even his unwritten words in our place, the analogy can only hold by way of a certain aggression and death grip. Mordecai doesn't just settle for a posterity under his partial influence; he forces the issue, tries to set himself in spiritual place after all, by the very displacement of his elective alter ego. He pays no mind to otherness, let alone to other minds. And so it is that this happenstance of in-class recitation (available as well, of course, to silent enunciation) reaches back not just to my first poetry reading but to the later motivation for this whole book. It does so by bringing out a certain disciplinary regret that helped spur its conception. For whereas a cognitive *ethics* of literature in the "other minds" school might be inclined to notice how Mordecai wants to be as transparent to Daniel as if the latter has inherited the former's thoughts simply by reading of him, only a complementary *ethic* of reading could audit in Eliot's prose (or, more to the point, in her language) the recognition—even critique—of this spiritual ghoulishness across the frictional semiopacity of word sequence per se. In Jameson's sense above, though at a linguistic scale not ordinarily probed in the broader strokes of his response to form, "themes" and "ideas" are here stylistically "relativized"—in particular a Zionist ideology and its transpersonal egoism—"to the benefit of formal demonstrations" that are available in textual process before the onset of any hermeneutic decoding.

The ectoplasticity of phrase at this terminal turn in *Deronda*, together with the diaphanous (but still phonic) alternatives it summons as if in an ephemeral prose séance, is no less exemplary for being—what?—improbable. Of course I am not saying that George Eliot actually says this: this about the ghostly perpetuity of rhetorical power in a double but unwritten pun. Or that it would, in any case, even be George Eliot who did. Out of her insinuated skeptical distance from Mordecai's vampiric ambition as the undead nationalist Word, what happens is rather that her desubjectified language produces this effect. And by that I mean again her English, not her fine-tuned and high-toned narrative prose. "Ghost" is not at the end said at all, let alone in spectral echo. Rather, its lexical span is seeded, and twice over, as a linguistic, a phonemic, possibility ("Is it not begun?")—not of what might have been, but of what might now be: be there for you in reading, be therefore yours alone to say.

Let such an intermesh and aftermath of wording complete this endpiece, then, as an extended coda to Chapter 6. In the give and drift of one word into the next, Morrison's Florens is about to give up her writing altogether to the torch. This we learn only after discovering that she has been written into being to begin with at nail point. In the form of prose *friction*, such writing, restaged under the character's own deep-dug impress in that novel, is a communicative act by means of which, so far from going unsaid in what is said, language is doubly installed under the sign of its formative ambivalence and its pending loss at once. Same with Mordecai's final utterance, as channeled through the hearse and hearsee of Eliot's own language. As his last words give way to a posthumous transfusion into Daniel, we audit their very dissipation in the alternate modes of impetus and elegy, quaver and fade-out. From this final speech, once again, and for all its coercive will to power, emerges the fact of a character's being spoken for in writing. In this way the prose of Eliot, like the prose of Morrison—passing through the very provisions of language in continually renewed embryo—shapes itself again in us, marked by its own oscillating verbal event. To repeat an entitling notion one last time, prose of this sort seals in syntactic process the vocally subcontracted (or call it the often subvocally redrafted) deed of reading.

And so the most commonplace way of putting it—in holding out for what one might wish to retain as literary in literary study, or, say, linguistic in the language arts—is also (as I hope both this book's own holding actions and its attempted advances have shown) actually the most philosophical way of putting it. That way is this: that in literary reading, *language doesn't finally go without saying*. Some such intuition must have been obvious from the start, from this book's first extended anecdote of fumbling self-tutelage. Writing is at its deepest, if not greatest, when it is manifestly writing, when it is felt being written, offering not an emulative writing lesson as such but a more pervasive lesson in language's inherent mutation. One isn't always as unsure and untutored as a novice reader, of course, but one is always reschooled by text. When writing thickens to itself, seems to be taking on more than it can spell out, or letting out more than it can quite pin down, difficulty becomes a filter—and relay—for the otherwise unsaid of language as language.

At such moments—when we may find ourselves caught up short and asking, "What is going on here?"—we nonetheless feel less frustrated by an unsettled density of phrase than entrusted with it. What is going on, in prose as in poetry, is that *language is happening*. Going on and going forward, taking place by increments of recognition. To cast our point of departure in the form of a final syllepsis, then: the beautiful, like so much else taken up in writing, changes from moment to moment and one thing to another. But whether any one change is transitive or not, the grammar of reading is always transactive, our commitment to it an ethic—though as far from doxa as it is from relaxation. All alphabetic and syntactic sequencing registers its changes in the beat of attention, the budge and lunge of text under renewed articulation and secondary vocality. And to put this crucial literary intuition in its most philosophical form: such change is *the present tense of potentiality*—with uncertainty its mode, language its medium, and medium itself its ongoing disclosure.

Isn't this, finally, where all the theoretical voices arrayed here—with whatever degree of vehemence they might in some cases deny that plural noun for their written words, might resist the metaphysics seemingly pandered to by any notion of literate "voices"—would still come to some kind of choric consensus? And precisely in the matter of literature writing language philosophy? Varying Cavell on the putting out of light and life together in the beautiful fury of Shakespearean lexical changes, have it this way: an ontology of human language founders on any proof except in the putting forth of speech. And literature is the proving ground of the most sensible, because sensed—and not least the most ethic-imbued, and ultimately philosophical—intuition one can have in this regard: that language is as language does.

NOTES

Fore Word

1. Barbara Dancygier, "Language, Cognition, and Literature," in *Creating Consiliance: Integrating the Sciences and the Humanities*, ed. Edward Slingerland and Mark Collard (New York: Oxford, 2012), 409.

2. Geoffrey Hartman, "Ghostlier Demarcations," *Literary Criticism—Idea and Act: The English Institute, 1939–1972; Selected Essays*, ed. W.K. Wimsatt (Berkeley: University of California Press, 1974), 226. The assumption of bodily mediation via a muted *oratio* is not returned to explicitly (though it is everywhere implicit in Hartman's emphasis on phonetic reading) in his later and much reprinted essay, "The Voice of the Shuttle: Language from the Point of View of Literature" (1969), in *Beyond Formalism* (New Haven, CT: Yale University Press, 1970), 336–54, whose subtitle is noted by Susan J. Wolfson in her contribution to "About Geoffrey Hartman: Materials for a Study of Intellectual Influence," a special issue of *Philological Quarterly*, forthcoming, for an emphasis central in fact to the present book as well. Spotlighted by that subtitle is not merely a linguistic lens directed at literature (sine qua non of any such formal attention) but the further optic (always aurally focused as well, so to speak) that literature applies to the very working of language—or, as I will be emphasizing it here, that finds audiovisual resolution in "literature writing language philosophy."

3. See Derek Attridge, *Moving Words: Forms of English Poetry* (Oxford: Oxford University Press, 2013), where his opening chapter's titular gambit—"A Return to Form?"—is answered in the affirmative with a thumbnail bibliography of what is often dubbed neoformalism (18–19)—beginning with Susan J. Wolfson and Marshall Brown's 2000 anthology, *Reading for Form*, as preceded importantly for Romantic studies, Attridge also notes, by Wolfson's 1997 monograph, *Formal Charges*. Of further, and not entirely incidental interest here, is that Attridge also chooses to open, as will my own first chapter, with a brief gesture of "autobiography," his first sentence recording a "moment of intellectual satisfaction I remember with particular vividness from my teenage years" (1). In his case this "occurred when, in high school, I was introduced to the principles of Latin scansion" and, struck by a reliability so different from English meter, found himself captivated by their "lucid and pleasing pattern" (1). As will be clear, my own American high school curriculum left me, to say the least, more to my own devices in any and all such matters. But I am tempted to think, as will also emerge, that something about the rhythmic enunciation of poetry does tend to send one back—as far as the mind can travel—to early sensory as well as later "intellectual" experience in the acquisition of linguistic as well as literary competence, back to something that I would therefore wish, in this respect as well, to call formative as well as formal.

4. My title's emphasis is also to be distinguished, but mainly as complementary, from Richard Poirier's "Prologue: The Deed of Writing," in *The Renewal of Literature: Emersonian Reflections* (New Haven, CT: Yale University Press, 1988), 3–66. Matching Poirier's sense that writing is an "event" of textual labor, a mode of verbal work rather than a spontaneous expressive vent, is the demand this places on the reader in apprehending, among other textual action, the linguistic leverage thus exerted.

5. See Wolfson in "About Geoffrey Hartman."

6. See T. J. Clark, "More Theses on Feuerbach," *Representations* 104, no. 1 (Fall 2008): 4–7.

7. One is pleased enough, from a departmental or disciplinary vantage point, to hear Clark celebrating the formal analysis of Breughel by English professor Edward Snow as a case in point for the "moment of practical criticism" (7) that art history has not fully enough passed through. But in light of my present "formative" stress, I gravitate more immediately to Clark's passing analogy of formalist aperçus to the unearthed structures of trans*formational* grammar, with Snow's intensity of perception "as productive of nonobvious findings as the young Chomsky at full steam" (7).

8. J. Hillis Miller, *The Linguistic Moment: From Wordsworth to Stevens* (Princeton, NJ: Princeton University Press, 1985), xiv.

9. By just these often adduced routes, these referential detours, texts put under inspection their own origin, become their own choric double (para-basis), displacing their descriptive scene onto its own writing as performance; or shift ("over and above" any textual message) between the telling and the told (meta-lepsis); or indulge the mis-use of one word for another (cata-chresis) when in fact there is no proper, no original term, nothing literal behind the petrified metaphor; or speak the linguistic fact behind the nontruth of all fiction, the sheer personification or prosopopeia (giving face) in the face of absence.

10. Garrett Stewart, *Reading Voices: Literature and the Phonotext* (Berkeley: University of California Press, 1990); Stewart, *Novel Violence: A Narratography of Victorian Fiction* (Chicago: University of Chicago Press, 2009), where, in the latter book's emphasis on the prose of prose fiction, I sought to stress the revealing nature of stylistic deviance at the level of word, syntax, and metaphor.

11. This was the work of Édouard-Léon Scott de Martinville. On the limited intent of his method (without audial playback), see Patrick Feaster, "Framing the Mechanical Voice: Generic Conventions of Early Phonograph Recording," *Folklore Forum* 32, nos. 1/2 (2001): 57–102; and Jonathan Sterne, *The Audible Past: Cultural Origins of Sound Reproduction* (Durham, NC: Duke University Press, 2003), 31–85. See also Jonathan Sterne and Mitchell Akiyama, "'The Recording That Never Wanted to Be Heard' and Other Stories of Sonification," in *The Oxford Handbook of Sound Studies*, ed. Trevor Pinch and Karin Bijsterveld (Oxford: Oxford University Press, 2012), 544–60.

12. As, for instance, in the title of Lisa Gitelman's *Scripts, Grooves, and Writing Machines: Representing Technology in the Edison Era* (Stanford, CA: Stanford University Press, 1999).

13. While the newer formalisms are happily pushing back here and there at interpretation's slackened interest in such matters (such verbal materiality), a formative emphasis within this approach would, at a certain level, try starting over—from the linguistic ground up.

14. Stanley Cavell, *Little Did I Know: Excerpts from Memory* (Stanford, CA: Stanford University Press, 2010).

15. Garrett Stewart, "Reading Feeling and the 'Transferred Life': *The Mill on the Floss*," in *The Feeling of Reading: Affective Experience and Victorian Literature*, ed.

Rachel Ablow (Ann Arbor: University of Michigan Press, 2010), 179–206, an essay with an emphasis on subvocal irony in George Eliot, to which I'll be returning, with a different novel under audition, in "After Wording" below.

16. Elisha Cohn, *Still Life: Suspended Development in the Victorian Novel* (New York: Oxford University Press, forthcoming). Affect is found instead, in her reading, to mark a nineteenth-century aestheticism all its own: a remission or lapsed vigilance in the demands of self-culture that goes so far as to valorize sensation over perception, let alone feeling over thought, and that gravitates as a result to episodes of prose extricated from plot drive and given over to a poetics of dreamlike, impersonal rhythm. Her analysis is thereby drawn to many a plotless passage of recessively inflected prose whose very resistance to regimes of concentrated purpose still has a way of inviting a nonteleological readerly attention—or attunement. It is this mode of reading, in response to spells of disengaged action and diffuse sensory responsiveness, that I would include within an ethic of verbal affect—one that leads a cognitive life of its own before leading on in turn, as it often does, to fuel an implied (but not subsuming) ethics of personhood and sympathetic recognition.

17. The corrective emphasis in Cohn, as taken up in my sense of a linguistic ethic rather than a communal ethics, is not unrelated to what one may well want to resist, as regards lyric writing earlier in the century, in the intentionalist proposals of Zachary Leader in *Revision and Romantic Authorship* (Oxford: Clarendon Press, 1996). His argument privileges, for instance, late-life changes in verse texts over earlier published versions. He does so according to a telltale "ethical" and even quasi-legal mandate in honoring the dead's last wishes (76–77)—and thus, more broadly, disempowering a traditional mainstay of criticism altogether in those "against-the-grain" readings that refuse a supposed direct transfusion of writerly intent (as well as being diametrically opposed to such editorial critics of revisionary textual genetics as Susan Wolfson, Peter Manning, and others). Again: the rule of expressive personhood rather than of linguistic encounter. Treating the personified authorial "other" under this legislated ethics of alterity runs counter to the more targeted ethic of reading stressed in my chapters, which does not owe obedience to the meant so much as it honors a cognizance of the meaning process—on alert for how language does its work in speaking (through any particular writer) of its own being-written, once or once over. Unlike a last testament, the implied referential contract in the deed of reading is not legal and binding, but freed to latency and even at times lexically unbinding, syntactically disbanding.

18. See Stephen Best and Sharon Marcus, "Surface Reading: An Introduction," "The Way We Read Now," ed. Stephen Best and Sharon Marcus, with Emily Apter and Elaine Freedgood, special issue, *Representations* 108, no. 1 (Fall 2009): 1–21. Even setting aside this essay's question-begging assumption that, in the heyday of "symptomatic" reading, textual surface was presumed either "superfluous" (1) or discountably "superficial" (2)—rather than constituting the very field of diagnostic labor, from whose discrepancies the hidden (or unconscious) ideological agenda could be assessed—still the call for a less suspicious, a more descriptive, appreciative, immanent, and thus ultimately affective investment in texts, rather than a mastery of their buried political contradictions, remains rather far from the specific impulse of this book. That's why it has seemed necessary to insist on something preliminary and elementing, called an ethic of attention, that facilitates, rather than excuses from the room, an equally watchful ethics and politics of literary imagining. The authors of that position paper invoke the recent initiatives of neoformalism, to be sure, where they find the superfice restored to its own inherent complexity in a mode reminiscent of New Criticism, albeit differently contextualized in a social and noncanonical breadth of reception—instancing all this

as a leading example of the titular "way we read now." But their italicized stress (as one of several leading new options) on an "*embrace of the surface as an affective and ethical stance*" (10) is to be distinguished from the level(s) of attention proposed (or let's just say attempted) here, whether in the "graphonic" reading of poetry and its prose equivalents or, more broadly, in the "narratographic" reading of fiction—each yielding up a conditioning linguistic possibility not to be "embraced" or otherwise celebrated (or even just cerebrated) but to be plumbed, philosophically before ideologically, for the "structuring absence" of linguistic potential itself. The "valorization of surface reading as willed, sustained proximity to the text" (10) would seem, in contrast, to privilege almost claustrophobically the time-tested paradigm of closeness in reading ("proximity"), open as always to charges of cultural myopia, over a constitutive deep focus on the shaping energies rather than produced effects of verbal phrase. Instead, these chapters proceed as if literature were a sign or symptom, which it is, of foundational linguistic options manipulated, suspended, overruled, and renegotiated in the writing, and then the reading, act. See, as it happens, Fredric Jameson's entirely tacit rejoinder to the supposed limits of his own version of a symptomatic method in "After Wording" below, note 1.

19. Charles Altieri, *Reckoning with the Imagination: Wittgenstein and the Aesthetics of Literary Experience* (Ithaca, NY: Cornell University Press, 2014). In clarifying his interest in literary value over literary ethics, Altieri's penultimate chapter, "What Literary Theory Can Learn from Wittgenstein's Silence about Ethics," notes in passing how the deconstructive work of J. Hillis Miller in *The Ethics of Reading: Kant, De Man, Eliot, Trollope, James, and Benjamin* (New York: Columbia University Press, 1987) has mostly been subsumed to more political models (even when adopted from Derrida and Levinas) of encountered otherness in poststructuralist ethics.

20. This catalogue essay accompanied the retrospective called "Brian Dettmer: A Decade of Book Sculpture" at the Herman Geiger Foundation in Cecina, Italy, in the summer of 2014, following on from my earlier treatment of Dettmer's work in *Bookwork: Medium to Object to Concept to Art* (Chicago: University of Chicago Press, 2011).

1. Induction

1. See Michael Riffaterre, *The Semiotics of Poetry* (Bloomington: Indiana University Press, 1980).

2. Geoffrey H. Hartman, "The Voice of the Shuttle: Language from the Point of View of Literature," in *Beyond Formalism* (New Haven, CT: Yale University Press, 1970), 341.

3. Heard in audio version from The Poetry Foundation: http://www.poetryfoundation.org/features/audioitem/630. Another poem by the same title, *Some Words within Words*, appears "(for children and others)" in Richard Wilbur, *Anterooms: New Poems and Translations* (Boston: Houghton Mifflin, 2010), 51–52.

4. Unpaginated examples from Richard Wilbur, *The Pig in the Spigot*, illustrated by J. Otto Seibold (San Diego, CA: Harcourt, 2000).

5. *The Collected Poems of Wallace Stevens* (New York: Vintage, 1982), 171.

6. I'm thinking here in particular of T. J. Clark's *The Sight of Death: An Experiment in Art Writing* (New Haven, CT: Yale University Press, 2006), where, in his scrupulous "viewing" rather than mere "reading" of two Poussin masterworks, Clark places repeated stress on the "ethical" force of disclosed pigment and brushwork in the

"episodes" of paint itself that pace these quasi-narrative canvases. Clark's would thus count for me as a "narratographic" apprehension of the medium.

7. Martin Heidegger, "The Thing," in *Poetry, Language, Thought*, trans. Albert Hofstadter (New York: Harper & Row, 1971), 177.

8. Wallace Stevens, "The Course of a Particular," in *The Palm at the End of the Mind*, ed. Holly Stevens (New York: Vintage, 1967), 367.

2. Secondary Vocality

1. Wallace Stevens, "An Ordinary Evening in New Haven," in *Collected Poems of Wallace Stevens* (New York: Vintage, 1954), 473.

2. Thus Walter Ong, *Orality and Literacy: The Technologizing of the Word* (London: Methuen, 1982; New York: Routledge, 1988): " 'Reading' a text means converting it to sound, aloud or in the imagination, syllable by syllable in slow reading or sketchily in the rapid reading common to high-technology cultures" (8). But this admission of the temporal is rare in his emphasis on writing's "commitment of the word to space" (7), a point reiterated later as the alphabet's "ruthlessly efficient reducer of sound to space" (100). On occasion, though, Ong admits that in this space of inscription "the spoken word still resides and lives" (8)—but manifest only in transit, we've already been told, ephemeral, never abiding: more like crests upon the alphabetic tide and backwash than what somehow resides there, or say, "resides" more in the etymological sense (which Ong may well have meant to invoke) of the merely *residual.* Orality is lost to time in the first place, and then its duration is lost to space when its event is petrified into script. As the essence of "verbomotor culture" (68), sound exists only when it is "going out of existence" (32), a maxim later exactly repeated (71). And not just repeated but exemplified the first time around, his chosen example offering a nice irony on the very notion of evanescence: "When I pronounce the word 'permanence', by the time I get to the '-nence', the 'perma- is gone, and has to be gone" (32). Same, backing up along the lexical extension, with the very "per" of "impermanence"—unless, that is, the "imp" has refused its mandatory exit en route (as Poe lets happen in Chapter 4 below).

3. Garrett Stewart, *Reading Voices: Literature and the Phonotext* (Berkeley: University of California Press, 1990), where my drawing on the neural and anatomical science of subvocal speech production is tacitly renewed by a recent French commentary on Flaubert's sense of prose music. Pierre-Marc de Biasi writes in "LA VOIX: Le gueuloir de Flaubert," *Le Magazine Littéraire*, no. 401 (September 2001): "For Flaubert, during the most silent of readings we do of course read with our eyes but always also with our throat in that, at its prompting, we feel a genuine virtual music of words: the music that could become audible if we endowed with the least of breaths what is, in us, an infinitesimal but precise sketch of an articulation. *Contemporary science seems very much to prove him right*" (31; emphasis added). It is the "gueuloir" ("yelling out") of that title that actually renders this sometimes too-tuneful music audible: namely, Flaubert's habit of forcefully reading aloud his texts in the act of revision, with the intent to strip away such extraneous phonetic recurrence as assonance and alliteration. This is the subject of Michael Fried's searching book by the title *Flaubert's "Gueuloir": On Madame Bovary and Sallambô* (New Haven, CT: Yale University Press, 2012), where he quotes de Biasi (153–54 n. 16). For my purposes, the French critic's phrase "sketch of an articulation" is nicely poised as metaphor between script and muscular tracing—recalling the more faintly metaphoric sense in Ong (*Orality and Literacy*, 8) of word sounds imagined "sketchily in . . . rapid reading."

In this same vein, and although I am less convinced by the function of "mirror neurons" in our relation to textual phenomena than are some recent cognitive students of literature, I would be ready to entertain "echo neurons" as a metaphor for the firing mechanism of secondary vocality. Or put it, in the French spirit of these issues here, that such an aural mirroring of phonetic text in the deed of silent enunciation, such a somatic sketch of sound forms, offers the readerly potential *pour voir un voix*.

4. Giorgio Agamben, *The End of the Poem*, trans. Daniel Heller-Roazen (1996; Stanford, CA: Stanford University Press, 1999), 115.

5. Michel Foucault, *Death and the Labyrinth: The World of Raymond Roussel*, trans. Charles Ruas (1963; New York: Doubleday, 1986).

6. Giorgio Agamben, *Language and Death: The Place of Negativity*, trans. Karen E. Pinkus with Michael Hardt (1982; Minneapolis: University of Minnesota Press, 1991), xi-xii, 45.

7. Steven Connor, *Beckett, Modernism and the Material Imagination* (Cambridge: Cambridge University Press, 2014), where his chapter on "Writing the White Voice" begins with the scholarship on the putative evolutionary break from oralized to strictly silent reading that I reviewed in *Reading Voices* (see note 3 above), though including some notable debate on this history since.

8. Geoffrey Hartman, "Words, Wish, Worth: Wordsworth," in Harold Bloom, Paul de Man, Jacques Derrida, Geoffrey Hartman, J. Hillis Miller, *Deconstruction & Criticism* (New York: Continuum, 1979), 193, a passage anchoring Susan Wolfson's appreciation of Hartman's poetics in a cluster of essays on the critic's influence in *Philological Quarterly*, forthcoming 2015.

9. The ultimate question is whether Heidegger's concept of *Dasein* really makes the advance it claims over "the medieval *Haecceitas*, not to mention the I of modern subjectivity" (Agamben, *Language and Death*, 5)—or whether, because in the *Da* there's no real *there* there, it doesn't fall back into the negative dialectic of Hegel. It is this question, in effect, that will eventually lead Agamben to a prolonged scrutiny of the *t/here* in linguistics, or, in other words, the place of deictic shifts in the constitution of reference's virtual space.

10. An intricate if tacit bond exists between Agamben's "Philosophy and Linguistics," in *Potentialities: Collected Essays in Philosophy*, trans. Daniel Heller-Roazen (Stanford, CA: Stanford University Press, 1999), 62–76, and his account of Aristotelian "potential" as the inherent presence of an alternative (so that, for instance, the practicing poet, achieving his gift, retains "potential in so far as he has the potential to . . . not-write poems" ["On Potentiality," in *Potentialities*, 179]). Here is a contingency, whether positive or negative, that is not "annulled in actuality" but "that conserves itself and saves itself in actuality" (184), always pending there. Whereas linguistics takes language as an axiom, studying its essence, the attempt to philosophize instead the existence of language, its very being as potential in each speaker, becomes a model for philosophy at large. In any such "literalization of the voice" (74), its letteralizing, which is the very definition of language, one immediately encounters "the transformation of the *factum loquendi* into a presupposition that," for its science, "must remain unthought" (75). But not for its philosophy, the task of which, as Agamben's closing paragraph has it with his own italics, is "to consider no longer the *presupposition* of Being and potentiality," including the being of language and its founding possibility, "but their *exposition*" (76). In the present context, it isn't just that poetry is a testing ground for such an exposure ("exposition") of language's being. What the present chapter pulls together from Agamben's separate essays in poetics is a complementary emphasis on the way the contingencies of reading (as *re*reading) locate

the potential (always present, always overcome in the "taking-place of language") of not-reading. Or, more to the literary point, of reading otherwise. In any case, as discussion to come—sampling and supplementing Agamben's verse analysis—should make clear, an Empsonian reader might be the first to say that ambiguity itself *exposes* more than *presumes* language.

11. Gilles Deleuze, *Cinema 2: The Time-Image*, trans. Hugh Tomlinson and Robert Galeta (Minneapolis: University of Minnesota Press, 1986), where this notion is a kind of conceptual refrain, having found its definitive statement years before in his 1968 work, *Difference and Repetition* (London: Athlone, 1994), in an explicit allusion to time and memory in Proust: "The virtual is opposed not to the real but to the actual" (208).

12. Giorgio Agamben, *Homo Sacer: Sovereign Power and Bare Life*, trans. Daniel Heller-Roazen (Stanford, CA: Stanford University Press, 1998).

13. The double bind Agamben finds in philosophy's most stringent retreat from its own limits is summarized at one point as follows in *Language and Death*: "The mythogeme of the Voice is, thus, the original mythogeme of metaphysics; but inasmuch as the Voice is also the original place of negativity, negativity is inseparable from metaphysics. (Here the limitations of all critiques of metaphysics are made evident; they hope to surpass the horizon of metaphysics by radicalizing the problem of negativity and ungroundedness, as if a pure and simple repetition of its *fundamental* problem could lead to a surpassing of metaphysics" (85; Agamben's emphasis).

14. Mladen Dolar, *A Voice and Nothing More* (Cambridge, MA: MIT Press, 2006), whose lucid fleshing out of the metaphysical history of Voice along Agamben's lines (crossbred with Lacan) is also noteworthy, together with many other recent studies, for citing none of Agamben's literary-critical work.

15. *Language and Death*, 45. Across the divide of the genitive, Agamben finds again, and this time at ground zero, the "place of negativity," for the voice of death doesn't just index death but symbolizes it when "interpreted" as such. In this double possession of the genitive—as in fact a vocal dispossession—on the one hand "the voice is death, which preserves and recalls the living as dead," while "at the same time," as sign rather than evidence, it is "an immediate trace and memory of death, pure negativity" (45)—like all language when understood according to the dialectic of sense-certainty over against its decimating abstractions.

16. See Giorgio Agamben, *Stanzas: Word and Phantasm in Western Culture*, trans. Ronald L. Martinez (1977; Minneapolis: University of Minnesota Press, 1993), 154, where that elusive term "vocal image" is quoted from a passage in Saussure in which the founder of modern linguistics despairs of his "science" having any real subject matter except such differentials—such glyphs of absence, such alphabetic figments.

17. See, for instance, Jeffrey S. Librett, "From the Sacrifice of the Letter to the Voice of Testimony: Giorgio Agamben's Fulfillment of Metaphysics," *Diacritics* 37, nos. 2–3 (Summer–Fall 2007): 11–33. Without noting the original comparison between voice under linguistic erasure and the obscure Roman practice of the excluded subject as systemic social purge, Librett mounts a closely argued critique of Agamben's Holocaust studies in the *homo sacer* project by, in effect, inverting the philosopher's metalinguistic orientation and turning it against him. In contrasting the testimony of survivors to the abjection of silenced victims, Agamben understands genocide to be replaying not just Roman barbarities (in political more than religious forms) but the Hegelian death of the animal body into meaning. Yet for Librett, Agamben's minimizing of a quasi-religious ritual involved in the ethnic slaughter of the Jews results in sacrificing, on Agamben's own part, the people of the book to a more Christianized and supposedly phonocentric Logos where something like the newly "crucified" body is survived by the Word as

Witness. Precisely by being detached from an account of Agamben's linguistic work, the critique may end up seeming one-sided. Rather than celebrating the Living Word in some transcendental sense, Agamben is engaged in tracing modern cultural depravities back, by homology rather than causality, to the privative nature of language as excluded body in Western metaphysics, all bio-graphy as the figurative encorpsing of its biology.

18. This is the stress applied by Agamben's most recent exegete. As contrasted with Librett's resistance to what he sees as a closet Christian ideology in Agamben's work (see note 17 above), Leland de la Durantaye, glossing Agamben's *The Church and the Kingdom* (London: Seagull, 2012), in "Afterword: On Method, the Messiah, Anarchy and Theocracy" (63–79), stresses the profane nature of the philosopher's evocatively theological paradigms. According to this account, Agamben's is a (Benjaminian) messianism without Second Coming. The question is one not of waiting—but of biding, abiding in, one's time. It depends, one may say, upon a sense not of expectation but of *present possibilities*. Yet even here, in de la Durantaye's commentary, there is no concerted effort to deliver the quasi-religious inference over to the method, theological to theoretical formats. A term and its concept are available but unclaimed: namely, and again, *potential*—potential as a paradoxically indwelling fact, not a prefiguration: a doubling over of the now and the if-only in the gesture of the emergent. As such, this emergence would have in particular its immanent linguistic register: its poesis as well as its less formal, its more amorphous, politics. For repeatedly in Agamben, this emergence is a gesture modeled by, and instanced in, the realized latencies of poetic language—realized in both "formative" senses together, activated as event by their recognition as potential.

19. See *The End of the Poem*, 100, where Agamben stresses enjambment and caesura as "limiting elements" not found in unmetered prose, a point reiterated in several of his other essays on verse.

20. This analysis by Agamben, from *Language and Death*, receives a deserved and extended gloss in a study of the philosopher's literary explorations to whose central tenet this chapter also subscribes: that the first half of his career in philologically inflected literary analysis and the second half in political philosophy, roughly two decades each, are sequential sides of the same coin of postmetaphysical exploration. See William Watkin, *The Literary Agamben: Adventures in Logopoiesis* (London: Continuum, 2010) for the way in which the chronologically sequenced questions "What does it mean to have language?" and "What does it mean to be human?" are inextricable (8). Later in his commentary, Watkin hews quite closely to Agamben's developing emphases in the reading of Leopardi (124–34), which he finds arriving at "one of the most profound reflections on the literary ever penned in any language at any time" (129). Allowing for hyperbole, it is indeed the power of Agamben's analysis that moves my coming paragraphs on Leopardi's sonnet to essay something further along the lines Agamben has laid down, though in a broader register of lexical and sublexcial effects: not a summary of Agamben's reading, of the sort Watkin provides, but a complementary "graphonic" tracking along similar philosophical lines. In this, still, my response does overlap with that deliberately circumscribed focus of Watkin's study, devoted not to the full reach of Agamben's poetic thinking, his philosophical thinking through poetry, but rather, and more specifically, to the way it gets us closer to literature's own "intimate experience with the semiotic materiality of language as such" (200). Yet for me "potential" in Agamben's philosophical work suggests one undertrafficked bridge between the two phases of his thought.

21. Writing on *Tintern Abbey*, British poet-critic J. H. Prynne has commented in his own way on how "all the eight pointing gestures with 'these' and 'this' confirm by their

incremental cadences, as proxy for the reader, the focus of viewpoint and visible scene: the steadily intensified here and now of where we are." See J. H. Prynne, "Tintern Abbey, Once Again," *Glossator* 1 (Fall 2009): 3, http://solutioperfecta.files.wordpress.com/2011/10/prynne-tintern-abbey-once-again-8x10.pdf. I would simply stress (more in the spirit of Agamben) that, behind the rhetoric, "where we are" is, as it were, only reading. In *Moving Words: Forms of English Poetry* (Oxford: Oxford University Press, 2013), Derek Attridge discusses Prynne's idiosyncratic criticism in a chapter called "Sound and Sense in Lyric Poetry," which in its own right is certainly a probing new contribution both to the mimetics and the broader semiotics of phonic play. In contrast, my emphasis falls more on what could be called "the sense of sound" in writing, the possibilities of enunciation I have called "evocalization," including the sometimes sprung rhythms of the undertext. In this respect, I am drawn to what Attridge highlights in Prynne's work: a stress on phonology rather than phonetics as the proper domain of poetic study, a matter not of acoustics but of semiabstract linguistic patterns (87). Without Prynne's specific preoccupations (close to Agamben's in this one regard) on deep etymology and "historical phonology" (87), my own sense of the "formative" linguistic philosophizing latent in phonemic as well as syntactic operations would indeed gravitate to such an *ology* rather than simply to its manifest phonetics (or phonemic tactics). See Prynne on "evolutionary phonology" in "Mental Ears and Poetic Words," *Chicago Review* 51, no. 1 (2009): 133, where his summary emphasis on consonantal stops (a specific subclass, so to speak, of Agamben's caesurae) renders, from within such predetermined instances, the very principle of linguistic segmentation. When Prynne finds these rhythmic effects isolating "states of being to be interrupted or broken into, opening faults and cleavages within the representation of language and thought in action" (140), his metaphors echo the seismic tropology of another contemporary poet in allusion to my own earlier work (see Craig Dworkin, in "After Wording" below).

22. One benefits, as always, from Jonathan Culler's "Apostrophe," chap. 7 in *The Pursuit of Signs: Semiotics, Literature, Deconstruction* (Ithaca, NY: Cornell University Press, 1981), 135–54.

23. See Paul de Man, "Hypogram and Inscription: Michael Riffaterre's Poetics of Reading," *Diacritics* 11, no. 4 (Winter 1981): 17–35.

24. Christopher Ricks long ago noticed this genitive richness in Wordsworth as part of the power of his prepositions, singling out remarks of C. C. Clarke on the "ambiguous" waver in "thoughts of more deep seclusion" (among other such bifocal uses of *of*) without noticing this grammatical trope also at work in the more elusive "picture of the mind." See Christopher Ricks, *The Force of Poetry* (Oxford: Clarendon Press, 1984), 119.

25. The lost letter of such contractions, such idiomatic elisions, becomes less neutral, more urgent, in its work when read against the chapter "Endangered Phonemes" in a book by Agamben's former student and frequent translator, Daniel Heller-Roazen, called *Echolalias: On the Forgetting of Language* (New York: Zone, 2005), which includes mention, among "problematic," "threatened," or "endangered" phonemes, of the *e* sound following the semiconsonant *j* even in the essential first-person French shifter *je*. This is a place-holding *ə* deemed "obsolete" (29) by modern phonology, yet whose eclipse in enunciation, as Heller-Roazen sees (without hearing) it, may emerge in a given poetic context as "haunting" the line (32) with its disallowed vowel. What this comes to, in light of Agamben's here uncited work, is a kind of exacerbated parable of language formation more broadly: a sound lost altogether, rather than only partially, to the meaning that exceeds it, a voicing wholly unrecoverable but (even at that) still virtual (still phantasmal) in the work of script.

26. Giorgio Agamben, "*Se*: Hegel's Absolute and Heidegger's *Ereignis*," in *Potentialities*, 116–37.

27. Agamben shows further ("*Se*," 131) that the *es* in a German phrase like "es gibt Zeit," "es gibt Sein" (it gives time, it gives being)—and thus distant equivalent to the circularity of an English idiom like "there is time" or even "there is being"—is in fact, by circuitous derivation, a detached genitive suffix of sorts, like the "of itself" of *se*, marking more or less that which is "*of* it," rather than being it: a reflex, in short, of the de-essentialized. And so again we encounter a neuter deflection of the nominative into what is only obliquely proper to it, and which, when further given over to grammar in the closed circuit of a phrase like "time is given," redraws the loop of reflexivity more openly than in a more routine English intensifier like "time itself." So, too, as Agamben notes, with the nearer equivalent of Italian and English in a phrase like *si dice* (it is said).

28. Alluding there to the landmark work of Friedrich Kittler, *Discourse Networks 1800/1900*, trans. Michael Metteer, with Chris Cullens (Stanford, CA: Stanford University Press, 1990)—and to the field of media theory it redefined.

29. Giorgio Agamben, "Bartleby, or On Contingency," in *Potentialities*, 243–74.

30. It is important to note here, especially because Agamben doesn't, a shift in emphasis within his own terminology. The release of thought into the unsourced site of its palpable mediation, that release that poetry draws on and then draws out from us in reading, is here a "desubjectifying" moment, in Agamben's poetics, that has become, in the next decade of his thought, a negative valence of media technology. At that later point, in his explicit debt to Foucault, he sounds more like Kittler (see note 28 and the coming chapter) than like a poetician. What "we are now witnessing," Agamben writes, in answer to his titular question about a prominent usage of Foucault's in *What Is an Apparatus? and Other Essays*, trans. David Kishik and Stefan Pedatella (Stanford, CA: Stanford University Press, 2009), amounts to defining the apparatus as a prosthetic *subjection* in which "processes of subjectification and processes of desubjectification seem to become reciprocally indifferent" (31), so that the user "who lets himself be captured by the cellular telephone" has become "only a number through which he can, eventually, be controlled," just as the TV spectator "gets, in exchange for his desubjectification, the frustrated mask of the couch potato, or his inclusion in the calculation of viewership ratings" (31). What once made the receiving mind permeable to something like its own native element, language itself, is now a more technological submission to the discourse network across all its channels and wavelengths. My return to Agamben's poetics, here and by extension in the next chapter, is a return to a cognitive feedback loop in reading that, by the tacit inference of his own later political critique, has been machined away by communication devices—or say, inscription technologies—other than phonetic language.

3. Errands of the Ear

1. Percy Bysshe Shelley, "A Defence of Poetry," in *The Longman Anthology of British Literature*, ed. Susan J. Wolfson and Peter J. Manning, 3rd ed., vol. 2a (New York: Longman, 2006).

2. Friedrich A. Kittler, *Discourse Networks 1800/1900*, trans. Michael Meteer, with Chris Cullens (Stanford, CA: Stanford University Press, 1990), 3.

3. James Joyce, *Finnegans Wake* (Harmondsworth, UK: Penguin, 1992), 258.

4. Andrew Elfenbein, *Romanticism and the Rise of English* (Stanford, CA: Stanford University Press, 2009).

5. Where, in *Reading Voices: Literature and the Phonotext* (Berkeley: University of California Press, 1990), the guiding principle of "evocalization" is what I am now identifying as well by the notion of secondary vocality. It should also be said, in light of subsequent chapters in the present book, that though Elfenbein's point is well taken about the foundational divide between cited (often parodied) elocution and impersonal exposition—a divide that organizes the novel as genre (in the difference between dialogue and narration especially)—one often notes a potent byplay between phonemic and syntactic effects, aurality and inscription, in the narrational (rather than citational) prose of prose fiction, especially in writers saturated in Romanticism like Charles Dickens and George Eliot, to say nothing of Toni Morrison's later and career-long fascination with this bridged divide.

6. Mladen Dolar, *A Voice and Nothing More* (Cambridge, MA: MIT Press, 2006), 73.

7. Kittler, *Discourse Networks*, 246–47.

8. Giorgio Agamben, "Philosophy and Linguistics," *Potentialities: Collected Essays in Philosophy*, trans. Daniel Heller-Roazen (Stanford, CA: Stanford University Press, 1999), 69.

9. Jean-Claude Milner, *Introduction à une science du langage* (Paris: Seuil, 1990).

10. Stanley Cavell, *Must We Mean What We Say? A Book of Essays* (Cambridge: Cambridge University Press, 1976).

11. F. J. Sypher, ed., "Sappho's Song," in *Poetical Works of Letitia Elizabeth Landon "L.E.L."* (Delmar, NY: Scholars' Facsimiles & Reprints, 1990), 5.

12. See Gyles Brandreth, *The Joy of Lex: How to Have Fun with 860,341,500 Words* (New York: William Morrow, 1980, where the phenomenon of the "oronym" is placed under the sign of the quizzical in the subsection "What Did You Say?" (58–59). Brandreth's obscure and unexplained coinage (alluding to an either/"or" ambiguity, perhaps, rather than to the technical term "oronymy" for the onomastic class "names of mountains"), a term that has nonetheless had considerable circulation since, is defined as follows: "Oronyms are sentences that can be read in two ways with the same sound"—as in the rather self-exampling "Are you aware of the words you have just uttered" vs. ". . . just stuttered." Or more fully discrepant: "The stuffy nose can lead to problems / The stuff he knows can lead to problems." All of his examples, however, turn in this way on the junctural equivocation of two (or three) abutting words, so that such phrasal alternatives (rather than full-sentence variants) are predominantly dependent on what I have called the wavering phonemic juncture of a "transegmental drift." See Stewart, *Reading Voices*, for a sampling of such effects from Shakespeare to Joyce and beyond.

13. Eric Griffiths, in *The Printed Voice of Victorian Poetry* (Oxford: Clarendon Press, 1989), argues both against Ong (35) and Derrida (48–59) on the score of voicing's absence from the grapholect (and idiolect) of verse enunciation. Later, he cites *In Memoriam*'s grief over Hallam's precipitous loss—"all he *was is* overworn" (st. 34; emphasis added)—as proof that Tennyson, so concerned about undue sibilance (hating, for instance, Pope's "offence from amorous causes springs" in *The Rape of the Lock*), could only have wanted the effect that "crowds together" the monosyllabic antithesis of "was is" (Griffiths, 110–11)—as in fact it serves also to mourn with feeling inelegance (one might add) the causal wrench of tense from being to its own past. On the question of sibilance, Tennyson is also cited by Griffiths as railing again the cacophonous printed voice induced by a typo when his "earth's invention stored" was given in the *Times* as "earth's intensions stored." Objected the laureate: "I should never have written so unmusically as ntions st" (*sic* in original; Griffiths, 111)—unless

perhaps, in my example, when needing to rescue absolute "silence" for human music in his reading of Hallam's "silent-speaking" letters, as conjured by their own cramped vocality and paradoxical self-release.

14. The effect here is a function of hendiadys, the figure of twinning, which I illustrate at greater length in my chapter on diction in *The Oxford Handbook of English Poetry*, ed. Matthew Bevis (Oxford: Oxford Univesity Press, 2013).

15. Robert Bridges, ed., *Poems of Gerard Manley Hopkins* (London: Humphrey Milford, 1918), 119.

16. Emily Dickinson, *Complete Poems*, ed. Thomas H. Johnson (New York: Little, Brown, 1960), no. 83.

17. This thread of his historical overview is summarized, apart from individual genres, as "the inward turning of the psyche produced by writing and intensified by print" (Ong, 151).

18. Kittler's complex argument develops across the entire chapter of *Discourse Networks 1800/1900* called "The Mother's Mouth," 25–69. On Kristeva's distinction between the semiotic and the symbolic, see Stewart, *Reading Voices*, 270–71, as well as further discussion of her approach throughout.

19. On this "introspection" in James, Wittgenstein quotes the American philosopher's sense of "self" as "consisting mainly 'of peculiar motions in the head and between the head and throat' " in enunciating that very monosyllable. Ludwig Wittgenstein, *Philosophical Investigations*, trans. and rev. P. M. S. Hacker and Joachim Schulte, 4th ed. (Oxford: Wiley-Blackwell, 2009), 132, no. 413. No definition emerges from uttering this concept, this abstract noun, except "the state of a philosopher's mind" in reflecting on it. Thus Wittgenstein in a closing parenthesis: "(And much could be learned from this.)" Among other things to be learned: that the thought of self, which is also to say the self of thought, inseparable from the radical ontological abstraction of its name, is also inseparable from the silent enunciation—somewhere between brain and musculature, mind and body—by which both the word and the very idea are posited.

20. G. W. F. Hegel, *Aesthetics: Lectures on Fine Art*, trans. T. M. Knox (Oxford: Clarendon Press, 1975), 1:89.

21. See Geoffrey Winthrop-Young, "Implosion and Intoxication: Kittler, a German Classic, and Pink Floyd," *Theory Culture Society* 23 (2006): 75–91.

4. Imp-aired Words

1. See "The Murders in the Rue Morgue," in *Complete Tales and Poems of Edgar Allan Poe* (New York: Vintage, 1975), 161.

2. Citations not given by Cavell are from Ralph Waldo Emerson, "Self-Reliance," in *Essays and Lectures*, ed. Joel Porte (New York: Library of America, 1983), 257–82.

3. Keats to John Taylor, February 27, 1818, in *The Letters of John Keats, 1814–1821*, ed. Hyder E. Rollins (Cambridge, MA: Harvard University Press, 2002), 1:239.

4. Both Poe stories are discussed from a different perspective, and with only intermittent reference to Cavell, in the second chapter, "Attention Surfeit Disorder," of my *Novel Violence: A Narratography of Victorian Fiction* (Chicago: University of Chicago Press, 2009), where Poe's stylistic excess stands in antinovelistic contrast to Victorian sacrificial plotting and its dubious rhetorical alleviations. Since then, I have returned specifically to Cavell's interest in Poe in my "The Word Viewed: Skepticism Degree Zero," in *Stanley Cavell and Literary Studies*, ed. Richard Eldridge and Bernard Rhie (New York: Continuum, 2011), 78–91.

5. Stanley Cavell, *The World Viewed: Reflections on the Ontology of Film* (1971; Cambridge, MA: Harvard University Press, 1979), 72.

6. A rhetorical question. Two books of mine, *Between Film and Screen: Modernism's Photo Synthesis* (Chicago: University of Chicago Press, 1999) and *Framed Time: Toward a Postfilmic Cinema* (Chicago: University of Chicago Press, 2007) do attempt a continuous answer as to why the rudimentary technologies of visual mediation on screen *are* enfolded into questions of one's relation to the world unfolded by the drama of plot.

7. Stanley Cavell, *Disowning Knowledge in Six Plays of Shakespeare* (Cambridge: Cambridge University Press, 1987), 140.

8. Stanley Cavell, "Being Odd, Getting Even: Descartes, Emerson, Poe," in *In Quest of the Ordinary: Lines of Skepticism and Romanticism* (Chicago: University of Chicago Press, 1988), 105–49.

9. See Stewart, *Novel Violence*, 77–81.

10. See "A Tale of the Ragged Mountains," in *Complete Tales and Poems*, 679–87.

11. I allude with that phrase to the title of the last chapter, "The Gothic of Reading," in Garrett Stewart, *Dear Reader: The Conscripted Audience in Nineteenth-Century British Fiction* (Baltimore: Johns Hopkins University Press, 1996), where I explore (with no attention there to Poe) certain macabre transferential exchanges in late Victorian fiction.

12. Georges Poulet, "The Phenomenology of Reading," *New Literary History* 1 (1969): 58, where the point is, for instance, that a grammatical "I" is spoken for by the reader in the course of a given enunciation.

13. Anyone thinking along these lines, and trying to think through their transferential assumptions, is indebted to the sense of "reading as being read" in Timothy Gould, *Hearing Things: Voice and Method in the Writing of Stanley Cavell* (Chicago: University of Chicago Press, 1989), especially as this central emphasis in Cavell's work on Emerson and Thoreau is given full scope in the analysis of Gould's last two chapters, "Models of Reading" and "Reading and Its Reversals." The influence of this analysis is also acknowledged in my approach to the matter of reversible intersubjectivity, as implicated in our response to Cavell's own style, in "The Avoidance of Stanley Cavell," *Contending with Stanley Cavell*, ed. Russell Goodman (New York: Oxford University Press, 2005), 140–56.

14. Gérard Genette, *The Work of Art: Immanence and Transcendence*, trans. G.M. Goshgarian (Ithaca, NY: Cornell University Press, 1977).

15. On this slip of Emerson's, see *Collected Works of Ralph Waldo Emerson*, vol. 2, *Essays: First Series*, ed. Alfred R. Ferguson and Jean Ferguson Carr, with introduction and notes by Joseph Slater (Cambridge, MA: Belknap Press, 1979), 230.

16. On this point of self-nomination as palindrome in *Great Expectations*, see Peter Brooks, *Reading for the Plot: Design and Intention in Narrative* (New York: Knopf, 1984), 142.

17. Stanley Cavell, *Must We Mean What We Say?* (New York: Scribner's, 1969).

18. "The Imp of the Perverse," in *Complete Tales and Poems*, 280–84; 284.

19. This is a formula summoned under deflection, in fact, by Hamlet's hinted sense of "speak out" in "For murder, though it hath no tongue, / Will speak with most miraculous organ" (2.2.593–94).

20. Gilbert Ryle, *The Concept of Mind* (London: Hutchinson and Company, 1949), 22, his example coming from chap. 39 of *Pickwick Papers*. I've given a somewhat fuller account of the splintered logic of syllepsis in connection with Ryle's critique of Descartes in "The Ethical Tempo of Narrative Syntax: Sylleptic Recognitions in *Our*

Mutual Friend," *Partial Answers: Journal of Literature and the History of Ideas* 8, no. 1 (January 2010): 119–45.

21. Stanley Cavell, *The Claim of Reason: Wittgenstein, Skepticism, Morality, and Tragedy* (New York: Oxford University Press, 1979), 180.

22. Ludwig Wittgenstein, *Philosophical Investigations*, trans. and rev. P. M. S. Hacker and Joachim Schulte, 4th ed. (Oxford: Wiley-Blackwell, 2009), 190, vi, no. 35.

23. See my extended microstylistc reading of this episode, together with an account of its treatment by Deleuze, Agamben, and the latter's fellow Italian philosopher Roberto Esposito, in "Lived Death: Dickens's Rogue Glyphs," in *Dickens's Style*, ed. Daniel Tyler (Cambridge: Cambridge University Press, 2013), 231–52.

24. Giorgio Agamben, "Difference and Repetition: On Guy Debord's Films," in *Art and the Moving Image: A Critical Reader*, ed. Tanya Leighton (London: Tate, 2008), 330.

25. Agamben's notion, after Valéry, of sound postponing sense recalls Geoffrey Hartman's definition of a "pun" either as "two meanings competing for the same phonemic space" or as "one sound bringing forth semantic twins." Hartman, "The Voice of the Shuttle: Language from the Point of View of Literature," in *Beyond Formalism* (New Haven, CT: Yale University Press, 1970),347. The inevitable deferral of one meaning by the other is only the clearer in the distributed, skewed fusions of syllepsis.

26. In this, one agrees with Charles Altieri, in "Taking Lyrics Literally: Teaching Poetry in a Prose Culture," *New Literary History* 32, no. 2 (Spring 2001): 259–81, that the power of lyric (and, I would add, of a prose equally marked by Altieri's crucial values of "intensity" and "plasticity" [267]) is not epistemic but performative, not a way of knowing but a way of experimental participation in states of feeling that writing draws out in us rather than merely depicts—and so draws us into. In Cavellian terms, literature offers a defeat of skepticism, then, not by the epistemological route of proof but not just by suspended disbelief either; rather, by a linguistic experience keyed to exceed what it names, to enact what waits unsayable—though still formally articulated—in its run of words.

27. J.L. Austin, *How to Do Things with Words*, ed. J.O. Urmson and Marina Sbisà, 2nd ed. (Cambridge, MA: Harvard University Press, 1979), 124.

28. This is a touchstone of metaphoric displacement discussed by de Man in his essay "Epistemology of Metaphor," in *On Metaphor*, ed. Sheldon Sacks (Chicago: University of Chicago Press, 1979), 13–30.

29. In this regard, another addendum to Cavell's initial lecture applies to "A Tale of the Ragged Mountains" as much as to "The Imp of the Perverse"—when that postscript sums up the linguistic constitution, or in Cavell's terms "creation," of the self as follows: "Users of language, humans are creatures of language, exist only from it, as equally it exists only from us" ("Being Odd," 141). It follows for Cavell, and all the more so with the allegory of simultaneous transcription in "A Tale," that the question of identity is "modeled by Poe as the existence of a writer, who exists simultaneously with the writing, as it is being written, uttered" (141). The freakish extension of this model, in Cavell's sense again its philosophical "parody," comes when the displaced reader, too, not only "exists simultaneously with the writing, as it is being written," but nearly dies by it. Here is Emersonian intersubjectivity gone eradicating.

30. Cavell, *The Claim of Reason*, 495.

31. Donald Davidson, "What Metaphors Mean," in Sacks, *On Metaphor*, 29–46.

32. Paul Ricoeur, *The Rule of Metaphor: The Creation of Meaning in Language*, trans. Robert Czerny, with Kathleen McLaughlin and John Costello SJ (London: Routledge Classics, 2003).

5. Splitting the Difference

1. Miss Bolo's precipitous departure "in a flood of tears and a sedan chair" finds, a century after *Pickwick*, a complicated homage from Groucho Marx in *Duck Soup* (1933), where he doubles the ante with a second prepositional spin: "You can leave in a taxi, and if you can't get a taxi, you can leave in a huff. If that's too soon, you can leave in a minute and a huff." Only the first sentence is given—as metaexample—by Steven Pinker in *The Sense of Style: The Thinking Person's Guide to Writing in the 21st Century* (New York: Penguin, 2014), 65. He is not commenting on syllepsis as a stylistic gesture, but rather noting how a specialist term of that sort benefits in writing from an example, preferably two—to triangulate understanding with a second "such as." His alternative instance, from Benjamin Franklin: "We must all hang together, or assuredly we shall all hang separately" (65).

2. Jean Epstein, *The Intelligence of a Machine*, trans. Christophe Wall-Romana (Minneapolis, MN: Univocal, 2014), 5, where, the name of the publisher aside, there is nothing "univocal" about this passing satiric barb.

3. An example from *Windsor Forest* that is given again, though this time indicated as involving "prozeugma and hypozeugma," in *The Princeton Encyclopedia of Poetry and Poetics*, ed. Roland Green et al. (Princeton, NJ: Princeton University Press, 2012), 1553, in a discussion nonetheless quick to admit the lack of consensus in the attribution of zeugma vs. syllepsis.

4. To sample the terminological quandaries in which this chapter has no need to mire itself, H.W. Fowler cites syllepsis ("taking together") as the grammatical "doubling" of Augustan wit, zeugma ("yoking") as its ungrammatical cousin (*The New Fowler's Modern English Usage*, ed. R.W. Burchfield, 3rd ed. [Oxford: Clarendon Press, 1996], 758, 863). Richard A. Lanham, following Puttenham, reverses the priority, so that zeugma ("single supply") covers Pope's "stains her honour or her new brocade," whereas syllepsis applies to such "double supply" problems of incongruent verb number as "the Nobles and the King was taken" (*A Handlist of Rhetorical Terms*, ed. Lanham [Berkeley: University of California Press, 1991], 160, 145); so, too, *The Oxford Companion to the English Language*, ed. Tom McArthur (Oxford: Oxford University Press, 1992), 1146. That's just for starters. Other sources, increasingly online, exemplify syllepsis with the same salient discrepancies in phrasal expectation, strictly grammatical or not, that are given elsewhere as instances of zeugma.

5. See Jacques Derrida on this reciprocal contradiction of reference from the aptly named "Double Session," in Derrida, *Dissemination*, trans. Barbara Johnson (Chicago: University of Chicago Press, 1981), 221. In prototypical Derridean terms, the *différence* to be lifted in the marital bond is the coming-between not of union but of its anatomical deferral. What the reciprocal cancellation of this phrasing amounts to, for Derrida, is in effect an unraveling (a deconstruction) of the very seam between definition and functional context, diction and syntax. In Michael Riffaterre's lexical rather than syntactic version of this trope, however, syllepsis is meant to topple New Critical ambiguity and its cult of multivalence, as well as to elude Derridean undecidability, by erecting in its place a functional semiotic "overdetermination." I give the italicized summary from Riffaterre's seed essay, "Syllepsis," *Critical Inquiry* 6 (1980): 635–38, where the familiar split between concrete and abstract in syllepsis is translated into the divide between obvious mimetic reference and semiotic overtone: "Syllepsis is a word understood in two different ways at once, as meaning and as significance. And therefore, because it sums up the duality of the text's message—its semantic and

semiotic faces—syllepsis is the literary sign par excellence" (638). For my thematically framed attempt to align Riffaterre's intertextuality with Fredric Jameson's "political unconscious" in a reading of the metaphorics (as well as sylleptic syntax) of colonial horizons in Dickens and E. M. Forster, see "The Foreign Offices of British Fiction," in *Reading for Form*, ed. Susan J. Wolfson and Marshall Brown (Seattle: University of Washington Press, 2006), 181–206.

6. Gérard Genette, *Narrative Discourse: An Essay in Method*, trans. Jane E. Lewin (Ithaca, NY: Cornell University Press, 1980), where syllepsis is first introduced (85) in distinction from analepsis and prolepsis, and where the "iterative syllepsis" (155) is later described in its tendency to abolish the norms of sequence by the forms of similarity, with the parallelism of the mode in general aimed at "a fully paradigmatic importance" (111).

7. William H. Gass, "The Ontology of the Sentence," in *The World within the Word* (Boston: David R Godine, 1988), 308–38.

8. "What Metaphors Mean," in *On Metaphor*, ed. Sheldon Sacks (Chicago: University of Chicago Press, 1979), 33.

9. Giorgio Agamben, "The Idea of Language," in *Potentialities: Collected Essays in Philosophy*, trans. Daniel Heller-Roazen (Stanford, CA: Stanford University Press, 1999), 40–41, in a passage directly alluding to Wittgenstein.

10. Paul Ricoeur, *The Rule of Metaphor: The Creation of Meaning in Language*, trans. Robert Czerny, with Kathleen McLaughlin and John Costello SJ (London: Routledge Classics, 2003).

11. Slavoj Žižek, *The Indivisible Remainder: On Schelling and Related Matters* (New York: Verso, 1996); see "'And' as a Category," 103–6; Marx adduced, 104, with Bentham's appearance in the series called "supplementary" in a deconstructive sense. See Karl Marx, *Marx/Engels Collected Works* (New York: International Publishers, 2005), 35:186.

12. Roland Barthes, *S/Z: An Essay* (New York: Hill and Wang, 1974), 58, where there is also, beyond Barthes's point, a kind of deflating broken parallelism (suddenly other-directed) at the end of Proust's rigorously nominalized series in explanation of an unanswered remark: "either because of astonishment at my words, attention to his work, a regard for etiquette, hardness of hearing, respect for the surroundings, fear of danger, slow-wittedness, or orders from the manager" (58).

13. Quoted in Barthes, *S/Z*, 236.

14. Roman Jakobson, "Linguistics and Poetics," in *Essays on the Language of Literature*, ed. Seymour Chatman and Samuel R. Levin (Boston: Houghton Mifflin, 1967), 303.

15. Maria Edgeworth, *Belinda*, ed. Kathryn Kilpatrick (New York: Oxford World Classics, 2008), 40.

16. Michael Wood, "Time and Her Aunt," in *A Companion to Jane Austen*, ed. Claudia L. Johnson and Clara Tuite (Oxford: Wiley-Blackwell, 2009), 195, where Wood, in unspoken deference to scholarship on Austen's own eighteenth-century predecessors, uses the alternative and older vocabulary to highlight, and by assonance at that, the phrasing's "beautiful zeugma."

17. Charles Dickens, "Shops and Their Tenants," in *Sketches by Boz*, with gratitude to Daniel Tyler for alerting me to its sylleptic traffic jam.

18. Henri Bergson, "Laughter: An Essay on the Comic," in *Comedy*, ed. Wylie Sypher (New York: Anchor, 1956), 61–190; see especially 123.

19. For a fuller sampling of the sylleptic habit in this last finished novel by Dickens, see my "The Ethical Tempo of Narrative Syntax: Sylleptic Recognitions in *Our Mutual Friend*," *Partial Answers: Journal of Literature and the History of Ideas* 8, no. 1 (January 2010): 119–45.

20. For very different examples from these later novelists, see Stewart, "The Ethical Tempo," 129–30.

21. Henry James, *"The Turn of the Screw" and "In the Cage"* (New York: Modern Library, 2001), 172.

22. In this sense my reading complements, at the level of style rather than genre—linguistics (or prosaics) rather than realist poetics—the approach to James's story in Richard Menke, *Telegraphic Realism: Victorian Realism and Other Information Systems* (Stanford, CA: Stanford University Press, 2007), 163–90.

23. See my discussion of le Carré's forked syntax in "Syllepsis Redux and the Rhetoric of Double Agency," *Partial Answers* 10, no. 1 (January 2012): 93–120, where I sample in passing, in comparison with Dickens and others, half a dozen of his novels for this recurrent effect (often added or finessed in revision on the way to press, as I have found since publication in examining his manuscripts and edited proofs donated recently to the Bodleian Library at Oxford). In *Our Kind of Traitor* (New York: Viking, 2010), amid instances more routine (like an image of indoctrinated spies who "abandoned themselves and their common sense to the embrace of their virtual world" [242]), we find two loosened variants of sylleptic mismatch deployed in a single long paragraph—once of the prepositional, once of the cross-phrasal, variety. Concerning "Ollie with his camp ways and single earring and overintelligence" (182), prose is seen forcing behavioral, material, and mental qualities together into the same anti-Cartesian, body-mind continuum. And this is the same Ollie who, as if prose itself were transferring its dexterity from description to characterization across a switch from predicate adjective to phrasal verb, was a "born educator . . . determined to make every lesson fun and every lesson stick" (183).

24. Muriel Spark, *The Abbess of Crewe* (New York: New Directions, 1974), 94, 26.

25. Shirley Hazzard, *The Bay of Noon* (New York: Picador, 1970), 74.

26. Kingsley Amis, *Girl, 20* (New York: New York Review of Books, 2009), 23, 44.

27. Robert Penn Warren, *All the King's Men* (New York: Harcourt, 2006), 31.

28. Toni Morrison, *A Mercy* (New York: Knopf, 2008), 32.

29. P. D. James, *The Children of Men* (New York: Knopf, 1993), 148.

30. Geoffrey Galt Harpham, *Getting it Right: Language, Literature, and Ethics* (Chicago: University of Chicago Press, 1992), 23.

31. Charles Dickens, *A Tale of Two Cities*, ed. Richard Maxwell (New York: Penguin, 2000).

32. Peter Brooks, *Reading for the Plot: Design and Intention in Narrative* (New York: Knopf, 1984), 129.

33. "Between Shakespeare and Joyce," writes William H. Gass in an essay called "The Sentence Seeks Its Form," there is "no one but Dickens who has an equal command of the English language" (*A Temple of Texts: Essays* [New York: Knopf, 2008], 275)—and he means by this to stress the aural dimension of the novelist's effects. "Language is born in the lungs and is shaped by the lips, palate, teeth, and tongue out of spent breath. . . . It therefore must be listened to while it is being written" (273). Written—and then read, its origins thus recovered in its destination. There is nothing undeconstructed in this. As Mladen Dolar would agree, and before him Agamben, and of course Kittler too (in his commentary on Goethe), speech is not the work of spirit but strictly enunciation, "spent breath" and its articulated filtering. In Dickens, long before he reaches the podium with it, such printed language waits to be audited by—precisely in being silently released from—typography's pent breath. Gass's most striking evidence from Dickens is a sentence that carries a slight additional interest for the present chapter, rather than for his, in the way it is sustained upon the

nonapostrophic and recursive lowercase moan of the letter *o*. David Copperfield's lament is given here with my typographical highlights on the kinds of anaphoric returns and alphabetic reversals by which Gass is intrigued: "From Monday morning until Saturday night, I had *no* advice, *no* c*o*u*nsel*, *no* encouragement, *no* c*o*n*s*o*l*a*tion*, *no* assistance, *no* support, of any kind, from any one" (275; emphasis added). Gass's own stress falls not on the negative trailing off of the nonechoic "one" (with its slant reprise of the opening "M*on*day") but rather, before that syllabic denouement, on the overt graphic flips from "no" to "on" and the alphabetic and half-phonic return of the latter twice over, after the aggrieved "no counsel," in the impacted nugatory parallel of "no c*on*solati*on*."

34. On the encompassing parallel between Rogue's life "in abeyance" and the echoing of this legalistic phrase concerning the return from supposed drowning of the hero John Harmon, see Stewart, "Lived Death: Dickens's Rogue Glyphs," in *Dickens's Style*, ed. Daniel Tyler (Cambridge: Cambridge University Press, 2013), 231–52, where I cite Roberto Esposito's follow-up to Deleuze and Agamben on this near-death episode. Esposito sees the guttering life of Riderhood as offering a Deleuzian case study in "potentializing and depotentializing flow" that simultaneously moves, in Agamben's terms (though undeployed in this case), between *zoe* (sheer animation) and *bios* (human life) and that engages, in the form of suspended animation, the "classic and controversial Deleuzian theme of the 'virtual' " (see Roberto Esposito, *Bíos: Biopolitics and Philosophy*, trans. Timothy Campbell [Minneapolis: University of Minnesota Press, 2008], 193), with its overtones here, for Esposito, of an "affirmative biopolitics."

6. Talking Room

1. A previous essay of mine informs this approach to an audiovisual literary effect in Morrison that recruits graphic and spatial metaphors for what we find her calling in *A Mercy* the "talking room" of her text. I had no space, as it happens, to discuss the luxuriant contralto of Morrison's audiobook mastery in my article on recorded fiction ("Novelist as 'Sound Thief': The Audiobooks of John le Carré," in *Audiobooks, Literature, and Sound Studies*, ed. Matthew Rubery [New York: Routledge, 2011], 109–26), where le Carré's novel *The Mission Song* is shown to involve a thematics of verbal transmission quite similar, one could further note, to that in Morrison's *A Mercy*. Certainly her performances merit a place alongside the recorded novels of writers from Dickens to le Carré in any account of the interplay between media—textual versus audial—as such attention serves to isolate not only latent phonetic effects in these writers but also certain broader motifs (rather than just secondary means) of orality and dissemination.

2. Peter Kivy, *The Performance of Reading: An Essay in the Philosophy of Literature* (Oxford: Blackwell, 2006). His claims have to do with the private reading encounter, not to be confused with the actual recitation (performance in this "theatrical" sense) of a text, as, for instance, in Toni Morrison's audiobook recordings.

3. Toni Morrison, afterword to *The Bluest Eye* (New York: Plume, 1993), 209–16.

4. I have examined Morrison's propensity for this sylleptic figure, along with that of many other writers, in "Syllepsis Redux and the Rhetoric of Double Agency," *Partial Answers* 10, no. 1 (January 2012), 115, though without citing a curious version of its divisive phrasing in Florens's last monologue, where she spells out her defiance against those "who believe they have claim and rule over me" (*A Mercy*, 184). The nonidiomatic "have claim" twists the grammar so out of joint that it seems to slip from

a compound object into the syntactic bifurcation of phrase over against clause: resisting, as if in the clutched knot of language itself, those who, it might otherwise and more patiently have been said—in a shift from noun to verb—"believe they have claim over me and so rule over me." Traced across this tensed skid from premise to oppression is, of course, the whole history of enslavement in a single racist dyad.

5. Toni Morrison, *Jazz* (1992; New York: Vintage, 2004), 8.

6. See Garrett Stewart, *Dear Reader: The Conscripted Audience in Nineteenth-Century British Fiction* (Baltimore: Johns Hopkins University Press, 1996).

7. As, for example: "We must separate awhile—Here! Take from my lips this kiss, / Whoever you are, I give it especially to you" ("To the Reader at Parting," in *Leaves of Grass*, 1871, p. 120, lines 2–3, The Walt Whitman Archive, ed. Ed Folsom and Kenneth M. Price, http://www.whitmanarchive.org). Or, closer yet to Morrison's trope in *Jazz*:

> It is I you hold and who holds you,
> I spring from the pages into your arms—decease calls me forth.
> O how your fingers drowse me. . . .
>
> ("So Long!" in Leaves of Grass, 1872 ed., p. 383, lines 15–16, Walt Whitman Archive)

8. See Catherine Gallagher, *Nobody's Story: The Vanishing Acts of Women Writers in the Marketplace, 1670–1820* (Berkeley: University of California Press, 1995).

9. Catherine Gallagher, "The Rise of Fictionality," in *The Novel*, vol. 1, *History, Geography, Culture*, ed. Franco Moretti (Princeton, NJ: Princeton University Press, 2006), 336–63.

10. Michel de Certeau, "Reading as Poaching," in *The Practice of Everyday Life* (Berkeley: University of California Press, 1984), 165–76. The present chapter began as a lecture at that English Institute meeting, and a version of the argument, now amplified here, has appeared as "The Deed of Reading: Toni Morrison and the Sculpted Book," in "Selected Essays from the English Institute (2011)," ed. Joseph R. Slaughter, special issue, *English Language History* 80 (2013): 427–53. The earlier article, however, develops a more extended and fully exemplified comparison between Morrison's tropes of the codex and the range of contemporary art in the altered book mode. Of particular relevance there are the text-canceled *bibliobjets* as well as hypertrophic spatial inscriptions discussed in my *Bookwork: Medium to Object to Concept to Art* (Chicago: University of Chicago Press, 2011).

11. See Roland Barthes, *S/Z: An Essay* (New York: Hill and Wang, 1974), in a little-cited early passage summed as follows: "Yet reading is not a parasitical act, the reactive complement of a writing which we endow with all the glamour of creation and anteriority. It is a form of work (which is why it would be better to speak of a lexeological act—a lexeographic act, since I write my reading)" (10). This is not selective "poaching," let alone parasitism, but a phrase-by-phrase collaboration, phrased in a way that might make it seem edging toward Barthes's modernist category of "the writerly." Instead, he wants to insist that this "work" of writing-as-one-reads is solicited even by the limited plurality of the classic text.

12. Toni Morrison, interview by Angels Carabi, *Belles Lettres* 10, no. 2 (1995): 40–43.

13. Roland Barthes, *The Preparation for the Novel: Lecture Courses and Seminars at the Collége de France, 1978–79 and 1979–80*, trans. Kate Briggs (New York: Columbia University Press, 2011), where Barthes suggests that the heraldic origins of

the term *mise en abyme* betray a certain graphic constraint, so that "what's at issue is a flat, static presentation" (169)—presumably even when a nested one. In the alternate paradigm Barthes proposes, a kind of reflexive self-modeling, "the work-as-maquette presents itself as its own experimentation; it stages a production" (170). According to this distinction, not just the self-cited inscriptive labor of *A Mercy* but the closing of *Jazz* might well, and quite apart from the analogy with McLuhan's page-spread regress in the case of *Jazz*, yield another example of the book enacting its own drive.

14. Toni Morrison, *Beloved* (1987; New York: Vintage, 2004), 84.

15. Garrett Stewart, *Novel Violence: A Narratography of Victorian Fiction* (Chicago: University of Chicago Press, 2009), 29.

16. As discussed in Chapter 2, see Steven Connor, *Beckett, Modernism and the Material Imagination* (Cambridge: Cambridge University Press, 2014), where the subtitle of his seventh chapter, "Writing the White Voice" (alluding to the white noise of signal theory), offers one of the closest parallels I know in print to my earlier notion of the "phonotext"—and since then to the logic of "secondary vocality." For Connor, in a related figuration, the book form opens upon a secondary spatiality: an "inner auditorium" (110) whose parameters offer the "white architecture of vocality" (111), traversed by "phonic ghosts" (112). Florens's "talking room" by any other name.

17. See Paul de Man, "Hypogram and Inscription: Michael Riffaterre's Poetics of Reading," *Diacritics* 11, no. 4 (Winter 1981): 17–35.

18. Henry James, *The Art of Fiction: Critical Prefaces*, ed. R.P. Blackmur (New York: Scribner's, 1934), 46: a "house" with, famously, a "million windows" (46) looking out from various vantage points.

19. Giorgio Agamben, *Stanzas: Word and Phantasm in Western Culture*, trans. Ronald L. Martinez (Minneapolis: University of Minnesota Press, 1993). xvi. Agamben is requoting Dante from the epigraph and later mentions the "philosophical topology" (xviii) required by his approach.

20. Agamben, as we know, is interested in the space between "the experience of a mere sound" and "the experience of meaning," an interspace in which transpires "the pure taking place of an instance of discourse without any determinate accession of meaning" (*Language and Death: The Place of Negativity*, trans. Karen E. Pinkus with Michael Hardt [1981; Minneapolis: University of Minnesota Press, 1992], 35): call it the place, if never firm ground, of language coming to be and of being coming to itself in language. The passage from the noise of voice to the sound of speech is often less than pure. In a July 2013 keynote address at "Modern Soundscapes," a conference at the University of New South Wales, Steven Connor—before the appearance of his book on Beckett, mentioned above in connection with the "white voice" of reading—pointed to the way literature, even when understood on the model of information theory, may find the emergence of signal from the flux of information as still carrying with it at times "a fringe of noise."

21. As Agamben puts it in *The End of the Poem*, trans. Daniel Heller-Roazen (Stanford, CA: Stanford University Press, 1999)—phrased indeed as literature's eponymous destiny—the work of poetic art is in fact the effort "to let language finally communicate itself, without remaining unsaid in what is said" (115).

22. Gérard Genette, *The Work of Art: Immanence and Transcendence*, trans. G.M. Goshgarian (Ithaca, NY: Cornell University Press, 1997).

23. With material equivalents of this trope in some of the conceptual artworks discussed in my article "The Deed of Reading: Toni Morrison and the Sculpted Book."

24. Paul Ricoeur, *Time and Narrative*, trans. Kathleen McLaughlin and David Pellauer (Chicago: University of Chicago Press, 1984–88), 1:71, with this outreach of

the narrative understood on the model of oral storytelling. I previously explored this model in *Dear Reader*, 62–63, arguing that the "pact of reading" (Ricoeur, 3:162) suggested by Ricoeur's third dimension of mimesis finds, in print texts, one marked point of impact in direct reader address. In contrast, what this book has identified as the deed of reading is distributed evenly—or unevenly, as the case may be—across the ridged terrain of style more generally.

25. Régis Debray, *Transmitting Culture*, trans. Eric Rauth (New York: Columbia University Press, 2000), where Debray argues that the sender-receiver model of communication transfer is insufficient to explain the broader mediatory circuits necessary for the transmission of culture and its values. One may think of Florens's letter to the future as the figuring of the latter in the trope of the former: legacy as addressed text.

26. See Henry Louis Gates Jr., "The Trope of the Talking Book," in *The Signifying Monkey: A Theory of African-American Criticism* (New York: Oxford University Press, 1988), 127–69. Compare Lena Hill's complementary claims for the prominence of "the trope of the picture book" (a phrase she uses as the title of the introduction to *Visualizing Blackness*) in subsequent African American self-representation from Phillis Wheatley in the mid-eighteenth century down through Ralph Ellison, in Hill, *Visualizing Blackness and the Creation of the African American Literary Tradition* (Cambridge: Cambridge University Press, 2014), 1–20. Morrison clearly has her own thematic reasons for returning to the alternative and earlier trope in her seventeenth-century setting.

After Wording

1. Fredric Jameson, *The Antinomies of Realism* (New York: Verso, 2013), 311, as if form and content were among the foremost "antinomies" meant to be dissolved (if not resolved) by his method—this being very much the emphasis as well, and very much under his influence, of my "Lukácsian stylistics" in *Novel Violence: A Narratography of Victorian Fiction* (Chicago: University of Chicago Press, 2009). No touted neoformalism can get out ahead of Jameson's procedures in some supposedly more vital traction with the inferences of literary technique, certainly no so-called surface reading.

2. James Joyce, *Finnegans Wake* (New York: Penguin, 1976), 143: a phrase giving the title to my chapter on Joyce's "modality of the audible" in *Reading Voices: Literature and the Phonotext* (Berkeley: University of California Press, 1990), 232–38, with an emphasis on what Joyce elsewhere evokes as the "phonoscopically" attuned reading act (250).

3. Jean-Michel Rabaté, "Lapsus ex machina," in *Post-Structuralist Joyce: Essays from the French*, ed. Derek Attridge and Daniel Ferrer (London: Cambridge University Press, 1984), 79.

4. Stewart, *Reading Voices*, with the Joycean phrase offering a subtitle for the book's first section (under the main title "Pronounced Defects")—and where the elided term "transegmental" is first defined (25).

5. Charles Bernstein, *Recalculating* (Chicago: University of Chicago Press, 2013), 93.

6. How much in all this, or in what specific ways, the poet's tongue is in his cheek about my term for the presumably cheeky silent tonguing of written lexemes is hard to say, given that Bernstein has earlier been hospitable in print to my notion of the "phonotext." See Bernstein's allusion to my subtitle in "Close Listening," in Bernstein, *My Way: Speeches and Poems* (Chicago: University of Chicago Press, 1999), 288.

7. See Craig Dworkin, "Shift," in *Strand* (New York: Roof, 2005), which begins with the fantastic reminder of how "tectonic grammar" has "so profoundly influenced linguistic thinking since the early 1970's" (9). In his subsequent grammatical machination, *Parse* (Berkeley: Atelos, 2008), with sentence diagrams on front and back covers, Dworkin "translates" sentence by sentence an 1874 text called *How To Parse: An Attempt to Apply the Principles of Scholarship to English Grammar*. He does so in the exhausting manner—to give the method, as it were, parse pro toto—of the three-word main title thus rendered: "ADVERB PREPOSITION OF THE INFINITIVE ACTIVE INDEFINITE PRESENT TENSE TRANSITIVE VERB INFINITIVE MOOD OBJECT AND SUBJECT IMPLIED . . ." (11). And so on for 270-some further pages.

8. With its inescapable play on the French for "words" plural, Dworkin's *Motes* (Berkeley: Roof, 2011) pluralizes (by pulverizing) chosen lexemes, as, for instance, when in a distich he unpacks "THE BRONX" into "I brought the bought wooden box from there" (34). Or—yes, transegmentally—plays "HYSTERIA" off against "his stereo" (44). Or forces us to rephoneticize the lowercase "i" of the "diva" in "Godiva, go" (43)—a curious instance of the garden-path noun rather than sentence. Or in a syllabic anagram frees up "FREE REIGN" into the countermusical pun "no refrain from singing around here" (48). Then, too, in a loop back to the phonetic comedy of none other than Richard Wilbur, Dworkin couldn't sound more like the acrobatic punster of *The Pig in the Spigot* than when uppercase "THUNDERCLOUDS" precipitate "clearly loud under there" (24): an effect further reminiscent of Faulkner's "loud cloudy flutter of the sparrows," muted by a sheltered retreat from the broiling day, on the opening page of *Absalom, Absalom!*—where a synesthetic prose embeds and baffles the unseen external commotion. From farcical verses for children through canonical modernism to aggressive conceptualism: as I close with below (but you can say you heard it here first), language is as language does.

9. See *Novel Violence*, picking up in part on tracks laid down in *Reading Voices*.

10. Joseph Conrad to R. B. Cunninghame Graham, August 5, 1987, in *The Collected Letters of Joseph Conrad*, ed. Frederick R. Karl and Laurence Davies (Cambridge: Cambridge University Press, 1988), 4:370.

11. We may take as example a time-lapse phrasing from the start of *Heart of Darkness* that I've remarked upon in commentary elsewhere but linger over now for a (vanishing) moment longer, where the solar disk, in indiscernible stages and by transferred epithet, lowers its eventually diminished visible sliver beneath the horizon, its orb phrased away as follows: "And at last, in its curved and imperceptible fall, the sun sank low, and from glowing white changed to a dull red." Except perhaps in relation to the rotating curvature of the earth itself, it isn't the "fall" that is "curved" but the object itself. And beyond this latent double orientation of spherical bodies, the phrase stages an imperceptibility that it also corrects along the progress it makes linguistically palpable. It does so when the loss of the "glowing" is already perceived under erasure across the incrementally sparked arc of "glow" in "sank low." The reading eye is itself hazed as if by the described world's own optic mutability. Or say, that the sun sets between and beneath the words as well as below the horizon. In writing like this, the world is all words. See Joseph Conrad, *Heart of Darkness*, ed. Robert Kimbrough (New York: W. W. Norton, 1988), 8.

12. Jacques Rancière, *The Flesh of Words: The Politics of Writing*, trans. Charlotte Mandell (Stanford, CA: Stanford University Press, 2004).

13. For the manifestly strained gestures at embodiment sometimes made by textual omniscience when inclined to identify with characters the way a reader might—and the further discursive strain this exerts on the operations of the "stylothete" in the case

of Jane Austen's prose—see the phonemically attuned account by D. A. Miller in *Jane Austen, or the Secret of Style* (Princeton, NJ: Princeton University Press, 2003).

14. See my chapter "Mordecai's Consumption: Afterlives of Interpretation in *Daniel Deronda*," in *Dear Reader: The Conscripted Audience in Nineteenth-Century British Fiction* (Baltimore: Johns Hopkins University Press, 1996), 301–28.

INDEX